MATÉRIEL CULTURE

The twentieth century probably saw no more conflict than in previous centuries; increased global communication and media coverage have, however, heightened our awareness of it. The scale and intensity of war was greater than anything before and the human cost reached unprecedented and previously unimaginable levels. Following the end of the century the materiality of these many conflicts – from local skirmishes to world wars – is becoming accepted on to the heritage agenda as a valid form of cultural resource for the benefit of future generations. *Matériel Culture* describes these recent developments, and documents why the study of conflict is important – and to whom.

The term 'matériel culture' encompasses the material remains of conflict, from buildings and monuments to artefacts and militaria, as well as human remains. This collection of essays, from an international range of contributors, illustrates the diversity in this material record, highlights the difficulties and challenges in preserving, presenting and interpreting it, and above all demonstrates the significant role matériel culture can play in contemporary society. Archaeologists have led the way in understanding these remains, as the fantastic selection of case studies in this volume suggests. Among the many studies are: the 'culture of shells', the archaeology of nuclear testing grounds, Cambodia's 'killing fields', the Berlin Wall, the biography of a medal, the reappearance of Argentina's 'disappeared' and Second World War concentration camps.

In presenting this collection the editors challenge our perception of what constitutes cultural heritage, what is significant about it, and what is worthy of record and preservation. This new and exciting field of archaeology has a wide relevance for academics and professionals in many disciplines, most certainly in archaeology, heritage management, history and anthropology.

John Schofield is an Inspector for English Heritage's Monuments Protection Programme. **William Gray Johnson** and **Colleen M. Beck** are Associate Research Professor and Research Professor respectively at the Desert Research Institute in Nevada, USA.

ONE WORLD ARCHAEOLOGY

Series Editor: (Volumes 1–37): Peter J. Ucko
Academic Series Editors (Volume 38 onwards): Martin Hall and Julian Thomas
Executive Series Editor (Volume 38 onwards): Peter Stone

MATÉRIEL CULTURE

The archaeology of
twentieth-century conflict

Edited by

John Schofield, William Gray Johnson
and Colleen M. Beck

London and New York

First published 2002 by Routledge
11 New Fetter Lane, London EC4P 4EE

Simultaneously published in the USA and Canada
by Routledge
29 West 35th Street, New York, NY 10001

Routledge is an imprint of the Taylor & Francis Group

Typeset in Bembo by Bookcraft Ltd, Stroud, Gloucestershire
Printed and bound in Great Britain by
The Cromwell Press, Trowbridge, Wiltshire

British Library Cataloguing in Publication Data
A catalogue record for this book is available from the British Library

Library of Congress Cataloging in Publication Data
A catalog record for this book has been requested

ISBN 0–415–23387–9

Dedication

During the course of this project we have become increasingly aware of the degree to which our interest and enthusiasm for matériel culture have been shaped by our own lives, and by the experiences of close friends and family. It is almost as though the very act of studying modern military archaeology has become an encounter with our lives; our own pasts. No doubt this will also be the case for numerous of our contributors: it clearly is for Jody Joy and Gabi Dolff-Bonekämper, whose contributions are arguably the most intimate of this collection. It is for this reason that we dedicate this volume to those whose experience has contributed in a significant way to shaping our own interest in the past:

For JS, Group Captain Arthur Schofield (1920–2001); for WGJ, PFC W.M. Johnson (1924–) and Capt O.G. Rucker, Jr (1928–); for CMB, Lt Col, USAF, W.R. Beck (1919–), W.R. Beck (1924–) and MM2, USN, W.K. Kolb (1944–).

Without them our enthusiasm for and commitment to this subject would never have materialized, and this book, and other related articles, would not have been written.

JS, WGJ and CMB
July 2001

Contents

Figures

Tables

Acknowledgements

The editors are very grateful for the assistance given and the patience and co-opera-tion shown by all the contributors in bringing this volume to completion. We'd like to express our thanks in particular to Roland Fletcher for his encouraging words during the conference and his willingness to produce a concluding chapter for the volume. We would also like to thank members of the World Archaeological Con-gress, and in particular Peter Stone, for encouraging this project initially, and for providing support and advice during its execution, Richard Morris for his advice on the scope of the volume, and Julene Barnes and Polly Osborn at Routledge for their assistance during the compilation and editing process.

In our places of work numerous colleagues have unwittingly contributed to this project through their encouragement of our interest in this aspect of the heritage. For JS, Graham Fairclough, Jeremy Lake, Margaret Nieke, Deborah Porter and David Stocker deserve particular mention, having tolerated the obsession with good humour over the years, giving support and encouragement when needed. WGJ owes thanks to Stephen Wells and Robert Furlow. CMB is especially indebted to Fred Au, Barbara Yoerg, Robert Furlow, Dale Ritter, Claudia Miner and Stephen Wells.

On the domestic front JS is grateful, as ever, for the constant support and under-standing of Janet, Armorel and James. For WGJ, much thanks, love and respect to his lifetime companion, Marc Comstock, for unwavering support. To Keith, Logan and Alexa, CMB expresses her appreciation for their encouragement and continu-ing interest and involvement in her research.

Contributors

Michael J. Anderton, Rural Development Service, DEFRA, Block C, Government Buildings, Brooklands Avenue, Cambridge, CB2 2BL, UK (andertonmj@netscapeonline.uk)

Colleen M. Beck, Desert Research Institute, 1055 East Tropicana, Suite 450, Las Vegas, NV 89119, USA (colleen@dri.edu)

John G. Beech, Coventry Business School, Coventry University, 5 Priory Street, Coventry, CV1 5FB, UK (John@Beech.net)

John Carman, Department of Archaeology, University of Cambridge, Downing Street, Cambridge, CB2 3DZ, UK (rjc16@cam.ac.uk)

Henrik Christiansen, The Danish Forest and Nature Agency, Haraldsgade 53, DK–2100 Copenhagen, Denmark (hc70b2000@hotmail.com)

Kate Clark, 1 Ellerncroft Road, Wootton-under-Edge, Gloucestershire, GL12 7AX, UK (horton@lineone.net)

Zoë Crossland, Museum of Anthropology, Ruthven Museums Building, 1109 Geddes, Ann Arbor, MI 48109–1079, USA (zoecro@umich.edu)

Gabi Dolff-Bonekämper, Denkmalpflegerin, Landesdenkmalamt Berlin, Krausenstrasse 38/39, 10117 Berlin (Mitte), Germany (gabi@dolff-bonekaemper.de)

Roland Fletcher, Department of Archaeology, University of Sydney, NSW, Australia (roland.fletcher@archaeology.usyd.edu.au)

Anne George, West Yorkshire Archive Service, Bradford Office, 15 Canal Road, Bradford, West Yorkshire, BD1 4AT, UK (bradford@wyjs.org.uk)

Denis Gojak, National Parks and Wildlife Service of New South Wales, PO Box 1967, Hurstville, NSW 2220, Australia (denis.gojak@npsw.gov.au)

P. Bion Griffin, Department of Anthropology, University of Hawaii, Honolulu, HI 96822, USA (griffin@hawaii.edu)

Lisa Hoshower-Leppo, 600 Brown Avenue, Hopewell, VA 23860, USA (leppolm@yahoo.com)

Neil Jarman, Institute for Conflict Research, Unit 14, North City Business Centre, 2 Duncairn Gardens, Belfast BT15 2GG, Northern Ireland (deputy@conflictresearch.org.uk

Helen Jarvis, School of Information Systems, Technology and Management, University of New South Wales, Sydney, NSW 2052, Australia (h.jarvis@unsw.edu.au)

William Gray Johnson, Desert Research Institute, 755 E. Flamingo Road, Las Vegas, NV 89119, USA (billj@dri.edu)

Jody Joy, 51 The Green Road, Sawston, Cambridgeshire, CB2 4SN, UK (jodypatrickjoy@hotmail.com)

Ulla-Riitta Kauppi, Tutkija, Museovirasto, Rakennushistorian osasto, PL 169, 00510 Helsinki, Finland (ulla-riitta.Kauppi@nba.fi)

Jeremy Lake, English Heritage, 23 Savile Row, London, W1X 1AB, UK (jeremy.lake@english.heritage.org.uk)

Roger Leech, Department of Archaeology, University of Southampton, SO17 1BJ, UK (rl2@soton.ac.uk)

Antonia Malan, Department of Archaeology, University of Cape Town, Rondebosch, Cape Town, 7701, South Africa (amalan@beattie.uct.ac.za)

Nicholas J. Saunders, Department of Anthropology, University College London, Gower Street, London, WC1E 6BT, UK (nicholas.saunders@ucl.ac.uk)

Rebecca Saunders, Museum of Natural Science, 119 Foster Hall, Louisiana State University, Baton Rouge, LA 70803, USA (rsaunde@lsu.edu)

John Schofield, English Heritage, 23 Savile Row, London, W1X 1AB, UK (john.schofield@english.heritage.org.uk)

Crain Soudien, Department of Education, Private Bag, Rondebosch, Cape Town, 7701, South Africa (cs@education.uct.ac.za)

Mandy Whorton, Harding ESE, 1627 Cole Blvd, CO 80401, USA (mswhorton@mactec.com)

Foreword

One World Archaeology is dedicated to exploring new themes, theories and applications in archaeology from around the world. The series of edited volumes began with contributions that were either part of the inaugural meeting of the World Archaeological Congress in Southampton, UK in 1986 or were commissioned specifically immediately after the meeting – frequently from participants who were inspired to make their own contributions. Since then WAC has held three further major international Congresses in Barquísimeto, Venezuela (1990), New Delhi, India (1994), and Cape Town, South Africa (1999) and a series of more specialized 'Inter-Congresses' focusing on *Archaeological ethics and the treatment of the dead* (Vermillion, USA, 1989), *Urban origins in Africa* (Mombasa, Kenya, 1993), *The destruction and conservation of cultural heritage* (Brač, Croatia, 1998), *Theory in Latin American Archaeology* (Olavarría, Argentina, 2000), and *The African Diaspora* (Curaçao, Dutch West Indies, 2001). In each case these meetings have attracted a wealth of original and often inspiring work from many countries.

The result has been a set of richly varied volumes that are at the cutting edge of (frequently multidisciplinary) new work, and which provide a breadth of perspective that charts the many and varied directions that contemporary archaeology is taking.

As series editors we should like to thank all editors and contributors for their hard work in producing these books. We should also like to express our thanks to Peter Ucko, inspiration behind both the World Archaeological Congress and the One World Archaeology series. Without him none of this would have happened.

Martin Hall, Cape Town, South Africa
Peter Stone, Newcastle, UK
Julian Thomas, Manchester, UK
November 2000

Preface

This volume owes its origin to an exchange of correspondence between, and subsequent meetings among, the editors in 1996–8, culminating in our decision to jointly organize a session for the fourth World Archaeological Congress in Cape Town, South Africa, in January 1999. For a subject that is by definition global, and which impacts upon contemporary society in many contrasting ways, it seemed to us that the worldwide scope that the WAC provides was uniquely placed to present these issues and debate them in a way never previously attempted or envisaged. Furthermore it seemed wholly appropriate that, for a debate on conflict, repression, human suffering and hope, Cape Town could not be bettered as a venue. Indeed, during the course of the conference we (the editors, along with numerous of the contributors to our session) visited the townships outside Cape Town and District Six, from which some of their inhabitants moved in the 1960s; some of us also visited Robben Island. These visits fuelled our determination to secure contributions on these places for the volume, and to extend its scope from one exclusively on military conflict to embrace a wider definition of matériel culture.

The session ('Matériel culture: international perspectives on military remains') came towards the end of the conference and was well attended, including representatives from countries and contexts for which the subject matter is particularly close. We had hoped this would happen but were nonetheless surprised when it did. The timing also gave us the opportunity to attend various other sessions beforehand, which contained contributions touching on related issues: memories of a workshop entitled 'Healing the Social Wounds of War' remain with us still, for the emotional charge that it generated amongst speakers and audience alike. The intimacy and emotion evident in that session came too late to influence our own, but determined the balance of contributions we wished to achieve in producing this subsequent volume.

Of the chapters in the book, those by Anderton, Beck, Beech, Carman, Christiansen, Jarman, Johnson, Kauppi, N. Saunders, Schofield and Whorton began as presentations for our session at the conference and all were available on the WAC-4 website as pre-circulated papers. The chapters by Clark, Crossland, Gojak and Malan and Soudien owe their existence to contributions given in other sessions, or less formally, at the conference; Leech and Fletcher both attended our session and their involvement in the discussion made contributions to the book inevitable. With the conference over we turned our attention to publication, and agreed on obvious gaps, thematic, geographical and political, pursuing potential contributors relentlessly; most agreed to be involved. Chapters obtained in this way are those by Dolff-Bonekämper, George, Griffin, Hoshower-Leppo, Jarvis, Joy, Lake and R. Saunders. While gaps do remain (and these are mentioned briefly in the Introduction), we are confident that the range of material now included in the volume is sufficiently deep and broad to address the principal issues and debates to which modern matériel culture can usefully contribute.

1 Introduction: *matériel culture in the modern world*

JOHN SCHOFIELD, WILLIAM GRAY JOHNSON
AND COLLEEN M. BECK

As we contemplate this end-of-century world [...] may war at last be recognised as having lost its usefulness and deep attractiveness? War in our time has been not merely a means of resolving inter-state disputes but also a vehicle through which the embittered, the dispossessed, the naked of the earth, the hungry masses yearning to breathe free, express their anger, jealousies and pent up urge to violence. There are grounds for believing that at last, after five thousand years of recorded war making, cultural and material changes may be working to inhibit man's proclivity to take up arms.

(Keegan 1993: 56)

SCOPE AND DEFINITIONS

This is a book about warfare, and arguably the first book to draw together from around the globe insights into and examples of the materiality of conflicts, wars, battles, skirmishes and civil unrest that have dominated lives and experience over the past century. It is a critical archaeology of conflict, examining what survives, why that material record is important and what mechanisms exist for retaining it in a form that can benefit this and future generations, accepting the point that we can learn a great deal about culture and the manner in which it develops from how people fight (Howard 1994: 1; Carman 1997). It also examines different perceptions of warfare: cultural, social and personal. How do we feel about our troubled pasts, about a 'heritage that hurts'? How do former combatants and warriors react to a heritage they helped create? And how will the retention of objects, structures and sites of conflict contribute to a more peaceful and tolerant society? To address this, a variety of approaches and examples are presented. Some of the contributions are detached, objective, 'cold'; others are more immediate, intimate, hot and engaging. There is a place for both, we argue.

For all these reasons the volume is necessarily wide-ranging, encompassing the full spectrum of what we refer to here as matériel culture: the physical remains of human conflict – military and civil – broadly defined to embrace sites and monuments, artefacts and militaria, vehicles, vessels and craft, and human remains. It also embraces the experience of conflict as witnessed by the many millions of people who have been involved in and affected by it during the course of the twentieth century. We explicitly draw the definition widely to include civil conflict and unrest for the reason that these aspects of warfare have come to characterize the twentieth century every bit as much as military activity, notwithstanding the obvious and often considerable overlap that exists between them. In fact civil wars and conflict became increasingly significant as the twentieth century progressed. Following the World Wars, and the subsequent ideological conflict and proxy wars of the Cold War, civil conflict emerged in the form of disputes over identity, ethnicity and religion. And these wars are different. They are fought mainly within states not between them; the victims are predominantly civilians; and they are far more resistant to outside pressure or negotiated settlements (Judd 1998: ix). The practice and the politics of warfare and peacemaking are not explicitly covered in this volume; we leave that to political commentators and historians. We do however address in very explicit and often intimate terms the materiality of those wars and what it represents in terms of human experience, including personal tragedy and loss of life, and cultural history.

The focus of this volume is the twentieth century, for three related reasons. First, that the interest in the materiality of recent conflict, and the increasing pressure to reuse or develop twentieth-century military sites, saw a significant increase towards the end of the century, coincident with the timing of the World Archaeological Congress at Cape Town in 1999. The Congress therefore provided a timely opportunity to reflect on a century just ending, on its military history and the materiality of events which have shaped the modern world. Second, the twentieth century has typically been described by historians and social commentators as one defined by warfare and unrest, by human suffering and atrocity. The century in other words was one characterized by warfare, and particular (and new) types of warfare at that. As Keegan has observed

> When war came in the twentieth century its 'recalcitrant indecisiveness' [...] reasserted itself with even greater force [than previously]. The reaction of the rich states was to embark on an ever more intense militarisation of their populations from above, in an attempt to break the deadlock. As the tide of war spilled over into the poor world, militarisation began from below, as the leaders of movements dedicated to winning freedom from European empires and an equivalent to Western economic well-being compelled peasants to become warriors. Both developments were fated to end in frustration.
>
> (1994: 57)

The third reason was that the material record of warfare of the twentieth century sets it apart from earlier times; it has a distinctive material culture comprising the development of science and technology (including flight and the increasing sophistication and accuracy of weapons systems), the emergence of 'Total War', the global scale of conflict, and the acceleration of the process of war – the increasing speed at which decisions are made and actions taken. As Virilio said in 1983 (republished 1997):

We no longer have time for reflection. The power of speed is *that*. Democracy is that. Democracy is no longer in the hands of men, it's in the hands of computerised instruments and answering machines, etc. Today there is still reaction time. It was approximately half an hour in 1961. Andropov and Reagan have no more than several minutes.

(1997: 61)

That said, the volume doesn't constitute a complete record in any sense. Obvious gaps include the physical – structural – record of the many national and international conflicts to emerge in Eastern Europe following the ending of the Cold War (though examples of forensic archaeology in these areas are represented here); there were also the many local conflicts on every continent and many island countries which fed the view of the Cold War being 'red-hot' in some parts of the world; and there are specific aspects on the theme of warfare where significant work remains to be done: curating or recording military hardware such as components of the Russian Fleet for example. Finally, a coherent research framework for the subject matter is still needed. It is hoped that this volume will make a significant contribution to that process, as well as promoting wider awareness and interest.

By contrast are those areas where work has been concentrated over the last ten to fifteen years, since the significance of this area of study became more accepted amongst heritage professionals; since it started to become 'conventional.' Much work has been done in the United Kingdom (see chapters by Lake, Schofield and Anderton), as it has in the USA (Johnson, Beck and Whorton). However, the fact that countries such as Slovakia, Guatemala, Finland, Denmark, Germany, Vietnam, Australia, South Africa and Cambodia are also represented is a clear sign that the values inherent within twentieth-century matériel culture are gaining acceptance amongst a wider and more diverse community, albeit for often very different reasons: for education and cultural benefits including tourism; for reasons of justice (so-called redemptive archaeology); for personal memory. And in thematic and chronological terms there are different emphases too. Virilio (1997: 175) defines three ages of military strategies and technology, the first two of which are covered in depth in this volume, the third only in part. First, strategies and weapons of *obstruction*, represented by built defences – the rampart, the pillbox and emplacement, lines of defence or defended locales (see for example the chapters by Schofield and Kauppi). Second are weapons of *destruction*, particularly artillery (N. Saunders) and on to thermonuclear devices (Beck). And third, weapons of *communication*, such as radar systems and satellites (Whorton). This third 'age' equates to what Virilio calls 'the power of Disappearance': under the sea with nuclear submarines, in the air with spy-planes, and even higher with satellites and the space shuttle (1997: 144). Returning to the Russian Fleet and similar issues around the globe, this is one topic where further research is needed and which is likely to represent a subsequent phase in military archaeology.

In this short introduction we will outline some of the principal themes emerging from the contributions that follow, and provide a context for them, notably: the diversity and form of this material record; the value of matériel culture; a contribution to contemporary society. These themes are not inclusive, but are we believe indicative of current trends.

DIVERSITY AND FORM

The materiality of twentieth-century warfare is a vast and diverse subject, from entire landscapes whose personalities bear the traces of military activity or presence, to specific places – sites, structures, buildings, monuments – where events occurred or where soldiers sat, waiting for invasions that in some cases never came. Matériel culture takes in the artefacts of conflict, from the shells that killed people and which became objects of art and remembrance after the war (N. Saunders), to the medals awarded to survivors or posthumously to those who showed bravery (Joy), to the remains of servicemen killed on active duty and civilians slain by the hand of their own countrymen, identified through the practice of forensic archaeology (Hoshower-Leppo; Crossland; R. Saunders; Jarvis).

Whatever their precise form, artefacts – the objects of war – have immense interpretative value and will often provoke strong reactions amongst those who view them. Museum displays of the Holocaust, showing the clothes, toys, the hair of victims, are powerfully symbolic of the worst atrocities of the Second World War (see for example Weinberg and Eliele 1995); a child's lunchbox does the same in portraying the consequences of the atomic bomb at Hiroshima. On a personal level, militaria belonging to family members or friends will become precious heirlooms, however insignificant they may have been in purely functional or monetary terms.

But places provoke emotions too, especially places of war, conflict, or of personal trauma. One of the places in southwest England from which American servicemen embarked for the D-Day landings means a great deal to the Normandy Veterans, who hold their commemoration service there every four years (Schofield). District Six, Cape Town, has remained largely empty since its inhabitants were forcibly removed under the Group Areas Act in 1966; but that empty space, a scar within the modern city, is arguably the strongest symbol of the apartheid era and its effects on South African citizenry. As a consequence the question of what to do with that scar is a matter of continuing debate (Malan and Soudien). The removal of another monument to socio-political segregation – the Berlin Wall – has also left scars within the modern city (Dolff-Bonekämper), just as the old Iron Curtain has between eastern and western Europe. And as with District Six it is a scar that generates controversy and evokes different perceptions depending on the emotional attachments of individuals to these places of memory.

As w⸱·   ersonal attachment and the associated layers of meaning attributed to
th⸱   ⸱ts of war, sense of place is significant at a community level too.
            ⸱as been a significant feature of the twentieth-century world, and
            ⸱orld have been influenced greatly by a military presence, if not
            ⸱he personality of these areas betrays that presence, that influ-
            ⸱ Cold War presence of US airmen on airbases in East Anglia,
            ⸱ influenced the character of this region, with the degree of

influence decreasing with distance from the main foci. Some American airmen and their families remain in the region, while the types of car, alongside a tendency more towards North American lifestyle pursuits, betray their long-lasting influence. Similarly, the personality of Greenham Common, and that of the nearby town of Newbury, England, owes much to the Cold War presence of missiles, and the protests that occurred here as a result. Interestingly, attitudes to the Common, as expressed by servicemen, protesters, local residents and businessmen illustrate the degree to which these 1980s social and political divisions continue to influence the local scene (Schofield and Anderton 2000).

In fact the relationship between matériel culture and society is rarely straightforward, something Fletcher puts into long-term perspective in the final chapter, and which forms the subject of numerous chapters in this volume. In Slovakia, the memorial at the famed Dukla Pass appears to have lost much of its earlier significance to the local populace (Leech). Australia's coastal defences attest to a haphazard development scheme designed to calm the local population more than secure any real defensive strategy (Gojak). In the Marshall Islands, the Japanese and US Second World War remains on the atolls have significance to Japan and the USA, but are not important to local Marshallese because they are not integral to their culture (Christiansen). A stronger and highly complex series of relationships can be seen in the state of Nevada where the presence of the Test Site, for the second half of the century, overshadowed life in Las Vegas some 120 km away, with some residents proud of 'their' test site, and its contribution to world peace (Beck). There was a darker, more ethereal aspect to this however, with an apparent contradictory cultural response to the growing threat of nuclear war reflected in the domestic architecture of the time (Johnson). There is also the fact that the test area deprived native communities of their traditional territories (Kuletz 1998), a factor which may also be true – albeit on a smaller scale – of the radar installations in Alaska (Whorton). Similar examples of displacement can be found the world over, the example of Ilois natives on Diego Garcia having generated much popular and media attention (see for example Benson 1990).

Some classes of monument reflect the significant and expanding role of science and technology in warfare (its increasing 'speed' as Virilio puts it) through the course of the century. Early experimental sites in southern England bare the traces of early military flight (Lake), while others have the remains of trench systems in which soldiers trained for the Western Front. Munitions factories, and the development of the explosives industry, have a rich and diverse material record, from gunpowder to atomic weapons testing (Cocroft 2000). On the other hand, bases for the deployment of such weapons may not be so varied but the remains can be quite rich, as is the case for example at various places in the Pacific (Christiansen). Above all, this scientific and technological resource is perhaps the most challenging material record to assess and to manage, for two reasons: first, because many of the sites and areas used for testing and experimental work, and for production, were unique in the combination of structures and remains surviving within them. The Nevada Test Site exemplifies this, presumably alongside Semipalatinsk in Kazakhstan, and the Novaya Zemlya test site above the Arctic Circle (Beck). Second, because the industrial production process, embracing scientific experimental research, is key to interpretation, and that process will typically embrace many sites, often in different countries or continents. Structures will range from the spectacularly monumental – such as weapons' testing stands – to mundane laboratory buildings and factories of standard design. The production of Blue Streak, an intercontinental ballistic missile delivery system, in the mid- to late 1950s involved a range of such sites in England and Australia for example (Cocroft 2000: 255–61). To understand the process at one site therefore, visitors must be encouraged to think big, to think global. This of course will be true ultimately for all sites relating to global conflict; visitors can't fully understand part without an appreciation of the whole. They see the 'soldier's eye' view perhaps, but not the wider cultural or political scene of which that soldier was undoubtedly aware.

VALUING MATÉRIEL CULTURE

What values we place on the sites and the materiality of recent conflict are equally diverse, engaging a plethora of emotional, objective and conservation-led arguments which are reflected on in a number of the chapters that follow. First is the point about long-termism; the fact that warfare in the twentieth century forms part of a continuum and although distinctive in many ways it is merely part of the story, not a story in itself (Virilio 1997; Carman this volume; Fletcher this volume). In terms of cultural history therefore, the material record – whether it be monuments and buildings (Lake; Schofield), testimonies or archives (George), or artefacts and hardware (N. Saunders) – has historical and interpretative significance; it tells us about the past, about historic events and people. Yet in heritage management terms, in deciding which sites to retain for interpretation, which archives to present, there needs to be a more detached, objective assessment; there needs to be an understanding of what exists and what is important before such decisions can be taken. In terms of sites and monuments, not everything can be kept, whatever emotional attachments and historic arguments may exist. In a world where sustainability is a central tenet of conservation theory and practice, selection has to be made on the basis of sound understanding and judgement, and that judgement will sometimes necessarily sit apart from the more engaging and emotive ties that sites have to people and events. Examples of how that understanding can be achieved are numerous in this volume (Griffin; Lake; Beck; Clark and others).

At the more engaging level of communities and those personally affected by war and conflict, sense of place and local character are important considerations, as is the use of places and sites for remembering. This is relevant for all recent heritage sites, though the ties and justifications are stronger and more compelling for places which saw conflict, witnessing suffering, loss of life or damage to cultural property; and sacred sites. Again examples are numerous: District Six in Cape Town (Malan and Soudien); the Berlin Wall (Dolff-Bonekämper); the bombed churches of London (Schofield); and Second World War concentration camps (Beech). All are visitor attractions to some extent, but all also have value to the communities and people whose lives these sites have affected, whether at the time or subsequently, and even today. All of these examples are powerfully symbolic sites that now provide places for quiet reflection, for remembering. Associated museums will contribute to understanding past atrocities and violent events, with the best – the most affective, the most engaging – documenting personal experiences of the places they describe, and the consequences of those past events.

Indeed this theme of presentation was a significant factor in determining the scope of the original conference session, and an emphasis that has been retained for the volume. At one level, should sites that will serve to remind people of past troubles be retained or removed? Is it better to confront this materiality, or ignore and forget it (Jarman)? Then, what is an appropriate way of presenting and interpreting sites of conflict? To leave things as they are, as 'monuments' clearly displaying the effects of time and neglect (as can be seen in pictures of District Six and the area of the former Nordbahnhof in Berlin), or to provide clean, managed sites where tourists and visitors are presented with a finished product, a visitor experience, engaging to a greater or lesser degree? The arguments and options are complex and extend of course beyond heritage management considerations, drawing in for example economic, political and social dimensions too. The complexity of these arguments is evident in several contributions (Beech; Clark; George; Jarman, for example).

Value also has relevance in the context of social historical research. Some material records are central to developing a knowledge of warriors and societies at war that official histories and some archives don't address. What were these combatants like; how did they behave in time of war; how was the world through their eyes? Diaries and personal accounts can help here, contributing to a valuable social archaeology of communities at war (Anderton). However, as John Steinbeck noted in his journals as a war correspondent, this will only extend so far. Warriors will often not remember their experiences in battle, and the worse the battle the less they remember. As he says, 'under extended bombardment or bombing the nerve ends are literally beaten. The ear drums are tortured by blast and the eyes ache from the constant hammering' (1975: 163). This emotional battering is likely to prevent recall in any logical sense, at least for the types of conflict Steinbeck witnessed. We may not therefore witness a warrior's experience 'at war', in the teeth of battle, but the information from 'behind the lines' can also provide significant insight (Anderton). Then there's the passage of time, which inevitably distorts fact. Testimonies, archives and journals are valuable resources, but as with all evidence they need to be interpreted in an objective and discerning way (George).

MATÉRIEL CULTURE IN THE CONTEMPORARY WORLD

Beyond all else this volume is about values and significance, whether as a historic resource for purposes of research and understanding, to promote awareness, or to enable this and future generations to confront their troubled pasts, for remembering, for justice, or to ensure a more peaceful and tolerant society in the future. It is also about the role of archaeologists in our modern world. Too often we are relegated to a role of only being able to illuminate prehistory or history so distant that no living persons exist to tell about it. In this volume we highlight the strides of archaeologists to challenge this role. Whether it is about the conduct of archaeological data gathering (Beck, Hoshower-Leppo, R. Saunders and others) or theorizing about relationships between sets of material culture (Johnson), we believe the discipline as a whole is expanded and improved.

The examples included here do not cover in depth all the types of twentieth-century conflict and its materiality, but they do indicate the breadth both of human experience, and the fabric that survives to relay these experiences to future generations. From London to Slovakia and the Marshall Islands in the 1940s, from Cape Town to Berlin in the 1960s, from Robben Island to Northern Ireland in the 1980–90s, matériel culture is everywhere, both in a strictly material sense, in the built environment, written words, pictures and film, and in terms of human experience. This record, characterizing much of what the twentieth century was about, will inevitably diminish with time. But in documenting its significance, in describing what it is and what it means, by drawing it into the scope of mainstream historical and archaeological research, the rate of decay can be slowed contributing in some small way to interpreting a violent twentieth century, and we hope to a future in which, as John Keegan states, 'man's proclivity to take up arms' is inhibited.

REFERENCES

Benson, P. (1990) *A Lesser Dependency,* London: Penguin.

Carman, J. (ed.) (1997) *Material Harm: Archaeological Studies of War and Violence,* Glasgow: Cruithne Press.

Cocroft, W.D. (2000) *Dangerous Energy: The Archaeology of Gunpowder and Military Explosives Manufacture,* London: English Heritage.

Howard, M. (1994) 'Constraints on warfare', in Howard, M., Andreopoulos, G. and Shulman, M. (eds) *The Laws of War: Constraints on Warfare in the Modern World,* Yale: Yale University Press, pp. 1–11.

Judd, Lord of Portsea (1998) 'Foreword', in Rupesinghe, K. (ed.) *Civil Wars, Civil Peace: An Introduction to Conflict Resolution,* London: Pluto Press, pp. ix-x.

Keegan, J. (1993) *A History of Warfare,* London: Pimlico.

Kuletz, V.L. (1998) *The Tainted Desert: Environmental Ruin in the American West,* New York and London: Routledge.

Schofield, J. and Anderton, M. (2000) The queer archaeology of Green Gate: interpreting contested space at Greenham Common Airbase, *World Archaeology* 32(2) 236–51.

Steinbeck, J. (1975) *Once There Was a War,* London: Pan.

Virilio, P. and Lotringer, S. (1997) *Pure War* (Revised edn), New York: Semiotext(e).

Weinberg, J. and Elieli, R. (1995) *The Holocaust Museum in Washington,* New York: Rizzoli.

2   Paradox in places: twentieth-century battlefield sites in long-term perspective

JOHN CARMAN

The 'Bloody Meadows' project (Carman 1999a, b) investigates the category of the 'historic battlefield' as a culturally constructed locale. It approaches battlefields from the premise that such places have something to tell us about the nature of human violence as expressed in war, and this makes them important. As a consequence, the project is inevitably concerned with issues surrounding their preservation.

A 'historic battlefield' is a defined space in which organized groups of armed people did regulated violence upon one another. Such places are the main focus of attention for military historians of all periods (Keegan 1976; Weigley 1991) and are increasingly being taken up as part of a nation's 'official' cultural heritage (for example, the preservation of US battlefields as National Monuments: Scott *et al.* 1989; English Heritage 1995; Foard 1995; Schofield 1998). Bloody Meadows, however, moves beyond the conventional discourses of military history and indeed much 'military archaeology' into a frame where cultural attitudes to battlefields come to the fore. In the twentieth century war was less concerned with defined spaces, and extended its reach. Accordingly, this chapter will examine twentieth-century war from the perspective of the long term in human history and will to some extent provide a justification for a preservationist project in the 'archaeology of war' that comes no closer to our own time than the year 1900. In doing so, it will place the interpretation and understanding of twentieth-century war at the heart of any concern with the preservation of its physical remains.

PRESERVING THE EVIDENCE OF WAR

The process of preservation in archaeological resource management (ARM) classically involves the two preliminary stages of identification and evaluation. Identification involves a process of survey and recording with the intention of establishing the quantity and types of the material available. Evaluation involves a process of giving value to material such that the value given to any one example can be compared with the value given to another. From this, choices can be made as to which examples are to be kept for posterity and which others are to be investigated or abandoned (Cleere 1984: 126). This is the system generally applied and which allows schedules or lists of important places and monuments to be compiled in the various countries of the world. It is a general approach that can be applied to upstanding buildings, to field monuments of various kinds and to places. Resource managers are increasingly aware that what they seek to preserve today will become the material record of the past for the future (Lipe 1984: 3). The general trend in the twentieth century towards the public preservation of all kinds of everything from the past has given rise to some criticism that it stifles new initiatives (Strong 1990: 221–3) and serves to blind people to the realities of their own lives by allowing the creation of 'comfortable' nostalgic pasts (Hewison 1987).

The kind of monument creation that emerged from the major wars of the last century can, however, be seen in a different light. They mostly do not represent the efforts of 'detached' professionals at public preservation, but the efforts of those directly involved to make some kind of sense of, and to help overcome, the horrors of which they were a part. First World War memorials to the dead – constructed throughout Europe in to the 1920s – were frequently not official 'public' constructions, but local initiatives designed to commemorate those personally known to the builders (Tarlow 1997: 113–15). A contrast can be drawn with, for example, the Vietnam Memorial in Washington DC, but this too was achieved through the pressure of those directly involved in that conflict. The Commonwealth War Graves Commission was a similar initiative to commemorate the dead who found their last resting place a long way from home: lovingly tended, these cemeteries remain moving testimony to the human cost of war. The battlefields of the First World War Western Front (1914–18) and of Western Europe after D-Day (1944) were not originally marked as 'historic battlefields' because to their visitors in the years immediately following those wars they represented not history but current events. They were primarily meant as mass cemeteries for the people of all countries who had died there, as are the cemeteries for American aircrew and others located in various parts of England. Whatever the main reason most have for visiting such places today – and many people still go to them as burial places – at the time of their creation they were seen as graves. Other initiatives concerned with ongoing life rather than past death were also evident in the preservation of the bombed-out cities of the Second World War. Some cities retained for decades their empty centres due to the vicissitudes of international politics (Berlin). Some were preserved by rebuilding, possibly as replicas of themselves prior to the war (Warsaw, Prague, Dresden); others were rebuilt deliberately anew (parts of London, Rotterdam); yet others were rebuilt as a mixture of old and new incorporating evidence for the wartime destruction (Coventry).

None of these examples represents the kind of preservation undertaken by professionals in archaeological resource management. The ARM approach is inevitably and quite properly academic, which categorizes material as 'of historic interest or importance' rather than as the stuff of our own direct experience. This is also the kind of approach taken to the preservation of battlefields, which categorizes them as phenomena from the past to be studied, not as the stuff of direct human experience. This kind of preservation represents a very different approach from that of the builders of war memorials and cemeteries, even though academic attention may turn to such structures (Bushaway 1992). They are no longer seen as war memorials and as cemeteries but as historical monuments, as distant from us as a medieval 'Eleanor Cross' or a prehistoric standing stone. The kinds of things created under such a programme are different from those of commemoration, even though some of the motives may be the same. Lines of First World War trenches have, for example, been preserved or reconstructed in an effort to retain some idea of the physical changes to the landscape wrought across Europe in that conflict. Inevitably such features become grass-grown, the trees are restored, nearby settlements are rebuilt and reoccupied and the fields are once more used for agriculture; thankfully, nobody is being killed there any more (but see N. Saunders, this volume). In this process, vital elements of the experience of being in that war – unsanitary conditions, alienation from the landscape and from fellow human beings, fear, pain, violent death – are lost to visitors and future students of war. Also inevitably, only parts of the system of trenches that ran from the North Sea coast to Switzerland are capable of preservation: the scale is reduced from the continental to the very local, and while this may reflect the short-term experience of individual soldiers occupied with a relatively narrow and restricted sector of the front, it inevitably denies a crucial aspect of that experience which lay in the knowledge of its extent. Elsewhere, the signs of past war may be preserved on the walls of buildings as bullet-holes or scarring caused by bomb and shell fragments (Athens, the Fix Brewery; London, Embankment; Cambridge, Trinity College, Sidney Street): they become 'features of historic interest' rather than part of an experience of terror and pain. The same applies to any deliberately preserved battlespace of twentieth-century war: the true nature of the experience has to be masked and the scale to be reduced simply to allow any conception of the events represented. Other preservation initiatives concern the technology of war. Examples of the types of weapon used in various conflicts, of armoured vehicles, amphibious vehicles and aircraft are accordingly kept in museums and by volunteer enthusiasts. Similarly, the last surviving 'big gun' warship of the Royal Navy is now on show on the Thames in London. All these devices for killing are thus made safe and available as things to visit.

The focus of professional and academic preservation is inevitably upon objects which become divorced from their contexts of construction and use. It is the same whether one is dealing with a portable object or a vehicle or a place. In treating battlefields, weapons, ships, aircraft or tanks the thing is treated as if it can be separated out from all other categories of things and retained, examined and understood as something separable from the rest of experience. This seems to work quite well as an approach for the more distant past where our own emotional and experiential involvement is limited, but it presents problems when dealing with the warfare of our own age. This is the 'paradox' of my title: the separation of the sense of recent or contemporary lived experience from the objects that were an integral part of creating that experience.

TWENTIETH-CENTURY WAR

The shape of late twentieth-century warfare as we came to know it (and even of twenty-first century warfare as we can foresee it) emerged as early as the closing months of the Second World War (1939–45). Jet fighter aircraft engaged bomber fleets, missiles struck at city populations, guided missiles sank warships, communication systems tracked enemy movements, and the very end of the war saw the first use of nuclear weapons. That war saw a heavy investment in scientific developments and new ways of waging war – that is, ways not limited to the use of bodies of infantry backed by artillery and more mobile forces, even though much of the 'battlefield' action was of just such a kind (Keegan 1976: 285–9). Much of the action of that war was also located away from traditional battlefield spaces. The seat of action of mid-twentieth-century warfare physically extended beyond the conventional temperate zones into the desert, the jungle and the arctic regions; it penetrated below the surface of sea, into the sky and even into outer space. Keegan's (1989) discussion of the Second World War abandons a detailed chronicle of events in favour of discussions of the main forms of military action experienced and the 'themes' of the war: the search for supremacy in the air; the airborne delivery of forces by land and sea; fighting in and for cities; amphibious landings; the military occupation of conquered territory; long-range aerial bombardment; Special Operations, resistance to occupation and espionage; and the development of secret weapons. The action of the war thus extended conceptually beyond the battlefield proper, to civilian populations and their governments, into the realms of science and technology, and the beginnings of computerdom, the infosphere and cyberspace. This is the pattern of warfare we have come to know during the Cold War and since its end: it is what Gray (1997) calls 'postmodern war'.

Elsewhere (Carman 1999b) I have suggested a tentative three-period 'model' for understanding battlefields. Although it is evident that within each of these stages there are further more complex processes at work (Carman 1999a), and which it is one of the purposes of Bloody Meadows as it develops to reveal, the model as a whole appears to stand the test of scrutiny. The style of battle common throughout much of antiquity, through the medieval and well into the early modern period was like a formal duel, deliberately fought on flat ground with as few features as possible. This set-piece engagement on flat ground displays a very different attitude towards the kinds of places where battles were allowed to be fought than later in history, for by the end of the seventeenth century places were actively being sought for battles that had recognizable features: high ground, wooded areas, defensible lines of stream or wall, or buildings in which to enclose troops. During the eighteenth and nineteenth centuries the search for featured ground came to be an important part of military practice, so that this period from the seventeenth to the early nineteenth centuries was, as one military historian has put it, 'quintessentially the age of battles' (Weigley 1991: xi) – the period inspiring Clausewitz to write his monumental book *On War* (Clausewitz 1976 (1832)) which argued the case for the single, decisive clash of arms.

Day-long battle over shaped landscapes was to give way to 'the nightmare of endless grappling in the sodden trenches of … the American Civil War, and then the First World War' (Weigley 1991: xi). Keegan (1976: 308) chronicles 'the transformation of the environment of the battlefield into one almost wholly – and indiscriminately – hostile to (human beings)'. But the idea of total destruction was also transferred elsewhere: beyond the battlefield space to other seats of war. Large-scale destruction by aerial bombardment of warmaking potential was seen as a way of avoiding the horrors of the modern battle. This was the idea that lay behind the Japanese attack on Pearl Harbor (1941), behind the German *blitzkrieg* (1939–40) and British and American strategic bombing campaigns (1940–5). Brodie (1973: 51) is at pains to point out that the firestorm was a technique first developed by the allies against the cities of Germany and Japan: we remember the civilian population of Dresden as a victim of the firestorm, often forgetting that the technique was perfected against the marshalling yards and port facilities of Hamburg and the wooden buildings of Tokyo. All of Japan's major cities were subjected to such attacks by mid-1945, with the exception of Hiroshima and Nagasaki. The atomic bomb was constructed and used as a relatively cheap means – both in lives and treasure – of delivering the firestorm to these last remaining enemy cities. By the time of its use, such was American air superiority that a single aircraft accompanied by a single fighter could fly safely over Japan; a single aircraft carrying a single bomb was then able to destroy an entire city (Brodie 1973: 45–56).

This notion of complete destruction has found its way into our own age. The Nazi Holocaust was an attempt to wipe out an entire population, and others (for example, the efforts of Pol Pot in Cambodia and 'ethnic cleansing' in former Yugoslavia and Rwanda) have sought to emulate that example. The theory that lay behind Cold War strategies was that an attempt to strike at any ally would trigger worldwide nuclear devastation, and few had doubts that this would mean the effective end of humanity. In the Vietnamese jungle (1961–73) there was widespread use by American forces of defoliant chemicals; the 'free-fire' zone was an area where complete destruction was specifically authorized to annihilate enemy forces; and aerial bombing campaigns such as 'Rolling Thunder' which deliberately targeted civilian populations were specifically intended to bomb North Vietnam 'into the stone age' (Le May, quoted in Brodie 1973: 179) or to 'flatten the country and (allow us to) pave it over' (Reagan, quoted in Brodie 1973: 179). As this chapter is being written (January 2000), Russian forces are systematically razing the Chechen city of Grozny and virtually every other part of the world can cite an example of a major war involving some kind of attempt at mass destruction since the end of the Second World War (Laffin 1995: 23–4). There is every reason to believe that the twentieth century is the bloodiest in human history and in the twenty-first century we all still live under the threat of nuclear war.

INTERPRETING TWENTIETH-CENTURY WAR

Changes in warmaking style represent more than mere technological advance or simply changes in tactics, and there are echoes in the changes on battlefields of other changes in society (Carman 1999b: 238–9). Gray (1997: 195–210) charts the late-twentieth-century rise of the 'cyborg-soldier', increasingly dehumanized by a reliance on advanced technology and the use of drugs to overcome the stresses of battle, developments which are reflected also in civilian life. Such phenomena highlight the almost unnoticed ubiquity of war in our world, and the increasing power of the discourse of war to dominate other discourses (Gray 1997: 247–54).

The Bloody Meadows Project has developed a set of parameters for the analysis of battlefields in the past which allows an understanding of battle in a particular period to be developed (Carman 1999a). The analysis is split into two broad but interacting fields: the 'rules of war' applying in a particular period; and the specifics of a particular battlefield landscape. The rules of war cover such things as the degree of mutual agreement needed before fighting could commence, whether the two sides were required to see each other as 'legitimate' enemies or whether anyone could participate in a battle, some assessment of the level of violence employed, and how (if at all) the battlesite was remembered afterwards. They are a measure of how 'formal' battle was regarded and how distinctive it was from other forms of conflict at that time. The characteristics of the battlefield landscape are addressed in order to identify features present in the battlespace and how they were used by combatants. This gives some insight into attitudes to the battlefield as a place. The query as to whether structured formations were present (ordered columns or lines of troops) gives a clue to how participants moved through the battlefield space: if the landscape is seen as architecture, so too can the forces engaged be seen as a kind of 'mobile architecture'. The two final sections attempt to summarize our expectations as filtered through an understanding of 'good military practice': it is the dysfunctional behaviour (the apparent mistakes or omissions) which can give a clue to cultural attitudes and expectations of the battlefield space. In applying this analysis to two distinctive examples of twentieth-century warfare, the difference of 'post-modern' war from that of earlier periods becomes evident. Taking such a long-term perspective, late-twentieth-century 'post-modern' war can be seen to be as different from modern war as modern war was from ancient war.

The Battle of the Atlantic 1939–43

Although technically a battle as long as the war of which it was a part, the consensus of historical opinion marks the German attempt to prevent essential supplies to Britain during the Second World War as won by December 1943 (Keegan 1989: 103–23; Syrett 1994). Using a combination of surface vessels, air attacks and especially submarines (U-boats) operating in 'packs', the Germans sought to prevent supply ships reaching British ports and to destroy others that could be used for the purpose. In response, the British and their allies instituted a system of protected convoys. Action ranged over the expanse of the Atlantic Ocean, from the coasts of

Table 2.1 The Battle of the Atlantic 1939–43

Rules of war	*Battlefield architecture*
Agreement to fight: Y	*Features present*
	Surface
	Subsurface
	Large extent of ocean
	Shipping lanes/convoy routes
	Radio links
	Weather systems
	Tides/currents
Mutual recognition as 'legitimate' enemies: Y	*Type of feature used*
	Surface
	Subsurface
	Large extent of ocean
	Shipping lanes/convoy routes
	Radio links
	Weather systems
Level of violence: high	*Type of feature not used*
	Tides/currents
Marking of battlesite: none	*Use of terrain:*
	as cover Y
	to impede visibility Y
	to impede movement Y
	all by convoys
Participants: naval personnel and civilian crews	*Structured formations:* Y
Ultimate target: civilian population of the UK	

Functional aspects

Recognition by both sides of the importance of the sea-lanes to the outcome of the war. Effective and imaginative use of existing technology to find and attack targets. Development by Allies of effective anti U-boat techniques and effective deployment of resources.

Dysfunctional aspects

Failure of Germans to develop effective anti-convoy tactics. Unwillingness of German air forces to provide reconnaissance and cover for U-boats. Involvement of civilian crews as targets. Distance of ultimate target: UK home population and warmaking potential. Different measures of success: for U-boats, destruction of enemy shipping; for convoys, avoidance of loss of shipping and cargo.

Britain and the United States, over the central ocean and to the sea off Gibraltar. The combined use of electronic tracking devices and air cover allowed allied convoys and their naval escorts either to avoid U-boats or to pin them in position and destroy them.

Analysis of this long and complex conflict indicates a surprisingly large number of 'features' present in the battlespace which played a large part in the battle as it unfurled: the majority of these are conceptual or technological rather than physical 'terrain' to be experienced directly. The failure of the Germans to develop effective means of countering the defensive power of the convoy or to combine resources (such as submarines and air power) is suggestive of a belief in merely putting pressure on an enemy to cause surrender. However, the ultimate target of these operations was not ships and their crews, but the civilian population relying on the supplies carried (Syrett 1994: 259) who were geographically very distant and entirely detached from the action at sea.

'Rolling Thunder': the American air war against North Vietnam 1965–8

In response to attacks on American forces providing aid to South Vietnam in its war against insurgents supported by North Vietnam, the US instituted a series of air attacks on North Vietnamese targets. Beginning with attempts to destroy North Vietnam's military logistical and supply capacity, the raids increased in intensity over three years to include civilian industrial targets (Thompson 1980: 40–3). The North Vietnamese responses included increasing air defences, dispersal of industrial production into the countryside and increased reliance upon foreign aid to provide essential supplies and war matériel (Smith 1994: 201–2). The launch of the so-called 'Tet Offensive' in January 1968 proved the warmaking capacity of North Vietnam was unaffected by the bombing (Smith 1994: 213; Thompson 1980: 42) and – together with a shift in American public opinion against the war – brought a gradual end to the bombing campaign.

Air war provides few 'features' identifiable in the battlespace. Clearly, as in the case of the German submarine war in the Atlantic, the US forces believed in winning a war by placing pressure on populations at large rather than defeat of an enemy 'in the field'. The ultimate enemy was also, again, detached from the action (Smith 1994: 233, 235): South Vietnamese insurgents were not directly targeted by bombing. Finally, there was a variance in understanding of what was at stake: for the US Vietnam was a limited 'brush-fire' war on the fringe of the broader Cold War struggle; but for the North Vietnamese it was a war for survival and national liberation and therefore 'total' (Smith 1994: 239).

Twentieth-century battle in long-term perspective

These distinctive battles of the twentieth century share elements in common, and these elements may be typical of the shift to a new style of war in our age. Both battles extended beyond the land to environments hostile to humans unsupported by technology: the open sea and the air. Such features as were present can be apprehended conceptually but cannot physically be experienced, which distanced

Table 2.2 'Rolling Thunder': the American air war against Vietnam 1965–8

Rules of war	Battlefield architecture
Agreement to fight: Y	*Features present:* None
Mutual recognition as 'legitimate' enemies: Y	*Type of feature used:* None
Level of violence: high	*Type of feature not used:* N/A
Marking of battlesite: none	*Use of terrain:* as cover N/A to impede visibility N/A to impede movement N/A
Participants: military personnel (both sides) and civilian population of North Vietnam	*Structured formations:* Y

Functional aspects

Effective use of resources available to both sides:
    US – high-tech weapons and air power;
    North Vietnam (NV) – dispersed population, low-tech needs.
Attempt by US to win a war by cheapest and quickest means available. Effective use by NV of access to overseas support and material aid. High morale and 'will to win' among all participants.

Dysfunctional aspects

Failure of US to appreciate NV strategy of pulling US into a long war. Over-reliance of US on air power alone. Willingness of both sides to inflict and bear civilian casualties. Distance of ultimate target of raids from action: South Vietnamese insurgents. Different measures of success: US, damage to NV warmaking capacity and undermining of will to continue; NV, avoidance or absorption of damage. Different measures of scale of the war: while a limited war for the US, for NV it was a 'total' war.

fighters from their 'terrain'. Also, the targets at which action was directed were not those directly engaged in combat: in the 1940s Atlantic, it was the civilian population of the UK; in 1960s Vietnam, it was South Vietnamese insurgents. In both cases, the measures of success of the two sides were at variance: for one, destruction of the enemy; for the other, merely to absorb or avoid harm. This differs from the battles of other ages, where the aims of both sides would be identical: victory here and now over the opposing force. Ultimately, rather than the physical destruction of enemy forces as advocated by Clausewitz (1976 (1832): 258), what was sought was to persuade the enemy population to cease fighting.

Accordingly, the battlefields of our own time are not only more extensive than those of earlier periods with fighting persisting over a longer time (Keegan 1976: 302–5), but are simultaneously and disconcertingly at once everywhere and nowhere, involving everybody both at home and in the front line. As Herr (1977: 207) puts it for his generation and ours, 'Vietnam, Vietnam, Vietnam: we've all been there'. In considering the preservation of the material remains of the last century's wars, we need to consider very carefully what it is exactly that we wish to preserve and what we do preserve in the act of preservation.

CONCLUSIONS: PRESERVING THE MEMORY OF TWENTIETH-CENTURY WAR

The choice of what we preserve from the wars of our age will inevitably become the measure in the future of what those wars were about and what they were like. The record left by those involved is one of cemeteries and memorials to the dead, and reconstruction to continue life. The record of the preservationist is that of carefully conserved areas where organized and regulated fighting once took place and of the implements and technology of war. Cemeteries and memorials contain a powerful involvement of emotion and feeling – the direct stuff of human experience; and the will to rebuild and carry on for the future is the product of that investment of feeling. By contrast, the professional preservation record tends to be that of the professional military perspective on war: an emphasis on technology, on the specifics of military means, and indeed on the military ideology of war that focuses on the rational control of irrationality (Gray 1997). For past ages – in which the military and civilian areas of life can conveniently be set apart (cf. the 'age of battles' which ended in 1815 (Weigley 1991: xvii)) – this is an approach that can make a great deal of sense. But for our own age – in which military activity inevitably involves the civilian sphere, in which civilian populations are subject to deliberate military attack, and where total and Cold War subsumes all other activity – this separation denies the reality of war as experienced. The remains of twentieth-century war cannot then be treated like the military remains from any other period. The myth of 'peace' since the end of the Second World War belies the truth of experience outside the countries of Western Europe and North America: it has been pointed out that 'the Cold War was red hot in the Third World' (Childs, quoted in Gray 1977: 27). The remains of twentieth-century war are supremely culturally significant because – almost more than anything else we may pass to our descendants – they represent what the twentieth century has very largely been about. We have lived, and still live, in an age of almost permanent war. Where war is not directly affecting us, it is affecting us indirectly. It is this fact that somehow must be reflected in the project of preserving the evidence for twentieth-century war.

It seems to me that there are two different ways forward. One is not to attempt to preserve the remains of our wars. Instead, we leave as their legacy the artefacts of those involved – cemeteries, War Graves, monuments and memorials, the evidence of destruction, the rebuilt cities – for future archaeologists to make of what they can. Some of those specifically military remains with which the professional preservationist project is directly concerned will also survive accidentally to be available to our professional successors. This approach has the advantage that we need not pre-interpret the stuff of our own time. We need make no choices about what is significant, about what can or should be preserved, and we do not thereby dictate to future generations what they should think of us. We need not try to be 'objective' about our own age. Instead the future can make up its own mind about us from whatever it can glean of our accidental remains.

The alternative is to deliberately incorporate a sense of the experience of war into our preservationist project. We need to go out of our way to preserve material that can give as full a picture of twentieth-century war as possible. It means that we need first to develop that picture. We cannot do this from an 'objective' standpoint, because we are not objective about our own lives. But we do know our own experience and can draw on the experience of others. What we could aim to pass on to the future is a sense of what it may have been like to be us in our time, as complete as we can make it, with as many different perspectives on what it was like as we can include. This is not an easy task. It is not an easy task because completeness of this kind is by no means easy to achieve, if it can be sought at all. It is even more difficult because it is inevitably also a supremely uncomfortable task. We cannot afford to allow the myths of recent history to overtake us: and we shall need to go out of our way to incorporate in our project the perspective and experience of those whose actions we find morally repugnant. We cannot afford to be squeamish, nor to select only the morally justifiable as worthy of remembrance. It means taking a proper responsibility for understanding what our age has been like and passing this heightened personal knowledge on to our descendants.

This chapter has sought to consider some of the issues surrounding the preservation of the remains of the wars of our own time. It has done so by distinguishing the 'professional' preservation project from the responses of those more directly involved. It has also sought to demonstrate the importance of first understanding the war of our age. As professionals we have important and serious choices to make about whether to attempt to deliberately preserve the evidence for the wars of our age, and if so what we consider suitable to mark as worthy of remembrance. My own view is that we should endeavour to pass on to our descendants some idea of what our period of history has been like. I believe that to do so we need to choose carefully, to be fully professional and ultimately not to be frightened of what we may need to recognize of ourselves or our time. The tendency to gloss over the unpleasant or to be squeamish must be actively suppressed: the wars of our time are neither nice nor few and limited, and we have a duty not to make them appear so.

ACKNOWLEDGEMENTS

This chapter is written in memoriam of the author's namesake, Private Richard John Carman of the 8th Battalion Queen's Own (Royal West Kent Regiment), who died on Wednesday 20 March 1918 and is remembered with honour at the Thiepval Memorial, Somme, France in the perpetual care of the Commonwealth War Graves Commission.

The chapter has seen two previous incarnations with identical titles. The first was presented to the WAC4 session from which this volume derives. A second was published on the WAC4 website at: http://www.wac.uct.ac.za/wac4/symposia/papers/S040crm1.pdf

I am grateful to John Schofield for the opportunity to present the papers and for the chance to publish in this book a further development of these ideas. Thanks are also due to the McDonald Institute for Archaeological Research, Cambridge, for financial assistance supporting the fieldwork that helped the Bloody Meadows Project to develop. Clare Hall, Cambridge, provided valuable and generous assistance with the costs of attending WAC4, and both Clare Hall and the Department of Archaeology of the University of Cambridge provided the facilities where Bloody Meadows and this chapter were realized. As always, I owe an immeasurable debt to Patricia Carman, partner in battlefield research and life, for just about everything.

REFERENCES

Brodie, B. (1973) *War and Politics,* London: Cassell.

Bushaway, B. (1992) 'Name upon name: the Great War and remembrance', in Porter, R. (ed.) *Myths of the English*, Cambridge: Polity Press, pp. 136–67.

Carman, J. (1999a) 'Beyond the Western way of war: ancient battlefields in comparative perspective', in Carman, J. and Harding, A. (eds) *Ancient Warfare: Archaeological Perspectives*, Stroud: Sutton, pp. 39–55.

Carman, J. (1999b) 'Bloody Meadows: the places of battle', in Tarlow, S. and West, S. (eds) *The Familiar Past? Archaeologies of Britain 1550–1950*, London: Routledge, pp. 233–245.

Clausewitz, C. von. [1832] (1976) *On War,* edited and translated by M. Howard and P. Paret, Princeton: Princeton University Press.

Cleere, H.F. (1984) *Approaches to the Archaeological Heritage,* Cambridge: Cambridge University Press.

Doyle, P. and Bennett, M.R. (1997) Military geography: terrain evaluation and the Western Front 1914–1918, *Geographical Journal* 163: 1–24.

English Heritage (1995) *Register of Historic Battlefields,* London: English Heritage.

Foard, G. (1995) *Naseby: The Decisive Campaign,* Whitstable: Pryor Publications.

Gray, C.H. (1997) *Postmodern War: The New Politics of Conflict,* London: Routledge.

Herr, M. (1977) *Dispatches,* London: Picador.

Hewison, R. (1987) *The Heritage Industry: Britain in a Climate of Decline,* London: Methuen.

Keegan, J. (1976) *The Face of Battle,* London: Hutchinson.

Keegan, J. (1989) *The Second World War,* London: Hutchinson.

Laffin, J. (1995) *Brassey's Battles: 3,500 years of Conflict, Campaigns and Wars from A-Z,* London: Brassey's.

Lipe, W. (1984) 'Value and meaning in cultural resources', in Cleere, H.F. (ed.) *Approaches to the Archaeological Heritage*, Cambridge: Cambridge University Press, pp. 1–11.

Schofield, J. (1998) 'Character, conflict and atrocity: touchstones in the archaeology of war', in Jones, M. and Rotherham, D. (eds) *Landscapes – Perception, Recognition and Management: Reconciling the Impossible*, Sheffield: The Landscape Conservation Forum and Sheffield Hallam University (Landscape Archaeology and Ecology 3), pp. 104–107.

Scott, D.D., Fox, R.A., Connor, M.A. and Harmon, D. (1989) *Archaeological Perspectives on the Battle of the Little Big Horn,* Norman OK and London: University of Oklahoma Press.

Smith, J.T. (1994) *Rolling Thunder: The American Strategic Bombing Campaign against North Vietnam 1964–1968,* Walton on Thames: Air Research Publications.

Strong, R. (1990) *Lost Treasures of Britain: Five Centuries of Creation and Destruction,* London: Guild Publishing.

Syrett, D. (1994) *The Defeat of the German U-Boats: The Battle of the Atlantic,* Columbia SC: University of South Carolina Press.

Tarlow, S. (1997) An archaeology of remembering: death, bereavement and the First World War, *Cambridge Archaeological Journal* 7(1): 105–121.

Thompson, J.C. (1980) *Rolling Thunder: Understanding Policy and Programme Failure,* Chapel Hill NC: University of North Carolina Press.

Weigley, R.F. (1991) *The Age of Battles: The Quest for Decisive Warfare from Breitenfeld to Waterloo,* Bloomington and Indianapolis: Indiana University Press.

3   The ironic 'culture of shells' in the Great War and beyond

Nicholas J. Saunders

> The brains of science, the money of fools
> Had fashioned an iron slave.
>
> ('The Shell', Private H. Smalley Sarson, 1993)

THE SHELLS OF WAR

The Great War of 1914–18 was recognized at the time as 'the war of matériel' – a dramatic example of a world transformed by and constituted of its material culture (Miller 1985: 204–5). If objects make people just as people make objects (see for example Pels 1998: 101), then the defining objects of the First World War were the millions of artillery shells made in munitions factories across Europe and the United States from 1914 to 1918 and fired in huge quantities particularly along the Western Front. More shells were fired in the battle of Neuve Chapelle in March 1915 than in the whole of the Boer War (Gilbert 1994: 132). The dead and injured accumulated in vast numbers, forcing us perhaps to agree with Allain Bernède (1997: 91) that, 'the front … [was] … nothing but the continuation of the factory'. Shell production, warfare and death had been industrialized.

It is not surprising that artillery shells have come to symbolize the world's first experience of total war. Shells devastated landscape as well as people, transformed economies, altered gender relations through an industrialized military complex, became art and icon, and possessed symbolic resonances which ambiguously combined Modernism and pre-war realities. If the modern world was forged in the crucible of war, then shells were the catalyst, fragmenting peoples, places and institutions.

In writing a cultural biography of the shell (*pace* Kopytoff 1986), we can explore the complex relationship between human beings, the things they made and used, and the nature of the physical, spiritual, and metaphorical worlds they created through the agency of destruction (Saunders n.d.a). Rich in symbolism and irony, shells were mediators between men and women, soldiers and civilians, individuals and industrialized society, the nations which fought the war, and, perhaps most of all, between the living and the dead.

Shells gave birth to a geographical feature which has come to represent the Great War, and which itself possesses many implications for the study of landscape (Saunders 2001a). Military stalemate in the first few months of the war led to the digging of continuous lines of trenches, 760 km long, from the English Channel to the Swiss border (Keegan 1998: 147). To dislodge men from trenches, rather than killing them on open battlefields, high explosives rather than shrapnel-bearing shells were needed (Strachan 1998: 137). This shift of military emphasis had far-reaching consequences for the conduct of the war.

> Generals anxious to explain their failures in 1914 were quick to attribute all to a lack of high-explosive shell. In so doing they exacerbated the shortage of which they complained, effectively discouraging the search for tactical and operational solutions in favour of that for economic and industrial ones.
>
> (Strachan 1998: 138)

In a materiality-based view of the world, an individual's social being is determined by their relationship to the objects that represent them, the object becoming a metaphor for the self, a way of knowing oneself through things (Hoskins 1998: 195, 198). Through the various transformations of their 'social lives', artillery shells, and the experiences of all who came and continue to come into contact with them, offer new perspectives and insights into what Gell (1998: 74) calls the objectification of personhood in artefacts.

INDUSTRIALIZED IRONY

Munitions were metaphorically and physically conceived by women. As war progressed and more men were released to the front, women increasingly took on industrial jobs. Fuse- and cartridge-making saw an increase of some 424 000 women between 1914 and 1918 (Braybon 1995: 150), and the 400 women who worked at Woolwich Arsenal in 1915 had increased to 27 000 by the time of the Armistice (Ouditt 1994: 72). By war's end, Winston Churchill could comment that Britain had become an arsenal (Terraine 1996: 5).

An irony not lost on Edwardian society was that women furnished men with weapons of mass destruction (Woollacott 1994: 7). Justifications of this inversion of past practices and of the 'natural order', saw parallels drawn between making bombs and making babies, with references to the womb of the shell being loaded with its deadly charge (Hall Caine quoted in Ouditt 1994: 78–9). Working in munitions factories allowed approximately 1 million women to 'do their bit' (Woollacott 1994: 2,18) – it also changed their perspective in what had been a man's world of work. Working in a munitions factory was an opportunity to escape service 'below stairs', and enter better paid factory employment (Woollacott 1994: 4–5). Some 400 000 women left domestic service mainly for munitions and transport work between 1914 and 1918 (Braybon 1995: 148–9) (Fig. 3.1).

Women's achievements were at the price of producing shells, bullets and guns,

Figure 3.1 German women making shells in a munitions factory

Source: Author

which drove their menfolk into the bestial and dangerous underground world of trenches, dugouts and tunnels. The sense of irony, and injustice, was heightened by discrepancies in pay between women who made shells and men who endured them. 'A soldier might ... compare his bob a day [i.e. 1 shilling, or 5p] with the wages of munitions workers ... like Rosina Whyatt, who had earned 16s. [80p] a week as a farm labourer and got 70s. [£3.50] as a shell operative' (Winter 1979: 167). Shells, and other war matériel, stood at the crossroads of these developments, simultaneously embodying and creating social change.

Some women were proud and confident, equating their munitions work to soldiers' efforts at the front. 'Every time you fire your gun you can remember I am helping to make the shells,' reported one woman (Mrs Alec Tweedie, quoted in Ouditt 1994: 74). Others were less sure, believing they were 'working twelve hours a day towards the destruction of other people's loved ones' (Peggy Hamilton, quoted in Ouditt 1994: 77). More tragic still, though largely concealed from the public (then and since), were the sizeable numbers of British and Allied troops killed and maimed by backfire – shells which for various reasons exploded prematurely, or fell short and killed their own men rather than the enemy's (Regan 1995: 77–112). Shells made by British women killed British soldiers throughout the war, especially in the early years. The same was true in France, where 'General Percin estimated that seventy-five thousand French troops were killed or wounded by their own artillery' (Eksteins 1990: 153).

Shell shortages during the winter of 1914–15 led to an increase in production (Strachan 1998: 137), mainly by women. A subsequent decrease in the quality of shells and inspection standards led to premature shell explosion destroying over

600 French field guns in 1915. One British soldier recalled the bitter human cost of poor quality shells at Loos later the same year:

> They told us it would be a bit of cake and all we'd got to do ... was dawdle along and take these trenches which we'd find pulverised by our guns. Every other blooming shot was a dud, ... my battalion lost hundreds of men in the first hour ... The whole thing was a waste of lives.
>
> (Private C.H. Russell, quoted in Macdonald 1993a: 510)

On the Somme, almost a year later, things had changed little, with some 30 per cent of shells fired by British guns proving to be duds (Strachan 1998: 141–2). As deadly as these shells could be to their own side they were sometimes accompanied by notes written by munitionettes and which had been stuffed into their packing cases (Culleton 1995: 12) – a tender female accompaniment to the ambiguous weapons of mass destruction.

Equally devastating physically, and arguably more symbolic for the British, was the fact that while the majority of munitions workers were working-class women, it was often the daughters of their erstwhile middle- and upper-class employers who tended the results of shellfire as Voluntary Aid Detachment (VAD) nurses in field hospitals behind the battlefields (see Macdonald 1980; Wenzel and Cornish 1980). While it fell to women to mend what they had helped to break, the implications of the British class system worked their way through the newly-gendered socio-economics of shell production, to symbolically set different classes of British women against each other.

Not that women escaped the scarring effects of their own activities. When shells exploded they not only killed and maimed men at the Front but sometimes also women at home, as when an accidental explosion at a munitions factory in Faversham, Kent, killed 106 munitions workers, many of them women, on 2 April 1916. In 1917, 69 women were killed and another 72 severely injured when an accidental fire ignited 50 tons of TNT at a munitions factory at Silvertown in East London. Ironically, this caused 'more destruction than all the First World War air raids on the capital combined' (Gilbert 1994: 345). Home-made shells sometimes proved more deadly than enemy ones. Even when not killed or injured, shell-making marked the munitionettes by leaving them with yellow skin and orange hair characteristic of TNT poisoning (Woollacott 1994: 12) – which itself eventually accounted for the lives of 61 women (Gilbert 1994: 345).

British women and shells combined unexpectedly in the sphere of alcohol consumption. The shortage of shells and quantity of duds which, according to the authorities, were responsible for the military failures of 1915, were ultimately blamed on the drunkenness and slacking of (mainly female) munitions workers (Southall 1982: 44–5). In October 1915, the 'Defence of the Realm Act' (DORA) was used to place severe restrictions on drinking hours – laws which survive in altered form today. Ironically, as alcohol consumption at home decreased, and the quantity and quality of shells improved, soldiers' consumption of wine, beer, and spirits – especially the official rum ration – was increasingly regarded as indispensible in getting men to endure ever greater barrages and to engage the enemy (Ferguson 1998: 351–2).

THE 'STORM OF STEEL'

For their part, soldiers had an ambiguous relationship with shells, perhaps not surprising when almost three-quarters of wounds were shell wounds (Winter 1979: 117). Soldiers were often ambivalent about using the munitions their womenfolk had made, for they suffered from the deafening barrages that lasted for hours, sometimes days. Even worse, these bombardments called down on their own heads the enemy's response known as 'the hate' (see Dunn [1938] 1997: 116).

Preceding an attack, British bombardments frequently failed to cut the enemy's defensive barbed wire (often their primary purpose), yet invariably succeeded in churning the land, thereby seriously, and often fatally, impeding their own troops' advance (see for example Keegan 1998: 314). A sustained artillery barrage also warned the enemy of impending attack, allowing them to take shelter then man their machine guns as soon as it stopped (Brown 1997: 67). The deadly consequences for British soldiers of their own artillery's tactics on 1 July 1916 on the Somme are well documented (Macdonald 1993b; Middlebrook 1984).

In this sense, shells were ambiguous weapons that often worked against achieving the ends they were designed to gain. Their potential effectiveness against an entrenched enemy was neutralized then inverted by a failure to understand that industrialized war was more than amassing shells and firing them incessantly. Shells and artillery were the epitome of scientific and technological achievement in military hardware, but new ways of thinking and innovative strategies and tactics were required for their potential to be realized. The obsession with quantity of munitions and the corresponding inability to use them effectively was both tragic and ironic. While improvements and innovations, such as counter-battery fire and the 'creeping barrage' did occur, for various command and technical reasons, and more often than not, they were lethally ineffective (Keegan 1998: 314–5).

The monumentality of hardware conceived and built to deliver shells probably appeared to many soldiers of almost supernatural proportions. In preparation and firing of artillery, it was as if men had become the slaves of the shell. One example, the German 420 howitzer

> weighed twenty tons and was moved by nine tractors. The cutting and steel lining of the gunpit took four days. The gun itself took twelve men five minutes to load and fire, a light railway and crane getting the one-ton shell into position. Each shell went at 1,700 mph to a height of Mont Blanc, covered a distance of six miles horizontally and made a crater large enough to enclose a house.
>
> (Winter 1979: 115)

The intensity of barrage by these machines was such that an attitude of hopelessness overwhelmed many soldiers, inducing a feeling that 'Fate' was responsible, and every incoming shell inscribed with a man's name (Bourke 1996: 77). And incoming shells arrived in vast numbers. During the preliminary bombardment for the Third Battle of Ypres (often called Passchendaele) in July 1917, the Royal Artillery alone fired 4 283 550 rounds – at a cost of £22 211 389 14s 4d (Terraine 1992: 218); during the whole battle, the Germans discharged some 18 000 000 shells (Werth 1997: 329). Shells and their bombardments produced bizarre, horrific, yet uniquely symbolic images of war, such as an account of how a complete shell penetrated and lodged in a man's body, killing him instantly, but not exploding. Flying over the Somme in 1916, Cecil Lewis had a close encounter with a British howitzer shell hovering at the top of its trajectory before it plunged back to earth (Lewis [1936] 1993: 67). French artillerymen built altars of stacked shells for religious services held in the field.

In combat, soldiers were exposed to hitherto unimaginable quantities of bombs, mortars, shrapnel, bullets, and gas – a hail and miasma of death through which they were expected to advance – sometimes line abreast and at walking pace, as most notoriously on the first day of the Battle of the Somme in 1916 (see for example Brown 1997: 66). Such events were 'like black magic: bodies continued walking after decapitation; shells burst and bodies simply vanished' (Bourke 1996: 214). As Ferguson (1998: 340) notes, it was a form of mass suicide.

The barrage, the event which transformed industrialized shell production into industrialized death, possessed a unique dimension in creating a new world of phenomenological experience for soldiers (Saunders n.d.a), who were 'formed as subjects by the technology they used' (Gosden 1999: 161). It destroyed the body and mind of front-line soldiers, whose awareness of explosions 'was more of a compressed air punch on the ear drum than of sound' (Winter 1979: 107,115). As Griffith (quoted in Winter 1979: 175) recalled:

> The sound was different from anything known to me …. It seemed as though the air were full of a vast agonized passion, bursting now with groans and sighs, shuddering beneath terrible blows …. It was poised in the air, a stationary panorama of sound, not the creation of men.
>
> (Winter 1979: 175)

Eyes and ears also registered the split-second consequences of bombardment on the human body.

> Showers of lead flying about & big big shells its an unearthy (sic) sight to see them drop in amongst human beings. The cries are terrible ….
> (Papers of Miss Dorothy Scoles, quoted in Bourke 1996: 76)

After bombardment and battle, trenches, battlefields and rear support areas alike were strewn with spent shells, cooling shrapnel and unexploded ordnance which could explode unexpectedly, adding further to the toll of mutilation and death. Interspersed with the metal were the equally fragmented remains of soldiers. As Sergeant H.E. May (1997: 200) observed in the Ypres salient in 1917, such a scene

> was a vision indescribable in its naked horror. Pieces of metal that once were cannon; and, if good Krupp steel had been so shattered, what of the humans who served the steel? Heads, legs, arms, trunks, pieces of rotting flesh, skulls that grinned hideously, bones cleaned by exposure, lay about in hopeless riot.

Scenes like these were the product of the first great war of high explosive. To this must be added the invention and refinement of gas attack, first used by the Germans at Langemarck, north of Ypres, in April 1915. Subsequent technical advances which replaced awkward valve-release canisters with gas packed into shells added to the horrors of bombardment. Irony, as ever, was never far away. Soon, all along the front-line, empty shellcases were suspended over trenches to serve as warning gongs if there was a suspicion of a gas attack (Dunn [1938] 1997: 455; Winter 1979: 82,121) (Fig. 3.2). The killing shell had been transformed into a life-saving device and, in passing, it was noticed that the French 75 mm shell was a half-tone higher than the British 18-pounder.

ICONICITY AND FRAGMENTATION

The consequences of industrialized war focused on fragmentation, actual and symbolic. Ambiguity was everywhere. Shells were created by industrialization which divided up human labour, compartmentalizing manufacturing processes to permit mass production, yet simultaneously gathering people together into the 'superbody' of the factory to make ever greater quantities of munitions whose effects were to dismember and scatter individual human bodies (for example Whalen 1984), produce piles of freshly amputated arms and legs (see for instance Hayward 1997: 258), and frequently vaporize all traces of the body, thereby producing that other feature of the Great War – 'The Missing' (see Dyer 1995).

It often seemed as if everything had been sacrificed to the artillery shell – a multi-media cultic obsession with the object. Apart from innumerable brass shellcases brought home by soldiers as war souvenirs (for example Dunn [1938] 1997: 580), the shell icon was ubiquitous. Posters, postcards and advertisements displayed its image, and household objects such as shell-shaped money boxes, ornaments and cruets, were miniature forms handled by all. The heraldic china industry promulgated the shapes of war. These producers

> in their naivety … saw in the glut of artefacts of war suitable bases for their models and in the years during and following the war designed a large number

Figure 3.2 Trench gas gong made from empty shellcase, Ypres Salient 1915

Source: Imperial War Museum, London (Photo no. Q 56927)

of models of a martial character whose origins were on the battlefields of the First World War.

(Southall 1982: 8)

Everything was available in china – from grenades, tanks, aeroplanes and trench mortars to shrapnel and incendiary shells (see Welbourne 1998). Particularly ironic were shell-shaped salt sellars which, in imitation of shrapnel, were designed to shatter into a thousand pieces if dropped (Southall 1982: 44–5). Such items can be compared with real shellcases which were decorated as Trench Art (see below), mounted in a wooden framework, and placed in a hallway or dining room as table gongs to announce mealtimes. The popularity of the same forms in china and metal is indicative of British society's predisposition to accept and buy the shapes of death that so characterized romanticized civilian notions of the war.

Figure 3.3 Romantic irony: French postcard with a French 75 mm artillery shell

Source: Marie-Monique Huss

Ironic transformations of matter occured in both directions. When shell short-ages struck, civilians were exhorted to raid their homes for metal items which could be melted down and recast as armaments in munitions factories (Saunders n.d.b). In Germany and Austria, where shortages became acute, extreme efforts were made to collect cutlery, brass doorknobs and miscellaneous household metals (Terraine 1998: 272). Religious artefacts had no privilege – 'Over eighteen thousand church bells and innumerable organ pipes were donated to the war effort, to be melted down and used for arms and ammunition' (Eksteins 1990: 202).

Even the postcard played its part in the apotheosis of the shell (Huss 2000). In France, they often portrayed romanticized scenes of women dreaming of their sol-dier sweethearts and conjuring up an image of the ubiquitous French 75 mm shell. These were sometimes draped in the Tricolour or surrounded by flowers as a patri-otic symbol of French manhood and military aggression against the German foe (Fig. 3.3). Countless posters were produced which showed women accompanied by artillery shells (see for example Culleton 1995). A famous cartoon by Bruce Bairnsfather, captured the attitude that the war would go on forever. Looking forward to 1950, it shows two soldiers grown old in the trenches as a batch of new shells passes overhead.

The ironies and ambiguities of this material culture were part of wider notions and attitudes prevalent during, and especially after, the war. These concerned social and cultural dislocation. The war was seen as having ruptured time, driven a fault-line through the middle of civilization (Hynes 1990: xi, 116). It had shattered not just the landscapes of the Western Front (Saunders 2001a, b), and elsewhere, and the bodies of soldiers, but families, relationships and notions of art, as well as scientific progress, across Europe (see for example Silver 1989: 1–2, 8; Audoin-Rouzeau 1992: 136–7; Booth 1996; see also Saunders 2000a: 62).

After the war, Europe was a fragmented place – a land of invisible and incomplete people – the dead and the maimed so graphically pre-figured by Abel Gance in his film *J'accuse* (see Winter 1995: 15–17). In 1920 in Britain, there were 113 special hospitals, 319 separate surgical clinics, 36 ear clinics, 24 eye clinics, 19 heart centres and 48 special mental hospitals dealing with the effects of high-explosive shells on the human body (Winter 1979: 251). These anatomically distinct and geographically separated places symbolized the literal and metaphorical fragmentation of the human body. Eleven years after the war ended there were still 65 000 men in mental hospitals suffering shellshock (ibid.: 252).

In Britain, it was impossible to escape the presence of men broken by shellfire. In Stepney, London, Jim Wolveridge recalled

> a Mr Jordan who'd lost his right arm, my old man who'd been gassed, and the man at the top of the street who was so badly shell-shocked he couldn't walk without help. And there were lots of one-armed and one-legged old sweats begging in the streets.
>
> (Wolveridge, quoted in Bourke 1996: 35)

For many of these men, the most valuable item in rebuilding their lives was an artificial limb, especially the lighter, more expensive metal variety over the cheaper wooden kinds (Bourke 1996: 45–6). Those maimed by shellfire relied increasingly on limbs made by industrial processes refined to make the munitions which had inflicted their injuries. Metal was the common denominator in breaking and re-making men.

THE ARTISTIC TRANSFORMATION OF SHELLS

Shells and shellcases defined the Great War also by their capacity to be transformed into three-dimensional art objects – during the conflict, the inter-war years and up to the present. As Gell (1998: 74) notes 'Decorative patterns attached to artefacts attach people to things, and to the social projects those things entail.'

At the battlefront, stacked for use or already in the breech, shells were objects for graffiti. Gunners anticipated later artistic endeavours by chalking a caricature of the

Figure 3.4 Graffiti chalked on to shells before firing

Source: Author

Kaiser, Hindenburg, or a stereotyped 'Hun' on to the shell. Messages were written, such as 'Here's one for you Fritz' or 'Remember the *Lusitania*' (Fig. 3.4). Even before it was fired, the shell had been altered artistically, albeit in the simplest way.

After the empty casing had been ejected hot and smoking on to the ground, permanent artistic transformation began and with it a new chapter in the object's cultural biography (*pace* Kopytoff 1986). These altered shells, together with many other kinds of objects made by soldiers, civilians and POWs, are commonly known as Trench Art (Saunders 2000a, 2001c). Although items were of wood, bone, stone and textile, it is the metal objects which best capture the ironic *zeitgeist*. Of these, decorated 'shellcase vases' were the most popular, becoming the archetypal kind of Trench Art from the 1920s to the present.

Recycled from the waste of war (Saunders 2000b), these objects were neither 'distanced' from nor independent of the killing process – they were directly implicated. They were worked into different forms, as souvenirs, ornaments and sometimes for practical purposes. Analysing the diversity of manufacturing techniques and decorative styles reveals insights into their makers' lives and three distinct periods of manufacture (see Saunders 2000a, 2001c).

Trench Art 1914–19

This period saw shellcases made into Trench Art by soldiers and civilians (Fig. 3.5). For both groups these objects had the immediacy of war – of personal injury or loss for soldiers, and economic deprivation for civilians. In both cases, the

Figure 3.5 Trench Art shellcase souvenir: German shell decorated with Flanders Lion motif

Source: Author

artillery shell had been the agent of destruction and was transformed physically and symbolically into something economically positive by the people whose lives it had shattered.

Most shellcases made by soldiers were manufactured behind the lines, in safe areas where tools and time were available. Sophisticated examples, elaborately shaped and intricately decorated, were made by the Royal Engineers, and by units of the multi-ethnic allied army such as the Chinese Labour Corps. Many were made by Belgian metalsmiths who joined the army in 1914 and transferred their civilian skills to military hardware (Vermeulen-Roose 1972: 9–10). In their shaping and decoration, shellcases embodied and expressed an international variety of attitudes and skills united by war and its matériel. Soldiers carried on these activities also in front-line trenches and dugouts. One contemporary letter tells how 'The lads in the trenches while away the flat time by fashioning rings, crosses, and pendants out of bullets and the softer parts of shells' (LC: Letter from J. Laws).

Similar objects were made by French and Belgian civilians, many of whom were refugees from devastated areas. Economic hardship and loss of mainly agricultural livelihoods meant that working shellcases for sale as souvenirs became one way of making ends meet.

One irony which affected all who made these items was that such activities were technically illegal. For the British, Belgian, and possibly also French, German, and Italian armies, empty shellcases remained government property and were supposed to be gathered in dumps, refilled in munitions factories, then reused. Many Belgian soldiers did not sign their work specifically to avoid being reprimanded for stealing army property (Vermeulen-Roose 1972: 10). The realities of war, however, meant it was always easy to obtain these raw materials. The legality issue remains ambiguous. In Turkey, a shellcase from the Gallipoli battlefield is as much cultural heritage as a prehistoric artefact and both are subject to stringent laws.

Trench Art 1920–39

By 1920, soldier Trench Art had ceased, but its civilian counterpart flourished as refugees returned to homes devastated by war. The differences between civilian Trench Art made during and after the war had less to do with form and material than the changing relations of production and consumption associated with the temporal shift from war to peace (Saunders 2000: 50). Continuing economic hardships, landscapes full of raw materials and increasing numbers of battlefield pilgrims, gave new impetus to the market for Trench Art souvenirs – especially decorated shellcases.

During the 1920s and 1930s, shells made their way from battlefields into the homes and towns against which many had originally been fired. Now they were carried in, often by children, as constructive objects rather than agents of destruction. Shells which had wreaked so much devastation now became a central feature of economic reconstruction, collected and sold as scrap, or made into Trench Art souvenirs (Edouard Fierens, personal communication 1999).

These art objects are a complex kind of material culture. They were often made by the same people using the same techniques and designs as during the war. Yet, where previously sold to soldiers, they were now sold to the bereaved – widows and relatives of men who did not return. It is likely that some women bought Trench Art souvenirs of shells which they themselves had made in munitions factories during the war. Quite possibly, many paid for the visit and the object with money earned from making shells.

Shells which had embodied the terrors of barrage and so devastated men's minds and bodies often became treasured mementoes of a battlefield visit. As Susan Stewart (1998: 133) notes, in the distancing process between rememberer and remembered, 'the memory of the body is replaced by the memory of the object'. Shells which symbolized women 'doing their bit' towards industrialized killing had

Figure 3.6 Shells as living-room ornaments in a house near Ieper (Ypres), July 1999

Source: Author

become poignant objectifications of their own grief. Decorated shells 'authenticated' the experiences of the purchaser (ibid.: 134), and as Lloyd (1994: 185) says, allowed the pilgrims to 'carry home a tangible link with the memory, or even the spirit, of the dead.'

Taken home, brought within domestic space, decorated shellcases transformed into household ornaments, fabricated the past through their reordering of the material world (Radley 1994: 53) (Fig. 3.6). Attitudes towards these ornaments depended in part on whether a family's menfolk had survived the war. Some items, sent home as souvenirs by soldiers, became symbols of loss if the soldier did not return. Such was the case for the Goss family, the inventors of Heraldic Porcelain. In August 1916, outside Ypres, a shell exploded which killed their son Raymond. He had previously sent home a brass shellcase as a souvenir for his father. After his death, the family had it inscribed:

> French '75' Shell Case sent home by Sec. Lt. Raymond G.G. Goss 1/5th N. Staffs. Reg. 1915 killed near Hill 60 in Flanders August 1915.
>
> (Pine and Pine 1987: 137)

Shellcase vases accommodated themselves to the emotional atmosphere of a home which had suffered loss. The bereaved were linked by shared displays of objects whose presence ensured that treasured memories were always just a glance away. Shells which war had failed to deliver in any quantity to British soil were now conveyed by the peace and became a common feature of the home as 'indices of the past, ... objects to "remember by"' (Radley 1994: 52; and see Saunders n.d.b).

The enduring quality of these material objects was their ability to outlive their makers (Radley 1994: 58) and affect those with no direct experience of the war. In *Auntie Mabel's War* by Marian Wenzel and John Cornish (1980), a decorated French artillery shellcase 'released' the memory of Auntie Mabel, a wartime nurse, in the mind of her neice, Mrs Turner, some 60 years after the end of the Great War.

> Yes, that thing by the fireplace with the flowers on it is really a shell case .... She brought that back from France for her parents; I thought it was an awfully morbid thing .... It got to Granny's house and then it came here.... I often look at it and wonder how many men its shell killed.
>
> (Wenzel and Cornish 1980: 8)

Shellcases were often made of brass, which tarnishes quickly and requires frequent polishing. It is almost certain that as house ornaments such objects gave rise to a domestic routine of cleaning and polishing, and that, in many cases, this probably had therapeutic effects for the bereaved. Decades of often obsessive polishing erased the original decoration and inscription completely. While many British, French and Belgian families tended lovingly to these objects, for Germans the act of making, selling, and displaying decorated shellcases was a sacreligious if not barbarian act (Weixler 1938: 48–9; Eksteins 1998: 311). Such was the cultural relativity in attitudes towards the definitive objects of industrialized war.

Trench Art 1939–2001

The Second World War changed the meaning of the Great War, yielded its own crop of shells, and precipitated different attitudes to all shellcase Trench Art made between 1914 and 1939. Between 1945 and the mid-1960s Great War shells, decorated and undecorated, lost much of their poignancy as objects of memory, were seen as anachronisms, and, where not thrown away, were sold as scrap rather than curated as valued historical objects.

Shells which survived found a new lease of life from the mid-1960s onwards as interest in the Great War increased. Burgeoning numbers of battlefield visitors (Walter 1993: 63; Lloyd 1994: 289) saw an increase in the popularity of all kinds of Great War memorabilia and the ever popular decorated shellcases became a mainstay of the militaria trade. Most have had their original meanings displaced by a market whose fluctuating prices reflects the classificatory confusion which surrounds them. Regarded variously as antiques, militaria, souvenirs, bric-à-brac and curiosities, the qualities of completeness, distinctiveness and shiny appearance have replaced earlier emotional values.

Especially fine pieces are sometimes stolen from museums, while others are faked, either as old shells reworked today, or modern shells sold as Great War originals. There is also great rivalry between European collectors to possess the most impressive objects – a secretive world of intrigue, disputes, deceptions and even violence – an ironic twist to the ever-changing social lives of these objects (Saunders n.d.b).

Trench Art shells are undervalued in museums – still considered curious, if sometimes ingenious, ephemera of war, with little artistic merit. This despite Renoir, Rodin and Lalique having presided over wartime exhibitions of these objects in Paris (ENOA 1915), and the wider anthropological point that such objects represent 'the visible knot which ties together an invisible skein of relations, fanning out into social space and social time' (Gell 1998: 62). Despite being a unique historical resource for hands-on experience and exhibitions, most decorated shellcases today reside in museum storerooms (and see Baert 1999; Compère-Morel 2000; Coote *et al.* 2000). Only in the privately run café-museums along the old Western Front are they displayed in any numbers (Saunders 2001c).

LEGACY

Great War shells possess a seemingly limitless capacity to embody the war that gave them birth. Today, apart from the exposure of empty shellcases as art objects (Saunders 2000a, 2001c), live unexploded shells are a potentially lethal feature of the nascent archaeology of the Great War (Saunders in press). More widely, unexploded ordnance continues to threaten human life all along the old Western Front (Webster 1998; Saunders 2001a). In 1991, thirty-six French farmers died when their machinery hit live shells (Webster 1998: 29). In the late 1990s, an average year on the Somme yielded around 90 tonnes of dangerously volatile 'hardware' – known as the 'iron harvest' (Holt and Holt 1996: 12). In Belgium, around Ypres, up to 250 000 kg of such materials can be recovered in a year, which the Belgian army disposes of in controlled explosions twice or three times a day (Derez 1997: 443; Lt. Col. L. Deprez-Wouts, personal communication 1998). One estimate is that there are 400 million unexploded shells left along the old Western Front (Senior Captain Vander Mast, personal communication 1999). In some areas, the concentration of shells has created landscapes of dangerous liminality, to which public access is still denied or restricted. Such *villages détruits* are exemplified by Louvemont near Verdun and five ruined villages within the French army's training area of 'Camp de Suippes' in Champagne (Fair 1998). In the midst of some prohibited regions are signs announcing a safe, cleared area suitable for picnicking. In many parts of France and Belgium, Great War shells still shape the land and exact an annual toll in human life.

The Great War's 'culture of shells' was the pivot around which the human experience of the world's first industrialized conflict revolved, and in some senses, still revolves. On the battlefields, where once were bodies and shells, it is mainly the shells which remain intact – it is as if the souls of 'The Missing' have turned into metal. Through all their transformations, shells have become the most complex objectifications of that most ironic of conflicts – 'the war to end all wars'.

ACKNOWLEDGEMENTS

I am grateful to the following for their help during my research into this subject: Thomas Compère-Morel and Marie-Pascale Prévost-Bault of the Historial de la Grande Guerre, Péronne; Senior Captain Vander Mast, Poelkapelle; Susanne Küchler, University College London; and John Schofield. I would like to acknowledge the financial support of the British Academy through its award of an Institutional Fellowship and University College London, which funded fieldwork in France, Belgium and Bosnia between 1998 and 2000.

REFERENCES

Audoin-Rouzeau, S. (1992) *Men at War 1914–1918: National Sentiment and Trench Journalism in France during the First World War,* Oxford: Berg.

Baert, Koen (ed.) (1999) *In Flanders Fields Museum: Catalogue of the Objects,* Ieper: In Flanders Fields Museum.

Bernède, A. (1997) 'Third Ypres and the restoration of confidence in the ranks of the French army', in Liddle, P.H. (ed.) *Passchendaele in Perspective: The Third Battle of Ypres*, London: Leo Cooper, pp. 324–332.

Booth, A. (1996) *Postcards from the Trenches: Negotiating the Space Between Modernism and the First World War,* Oxford: Oxford University Press.

Bourke, J. (1996) *Dismembering the Male: Men's Bodies, Britain and the Great War,* London: Reaktion.

Braybon, G. (1995) 'Women and the War', in Constantine, S., Kirby M.W. and Rose M.B. (eds) *The First World War in British History*, London: Edward Arnold, pp.141–167.

Brown, M. (1997) *The Imperial War Museum Book of the Western Front,* London: Sidgwick and Jackson.

Compère-Morel, T. (2000) *L'Historial de la Grande Guerre et le Circuit du Souvenir,* Tournai: La Renaissance du Livre.

Coote, J., Moreton, C. and Nicholson, J. (eds) (2000) *Transformations, the Art of Recycling,* Oxford: Pitt Rivers Museum.

Culleton, C.A. (1995) Working class women's service newspapers and the First World War, *Imperial War Museum Review* 10: 4–12.

Derez, M. (1997) 'A Belgian Salient for reconstruction: people and *patrie,* landscape and memory', in Liddle, P.H. (ed.) *Passchendaele in Perspective: The Third Battle of Ypres*, London: Leo Cooper, pp. 437–458.

Dunn, J.C. [1938] (1997) *The War the Infantry Knew 1914–1919: A Chronicle of Service in France and Belgium,* London: Abacus.

Dyer, G. (1995) *The Missing of the Somme,* London: Penguin.

Eksteins, M. (1990) *The Rites of Spring: The Great War and the Birth of the Modern Age,* Boston: Houghton Mifflin.

Eksteins, M. (1998) 'Memory and the Great War', in Strachan, H. (ed.) *The Oxford Illustrated History of the First World War*, Oxford: Oxford University Press, pp. 305–18.

ENOA (1915) *Exposition Nationale des Oeuvres des Artistes Tués a l'Ennemi, Bléssés, Prisonniers, et aux Armées,* catalogue to exhibition, Salles du Jeu de Paume, Tuileries, Paris, 20 May– 20 July 1915, organised by 'La Triennale'.

Fair, C. (1998) The lost villages of the Camp de Suippes, Champagne: La journeé des villages détruits, *The Western Front Association Bulletin* 51: 32.

Ferguson, N. (1998) *The Pity of War,* London: Allen Lane.

Gell, A. (1998) *Art and Agency: An Anthropological Theory,* Oxford: Oxford University Press.

Gilbert, M. (1994) *The First World War,* London: HarperCollins.

Gosden, C. (1999) *Anthropology and Archaeology: A Changing Relationship,* London: Routledge.

Hayward, J.A. (1997) 'A Casualty Clearing Station', in Lewis, J.E. (Introd.) *True World War One Stories: Sixty Personal Narratives of the War*, London: Robinson, pp. 252–259.

Holt, T. and Holt, V. (1996) *Major and Mrs Holt's Battlefield Guide to the Somme,* London: Leo Cooper.

Hoskins, J. (1998) *Biographical Objects: How Things Tell the Stories of People's Lives,* London: Routledge.

Huss, M.-M. (2000) *Histoires de Familles: Cartes Postales et Culture de Guerre,* Paris: Éditions Noesis.

Hynes, S. (1990) *A War Imagined: The First World War and English Culture,* London: The Bodley Head.

Keegan, J. (1998) *The First World War,* London: Hutchinson.

Kopytoff, I. (1986) 'The Cultural Biography of Things: Commoditization as Process', in Appadurai, A. (ed.) *The Social Life of Things*, Cambridge: Cambridge University Press, pp. 64–91.

L.C..Liddle Collection/reference numbers, The Liddle Collection, Brotherton Library, University of Leeds.

Lewis, C. (1993) *Sagitarrius Rising,* London: Warner.

Lloyd, D.W. (1994) 'Tourism, pilgrimage, and the commemoration of the Great War in Great Britain, Australia and Canada, 1919–1939', PhD thesis, Cambridge University.

Macdonald, L. (1980) *The Roses of No Man's Land,* London: Michael Joseph.

Macdonald, L. (1993a) *1915: The Death of Innocence,* London: Headline.

Macdonald, L. (1993b) *Somme,* London: Penguin.

May, H.E. (1997) 'In a Highland Regiment, 1917–1918', in Lewis, J.E. (Introd.) *True World War 1 Stories: Sixty Personal Narratives of the War*, London: Robinson, pp. 199–206.

Middlebrook, M. (1984) *The First Day on the Somme,* Harmondsworth: Penguin.

Miller, D. (1985) *Artefacts as Categories,* Cambridge: Cambridge University Press.

Ouditt, S. (1994) *Fighting Forces, Writing Women: Identity and Ideology in the First World War,* London: Routledge.

Pels, P. (1998) 'The spirit of matter: on fetish, rarity, fact, and fancy', in Spyer, P. (ed.) *Border Fetishisms: Material Objects in Unstable Spaces*, London: Routledge, pp. 91–121.

Pine, L. and Pine, N. (1987) *William Henry Goss: The Story of the Staffordshire family of Potters who invented Heraldic Porcelain,* Horndean: Milestone Publications.

Radley, A. (1994) 'Artefacts, memory and a sense of the past', in Middleton, D. and Edwards, D. (eds.) *Collective Remembering*, Sage: London, pp. 46–59.

Regan, G. (1995) *Backfire: The Tragic Story of Friendly Fire in Warfare from Ancient Times to the Gulf War,* London: Robson.

Sarson, Private H. Smalley (1993) 'The Shell', in Stephen, M. (ed.) *Poems of The First World War, 'Never Such Innocence'*, London: J.M. Dent, p. 146.

Saunders, N.J. (2000a) Bodies of metal, shells of memory: 'Trench Art' and the Great War Re-cycled, *Journal of Material Culture* 5(1): 43–67.

Saunders, N.J. (2000b) 'Trench Art: The Recyclia of War,' in Coote, J., Morton, C. and Nicholson, J. (eds) *Transformations: The Art of Recycling*, Oxford: Pitt Rivers Museum, pp. 64–67.

Saunders, N.J. (2001a) 'Matter and memory in the landscapes of conflict: the Western Front 1914–1999', in Bender, B. and Winer, M. (eds) *Contested Landscapes: Movement, Exile and Place,* Oxford: Berg, pp. 37–53.

Saunders, N.J. (2001b) Materiality, space and distance: dimensioning the Great War, 1914–1918, *European Journal of Archaeology* (forthcoming).

Saunders, N.J. (2001c) *Trench Art: A Brief History and Guide, 1914–1939,* Barnsley: Leo Cooper.

Saunders, N.J. (in press) Excavating memories: archaeology and the Great War, 1914–2001. Antiquity.

Saunders, N.J. (n.d.a) The cosmology of war (ms. in preparation).

Saunders, N.J. (n.d.b) 'At home with war: restless objects in unstable places, from the Great War to Bosnia', in Saunders, N.J. and Küchler, S. (eds) volume on Reyclia (in preparation).

Silver, K.E. (1989) *Esprit de Corps: Art of the Parisian Avante-garde and the First World War, 1914–25,* London: Thames and Hudson.

Southall, R. (1982) *Take Me Back to Dear Old Blighty: The First World War through the Eyes of the Heraldic China Manufacturers,* Horndean: Milestone.

Stewart, S. (1998) *On Longing: Narratives of the Miniature, the Gigantic, the Souvenir, the Collection,* Durham: Duke University Press.

Strachan, H. (1998) 'Economic mobilization: money, munitions, and machines', in Strachan, H. (ed.) *The Oxford Illustrated History of the First World War,* Oxford: Oxford University Press, pp. 134–148.

Terraine, J. (1992) *White Heat: The New Warfare 1914–18,* London: Leo Cooper.

Terraine, J. (1996) 'The substance of the War', in Cecil, H. and Liddle, P.H. (eds) *Facing Armageddon: The First World War Experienced,* London: Leo Cooper, pp. 3–15.

Terraine, J. (1998) *The Great War,* Ware: Wordsworth Editions.

Vermeulen-Roose, G. (Comp.) (1972) *Van Obushuls tot Sierstuk: Studie over een Originale en Kunstvolle Vrijetijdsbesteding onder de Oorlog 1914–1918,* Zonnebeke: De Zonnebekse Heemvrienden.

Walter, T. (1993) 'War grave pilgrimage', in Reader, I. and Walter, T. (eds) *Pilgrimage in Popular Culture,* Basingstoke: Macmillan Press, pp. 63–91.

Webster, D. (1998) *Aftermath: The Remnants of War,* New York: Vintage.

Weixler, F.P. (1938) *Damals und Heute an der Westfront,* Berlin: Verlag Scherl.

Welbourne, P. (1998) Crested china and the First World War, *Western Front Association Bulletin* 51 (June 1998): 26–7.

Wenzel, M. and Cornish, J. (Comps) (1980) *Auntie Mabel's War: An Account of her Part in the Hostilities of 1914–18,* London: Allen Lane.

Werth, G. (1997) 'Flanders 1917 and the German soldier', in Liddle, P.H. (ed.) *Passchendaele in Perspective: The Third Battle of Ypres,* London: Leo Cooper, pp. 324–332.

Whalen, R.W. (1984) *Bitter Wounds: German Victims of the Great War, 1914–1939,* Ithaca: Cornell University Press.

Winter, D. (1979) *Death's Men: Soldiers of the Great War,* Harmondsworth: Penguin.

Winter, J. (1995) *Sites of Memory, Sites of Mourning: The Great War in European Cultural History,* Cambridge: Cambridge University Press.

Woollacott, A. (1994) *On Her Their Lives Depend: Munitions Workers in the Great War,* Berkeley: University of California Press.

4   The battlefield of the Dukla Pass: an archaeological perspective on the end of the Cold War in Europe

ROGER LEECH

In eastern Slovakia you are increasingly aware of the proximity of the Carpathian mountains and the steppes of Russia and the Ukraine to the east. The mountains crowd closer and there are now road signs to Odessa. It was here in October 1944 that the Soviet armies finally broke through the Carpathian chain to take Budapest and turn west across the Hungarian plain towards Germany. One of the hardest fought operations in this campaign was the taking of the Dukla Pass, the key route from southern Poland into Slovakia (Fig. 4.1).

Figure 4.1 The Dukla Pass in relation to the Carpathian frontier between Poland and Slovakia

Source: Author

It was to the area of this battlefield that my archaeologist wife Pamela and myself were heading in August 1998. It was nine years since the Velvet Revolution of 1989 and the creation of the independent Czech and Slovak republics. Our antennae were, we thought, attuned to an archaeological perspective on all that might have since happened.

The Dukla Museum in Svidnik and the battlefield at the Dukla Pass were fully described in our first edition of the *Rough Guide to Czechoslovakia:*

> Looking something like the Slovak equivalent of New York's Guggenheim Museum, the spanking white **Dukla Museum** at the beginning of the Bardejov road is under reconstruction, but when complete it should house a gruesome exhibition on the battle for the 'Valley of Death' (see 'Dukla Pass' below). Instead head about 1 km northwest towards Bardejov, where a gigantic **Soviet war memorial** commemorates the many thousands who fell in the fighting. It's an exceptionally peaceful spot, interrupted only by the occasional coachload of Soviet war veterans, who stagger up the monumental staircase to lay wreaths to the sound of Beethoven's Funeral March blasting out from speakers strategically hidden in the ornamental shrubbery ….
>
> **The Dukla Pass** (Dukliansky priesmyk) … was for centuries the main mountain crossing-point on the trade route from the Baltic to Hungary. This location has ensured a bloody history, the worst episode occurring in the last war, when over 80,000 Soviet soldiers and 6,500 Czechoslovaks died trying to capture the valley from the Nazis. There's a giant granite memorial at the top of the pass, 1 km from the Polish border, as well as an open-air museum – a trail of underground bunkers, tussling tanks and sundry armoured vehicles – strung out along the road.
>
> (Humphreys 1991: 345)

At the same time a note warned of the rapid pace of change within the region and welcomed comments or corrections. We were perhaps not fully prepared for the changes that might have occurred.

We had anticipated that the museum in Svidnik would be well signposted, a major attraction to tourists looking for the Eastern Front equivalents of the many Second World War museums to be found on either side of the English Channel. There were though no signs and, when at last we found the well-arranged entrance and reception area to the museum, officials told us that it was closed for temporary repairs. We headed then for the pass and the battlefield.

Here too there were no signs and no trace whatsoever of the trail of bunkers, tanks and sundry armoured vehicles. After an abortive trip to the border crossing with Poland, we parked in what appeared to be a large but almost completely empty lorry park and approached the sales hut on the opposite side of the highway. It was always possible that we might be able to purchase a guide or history for the battlefield of 1944. The hut proved to be the frontier liquor store, and evoked only the response that 'there is no history for this battle'. Not to be deterred, having come

Figure 4.2 The Dukla Pass looking south, from the battlemented war memorial to the now largely empty coach and car park

Source: Author

this far, we headed for the monument or war memorial beyond our lorry park, following into woodland a wide concrete path much encroached upon by vegetation. Slowly we realized that alongside this path were lamp-posts, now well hidden in the trees. More abortive searching led us ultimately to the observation tower; here a caretaker or curator was able to take us in the lift to the top of the tower. At last the details of the battle were there to see on a series of panoramas etched on perspex, the text in Russian.

It was now clear that this was a monument or museum no longer valued. One regime had replaced another and the presentation or maintenance of the Dukla Pass battlefield and its attendant monuments and displays was not a priority for Slovakia in 1998. How much longer would any of the landscape seen somewhat differently by the writer of the *Rough Guide* be visible? The rest of the afternoon was a rapid photographic recording exercise: first the observation tower, then the lamp-standards and 'lorry park', the last presumably to accommodate the tens of coaches bringing veterans to the battlefield (Fig. 4.2). Second we returned to Svidnik, to photograph the war memorial (Fig. 4.3). Finally we returned 16 km down the road to record the vast weed-infested car parks to the west of the town, which we realized retrospectively had served the same coachloads arriving in Svidnik. The tall lamp-posts, crowned with rusting red stars, had together with the car parks assumed a new archaeological significance (Fig. 4.4).

Detached from the events of 1944 or 1989 it was possible in the undertaking of

Figure 4.3 Part of the war memorial at Svidnik: a Soviet soldier and a partisan are welcomed by a Slovak woman

Source: Author

the fieldwork to see this as a valuable archaeological recording exercise. It was exciting to see that historical archaeology had here a role to play in the understanding of very recent socio-political change in Slovakia. In a wider context the recording of these abandoned museum landscapes leads to consideration of a range of issues relating to their interpretation and use by those concerned consciously or otherwise with the creation and maintenance of national consciousness.

Museums are much concerned with the creation and portrayal of national identity (Zedde 1998). The representation of the Dukla Pass battlefield was intimately bound up with Soviet identity, most especially with the victories of the Soviet army in the latter part of the Second World War. The cessation of support for the commemoration of the battlefield might similarly be linked to Slovak national identity, but here the situation is perhaps more complex. In the battle for

Figure 4.4 The weed-infested and abandoned coach and car park for the war memorial at Svidnik

Source: Author

the Dukla Pass, Soviet and Czechoslovak troops sought to link up with the uprising within Slovakia itself (Erickson 1983: 369). In this sense commemoration of the battlefield provided a link with Slovak identity and to the memory of the uprising against the Slovak government as constructed and supported by the Third Reich. But the Slovak uprising was not supported by the majority of the Slovak people and in 1945 over 10 000 Slovak people were imprisoned or executed by the Soviet regime in a bid to crush the movement for Slovakian independence. In the new flowering of Slovak independence, celebrating a Soviet victory might not be high on the agenda. A further dimension is the recent view of many that battles such as that for the Dukla Pass were the sites of needless slaughter (Drabek 1997).

National identity might also play a role in the low profile accorded in Western historiography to all but a handful of operations in the east. The principal histories of the eastern front and the Russian advance to Berlin mention the battle for the Dukla Pass only briefly. In Erickson's history of Stalin's war with Germany the forcing of the Dukla Pass merits but one brief mention (Erickson 1983: 369). Ziemke gives just a little more detail; in September 1944:

> Fourth Ukrainian Front's progress through the Dukla Pass was not encouraging; it had been slow from the start and at the end of the month the offensive was almost at a standstill.

After the turn of the month the Soviet attack into the Dukla Pass began to make headway, partly because Hitler had taken out a panzer division there for his striking force, and on 6 October the Russians took the pass.

(Ziemke 1968: 362)

The Dukla Pass is not a name that would spring readily to mind for those in western Europe and North America reasonably familiar with the history of the Second World War. Glantz, of the United States Army Foreign Military Studies Office, has argued that

The blinders and restrictions that inhibited the work of Soviet military historians must be explained and removed before they, or their Western counterparts, can achieve the credibility they deserve, and even more important, before the Soviet role in the war can achieve the stature which it deserves.

(Glantz 1998: 2)

The material culture of the battlefield might provide another perspective on this argument. The present-day locus of the battlefield might be a very important factor in providing or denying such stature. Much-promoted museums on either side of the English Channel, at Caen, London, Portsmouth and in many other places, contribute to raising an awareness of the Normandy landings and the subsequent campaign of 1944 in a way that would now seem impossible for the Soviet victories in Slovakia and other parts of eastern Europe. The last was well illustrated by a feature in the English newspaper *The Independent* on 22 October 2000:

To the east of the Carpathians the monument to the greatest of all Soviet victories now lies deep within the Ukraine at Stalingrad, renamed as Volgograd. The 250 feet high figure of Mother Russia is now cracking and may not stand for much longer. Government support is not forthcoming. Meanwhile the government has at the same time endorsed the building of an adjacent cathedral, to be built on the battlefield in time for the 60th anniversary of the German surrender. The surrender might now be more significant than the victory. The latter was after all a victory for the Soviet Union, not for the now independent Ukraine.

(Cockburn 2000: 1)

In Stalingrad itself and across the many thousands of square miles covered by the Soviet advance there must be many similar instances of once cherished monuments, memorials and museums now abandoned. These merit archaeological attention, not simply as a material record of the Second World War, but as a record of events in the very recent past, notably in the aftermath of the 1989 upheavals. The most intensive work on the battlefield of the Dukla Pass now appears to be that targeted at pyrotechnic enthusiasts:

VISIT SLOVAKIA TO TRACE THE SECOND WORLD WAR AND ITS AFTERMATH

You could touch relics of the Second World War with your own hand and with metal detectors. Remains of ammunition, still full of explosive strength, appliances of German Wermacht and Soviet Red Army are still hidden in the Eastern part of Slovakia known as a Dukla Pass. Fierce battles had happened in the region during the September and November 1944. Even now, 53 years after the Second World War, you could find here unique war relics. You need a metal detector to find them and professionals who guarantee a security of such adventurous exploring activities …

. . . . . Click Here

(Anon. 2000)

Interest in this battlefield might also well move to re-enactment. The re-enactment of Second World War battles is a growth area. German panzer troops now fight with (is it alongside or against?) American, Commonwealth, British and USSR units: you can even purchase a panzer Tiger tank. One such re-enactment group perpetuates the memory of the First Gebirgsjager Division of the German Wermacht (Denniston 1998: 1–2). This was a division that fought in the Dukla Pass – but not in the battle of 1944. This division was part of XIV Army Group South, capturing the Dukla Pass in operations in 1939 and forcing the surrender of the Polish city of Lemberg. We are reminded here that the commemoration of a nation's history through its material culture may suffer from what has been termed selective amnesia (Zedde 1998). Ignatieff related a discussion with a museum curator in reunified Germany. Disagreeing with the proposal that there might be a museum on the history and culture of East Germany, the curator asserted that museums should always be 'archives of success' (Ignatieff 1993: 74).

Passing from the former East into the former West, the traces of the Iron Curtain are not now easily or at all recognized from the autobahn. Doubtless the Iron Curtain will be traceable in the archaeological records of the *Landes* which it formerly separated. The Iron Curtain represented approximately the furthest extent of the Soviet advance. To the east, many more decaying monuments to the victories of the Soviet armies will merit study, not only by pyrotechnic enthusiasts but by archaeologists, not simply in relation to battlefields o+f the Second World War but to subsequent events, not least those that have followed the revolutions of 1989. The battlefields of the Second World War are complex and active historic landscapes with multiple meanings.

REFERENCES

Anon. (2000) *Visit Slovakia to Trace the Second World War and its Aftermath,* online, available HTTP: <http://www.pyrotechnics.sk> (accessed 30 November 2000).

Cockburn, P. (2000) Church rises as Soviet symbol of victory, *The Independent,* 22 October 2000.

Denniston, P. (1998) *1. Gerbirgs-Division*, online, available HTTP: <http://www.gebirgsjaeger.4mg.com/1gebdiv.htm> (accessed 30 November 2000).

Drabek, J. (1997) Putting pride in the Czech Army, *The Prague Post,* 17 September 1997.

Erickson, J. (1983) *The Road to Berlin: Stalin's War with Germany.* Volume 2, London: Weidenfeld and Nicolson.

Glantz, D. (1998) *The Failures of Historiography: Forgotten Battles of German-Soviet War (1941–1945),* Fort Leavenworth, Kansas: United States Army Foreign Military Studies office, online, available HTTP: <http://rhino.shef.ac.uk:3001/mr-home/rzhev2.html> (accessed 30 November 2000).

Humphreys, R. (1991) *Czechoslovakia: The Rough Guide*, London: Harrap Columbus.

Ignatieff, M. (1993) *Blood and Belonging – Journeys into the New Nationalism*, Toronto: Penguin.

Zedde, K. (1998) Societies in Conflict: Museums and the Creation of 'National Identity', International Council of Museums, online, available HTTP: <http://maltwood.finearts.uvic.ca/tmr/zedde.html> (accessed 30 November 2000).

Ziemke, Earl F. (1968) *Stalingrad to Berlin: The German Defeat in the East*, Washington DC: Center of Military History, United States Army.

5   The Salpa Line: a monument of the future and the traces of war in the Finnish cultural landscape

ULLA-RIITTA KAUPPI

In Finland, there appears to be a common feature in the conservation of fortifications from different periods and other sites of military history. Abandoned structures are first allowed to go to ruin, and not until the last moment do people wake up to their value as monuments and start to bring them back to life. The delay thus involved is generally at least one generation.

FORTIFICATION IN FINLAND: A BRIEF HISTORY

Castles, fortresses and other sites of military history have been constructed on Finnish soil over a period of almost 1000 years, witnesses to the power struggle between East and West – Sweden and Russia, and most recently, Soviet Russia and Germany. If they were lucky, the Finns were onlookers as the great powers slogged it out. In the worst case they were forced to join in the fighting. For this reason only the very first and the very last fortifications in Finnish history, the Iron Age hillforts of around 1000 years ago and the lines of bunkers from the Second World War, were built by the Finns themselves. The rest were built by a foreign power, generally using Finnish labour.

All the stages in between those first and last fortifications represented the importation of fortification theories to the periphery of Europe. First of all the Swedes built five Continental-style citadels with encircling walls in the thirteenth and fourteenth centuries to provide a modicum of protection for their sphere of influence. The first proper fortress was Olavinlinna in Savonlinna with its round gun turrets (donjons), founded in 1475 and nowadays known for its international opera festival. Vyborg was the only Finnish town where the Swedes built a medieval town wall in addition to a castle. But the wall was demolished at the beginning of the seventeenth century to make way for an eastward-facing fortress town, surrounded by bastions and built on a grid plan, the first of its type in Finland.

The European bastion system did not properly become established in Finland until the eighteenth century, introduced by the Swedes from the West and the Russians from the East. The towns of Hamina and Lappeenranta, which were built by the Swedes, and Taavetti, built by the Russians, were textbook examples of the art. Sveaborg, now known as Suomenlinna, was built by the Swedes on the approach to

Helsinki and exhibits the freer French fortification techniques of Marshal Vauban. This sea fortress with its galley dockyard was included in Unesco's World Heritage List in 1991, and celebrated its 250th anniversary in 1998 with a series of cultural events.

The remaining half-dozen bastion fortresses and the only caponier fortress were built by the Russians under General Suvorov at the turn of the nineteenth century in what is now southeastern Finland, an area that Russia had taken from Sweden in the wars of the eighteenth century. The fortresses were designed to provide a line of protection for the imperial capital, St Petersburg, against a Swedish revenge attack.

As a result of the Napoleonic Wars, Russia annexed all of Finland from Sweden, making it an autonomous grand duchy within the empire. This brought the longest period of peace in Finland's history, lasting over 100 years, during which time around twenty unfortified garrisons were built. These were to form an important chapter in Finnish urban history and a significant focus for today's conservation efforts. Apart from Suomenlinna (Sveaborg), the old castles and fortresses were turned into prisons, magazines or arsenals for the Russian army.

THE EARLY STAGES OF RESTORATION OF FORTIFICATIONS

As early as the end of the nineteenth century, the Finnish civilian administration paid attention to the need to conserve old castles and fortresses. There was only limited funding available for restoration work, and in Russia, Finland's overlord, there was not even that. Arguably, the lack of funds saved their originality from the ravages of the national and stylistic romanticism current at the time.

Only since the 1970s has concerted effort been put into the restoration of castles and fortifications. The National Board of Antiquities, which is under the Ministry of Education, has supervised a restoration programme that is largely centered on employment creation schemes and open prisons. In this way the budget has been shared with the Ministries of Employment and Justice. There was a thorough debate on restoration principles some twenty years ago and there is now an established procedure. Besides the shortage of funding, another problem is the northern climate and the special restoration techniques this demands. The winter can last six months, with temperatures dropping to around minus 30° Celsius.

FORTIFICATIONS IN THE TWENTIETH CENTURY

During the First World War, the Russians built a sea and land fortification around Helsinki, using as its centre the former Swedish sea fortress. Forming a perfect circle, this modern permanent fortification with its concrete bunkers and gun emplacements was designed to fend off a German attack on Russia. Helsinki was one of seven maritime fronts on the Gulf of Finland protecting St Petersburg. The strongest link in this system was at Tallinn, the capital of Estonia. The Russians thought that the Germans would attack St Petersburg from the Gulf of Bothnia

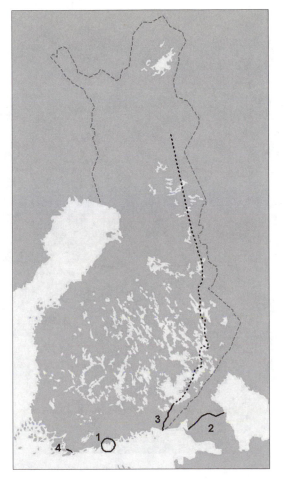

Figure 5.1 Map of the Salpa Line

Source: National Board of Antiquities

and via Finland, so an inland fortification system stretching up to Lapland was begun. But with the outbreak of the Russian revolution in 1917 and the confusion following Finnish independence, it remained unfinished. During the Finnish civil war in 1918 neither the Whites nor the Reds made use of the abandoned fortification system. After the war had been won by the Whites, under the command of Marshal Mannerheim, the maritime fortifications were incorporated into Finland's newly formed defence capability.

In the 1920s, construction began on the first Finnish fortresses since the Iron Age hillforts. A chain of bunkers named after Marshal Mannerheim was built near Vyborg, which at that time still belonged to Finland. In 1944 the bunkers were captured by the Soviet Union and still provide good service as a potato store for the Russians.

Figure 5.2 Soldiers digging the zigzag shooting trenches of the Salpa Line

Source: National Board of Antiquities

On the eve of the Second World War, the largest construction site in Finnish history was started – the Salpa Line. For political reasons this has been hushed up and rarely discussed even into the 1990s. The Salpa Line is the largest monument in Finland. It stretches for the entire 1200 km of the border with Russia (Fig. 5.1). In the south it has permanent fortifications, in the north field fortifications. The name Salpa in Finnish means bolt, implying something that has been securely barred shut, and with good reason. Besides its zigzag trenches, the Salpa Line contained 728 concrete or dug-out bunkers, around 3000 wooden field fortifications and between two and six rows of stone tank barriers stretching for around 200 km (Figs. 5.2–5.5). Overall it is at least comparable with the Maginot Line or the Atlantic Wall.

The Red Army poured over the Mannerheim Line, but the permanent fortifications of the Salpa Line were never fought over. With the collapse of the Soviet Union, documents from that period now give us the reason: Stalin had been

Figure 5.3 Marshal Mannerheim at the dragon-teeth line in 1943

Source: National Board of Antiquities

Figure 5.4 Typical Salpa Line dragon teeth

Source: National Board of Antiquities

Figure 5.5   Civil workers building a typical Finnish wooden dugout

Source: National Board of Antiquities

informed that it was a very substantial line of defence. Some of the bloodiest battles of the Second World War were fought just to the south of the Arctic Circle at Finland's narrowest part, where there were field fortifications. Stalin wanted to take Finland by splitting it in two, but Finland was able to repulse the Red Army despite the latter's vast superiority in numbers and weaponry.

CONSERVATION OF RECENT MILITARY HISTORY

Today Finland's castles and fortifications, including the Russian works of the First World War, are protected by the Law on Ancient Monuments (1963/295). Since the 1970s the National Board of Antiquities has been conserving and maintaining the mainland parts of this dilapidated wartime front to form a park encircling Helsinki. From the 1990s this work has been shared with the city of Helsinki. Although the maritime front is still operational, the National Board of Antiquities and the defence administration work closely together to conserve antiquarian sites even if they are in military use.

The legal position in regard to conservation of the fortifications, battle sites and mass graves of the Second World War is still open. But from the beginning of the 1990s, this situation has not prevented the National Board of Antiquities from considering them on a par with sites designated by the Law on Ancient Monuments, not to mention the field fortifications built during the year-long occupation by the Red Army of the southernmost tip of Finland and by the Germans in Lapland in the closing stages of the war. In this way even certain Second World War sites that are 'outside the protection of the law' have been renovated as an open air museum. At present we are seeking a solution to the partial conservation of the remnants of the Porkkala base to the west of Helsinki to provide a reminder of a traumatic but historical fact. The base was occupied by the Soviet Union between 1944–56 under the terms of the peace settlement.

The collapse of the Soviet Union produced a renaissance of interest in Second World War history in Finland. The enthusiasm of voluntary and veterans' organisations and local authorities to set up museums in the bunkers of the Salpa Line and to renovate the field fortifications of the forest campaigns has sometimes taken on stylistic tendencies which the National Board of Antiquities has had to diplomatically turn down.

Some of the permanent fortifications of the Salpa Line are still in military use. This has not prevented the defence administration and the National Board of Antiquities from working together. The Salpa Line has become a national monument, which in future will enjoy the protection of conservation law. Conservation can be furthered through planning, maintenance and tourism. Technically it has not presented a problem; after all, it is largely located in rural areas, partly in woodland, and the granite and concrete can withstand the elements. The defence administration has maintained the structures and the National Board of Antiquities has cleared the pines and spruce growing on top, while the five local authorities have organized trips in the summer months. The section that can be viewed is typologically meaningful and stretches from the Gulf of Finland to Joensuu.

The section to the north, with its field fortifications, is no longer in military use. In the former military areas in Kuhmo and Suomussalmi, a timber-braced dugout, trenches and gun positions have been restored as part of an employment scheme under the supervision of the National Board of Antiquities (Figs. 5.6 and 5.7). Nearby, historical exhibitions have been organized under the guidance of the Military Museum. Some of the field fortifications have intentionally been left in an authentic state.

At present a solution is being sought to the problems presented by the mass graves of Red Army soldiers. One example is a museum site stretching for 20 km along the Raate road in Suomussalmi in the Kainuu region, which was the scene of fighting in 1939–40. So far it has not been possible to locate the graves of some 20 000 soldiers belonging to a Ukrainian division destroyed by 2000 Finnish troops. The museum exhibition and the road are an annual pilgrimage for surviving veterans, Finns and Ukrainians.

The work, then, is just beginning, although parts have already been completed. Our problem is the vast size, its typological diversity, the winter climate and the

Figure 5.6 Restored shooting trenches at the outdoor museum in Kuhmo

Source: National Board of Antiquities

sparse population. At the ideological level, the problem has been the choice of the sections to be conserved; at the practical level the problems have been funding and organization, largely within employment creation budgets. The National Board of Antiquities has chosen to restore those sites that geographically and typologically will provide a comprehensive sample. The criteria used in the selection process were developed in Norway. The historical perspectives applied include the historical value of the event concerned, identity and symbolic value and pedagogical value. The physical qualities include originality, authenticity, museum qualities and environmental value. Macro and micro historical perspectives have also been taken into account: the site as a chapter in the conflict of interests between states; an art history study of style and period; international influences; and strategic resourcefulness (despite their brutal efficiency). Large fortifications represent an elite culture in military history. The micro historical aspects include the social structure of fortifications, whether as construction sites or as societies, the interaction between the military and civil life, and fortifications as building sites and a source of livelihood.

Military history, then, is not simply a matter of conserving objects. Military construction has always had a great influence on the social structure both in times of war and peace. We are therefore aiming at a concept of military history and military construction as part of the national cultural landscape. We term this concept militaria, which, besides fortifications and sites of battles, extends to garrisons as

Figure 5.7 Restored shooting trenches at the outdoor museum in Kuhmo

Source: National Board of Antiquities

recent as the 1950s. On this basis there has been a lively professional debate in Fästningsvård, the joint forum for Nordic antiquarian authorities. Recently the emphasis has been on twentieth-century military history. We have realized together how important the international debate is, both between the Nordic countries and further afield. This applies especially to the Second World War, which is particularly charged with emotions – in Finland perhaps unusually so – in order that excesses of both nationalism and neglect can be avoided.

6 Forgotten and refound military structures in the Central Pacific: examples from the Marshall Islands

HENRIK CHRISTIANSEN

INTRODUCTION

In 1914, when Japan took over the German possessions in Micronesia, they also became a threat to the American dominance in the Central Pacific (Miller 1991: 92). Micronesia was ruled under Japanese military governance until 1922, when the League of Nations trusted it to Japan as a C-mandate: that is, they were not to fortify the area. Later, this trust was guaranteed by the Washington Naval Treaty of 1922 between Japan and the United States (Peattie 1988: 60). In 1935, Japan withdrew from the League of Nations and sealed off her mandated areas to foreigners (Crowl and Love 1955: 201; Peattie 1988: 34). This action, of course, triggered suspicions regarding Japanese activities in the region. After the end of the Second World War, the debate continued as to whether or not the former Japanese-mandated areas in Micronesia were fortified before the outbreak of the war (Okumiya 1968). No decisive proof has so far been found.

One thing can be said for certain: in 1943, when the United States forces fought their way up through the Central Pacific, they found well-fortified military bases on the Marshall Islands, in the easternmost part of Micronesia. In accordance with the American amphibious doctrine, introduced by Pete Ellis in 1921, only a few of the Japanese bases were taken by military force (Reber 1977). The remaining bases were bypassed and left isolated in the American hinterland. After the war, the bypassed bases were abandoned by the Japanese garrisons and the remote atolls on which they were located remained relatively isolated until the 1980s when regular air service was introduced to the region.

Today the bases form a perfect time capsule for the study of the war in the Pacific. The objective here is to present a short overview of the former military bases and the initiatives taken to preserve them.

THE MARSHALL ISLANDS

The Marshall Islands are located in the eastern part of Micronesia, those thousands of islands scattered north of the Equator between Hawaii and the Philippines. The 1225 islands are grouped together in twenty-nine atolls, groups of islands each encircling a lagoon and five low islands. Together the atolls form two north–south running chains: the Ratak chain to the northeast, and the Ralik chain to the southwest. In the Ralik chain, the Kwajalein atoll forms the world's largest lagoon. One atoll, Wake or Einen Kio, is located between Guam and Hawaii more than 1200 km north of Kwajalein. Today the atoll is held by the USA, but the Marshallese government claims it to be a part of their nation.

THE BASES

In order to understand the function of the Japanese bases, it is necessary to view the Marshall Islands in a Second World War perspective. The Marshall Islands constituted the easternmost defence perimeter in the Japanese defence chain against the USA. The northern part of the area however, that is Einen Kio or Wake Island, has been a US-controlled outpost since 1898 and transfer location for civilian air traffic since 1935. The atoll was conquered by the Japanese shortly after the Japanese attack on Pearl Harbor in December 1941. The Japanese attack on Einen Kio took off from the Marshall Islands, of which they had been in control since 1914.

In 1941, the Japanese Navy headquarters in Chuuk established a subordinate command (the 6th baseforce) on Kwajalein, while the other bases were commissioned to the following duties. The Roi-Namur airbase on the Kwajalein atoll commanded all the other airbases in the Marshall and Gilbert Islands region. The base was taken by the US after heavy bombardment and attack on 1 February 1944. The Enewetak base on the Enewetak atoll was a former fuel storage depot that had just been turned into an airfield and lookout station, when it was destroyed by the advancing US forces in mid-February 1944. The Majuro base on the Majuro atoll was a base for small seaplanes. The US conquered the base on 1 February 1944. Torwa on the Maloelap atoll was strictly a land-based air-defence base with long-ranging land-based surveillance planes and fighter planes. Torwa was never attacked by the US and instead remained isolated and bypassed until the end of the war. The Emiej base on the Jalwoj atoll, a seaplane base with long-ranging Kawanishi H8K seaplanes, also remained isolated and bypassed till the end of the war. On the Wojja atoll, the Wojja base was a combined sea–land airbase primarily for seaplanes, while the airstrip was built to facilitate the fighters and bombers staging through from Kwajalein and Roi-Namur to Torwa and, later, Mili. Wojja, too, was never captured, but remained isolated and bypassed till the end of the war. Up to the beginning of 1943, Mili on the Mili Atoll was a forward air-lookout station. After the fall of Tarawa in the Gilbert Islands in 1943, the base was transformed into a major airbase for land-based fighters and bombers. As a result of this build-up, the base on Majuro was phased out. Mili was another base that was never captured, but remained isolated and bypassed until the end of the war.

Apart from a single US aircraft carrier attack in the early part of 1942, the bases were left relatively undisturbed during the early part of the war. Not until 1943, when the US forces commenced the Marshall Islands campaign under the code

Table 6.1 Results of the US strategic bomb survey of Wojja, Torwa, Mili and Jalwoj. The number of bombs found at each location is indicated on the left

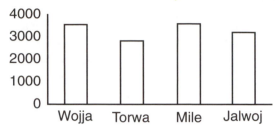

name 'Flintlock', did the bases come under heavy fire. This continued until February 1944, when the bases on Majuro, Kwajalein and Eniwetok were captured from the Japanese. Majuro was attractive from a strategic US point of view. The former Japanese base was conveniently located between the bypassed bases and could also serve as a staging point for aeroplanes from the newly conquered atolls in the Gilberts to Kwajalein.

The remaining Japanese bases, Torwa, Jalwoj, Mili and Wojja, remained isolated until the end of the war. For 18 months, between February 1944 and August 1945, these bases were left isolated in the middle of the American hinterland. Majuro and Kwajalein were turned into major US air and supply bases. Although the isolated bases were kept neutral through daily US strafing and bomb runs, new untrained pilots and fighter planes were also sent over the bypassed atolls in order to acquire some combat practice under relatively safe conditions before they were dispatched to the heavy combat zones closer to Japan.

When the war ended in August 1945, the Japanese garrisons on the bypassed atolls surrendered. Most soldiers had already died from starvation and diseases. These bases had been destroyed from a military point of view in early 1944 and subsequently as a result of daily strafing and bombings from surface ships and aeroplanes. The first attacks in 1944 concentrated on vital military threats to the US forces, that is, the aeroplanes and air defence systems. Later, the attacks concentrated on coast-defence facilities, and finally on other military structures such as barracks and other buildings. In all some 12 900 tons of ammunition were used on the bypassed bases during the war (Table 6.1).

THE BASES TODAY

Immediately after the war, the four bypassed bases were left uninhabited, but gradually the Marshallese returned to the atolls from other atolls and islands to which they had fled or been removed during the war. Not until recently were the atolls visited, except by copra boats, but today Air Marshall flies the atolls on a regular basis. As the Marshallese traditionally live close to the lagoons, heavy vegetation has covered the rest of the islands, except for the former Japanese airstrips, which are used by Air Marshall.

Immediately after the end of the Second World War, the Japanese garrisons did

Table 6.2 Sites on the bypassed atolls

Type	Torwa	Jalwoj	Wojja	Mili
Personnel	84	52	110	51
Storage	24	21	24	6
Transportation	15	5	7	23
Communication	5	2	8	0
Defence	21	11	26	23
Aviation	33	6	13	8
Total	**182**	**97**	**188**	**111**

some cleaning up, but still left large amounts of unexploded ammunition and ordnance behind. Later, in the 1960s, private scrap-dealer companies undertook clear-up work, which seems to have done more damage to the historic sites than the war itself. The dealers collected valuable scrap, for example copper and brass from the guns and other military installations, and left behind what they could not use. Often they were rather brutal in their efforts to obtain metal.

Between 1992–4 the four former military bases were surveyed in order to develop an historic preservation master plan (Christiansen 1994a–d). The structures and sites remaining are related to personnel, storage, transportation, communication, defence and aviation (Table 6.2). The personnel sites are buildings, barracks, mess halls, kitchens, laundries, bathhouses, toilet buildings, hospitals, power plants, water tanks, air-raid shelters and memorials. Sites related to storage are warehouses, workshops, water-cooler tanks, torpedo assembly buildings, ammunition buildings and fuel and oil tanks. Surveyed sites related to transportation are vehicles, trains, piers and ships. Communication-related sites are radio stations and radio towers. Sites related to defence are radars, fire control buildings, range-finder installations, search lights, anti-tank/anti-personnel walls, pill boxes, block houses, commando posts, observation bunkers, 25 mm anti-aircraft guns, heavy anti-aircraft, other anti-aircraft, howitzer guns, 15 cm field artillery emplacements, anti-tank trenches, 8 cm ships guns, armoured tanks, 12.7 mm dual purpose guns, 8 cm dual purpose gun emplacements, 12 cm coastal defence guns, 15 cm coastal defence guns and other types of coastal defence gun. Sites related to aviation are air control centres, hangars, aeroplane revetments, runways, seaplane ramps/aprons, fighter planes, bomber planes, dive bombers, aeroplane parts, seaplanes and US aeroplanes.

As Table 6.2 shows, the number of structures and sites differs from base to base. Thus it reflects a varied picture of what is left today. Judging from sites built in concrete, there is no doubt that the best designed base is located on Torwa on the Maloelap atoll. The military base with fewest concrete sites is Mili on the Mili

Atoll. It should be remembered that the Mili base was constructed at a time when the Japanese supply lines were unstable and about to be cut off.

It is obvious that the material military structures on the bypassed atolls only represent a small part of what was originally there. All wooden structures are missing as a result of time, war and other human activities. Sites and structures made of concrete are better preserved, although they are also marked by the traces of war. Today they appear as ruins or can be seen intact, covered with bomb craters and countless signs of strafing bullets. Regardless of this, it is still fairly easy to get an impression of the former bases. Structures made of metal, that is aeroplanes, vehicles, trains, engines and guns of all calibre, can still be found on the former bases, with the exception of Wojja. Hardly any of these movable objects have been found in situ as they were piled together during the post-war clear up.

Threats to these sites are numerous. Buildings made of concrete do not easily disintegrate, even though they are exposed to weather, time, human exploitation, shoreline retreat and the current problem of rising sea levels; they are still by far the best-preserved sites. Items made of steel and iron are in far worse shape. Local vegetation creates microclimates that corrode the guns and other metal objects. In addition, the position of these sites near the coast on the low-lying atolls exposes the remains to salt, increasing the corrosion. These sites are slowly deteriorating. Other threats are also approaching the sites, such as damage from looting. Theft by local people who take what they find necessary from the sites in order to reuse the items is a common thing, but more serious is grand theft where whole aeroplanes are removed and sold.

PRESERVATION OR NOT?

Although several attempts have been made since the war to clean up and remove the symbols of war, most of them are still in place. The question remains then: what should be preserved and for what reason? When we make attempts to preserve the past, it is usually because we want future generations to remember their historical roots. In the case of the Marshall Islands, however, it should be remembered that the war was basically a war between Japan and the USA. Naturally the former bases have meaning mainly for the history of these nations. However, the Marshallese could not care less. They just suffered, and the events that took place more than fifty years ago do not form an integral part of Marshallese culture. Consequently, the scholars who undertake studies of Second World War history in the region do not come from the Marshalls, but rather from Japan and the USA, with only a very few researchers from other countries, such as myself. The atolls and their military remains form a perfect time capsule for the study of Second World War history in the Pacific. The former battlefields at Kwajalein and Roi-Namur, as well as other battlefields in the Pacific region, have all been turned into well-kept parks where the guns and other military installations form a scenic picture amongst well-kept lawns, rather than showing the visitor the grim face of war. Only on the former bases in the Marshalls can this be studied, as the evidence is intact. It would, of course, be meaningless to protect everything. Now, when the sites are documented, it is up to the Marshall Island Historic Preservation Office to designate the sites that have the greatest historical value and identify the most interesting sites that tourists and others can benefit from. The story of the bases, including all the written records and documentaries, could easily be published on a CD-ROM in order to satisfy the needs of tourists and scholars.

The former military bases are of limited interest to the native Marshallese on the atolls. And yet they do profit from them. Wherever convenient, they move into the former fortified buildings. The blockhouses, ammunition buildings and radio stations should be mentioned as examples of sites that are inhabited and used today as homes, churches and typhoon shelters. Aeroplanes are stripped in order to use the metal in houses, and grenade boxes and fuel drop tanks are used for water storage. The former military airstrips are presently used by Air Marshall and piers in the lagoons by larger fishing ships.

But it could also be important to preserve sites if they can generate an income for the residents of the atolls. Attempts have been made by the Marshallese government to help the tourism industry promote the atolls as interesting places to visit. Tourism could provide a financial boost to the local economy if the tourists come to dive and to see Second World War sites. The traditional systems, where clan leaders rule atolls, however often seem to conflict with the government's attempts at preventing these intentions from becoming a success.

The government of the Marshall Islands has taken steps to prevent looting and to preserve certain parts of the historic remains. The Marshall Islands Historic Preservation Act of 1991 was introduced to mitigate the conflict between development and threats to historic sites, which also includes the military structures from the Second World War. A management conservation plan for the Second World War sites has been drawn up. Small-scale demonstration projects have been carried out on Wojja in order to learn how to protect metal objects from deterioration (Look and Spennemann 1994) and the bases have been carefully surveyed and described (Christiansen 1994a–d).

SUMMARY

On remote atolls in the Central Pacific it is possible to achieve first-hand historic information of the war in the Pacific. Four former Japanese military bases on remote atolls in the Marshall Islands have been surveyed. The bases are interesting for research as they are almost untouched since the end of the Second World War. Almost all other Second World War battlegrounds throughout the Pacific have been turned into well-kept combed resorts, deprived of their original surrounding and historical context. Today, however, threats to the sites on the bases are numerous. Natural degradation is progressing and man-made problems such as theft and pillaging are common. The Marshallese government has taken steps to prevent this by introducing a Historic Preservation Act, not only in order to mitigate conflicts between development and threats to the historic sites, but also to be able to promote tourism in the area.

ACKNOWLEDGEMENTS

Between 1992 and 1994, the author surveyed four former Japanese military bases, as part of a Historic Preservation and Tourism plan. The project was undertaken under the auspices of the Historic Preservation Office in Majuro, Republic of the Marshall Islands, through a financial grant from the Office of Territorial and International Affairs, US Department of the Interior. The author wishes to thank Dr Dirk Spennemann, former CEO of the Historic Preservation Office, and Alfred Capelle, former CEO of the National Museum of the Marshall Islands, for valuable help during this project.

REFERENCES

Christiansen, H. (1994a) *WW II Artefacts in the Republic of the Marshall Islands*. Volume I, *Torwa island, Maloelap Atoll*, unpublished government report, Historic Preservation Office, Majuro, Republic of the Marshall Islands.

Christiansen, H. (1994b) *WW II Artefacts in the Republic of the Marshall Islands*. Volume II, *Wojja island, Wojja Atoll*, unpublished government report, Historic Preservation Office, Majuro, Republic of the Marshall Islands.

Christiansen, H. (1994c) *WW II Artefacts in the Republic of the Marshall Islands*. Volume III, *Imiej island, Jaluit Atoll*, unpublished government report, Historic Preservation Office, Majuro, Republic of the Marshall Islands.

Christiansen, H. (1994d) *World War II Artefacts in the Republic of the Marshall Islands*. Volume IV, *Mili island, Mili Atoll*, unpublished government report, Historic Preservation Office, Majuro, Republic of the Marshall Islands.

Crowl, P. and Love, E. (1955) *The War in the Pacific: Seizure of the Gilberts and Marshalls*, Washington DC.

Look, D. and Spennemann, D. (1992) 'For Future Use: A Management Conservation Plan for the World War II sites in the Republic of the Marshall Islands' (HPO report 1992/19), unpublished government report, Historic Preservation Office, Majuro, Republic of the Marshall Islands Majuro Atoll, Republic of the Marshall Islands, and San Francisco, USA: RMI Historic Preservation Office and US National Park Service Western Region Office.

Miller, E.S. (1991) *War Plan Orange, The US Strategy to Defeat Japan 1897–1945*, Annapolis, Maryland: Naval Institute Press.

Peattie, M. (1988) *Nanyō: The Rise and Fall of the Japanese in Micronesia, 1885–1945*, Honolulu: University of Hawaii Press.

Reber, J.J. (1977) Pete Ellis: amphibious warfare prophet, *Proceedings* 103(1): 53–63, United States Naval Institute; Annapolis, Maryland.

7 The archaeology of scientific experiments at a nuclear testing ground

COLLEEN M. BECK

INTRODUCTION

A hallmark of the twentieth century was the exponential growth of technological innovation. With two world wars and a worldwide Cold War, international competition was intense to develop and apply new technology in order to maintain military superiority. The development of nuclear energy led to one of the most significant twentieth-century military inventions, the atomic bomb. During the Cold War, nuclear-related tests were conducted over forty-one years in the state of Nevada in the southwestern United States with the aim of refining nuclear capabilities. The built environment associated with this testing is a physical record of the events that occurred at this location, endeavours that were regionally, nationally and globally significant.

The archaeological study of nuclear testing provides an opportunity to document a class of historic constructions that, for the most part, are either unique or limited to only a few locations in the world. Over the past decade, research has been conducted on some of these structures providing information regarding the nature and scope of this class of recent historic sites at the Nevada Test Site, an operating government facility in the remote Nevada Desert under the jurisdiction of the United States Department of Energy.

ATOMIC BOMBS AND TESTING GROUNDS

United States scientists secretly developed the atomic bomb in the early 1940s (Smyth and Morrison 1990). The security around this project meant that the rest of humanity had no knowledge of the new level of devastation that would be possible with this technology. It was the actual use of this weapon on Hiroshima and Nagasaki in August 1945 that announced to the world the existence of the atomic bomb and alerted all to its destructive power, irreversibly changing world politics and the nature of international confrontations. After the Soviet Union successfully fielded their atomic bomb in 1949 (Walker 1999: 42), the world entered the era known as the Cold War. The United States and the Soviet Union, poised as enemies each ready to strike a deadly blow, dominated world events with their ever-increasing nuclear arsenal. These two superpowers engaged in a daily stale-mate, both awaiting and averting a war with atomic weapons until the ultimate col-lapse of the Soviet Union in the early 1990s.

Usually, new weapons are tested repeatedly to make certain that they are reliable. In the case of the atomic bomb, however, only one test was conducted before the bomb was initially used. In fact, at the end of the Second World War, this new weapon had been detonated on only three occasions, during the Trinity test in New Mexico (Szasz 1995) and twice in Japan (Hersey 1985). Due to the paucity of test-ing data, many scientific and military questions remained at the end of the Second World War regarding nuclear detonations. To address these issues, the United States began conducting nuclear tests in the Pacific Ocean in 1946 (Dibblin 1990; Weisgall 1994), tests which were difficult logistically and for which security issues were complex (Titus 1986: 55). Slowly momentum built towards establishing a continental nuclear testing location in the United States. This was a controversial proposal but with the inception of the Cold War, the initiation of the Korean War in 1950, and an increasing concern regarding national defence, political sentiment was swayed to go forward and identify potential locations (Fehner and Gosling 2000: 37–48; O'Donnell 2000).

On 18 December 1950, the Atomic Energy Commission received President Truman's approval to establish the Nevada Proving Ground (Lay 1950), now known as the Nevada Test Site. The chosen continental testing location is 105 km northwest of Las Vegas, Nevada, on land that was part of the Las Vegas–Tonopah Bombing and Gunnery Range, an Army Air Corps training locale created in 1940 (Office of History 1994). The following month, on 27 January 1951, inaugural nuclear testing on United States soil began with the Operation Ranger series of atmospheric nuclear tests. The first event was called Able (Miller 1986: 84–8).

Between 27 January 1951 and 2 October 1992, 928 nuclear tests were conducted at the Nevada Test Site, 904 by the United States and twenty-four joint tests by the United Kingdom and the United States. Of these, 100 were atmospheric tests and 824 were underground tests (Department of Energy 1994: viii). Additional tests were conducted in the Pacific and other locations. In a similar time frame, the Soviet Union conducted 715 tests with 216 in the atmosphere, 496 underground and three under water. All but forty (categorized as peaceful nuclear explosions) were conducted at the Semipalatinsk test site in Kazakhstan and the Novaya Zemlya test site above the Arctic Circle (Norris and Arkin 1996). The French and Chinese also conducted nuclear testing programmes, but these were much smaller in scope.

Nuclear testing at the Nevada Test Site was not continual over the forty-one years between 1951 and 1992. No tests were conducted in 1954 (Friesen 1995: 40–2) and in 1958 the United States ceased testing on 31 October with the Soviet Union following this lead on 3 November. These independent, self-imposed mor-atoriums were broken by the Soviet Union on 1 September 1961. The United States, caught off-guard by Soviet tests ending the moratorium, scrambled to resume testing on 15 September 1961 (Ogle 1985). Atmospheric tests then contin-ued until the United States, the United Kingdom and the Soviet Union signed the

Limited Test Ban Treaty on 5 August 1963, an agreement prohibiting these countries from testing nuclear weapons in the atmosphere, in outer space and under water (Friesen 1995: 6). Subsequently, all parties continued underground testing. Following the fall of the Soviet Union and the end of the Cold War, nuclear testing ceased at the Nevada Test Site when the first President Bush announced a unilateral moratorium on 2 October 1992 (Department of Energy 1994: ii).

THE NEVADA TEST SITE AND NUCLEAR TESTING REMAINS

In 1951 the Nevada Test Site encompassed 1761 sq km. Over the years its size has increased incrementally by annexation of adjacent United States Air Force lands, and today the facility is 3561 sq km. Two deserts, the Mojave and the Great Basin, and the transitional zone between them cross the Nevada Test Site. Terrain ranges from valleys and dry lake beds at an elevation of 1065 m to mountains and *mesas* at more than 2280 m. Based on the effects of the atomic bombs in Japan, most people expect the land at the Nevada Test Site to be barren and scarred from the years of nuclear testing; this isn't the case. Most testing was confined to three major physiographic locations: Frenchman Flat, Yucca Flat and the Pahute and Rainier *mesas*. Surprising to many, these areas resemble similar locations outside the facility; were it not for subsidence craters from underground tests and buildings for support infrastructure, it would be difficult to recognize this as a nuclear testing ground. In addition to the well-publicized detonations of nuclear devices at the Nevada Test Site, other programmes there focused on the effects of radiation and the application of nuclear energy for space exploration.

Before the 1990s, archaeologists surveying for sites at the Nevada Test Site would record all prehistoric and historic sites that pre-dated 1940, the date of the establishment of the gunnery range. Underground nuclear testing was ongoing at the time and no effort was made to document the associated artifacts and features. However, the fascination of seeing actual remains from a nuclear test was overwhelming, and visits were increasingly made to structures and buildings associated with atmospheric testing, especially on Frenchman Flat where the largest concentration of atmospheric testing remains is located. In time it was realized that these nuclear remains were vanishing and that, although recent, atmospheric testing was a significant historic event and it was important to begin documenting its material remains. This view was shared by the Department of Energy and was bolstered by the Nevada State Historic Preservation Office officially recognizing the historical significance of all nuclear testing in Nevada (Tlachac 1989).

Documentation of the historic structures has involved inventory and surveys of the structures built for testing and the testing support facilities. These surveys and inventories are ongoing and continue to record different aspects of this cultural environment. From work completed to date, the historical structures and remains can be assigned to three broad categories based on their association with either:

atmospheric and near-surface underground tests; contained underground tests; and non-explosive experiments related to radiation effects and the application of nuclear energy. Overarching these categories are support facilities, such as the town of Mercury. Located at the south end of the Nevada Test Site – where entry to the facility is gained – Mercury contained all basic services, including housing, a post office and scientific laboratories, as well as warehouses and buildings for associated activities. Many of the original buildings are still used today. In other parts of the test site, other places, known as camps, also served the workers' needs. In addition, a peace camp was established outside the test site as an outgrowth of anti-nuclear activism (Nevada Desert Experience 2000; Shundahai Network 2000). This make-shift camp has been occupied repeatedly over many years and contributes to the material record of nuclear testing in much the same way as the Women's Peace camp at Greenham Common, England (Schofield and Anderton 2000).

On the east side of the Nevada Test Site, atmospheric nuclear tests were con-ducted on Frenchman Flat and Yucca Flat between 1951 and 1964. During this test-ing era, the built environment was designed to assist with the implementation of the tests, to document the scientific data, to test the effects of the detonations, and to visually observe and record the tests. Atmospheric test devices were dropped from a plane, attached to a tethered balloon, attached to a metal tower, or placed at a shallow depth beneath the surface. Archival film footage shows imported trees, buildings and other items being destroyed by the shock waves. Beyond the ques-tion of survival is the knowledge that most atmospheric testing locations were cleaned up after the detonation and, in some cases, locations were used for multiple tests. This has produced an archaeological record that contains the structures and objects which survived the testing and were too massive or difficult to remove or relocate, were left at a location that was not reused, or were not included in the post-test clean-up activities. Considering all these factors, it is surprising that so many structures still exist. For example, a recent inventory in a section of French-man Flat recorded 157 structures associated with atmospheric testing (Johnson *et al.* 2000), many more than anyone expected.

There are two related factors that hinder creating effective descriptions of the nuclear testing constructions. First, nuclear testing consisted of experiments. The Nevada Test Site was an outdoor laboratory where scientists were constantly push-ing the edge of knowledge, creating and designing structures for effective experi-ments. Thus, many of the structures built for and used in nuclear testing were often unique to nuclear testing and were not common to Western culture. Second, there are no terms in our languages to accurately describe and convey the architectural presentation of some constructions.

This situation has produced a somewhat skewed public view of nuclear testing remains. A focus has been placed on structures that most resemble similar struc-tures in everyday life, such as a train trestle, a bank vault and a house. While these types of structures survive and were integral to testing experiments, they represent only a few of the remains and are not the common ones. Yet, they are the construc-tions that most people relate to easily, and, therefore, will continue to dominate the representation of Nevada Test Site remains. The categorization and description of

Figure 7.1 Stanchions that supported a tower for an atmospheric nuclear test

Source: Author

nuclear testing-related remains present an ongoing challenge, most effectively overcome by visual portrayals of the buildings and structures (Goin 1991). As with most archaeology, functional descriptions must be applied with caution, especially in such a unique environment. The language used here is thus intended to be descriptive.

Atmospheric testing remains

Atmospheric testing locations are most easily recognized by two features. On the ground surface, metal stanchions embedded in square cement blocks mark some of the actual ground zeroes, the points above which the nuclear detonations actually took place. Attached to these stanchions were wires that stabilized a tower to which the nuclear device or a balloon, buoying a nuclear device, was tethered until detonation (Fig. 7.1). The second feature is the single metal pole towers positioned around the ground zero (Fig. 7.2). Many are still standing and their purpose was to hold testing items, recording equipment and other instrumentation.

Other structures were built to house and protect equipment designed to record data from the tests. There are various underground bunkers scattered across the landscape, some copper-lined, which still have the original wiring and piping. Some problems occurred with the initial bunker design, as a few bunkers suffered blast damage and bunker design quickly evolved to create a structure that repeatedly survived nuclear blasts intact. Another structure is an electromagnetic pulse tower, resembling a child's playhouse or climbing apparatus rather than a critical

Figure 7.2 Single metal pole towers near an atmospheric nuclear test location

Source: Author

scientific instrument (Fig. 7.3). Yet these towers were integral to recording line-of-sight electromagnetic pulse information. Unique to the landscape is a navy ship's gun turret with its original base set below the surface. However, the gun had been reconfigured from a weapon to a scientific instrument designed to detect and record blast information, the turret providing a substantial structure capable of surviving the pressure waves from the detonations. Small rectangular concrete-block buildings on the flats and on the *mesas* also originally housed and protected scientific equipment, and small metal and wood containers scattered across the area may have been used for a similar purpose.

Experiments were conducted to study the effects of atmospheric tests and radiation on terrain, vegetation, animals, buildings, structures and objects. Boxes of wire and wood that held animals, such as pigs, dogs and rabbits, can be found at a few locations. Most striking are metal tubes with windows or apertures used as cages for animal experiments, their strength attested to by their intact condition today. Additionally, a variety of structures were built to test the durability of materials and

Figure 7.3 Electromagnetic pulse tower used in atmospheric nuclear tests

Source: Author

building types. Concrete skeletons of buildings, a rectangular brick structure, half-buried concrete Quonset hut-shaped buildings and various large pieces of constructed metal objects are dispersed across the landscape.

Complete mock towns, such as Survival Town and Doom Town, were constructed as part of the civil defence research and

> included industrial buildings and shelters, electrical power system, communication equipment, a radio broadcasting station, trailer homes, fire equipment, cars, and food supplies placed at varying distances from ground zero ... Only (two) two-storey houses and the frames of a few ranch-style homes survived.
> (Johnson and Beck 1995: 46)

In some cases, identical structures were built at increasing distances from a ground zero to measure the effects of the strength of blast as it moved across the landscape. Here scientists worked to determine what materials would survive and at what distances from a nuclear blast. A building type called the glass house falls into this category. Glass houses are single-storey wood-framed structures with various types of sheet glass framed and glazed into the sides of the buildings, forming a solid front of glass on all sides, with the interior of the glass covered by different styles and types of window shades. As expected, the glass house furthest from the ground zero test locations is more intact than the one closest.

In addition to materials testing, there were other concerns related to nuclear energy. In response to military commanders' lack of knowledge regarding the ability of troops

Figure 7.4 Wooden benches for observers of atmospheric nuclear tests that were detonated
on the Frenchman Flat dry lake bed in the foreground

Source: Author

to perform their duties in a nuclear battlefield situation, Camp Desert Rock was established near the entrance to the Nevada Test Site. Troops were housed here during their training in offensive and defensive nuclear combat conditions. Army troops participated in atmospheric tests between 1951 and 1957 (Edwards 1997). None of the tanks or armoured personnel carriers used by the troops has been found at the Nevada Test Site. However, some of the trenches that were built to shield troops from the atmospheric blasts are visible on the terrain and a few artefacts still exist where a cannon once stood. This cannon, now part of a museum at Fort Sill, Oklahoma, was designed for and successfully used, only once, to fire a nuclear weapon.

Acquiring data was paramount in the quest to understand nuclear weaponry. Much of it was recorded on film and photographs. Still standing is the original photographic station at a complex called the Control Point. Situated in the saddle between two key valleys, the Control Point had a commanding view of atmospheric tests in Frenchman and Yucca flats. This restricted access facility was the central location for monitoring the atmospheric and underground tests and was where the countdown to detonation was conducted. Remote camera and film stations near ground zeroes existed, but many have yet to be identified in the field. Other films and photographs were taken at two stations where military and civilian test observers, such as journalists, were allowed to watch the detonations. One observation station was at the south end of Frenchman Flat (Fig. 7.4) and the other, called News Nob, is at the south end of Yucca Flat. Here, sagging wooden benches in orderly lines still sit in place overlooking the testing areas.

One programme at the Nevada Test Site sought to determine if nuclear detonations could be effectively used for large land reconfiguration projects, such as building a new canal similar to the one across Panama. Here nuclear devices were placed at shallow depth so that the explosion would break through the surface and move dirt above and adjacent to the blast. This programme was called Plowshare with the biblical connotation quite purposeful, the goal being the peaceful application of nuclear detonations. One of the Plowshare tests, Sedan, produced a crater of such magnitude that it was used by Apollo astronauts in training for their work on the moon. It is also the only location at the Nevada Test Site listed on the United States National Register of Historic Places (Matthews 1998), though the significance of the entire testing facility is recognized (Tlachac 1989).

Contained underground nuclear testing

Nuclear testing remains are associated with two types of underground nuclear testing experiments configured to contain radioactivity below the surface: horizontal tunnel tests and vertical drill holes. Built into the face of Rainier *Mesa* at the north end of the Nevada Test Site, about thirty tunnels were built and used between 1957 and 1992 for 67 nuclear tests. These horizontal shafts were built large enough to enable equipment and people to enter and work inside effectively and to house the experimental package. The detonations occurred near the further end of the tunnels with containment plugs in place to hold the blast inside the structure. Material remains from this type of testing are the tunnels themselves and infrastructure; changes to the landscape above the tests also announce their location and strength. These types of nuclear explosions disintegrate the subsurface ground near the blast, creating a chamber, and when a chamber compressed the surface above occasionally sank, producing a crater. In those cases where no craters have appeared above tunnel tests; these locations are referred to as potential crater areas.

Contained underground testing, utilizing vertical drill holes, was conducted on Yucca Flat and on Pahute and Rainier *mesas* at the north end of the Nevada Test Site, taking advantage of different types of geology for various experiments. There were more than 600 of these tests. In contrast to atmospheric testing where reuse of structures was difficult due to the buildings near a test being directly affected by the detonations, the underground programmes utilized portable buildings and structures that were moved from one testing location to another. When the 1992 moratorium went into effect, some of these instrumentation support structures were either in place at a pending test location or at an equipment yard awaiting use. Trailers that sat near a ground zero are now redeployed. But multi-storied rectangular towers, used to assemble and house equipment for the drill hole and to lower the device into the hole, remain at two locations in Yucca Flat today.

The contained underground tests usually produced craters more dramatic in appearance than those from the tunnels. From the air Yucca Flat resembles a lunar landscape, yet none of these craters even closely compares in size to the Sedan

Figure 7.5 The test chamber used in the Huron King underground test. For scale, note the
person standing under the right hand side of the chamber

Source: Author

Crater mentioned previously. In the Sedan test, the sides of the crater were elevated
by the soil as it came to the surface and was redeposited. In contrast, with contained
vertical tests, the surface sinks below its natural contour.

A feature common at the drill hole craters is cable. At some locations, dozens of
specialized data cables emerge from the centre of the crater and extend up the sides
of the depression. Originally, these cables were attached to scientific equipment in
trailers surrounding the drill hole and transmitted the diagnostic information for
the experiment. Other cables from outside the test area brought power and communications to and from each test site.

One unusual object, a large, above-ground chamber, can be seen on Yucca Flat
(Fig. 7.5). In a test called Huron King, this chamber was placed directly over the
drill hole. Inside the chamber were a communications satellite and other experimental equipment in an atmosphere that simulated a space environment. The detonation reached and was contained in this chamber but, by means of a network of
mechanical closures, the pipe to the chamber was sealed before the shock wave
could reach the chamber; the chamber was then winched away rapidly before the
surface collapsed into a crater.

In all of the nuclear testing areas of the Nevada Test Site, there are miscellaneous
artifacts. These include empty cable spools, wood saw-horses, rope, boxes, nails,
lumber and other assorted metal, wood, glass and plastic objects. In some of the
craters, large metal pipes protrude from the bottom where drill-back activities were
conducted after the tests to obtain further data.

Non-explosive experiments

On Yucca Flat, there were two major non-explosive experiments pertaining to the effects of radiation. Operation BREN (Bare Reactor Experiment, Nevada) was conducted to determine the shielding characteristics of Japanese-style houses (Johnson *et al.* 1997: 22). In 1962, this complex of structures, simulating typical Japanese dwellings, was constructed in the desert 686 m from a tower that had a hoist car containing an open nuclear reactor. This tower, known as BREN tower, is 465 m tall and was the tallest government tower in the United States when it was built (Goldenberg and Beck 1991). The experiment was designed to determine the radiation doses received by the survivors of the atomic bombings of Japan in order to aid their health care. The Japanese houses now are wood-frame skeletons with only two left standing. To alleviate the effects of ground movement associated with underground testing, BREN Tower was moved to another location on the Nevada Test Site in 1966.

At the north end of Yucca Flat, a 14 ha experimental farm was built to study the effects of food exposed to radiation on animals, particularly cows (Beck *et al.* 1996: 30). The farm contained a well, reservoir, open paddocks, stalls, milking barn and laboratory building. Used for fifteen years and then decommissioned in 1981, the farm was dismantled in 1997, but alterations to the natural landscape remain visible.

On Jackass Flats in the southwestern corner of the Nevada Test Site are five facilities, built in the late 1950s and 1960s to develop nuclear-powered rocket engines for space exploration (see for example Beck *et al.* 2000; Drollinger *et al.* 2000). These were the Reactor Maintenance and Disassembly Facility, Test Cells A and C, the Engine Maintenance and Disassembly Facility, and the Engine Test Stand (Beck *et al.* 1996). These facilities contain massive structures, built to safely test nuclear reactors.

SIGNIFICANCE, VALUE AND PRESERVATION

In the 1950s, the inhabitants of Las Vegas identified with nuclear testing to the extent that a mushroom cloud was depicted in the centre of the official county seal. Tourists were provided with 'shot' calendars and maps to locations with views of the tests, while entertainment and industry attached 'atomic' to everything from drinks and hairdos to comedians and motels (Titus 1986: 94–5). Patriotism was strong as Las Vegans championed the Nevada Test Site and the role of the city in supporting a strong defence for the United States. Native Americans, on the other hand, felt that the establishment of the Nevada Test Site violated their claim to these ancestral lands and the nuclear testing activities were a desecration of the One Mother Earth (Shundahai Network 2000), with similar views held by others (Kuletz 1998). The public's perception of testing combined with controlled access to the Nevada Test Site have resulted in myths being generated about activities there, including claims of unidentified flying objects, aliens in captivity and other unbelievable stories that have found their way into modern culture. To demystify the Nevada Test Site, the Department of Energy today offers scheduled public tours of the testing remains in Frenchman and Yucca flats.

The Nevada Test Site figures prominently in the history of the Cold War. The efforts of the scientists, engineers and technicians who worked there developing and testing nuclear weapons, were integral to the stand-off between the United States, its Allies and the Soviet Union. The historical significance of the activities that took place at the Nevada Test Site is unquestionable. Pockets of testing structures exist today with isolated buildings and objects scattered across the landscape. Nuclear detonations are not commonplace in the world and, so far, have been mostly confined to only a few locations. Therefore, these vestiges of the Cold War at the Nevada Test Site are of a very limited class of material remains.

At the end of the year 2000, six facilities and 139 buildings, structures and objects at the Nevada Test Site had been recorded and determined eligible to the US National Register of Historic Places through consultation between the Department of Energy and the Nevada State Historic Preservation Office. Designation of the facilities and individual buildings, structures and objects as significant historical properties, besides documenting their importance, means that federal management of these locations is directed by requirements of the US National Historic Preservation Act. This law, while encouraging preservation of eligible properties, also allows dismantlement following a lengthy, written and visual documentation process.

When considering the applicability of preservation in regard to nuclear testing remains, the nature of the materials needs to be carefully scrutinized. For example, wind, rain and other natural processes slowly change many of the artificial landscapes created by the tests. These structural changes to the earth, in all likelihood, will exist for eons with no organized preservation efforts. On the other hand, the material remains that have survived a nuclear test should be protected from deliberate destruction because of their inherent significance. The structures built to survive tests, usually those related to test implementation and the acquisition of scientific data and the recordation of the tests, in most cases, are unique to nuclear testing as are the buildings associated with non-explosive research. Their preservation is important because they convey the scientific innovativeness of the nuclear testing endeavour. Other buildings were built to undergo a nuclear detonation. Stabilization of these buildings, structures and objects is appropriate and desirable. Restoration of structures originally built to be destroyed would not be in character with the intent of their construction. To see these nuclear testing remains in situ as they are is an experience that cannot be equalled by written word or in film. It brings home the cold, harsh reality of nuclear weaponry in the modern world and all that it influenced on the global front.

CONCLUSIONS

During the Cold War, there were three major continental nuclear testing grounds: the Nevada Test Site in the United States and two in the Soviet Union. These are the only places on earth where hundreds of nuclear devices have been detonated. Although there were no battles of engagement between the two Superpowers during the Cold War, a stalemate situation existed with each country testing nuclear weapons on their own soil as part of a strategy to maintain a strong defence and to be in possession of weapons superior to those of their counterpart. The nuclear testing era at the Nevada Test Site was a primary component of the Cold War, an era of a constant onslaught of threatening postures, coupled with world-wide fear of a nuclear war. Weapon capabilities and stockpiles were a primary concern with each country's emphasis on developing the best and most effective nuclear weapons.

Anyone who lived during this era remembers the spectre of a mushroom-shaped cloud that hung over the world as people wondered when nuclear war and potentially the annihilation of the human race might occur. The devastating effects of the bombs dropped on Japan haunted everyone; yet the inevitable nuclear war did not materialize. Instead, it seems that the fear of the devastating effects of nuclear weaponry kept the United States and the Soviet Union from participating in a nuclear war. In his book on the Cold War, John Lewis Gaddis (1997: 85–6) has presented this reflective interpretation well. He points out that in the history of warfare improvements in weaponry, including the atomic bomb, have had the result of causing (or having the potential to cause) more devastation and death; in other words, each invention is more efficient at what it is supposed to achieve. He believes that in the twentieth century, innovations in weaponry were major contributors to outbreaks of war, particularly in the First and Second World Wars. But as he states, 'It comes as something of a surprise, then, to realize that the most striking innovation in the history of military technology has turned out to be a cause of peace and not war' (Gaddis 1997: 85). Tens of thousands of nuclear weapons were built during the Cold War but none were used, even though there were events that made military confrontations seemed unavoidable.

> The ancient principle that if weapons are developed opportunities will be found to use them can, therefore, no longer be taken for granted, and that is a shift of major proportions in the long and lamentable history of warfare ... [The] new rationality grew out of the simple realization that as weapons become more devastating they become less usable.
>
> (Gaddis 1997: 86)

The nuclear testing grounds in the United States and the Soviet Union strongly supported the stalemate situation and probably contributed, indirectly, to saving thousands of lives. The Cold War was the last worldwide conflict of the twentieth century, yet, because there were no battles and no use of weapons, it has few associated remains. This aspect of the Cold War increases the importance of nuclear testing grounds and of the Nevada Test Site – the battlefields of the Cold War.

ACKNOWLEDGEMENTS

The US Department of Energy funded the research that formed the basis of this document. Special thanks are due to Robert Furlow at the Department of Energy, Nevada Operations Office, for his continuing support. However, all views presented here are mine alone. I would like to express my appreciation to Keith Kolb, Harold Drollinger and Evelyn Faulkner for their assistance. Recognition is due to the Desert Research Institute for its support during the preparation of this chapter.

REFERENCES

Beck, C.M., Drollinger, H. and Goldenberg, N. (2000) *An Historical Evaluation of the Test Cell A Facility for Characterization Activities Associated with Decontamination and Decommissioning, Area 25, Nevada Test Site, Nye County, Nevada,* Las Vegas: Desert Research Institute.

Beck, C.M., Goldenberg, N. and Johnson, W.G. (1996) *Nevada Test Site Historic Structures Survey,* Springfield, Virginia: National Technical Information Services.

Department of Energy (1994) *United States Nuclear Tests 1945–1992,* Springfield, Virginia: National Technical Information Services.

Dibblin, Jane (1990) *The Day of Two Suns: US Nuclear Testing and the Pacific Islanders,* New York: New Amsterdam.

Drollinger, H., Beck, C.M. and Goldenberg, N. (2000) *An Historical Evaluation of the Test Cell C Facility for Characterization Activities Associated with Decontamination and Decommissioning, Area 25, Nevada Test Site, Nye County, Nevada,* Las Vegas: Desert Research Institute.

Edwards, S. (1997) *Atomic Age Training Camp: The Historical Archaeology of Camp Desert Rock,* Masters thesis, University of Nevada, Las Vegas. Ann Arbor, Michigan: University Microfilms.

Fehner, T. and Gosling, F. (2000) *Origins of the Nevada Test Site,* United States Department of Energy.

Friesen, H. (1995) *A Perspective on Atmospheric Nuclear Tests in Nevada – Fact Book,* Springfield, Virginia: National Technical Information Services.

Gaddis, J. (1997) *We Now Know,* Oxford: Clarendon Press.

Goin, P. (1991) *Nuclear Landscapes,* Baltimore: Johns Hopkins University Press.

Goldenberg, N. and Beck, C.M. (1991) 'Historic Building Inventory and Evaluation: BREN Tower, Area 25, Nevada Test Site, Nye County, Nevada', Las Vegas: Desert Research Institute Cultural Resources Short Report no. 092791–1.

Hersey, J. (1985) *The Cold War,* New York: Henry Holt.

Johnson, W.G. and Beck, C.M. (1995) Proving Ground of the Nuclear Age, *Archaeology* 48(3): 42–9.

Johnson, W.G., Goldenberg, N. and Edwards, S. (1997) The Japanese Village at the Nevada Test Site, *Cultural Resource Management* 20(14): 21–2.

Johnson, W.G., Holz, B. and Jones, R. (2000), *A Cold War Battlefield: Frenchman Flat Historic District, Nevada Test Site, Nye County, Nevada,* Springfield, Virginia: National Technical Information Services.

Kuletz, V. (1998) *The Tainted Desert,* New York and London: Routledge.

Lay, J.S. (1950) Memorandum for the President, National Security Council, December 18, 1950, copy at the Coordination and Information Center, Department of Energy, Nevada Operations Office, Las Vegas.

Matthews, A. (1998) Making the list, *Preservation* 50(4): 64–73.

Miller, R. (1986) *Under the Cloud: The Decades of Nuclear Testing,* New York: Free Press.

Nevada Desert Experience (2000) *Archival Photos and Bits of History,* available HTTP: <http://nevadadesertexperience.org/JointPhotoElectronGraphichistory.html> (accessed 18 December 2000.

Norris, R. and Arkin, W. (1996) Known nuclear tests, *Bulletin of the Atomic Scientists* 52(3): 61–3.

O'Donnell, A. (1999) Transcript of interview by C.M. Beck and W.G. Johnson, on file at the Desert Research Institute, Las Vegas, Nevada.

Office of History, United States Weapons and Tactics Center (1994) *Brief History of Nellis Air Force Base, Nevada (Air Combat Command),* Las Vegas: Office of History, United States Air Force Weapons and Tactics Center, Nellis Air Force Base.

Ogle, W. (1985) *An Account of the Return to Nuclear Weapons Testing by the United States after the Test Moratorium 1958–1961,* Las Vegas: United States Department of Energy Nevada Operations Office.

Schofield, J. and Anderton, M. (2000) The queer archaeology of Green Gate: interpreting contested space at Greenham Common Airbase, *World Archaeology* 32(2): 236–51.

Shundahai Network (2000) *Shundahai Network,* available HTTP: <http://www.shundahai.org> (accessed 18 December 2000).

Smyth, H. and Morrison, P. (1990) *Atomic Energy for Military Purposes: the Official Report on the Development of the Atomic Bomb under the Auspices of the United States Government,* Palo Alto: Stanford University Press.

Szasz, F.M. (1995) *The Day the Sun Rose Twice,* Albuquerque: University of New Mexico Press.

Titus, A. (1986) *Bombs in the Backyard, Atomic Testing and American Politics,* Reno and Las Vegas: University of Nevada Press.

Tlachac, E.M. (1989) 'Nuclear Testing' in *Nevada Comprehensive Preservation Plan,* Section 25, pp. 1–24, Carson City: Nevada Division of Historic Preservation and Archeology, Department of Conservation and Natural Resources.

Walker, M. (1999) *The Cold War: A Military History,* New York: St Martin's Press.

Weisgall, J.M. (1994) *Operation Crossroads,* Annapolis: Naval Institute Press.

8   Missing in action: searching for America's war dead

Lisa Hoshower-Leppo

The US Army is designated as the Executive Agent for the Joint Mortuary Affairs Program and maintains a Central Joint Mortuary Affairs Office and the US Army Central Identification Laboratory, Hawaii (CILHI). The CILHI is the field-operating component of the Casualty and Memorial Affairs Operations Center, US Army Total Personnel Command.

The history behind the creation of the CILHI is a long one. For more than 150 years the US government has made a concerted effort to recover and inter the remains of American service members killed in war. The earliest endeavours date to the Seminole Wars of the 1840s; although many Civil War soldiers were buried where they fell, with little attempt at identification, the government had by then assumed an obligation to identify and bury war dead in registered graves. The Spanish–American War signalled a major policy change as servicemen interred on foreign soil were systematically disinterred from their burial sites in Cuba and returned to the United States for burial. The creation of the Graves Registration Service during the First World War reflected the US Government's desire to quickly return the remains of soldiers from Europe for interment on native soil.

During the Second World War Congress delegated the responsibility of returning the remains of US service members to the Secretary of the Army. Several temporary army identification laboratories were established and, for the first time, physical anthropologists and anatomists were retained to identify the remains. Congress had established a five-year time limit after the war's end for final resolution. When the congressional charter expired in 1951 the laboratories were disbanded.

During the Korean War a temporary identification laboratory was established – again by congressional charter – in Kohura, Japan to process United Nations Forces war dead. The laboratory closed in 1956, but some of the laboratory personnel remained in Japan and later assisted in the identification of service members killed in the Vietnam War.

During the 1960s two US mortuaries operated in South Vietnam to process and identify the remains of US service members killed during the Vietnam War. The closing of the mortuaries in 1972 and 1973 coincided with the withdrawal of US troops from South Vietnam. In March 1973 the US Army established the Central Identification Laboratory, Thailand (CIL-THAI) at Camp Samae San, Thailand, to continue the search for and recovery and the identification of the remains of US service members killed in the Vietnam War. As a result of the fall of the South Vietnamese government in 1975, the laboratory was relocated to Hawaii. On 8 November 1992 a new CILHI facility was built on Hickam Air Force Base, on the island of Oahu. Approximately 170 military and civilian personnel, operating in four major sections (Operations and Support; Search and Recovery Operations; Casualty Data Analysis; and the Laboratory) are under the command of a US army colonel.

The Support and Operations Section is responsible for pre-mission analysis and planning, post-mission evaluation, and between-mission management of the CILHI search and recovery teams. These teams travel the world to investigate and excavate crash and burial sites associated with the loss of US service members. A civilian CILHI anthropologist accompanies each military search and recovery team. The Casualty Data section researches, compiles and analyses the background data associated with each specific loss scenario and the individual(s) associated with that particular incident and also maintains personnel, medical and dental files on service members whose remains have not been recovered or identified.

Currently the CILHI laboratory scientific staff is comprised of twenty-five anthropologists and three forensic odontologists. All members of the scientific staff hold advanced degrees and training and several are board-certified in their specialties. The job of the CILHI anthropologists is twofold: (1) they are the recovery leaders on worldwide search and recovery missions to ensure that proper archaeological techniques and procedures are followed and that scientific integrity is maintained; and (2) they establish the identification of the CILHI-recovered remains or remains repatriated by foreign governments using standard recognized forensic anthropological techniques and procedures.

RECOVERY PROCEDURES

The majority of the CILHI search and recovery missions are conducted in remote, rugged and undeveloped mountainous terrain in Southeast Asia, specifically the Lao People's Democratic Republic (Laos), the Socialist Republic of Vietnam and the Kingdom of Cambodia. The CILHI excavations are generally complicated by a combination of unique factors. These complications include extreme environmental perils (for example unexploded ordnance, aberrant temperatures, monsoons, typhoons, flooding, poisonous reptiles and insects), physical dangers (the ever-present risk of fungal, parasitic and infectious diseases, together with unsanitary living conditions), geographic hazards (rugged mountainous terrain or dense jungle) and cultural factors (such as heavily scavenged sites, differences in cultural viewpoints, practices, attitudes and interpretations of the loss incident). Time and budget constraints, foreign government dictates and a politically and emotionally charged atmosphere exacerbate excavation conditions.

The goal of each CILHI excavation is to recover sufficient material evidence to identify the loss incident and the individual(s) involved through the archaeological recovery of human remains, life-support equipment, personal effects and aircraft wreckage. Before the anthropologists leave the CILHI they have had the opportunity to familiarize themselves with the loss incident from a case packet, assembled by the Casualty Data section, which holds all the information pertinent to the specific loss incident to which the anthropologist has been assigned. This packet contains maps, original message traffic from the time of loss, investigative reports, witness statements, biographic sketches of the individual(s) involved, information on the aircraft, and any other information relevant to case resolution. The anthropologist will study the case packet, form an initial excavation strategy and ascertain if standard excavation equipment and supplies are sufficient or if specialized equipment will be required.

Once in the host country every CILHI excavation, whether of an aircraft crash or burial site, begins with a survey of the project area by the anthropologist to estimate recovery time and size of indigenous labour force needed. The CILHI anthropologist incorporates witness statements, previous investigative and casualty data reports, alterations to the landscape and surface evidence distribution (for instance personal effects, life-support equipment, aircraft wreckage) to determine the area most likely to contain human remains. Core samples may also be taken to determine both the horizontal and vertical subsurface dimensions of the site. After the excavation area has been defined and an excavation strategy formulated, final preparations are made, and social and cultural obligations are met. The site preparation is completed and the datum point is established and recorded using the Global Positioning System (GPS). The excavation grid is placed around the datum and excavation by gridded units commences. All removed fill is screened for artefacts and remains. Provenance is recorded for all recovered items. Remains and artefacts are bagged by discrete units and transported to the CILHI with their immediate context retained during laboratory analysis.

Thirty years of taphonomic disturbances and cultural interventions by indigenous peoples have dramatically altered the majority of the excavation sites. Cultural alterations, including scavenging, ploughing, cultivation, deforestation and even the movement of people and animals over the land since the time of incident, can disturb and destroy evidence. Frequently cultural interventions so alter the landscape that there are no visible surface signs that an incident took place at all. Local villagers remove material from the archaeological context (crash site) and move it to a cultural context (their homes) – a process commonly referred to as scavenging. In most regions of Southeast Asia, crash sites have been extensively scavenged. Scavenging of aircraft crash sites varies among indigenous peoples based on their unique interpretations of the incident and the usefulness of the materials associated with it. Some items, such as life-support equipment and personal effects, are of no utilitarian value, but are retained as an oddity, a curiosity or as a reminder of the event. The wreckage that the CILHI recovery teams most frequently encounter on any given aircraft crash site is usually limited to aircraft fragments (Fig. 8.1). These remainders are either too small to be of any other practical use, such as oxidized aluminium, wires, and rivets, or are large parts, such as engines, that are too heavy or cumbersome to remove from the area.

Therefore, the precise spatial location of all material evidence at the site is not essential to reconstruction of the circumstances surrounding the loss incident.

Figure 8.1 Aircraft wreckage reduced to a small amount of 'scrap' after scavenging

High-speed aircraft impact crashes have one thing in common: the daunting magnitudes of the crater. Whether the aircraft impacted on a mountainside, in a rice paddy, or on level ground, the size of impact craters in combination with extensive scavenging, make it impractical, counter-productive and virtually impossible to minutely record provenance for each fragment of aircraft wreckage, human remains, life-support equipment or personal effects.

Prior to excavation, a metal detector is used to locate wreckage scatter outside the crater. If the type and concentration of wreckage warrants further investigation, then the excavation area is expanded beyond the crater's limits. Next, the datum is established and a 'hanging' grid is placed (Fig. 8.2). The walls of the crater are cleared of vegetation and loose soil using pickaxes and shovels. All fill is placed into buckets and transported by labourers to the screening area. Depth, as well as direction, of the excavation is dictated by the distribution of artefacts – typically a result of the trajectory or angle of aircraft impact. As one would expect, artefact distribution will mirror direction and mode of impact. For example, if the aircraft impacted the ground nose first, a large deep crater is formed with the majority of wreckage, life-support equipment and remains located at the lower depths of the crater. If the aircraft 'bellied' in and impacted the ground on a horizontal plane, then the majority of artefacts will scatter in a forward direction, frequently covering a great distance. Excavation proceeds by grid and each grid is screened and analysed for material evidence before the next grid is opened. Gross provenance is recorded for all recovered items. Excavation continues as long as aircraft wreckage identifiable by type or model, life-support equipment, personal effects or remains are encountered.

Figure 8.2 Field site featuring 'hanging grid'

In dealing with isolated burials, excavation is conducted in much the same manner as any forensic anthropological excavation of a buried body. However, unlike their contemporaries in forensic anthropology, the CILHI anthropologist reaches a burial site armed with the knowledge of the individual involved, the circumstances of loss and the facts surrounding the burial site. The majority of the CILHI buried-body cases in Southeast Asia are burials of individuals involved in aircraft fatalities. Southeast Asian nationalists were usually first on the scene; they either removed the remains from the aircraft or gathered the remains from the ground surface and interred them near the crash site. Personal effects and uniform items were more often than not removed and kept as souvenirs or turned over to the North Vietnamese Army. In some circumstances the remains were dug up and reinterred at a different location. In these instances surface or scattered remains may indicate evidence for a secondary burial episode. As a result each set of scattered remains represents a unique episode and must be handled as such, with flexible and adaptive recovery techniques. This is especially pertinent when surface finds believed to be associated with an isolated burial or air crash are encountered by the CILHI anthropologist. Given the nature of the incident and elapsed time, if any scattered remains exist, they have been subjected to almost three decades of taphonomic intervention. In isolated burial recoveries, surface finds typically indicate the most likely point to initiate excavation. The spatial distribution of bones, teeth and other items recovered in surface finds can help in determining the original location and position of the body. In aircraft crash sites, however, scattered remains are frequently just that, scattered. Thus, recovered remains and artefacts are documented by general provenance. In rare circumstances when an intact aircraft with remains is encountered, meticulous gridding, mapping and recording of all phases of site excavation are the norm.

CASE STUDIES

An isolated burial in Namh Ha province, Socialist Republic of Vietnam

In March 1994 a CILHI search and recovery team travelled to Nam Ha province, Socialist Republic of Vietnam (SRV) to conduct a search and recovery mission on an isolated burial site believed to be associated with a July 1967 loss incident. The loss event involved a SH-3A navy helicopter on a rescue mission over North Vietnam. While attempting to locate a downed pilot, the helicopter was repeatedly hit by flak and small arms fire. The helicopter caught fire, crashed on a hill, and was engulfed in flames. No one was observed exiting the aircraft before or after the crash. Three navy aircraft conducted individual visual searches of the crash site. No survivors were observed. Intensive ground fire in the area forced search and rescue attempts to be terminated. A Hanoi broadcast the same day of the incident reported that a helicopter came down on the hilltop killing all Americans on board. All individuals were listed as dead, body not recovered.

In October 1982 the SRV unilaterally turned over several sets of human remains to the CILHI. These repatriated remains were identified by the CILHI as three of the four individuals associated with the July 1967 SH-3A helicopter crash, leaving one individual unaccounted for.

In 1993 a Vietnamese source provided limited hearsay information concerning the alleged shooting down of an American helicopter in Nam Ha province. Casualty Data analysis at the CILHI indicated that this was the only helicopter loss involving unaccounted for individuals in this province.

In November 1993 a joint US–SRV investigative element travelled to Nam Ha province to investigate the case. The team interviewed two witnesses. One witness stated that he buried bodies that were subsequently exhumed (those remains repatriated to the CILHI in 1982). The other witness stated that he buried a body that was still at the site. This witness led the team to the alleged burial site and pointed out a 10 by 10 m area where he buried an American. No human remains or personal effects were found, but fibre-glass cloth, consistent with a helicopter crash site, was found. Based on this information the site was recommended for excavation.

In March 1994 a joint US–SRV excavation was conducted of the site associated with the July 1967 SH–3A helicopter loss. The site was located directly east of a karst base within flat cultivated fields interspersed with lava boulders. The original witness, who claimed to have buried the missing crew member in two ceramic burial containers typically used by the Vietnamese in their secondary interments, was brought to the alleged burial area. The witness walked directly to a lava boulder reference point and stated that he walked approximately 5 m due north from the centre of this boulder and buried the containers approximately waist deep. He relayed that at the time of burial the area had been deep forest with a thick undercover of shrubs, bushes and tall grasses. Since the time of the incident the landscape had been greatly altered by heavy machinery during deforesting of the area and years of cultivation. Because the area had been significantly transformed since the loss event, the anthropologist delineated a 15 by 12 m area around the alleged burial spot for excavation to compensate for any witness memory loss. The site was excavated using standard archaeological procedures. The project area grid was divided into 4 by 5 m excavation units. Excavation proceeded in 5 cm arbitrary levels and all fill was screened through quarter-inch mesh. Between approximately 45 and 50 cm below ground surface a layer of undisturbed limestone was encountered within each excavation unit. The anthropologist halted work and asked that the witness be returned to the site. The witness stated that he did not encounter this rock layer when he buried the remains and was visibly distraught that the team did not encounter the ceramic containers. As he was unable to provide any information or suggestions to direct the team to the correct burial location, the anthropologist closed the project area, recommended further investigation of the case and the team returned to their base camp.

That evening, a member of the Vietnamese Office for Seeking Missing Personnel (VNOSMP) came to the anthropologist with a piece of ceramic container. A villager had come forth and stated that during cultivation of her field several years ago she had encountered a ceramic burial container and left it undisturbed. She had been observing the joint field recovery team and rationalized that they were searching for the remains of an American involved in the Vietnam War. After the team left the site (on what would have been their last day of work) she returned to her field, probed the area, found a ceramic burial container, recovered a fragment for proof, reburied the container, and turned the fragment over to local village officials. These officials then sought out the search and recovery team and turned the fragment over to the VNOSMP working with the joint team.

The following morning the recovery team travelled to an area approximately 90 m north of the original excavation area. The woman and her family had spent the night in the field by the burial area to ensure that the container remained undisturbed. They had covered the area with a cloth and placed the probe directly over the container. The recovery team utilized standard archaeological procedures and encountered a crushed, fragmented ceramic burial container 50 cm below ground surface. An intact ceramic burial container was encountered 45 cm west of the first box at a depth of 44 cm below ground surface. In addition to human teeth and bone fragments, three pieces of flight suit consistent with flight suits worn by navy pilots were recovered. The original witness was present at the excavation and he confirmed that the two containers recovered were the ceramic burial containers that he had buried. The remains were repatriated to the CILHI for identification.

An isolated burial in Thanh Hoa province, Socialist Republic of Vietnam

In October 1995 a CILHI search and recovery team travelled to Thanh Hoa province, SRV to conduct a search and recovery mission on an isolated burial site believed to be associated with a 1967 loss incident. The incident involved the 1967 loss of an Air Force A-1E aircraft which was in a flight of two on a search and rescue mission over North Vietnam. During the mission the flight was attacked by four MIG-17s and the wingman observed that the loss incident aircraft had received hits on the left wing. The wing flew off the aircraft, which then rolled into a left spiral, crashed and exploded on impact. Search and recovery efforts were not possible due to heavy enemy aircraft and intense ground fire. A Hanoi radio broadcast on the same day of the incident reported the shooting down of an American rescue aircraft that was consistent with this loss event. Over the years, the continued hostile threat in the area precluded any visits or ground inspections of the site associated with the loss incident.

In September 1972 a Vietnamese source reported the shooting down of an American aircraft by a MIG-17 that was consistent with the events surrounding the 1967 loss of the A-1E. In July, August and November of 1991 three Vietnamese sources independently reported information and provided material evidence that correlated with the A-1E loss. These various statements and evidence were passed from the Vietnamese government to American officials and agreements were reached between government officials for a course of action.

In November 1992 and May 1994 joint US–SRV investigation teams travelled to Thanh Hoa province and interviewed witnesses concerning the incidents surrounding the loss event. Lack of physical evidence and insufficient witness testimony resulted in no new information. In November 1994 a joint investigative element travelled to Thanh Hoa province to investigate the 1967 loss of the A-1E aircraft. Two witnesses were interviewed who stated that they travelled to the crash site some time after the incident and buried the incomplete remains of an American pilot. The witnesses led the team to the alleged crash/burial site. Ordnance and numerous pieces of wreckage consistent with an A-1E aircraft were found. The site was recommended for excavation.

In October 1995 a CILHI recovery team went to the SRV to excavate the crash site associated with the loss incident. The joint US–SRV team travelled to Thanh Hoa province to investigate the case and meet with local officials for site co-ordination. Contracting for local labourers and landing zone preparations for the helicopter were discussed. A helicopter would be necessary to transport the team and their equipment to a base camp as the site was inaccessible by any other means.

An MI-17 helicopter transported the joint team and their equipment to the only flat dry area in the vicinity of the site, a hamlet of an ethnic mountain tribe. The joint team established their base camp in the backyard of the hamlet. The excavation site was a 3 km walk from the base camp across rice paddies, through a river, around an additional hamlet, and up a steep mountainside in double canopy jungle.

Two witnesses directed the team to the alleged crash and burial site, which was located on the side of a karst with an approximate 40° slope at an altitude of 1768 m.

Although they could not pinpoint the exact location and there was a small discrepancy in general area between statements, the areas pointed out by the witnesses did overlap. An area encompassing both witnesses' statements, measuring approximately 30 by 30 m was cleared of lush tropical vegetation.

Personal effects and pilot-related life-support equipment found during the surface search, combined with witness information, suggested that the burial location lay within an 8 by 12 m portion of the cleared area. The datum was established using the GPS and the area was divided into 4 by 4 m units. Between 20 and 50 cm of loose soil overlaid vertically faulted bedrock. This faulting exacerbated the dangers faced by excavating on a 40° slope with a sheer vertical drop. Footing was treacherous, walking across the site was laborious and maintaining balance during excavation was arduous. All units were excavated to bedrock and all fill was screened through quarter-inch mesh. Human remains, personal effects, life-support equipment and aircraft wreckage consistent with an A-1 series aircraft were recovered. The human remains were repatriated to the CILHI for identification.

An aircraft crash site in Savannakhet province, Laos People's Democratic Republic

In December 1968 a US Marine Corps F-4B aircraft was flying as leader in a flight of two on a night-combat mission over the Laos People's Democratic Republic (LPDR). The last transmission from the pilot was made as the aircraft approached its target area. The forward air controller and wingman watched the ordnance explode on the target area and then observed a secondary explosion shortly thereafter. The wingman attempted to contact the lead aircraft but no response was heard. The wingman believed the secondary explosion was the crash of the lead aircraft after being hit by enemy fire. Search and rescue efforts discovered no wreckage. Over the years, the continued hostile threat in the area precluded any visits or ground inspections of the site associated with the loss incident. The names of the two individuals associated with the incident and identification data were turned over to a four-party joint military team with a request for any available information. No response was forthcoming and the individuals were carried in the presumptive status of dead, body not recovered.

In March 1993 a joint US–LPDR team travelled to a village in Savannakhet Province, LPDR to investigate the case. Villagers led the team to an alleged crash site and informed them that they had salvaged the site for scrap metal in 1987 and had used explosives to blow up the wreckage into small pieces. A survey of the site found a large impact crater, some fragmented life-support materials and small pieces of wreckage scattered over a 50 m area. The site was recommended for excavation.

In early 1997 a joint recovery team initiated excavation of the crash site believed to be associated with the F-4 loss. The team recovered an extensive amount of life-support items and aircraft wreckage. Analysis of the life-support material tentatively indicated that two individuals were on board at the time of the crash. Aircraft wreckage was consistent with an F-4 series aircraft. Time constraints (the Laotian government dictates a maximum of thirty days in their country for the recovery teams per mission) did not allow for completion of the excavation.

In October 1997 a joint recovery team went to the LPDR to complete excavation of the site. The team travelled to the site from a semi-permanent base camp via Lao West Coast and Laotian military MI-17 helicopters. The crash site was located on a ridge in mountainous terrain at an elevation of 500 m above sea level. When the second recovery team arrived at the site the outside dimensions of the partially excavated crash crater were approximately 7 by 8 m and 2 m deep. The bottom of the crater had filled with water. Fifty local villagers were hired to help in the excavation. The datum was re-established and a hanging grid placed. Strings for individual units were attached to stakes on the rim of the crater and suspended across it. Plumb bobs were used to maintain provenance. Standard water pumps and hoses were transported to the site to remove the water from the bottom of the crater. The previously excavated walls of the crater were scraped to view the stratigraphy. The second soil stratum inside the crater consisted of an orange clay matrix heavily interspersed with quartz and sandstone inclusions. This matrix necessitated wet screening the excavated soil.

The excavation was conducted in a spiral, stepped fashion. Stepping the excavation helps to prevent undermining of the crater walls as the excavation proceeds – an important consideration given the sheer size of a high-speed aircraft crash crater. Spiral excavation allows the anthropologist to follow the contours of the crater and interpret evidence. After completion of the crater excavation (final dimensions were 10 by 12 by 9 m), the team excavated sixteen 4 by 4 m units surrounding the crater. The team also conducted a search of a 200 m area extending beyond the project area in all directions. No additional evidence was found.

Life-support equipment, personal effects and aircraft wreckage were recovered from the crater and the surrounding excavation units. The majority of evidence was recovered within the crater from the fourth stratum which ranged between 3.5–4.5 m below ground surface. Stratum four was a hard, dense clay layer with white, yellow, green and deep purple mottlings. The mottlings were an indicator of a disturbance. As with buried body cases where excavators are looking for disturbed soil as an indication of a disturbance, such indicators are also useful in buried aircraft crash sites. An extensive amount of life-support items, personal effects, and aircraft wreckage, but no human remains, were recovered by the two search and recovery teams at this site. This is an example of how thirty years of taphonomic disturbances and cultural interventions by indigenous peoples has dramatically altered an incident area. The combination of scavenging and explosives on the site by the local population along with natural taphonomic forces not only significantly disturbed the site, but also destroyed evidence – particularly fragile human remains.

CONCLUSIONS

These three case studies demonstrate the variety of procedures the CILHI follows to achieve their federally mandated task of the search for, recovery of and identification of all unaccounted-for US service members from all military conflicts and missions. The search agenda for the remains of these individuals will not end and the CILHI anthropologists work on a daily basis to fulfill this mission. While the goal of the CILHI is dedicated to the repatriation of service members from all conflicts, historically the main focus of the CILHI has been the return of the remains of US service members from a very unpopular military conflict – the Vietnam War. Even after thirty years the Vietnam War is an emotionally charged issue, particularly for family members who lost a loved one whose remains have yet to be repatriated. Some family members still express distrust of the Vietnamese government and its motives. The CILHI anthropologists work in this politically charged atmosphere to assure the families that the remains of their loved ones are treated in the most humane, honourable and ethical manner possible.

Not only must the CILHI anthropologists be aware of the political and emotional issues surrounding their mission, they must also work within the cultural parameters of the host countries. The anthropologists must remain vigilant and sensitive to the manner in which cultural implications and practices affect site excavations and interpretations as well as the interpretation of skeletal remains. Cultural customs and traditions affect site transformation and ultimately the methods and techniques utilized by the CILHI anthropologist in the recovery process. Differences in cultural practices, attitudes, viewpoints and interpretations of an event must be recognized and understood by the CILHI anthropologist before she/he can completely conduct the recovery and ultimately reconstruct the loss incident. The CILHI anthropologists are aware that certain cultural practices affect bone preservation and appearance and use this as circumstantial evidence in their evaluation of the case.

When the US combat forces withdrew from Vietnam, 2583 Americans were unaccounted for – 1500 in Vietnam, more than 500 in Laos, and almost 80 in Cambodia. Another 425 service members were lost off the coast of Vietnam. US officials first launched formal search and recovery operations in Vietnam and Laos in 1988 and Cambodia in 1991. At the time of writing, over 600 service members have been identified and repatriated as a result of joint US-host nation search and recovery efforts. Others remain lost – but never forgotten as the search continues.

ACKNOWLEDGEMENT

This chapter is dedicated to the memory of those who gave their lives in the search for the remains of fallen service members. The views expressed are those of the author and should not be construed to represent the US government.

9   Mapping Cambodia's 'killing fields'

HELEN JARVIS

After the overthrow of Democratic Kampuchea, Cambodia and Vietnam revealed to the outside world the horrors of Tuol Sleng, a high school in Phnom Penh where more than 15 000 people are reported to have been imprisoned and tortured before being executed on the outskirts of the city at Choeung Ek, often called 'the killing field'. Tuol Sleng became a Museum of Genocide, preserving the remains of the horror that took place there, and a memorial *stupa* was erected at Choeung Ek (Fig. 9.1 provides an example of a *stupa*). But these are only two such genocide sites of the many hundreds scattered throughout the country. During the three years, eight months and twenty days that the Khmer Rouge held power, more than 1.6 million people perished, over one quarter of the total population, dying in miserable circumstances of starvation and untreated illness, if not from brutal torture and execution, in one of the twentieth century's most destructive episodes (Kiernan 1996; Sliwinski 1996).

In November 1997, almost nineteen years after the Khmer Rouge was overthrown, for the first time one of the major organs of the United Nations acknowledged that massive human rights violations had occurred in Cambodia during the Democratic Kampuchea period of 1975–9. The General Assembly voted to accept the report of the Secretary General Special Representative on Human Rights for Cambodia, Thomas Hammarberg, which recommended a positive United Nations response to a July 1997 letter signed jointly by the then co-Prime Ministers Hun Sen and Norodom Ranariddh requesting assistance in bringing the Khmer Rouge to justice (United Nations 1999).

A UN Group of Experts was established to give an opinion as to whether sufficient grounds existed for convening a trial, and to explore the advantages and disadvantages of various types of tribunals, with different levels of international involvement. The Group of Experts' report, released in early 1999, recommended an international tribunal such as those already in operation for Rwanda and the former Yugoslavia. The Cambodian government response was rather to request international assistance for and involvement in a Cambodian domestic process. During the following years discussions continued with the United Nations as to the degree of international involvement in these judicial proceedings, while the number and identity of those to be indicted and tried are yet to be determined.

After two decades of delay in bringing the Khmer Rouge to justice, the tide was

Figure 9.1 Example of a *stupa*, located at Tuol Sleng Genocide Museum

decisively turning towards the setting up of a tribunal. Whatever form it may take, such a trial would almost certainly rely heavily on the unexpected plethora of documentation uncovered, catalogued and summarized over the past five years by the Cambodian Genocide Program (CGP) and the Documentation Center of Cambodia (DC-Cam), which reveals without a shadow of doubt the massive and systematic nationwide scope of the Khmer Rouge's human rights violations.[1]

DOCUMENTING THE CAMBODIAN GENOCIDE

The challenge faced by the CGP as we embarked on our work in early 1995 was to move beyond the authentic yet essentially reductionist images of skulls or black-clothed people slaving over irrigation canals to arrive at a deeper understanding of what took place in Cambodia from 1975 to 1979. So much has been invested by all parties and observers over more than twenty years of political disputation and discord. So much has been lost or destroyed. So much has been forgotten or covered up. How does one begin to provide the documentation for research and rescue of the evidence?

We began by seeking to locate and catalogue both known and previously unknown records in a variety of formats (paper records, photographs and film, oral testimony, physical geographic sites, remote sensing images, computer files) and in multiple languages (principally Khmer, French and English, but also in Vietnamese, Thai, Chinese and Russian) and locations (Cambodia, Vietnam, the United States, Australia and elsewhere), with the team of more than fifty individuals based in our three locations (Phnom Penh, New Haven and Sydney).

Existing international standards (such as machine-readable cataloguing formats and human rights classification codes) have had to be applied and frequently extended to handle this unusually broad range of data, and the software has been pushed to cope with new and challenging tasks (such as displaying Khmer script; linking retrieved records to associated image files; and displaying retrieved records and images on the Internet).

In addition to meeting our research objectives, we have had to place high regard on the integrity of all our data, its provenance and its security, due to the ever-increasing likelihood of its being used in evidence in a future trial. The continuous media spotlight, the intense political interest in the issue, and the continued presence and threat of the Khmer Rouge (particularly in the early years of our work) have demanded constant vigilance regarding the security of both staff and documents, as well as a high degree of responsiveness and sensitivity in presenting our results to the public, particularly as regards respecting the memory of those killed, and the privacy and integrity of the survivors.

The Cambodian Genocide Databases (CGDB)

We have developed a suite of databases, called the Cambodian Genocide Databases (CGDB), within which we manage bibliographic, biographic, geographic and image-based material.[2] At the time of its launch in January 1997, the CGP Bibliographic Database (CBIB) contained 2000 records covering a wide range of material and by mid-2000 it stood at 3400, with many thousands of documents awaiting processing.[3] The documents collected in Phnom Penh by the Documentation Center since the CGP began its work are turning out to be of great significance and the collection is of ever-growing dimensions, and greatly exceeds in number and significance what was aniticipated. These consist of such items as confessions, photographs, prison note books and personnel records from the central prison at Tuol Sleng in Phnom Penh, as well as from other parts of the Khmer Rouge security apparatus, and a complete set of the court documents presented at the 1979 People's Revolutionary Tribunal (DeNike *et al.* 2000). A virtual database of scanned images has been developed and is linked to the searchable databases.

A specific subset of the image database (CIMG) contains scanned images of more than 5000 photographs from Tuol Sleng prison – from one quarter to one third of the total number of people who were held there during the period of

Cambodian Genocide Sites
Mapping data 1995-9

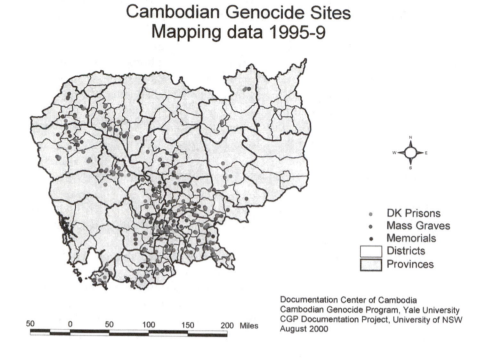

Figure 9.2   Cambodian genocide sites, mapped by Cambodian Genocide Program 1995–9, with spatial data from the Geography Department, Kingdom of Cambodia

Khmer Rouge rule, most of whom are believed to have been executed at Choeung Ek on the outskirts of Phnom Penh. (For reproductions of 100 of the photos and for introductory essays see Riley and Niven 1996; for more on Tuol Sleng see Chandler 1999.) CIMG also contains samples of photographs taken by the Documentation Center's mapping teams as they have visited the genocide sites throughout the country, as described further below in the section on CGEO.

The CGP Biographic Database (CBIO) in mid-2000 contained records on more than 10 000 people, with another 10 000 now in process. It contains data on those recorded as being members of the Khmer Rouge, but also on many other Cambodians, especially those known to have been victims of the Khmer Rouge, on whom biographical data were available in many sources, including interviews of hundreds of Cambodians, and from the more than 11 000 biographies and confessions of the Tuol Sleng prisoners.

Mapping the killing fields

One of the most significant aspects of the CGP's work, undertaken by field teams from the Documentation Center, is the mapping component under which we are recording details of genocide sites throughout the country, confirming by physical evidence the documentary accounts of the genocide. More than 500 genocide sites in twenty-one of Cambodia's twenty-four provinces have so far been recorded (Fig. 9.2), and the task is by no means complete. Every single province, district, subdistrict and almost every village in Cambodia appears to have some physical remains, indicating the widespread and systematic nature of the imprisonment, torture and killings carried out by the Khmer Rouge regime.

Using Global Positioning System (GPS) devices (Trimble Geo-Explorers creating Pathfinder files) the latitude and longitude of each site has been recorded, as well as the site's feature type(s) (burial site, prison or memorial) and further attributes for each type (such as grave pit, former school building or *stupa*). If such information can be found, then the probable date and the estimated number of people who were killed there are also noted.

These Pathfinder files are downloaded from the GPS recorder into PCs at the Documentation Center and then sent to UNSW over the Internet (using File Transfer Protocol) where they are processed using ArcInfo. We have been assisted extensively in this effort by the UNSW School of Geomatic Engineering, which has not only provided expert advice and data handling, but also access to software and hardware. The Cambodian genocide site data is combined with mapping coverages developed by the Cambodian Geographic Department, showing roads, rivers and political or administrative boundaries. The maps generated from ArcInfo, its interrogation and presentation package ArcView and its Internet Map Server, show locations of mass graves (giving the estimated number of victims per site ranging from two to 36 000), prisons and memorials. Roads, watercourses and district borders are also displayed.

As well as mapping the location of the genocide sites, the mapping teams have also found a number of documents and local informants who have provided information on the circumstances of the site from their personal perspective. In order to locate the sites we have relied on our accumulating documentary sources, and on advice from provincial authorities, particularly those from the Department of Culture, which had responsibility for erecting and maintaining the memorials and which in most cases still retain some kind of sketch map or list of sites in their province. The written documentation from the early 1980s is extremely important for locating and identifying the sites, and will become more so as the local informants gradually pass away.

Physically visiting all of the genocide sites in Cambodia is beyond what we have been able to do so far, so our priority has been to map the major sites in each province and district. However, some areas have been inaccessible due to security or transport considerations, and in some provinces we have only been able to make a preliminary survey, with sites selected for mapping on the basis of their accessibility.

The Documentation Center's field teams always need 4-wheel drive vehicles as roads, even in and around the capital, are shocking, and a few kilometres' distance off the main road to a site may take several hours. Sometimes resort is made to other forms of transportation, including ox-cart, motorbike, *remorque*, speedboat, very slow boat rowed by a single oar, and of course walking. Especially in the early years of this work, before the current stable government was formed in late 1998, our teams were frequently provided with armed escorts by the provincial or local authorities, due to fear of interference from residual Khmer Rouge forces, or from bandits. On one occasion in Kampot in 1996, our team left a site just 15 minutes before a Khmer Rouge unit crossed the only access road. Another ever-present danger comes from the estimated six million mines that litter Cambodia's countryside. As demining is a painfully slow operation, most of the areas visited carry some risk, making a local guide an imperative. Despite these obstacles, by the end of 1999 144 of Cambodia's 181 districts had been visited in twenty-one of the twenty-four provinces, and 506 sites had been mapped (comprising 270 burial sites, 158 prisons and 78 memorials).

Proposals for physical and social research (involving exhumation and forensic examination and exploration of the sites' place in cultural memory) have been outlined but as yet remain largely unfunded, although one aspect of this research – the cultural politics of the Cambodian genocide memorials especially relating to domestic and international tourism – is now being undertaken.

The vulnerability of Cambodia's genocide sites

Until we began this work, Cambodia had no national map of genocide sites, only schematic maps painted or chalked on blackboards in provincial or district administrative offices, or localized hand sketches of sites, such as that drawn in 1979 of sites along the road from Siem Reap town to the Angkor temples, used on the CGP Internet home page. The process of mapping the genocide sites has involved recording fragile evidence and interviewing ageing informants in the field. The physical vulnerability of both material and personal evidence has become all too clear during the five years of our work.

The graves were dug between twenty and twenty-five years ago. Every rainy season since then has washed parts of the physical evidence away, as over half of Cambodia is inundated for months every year, and the rivers are constantly changing their course. In October 1995 we took a small boat up the Mekong from Kampong Cham provincial capital to the Cham village of Trea 2. As we drew near we could see human remains protruding from the bank, exposed as the river has cut right into the mass grave. In several places the mapping teams have been told that graves were on islands that no longer exist.

Even sites on *terra firma* are vulnerable to jungle regrowth, to gradual collapse and rotting (especially the memorial structures made of wood) or to animal or human intervention. In the wake of liberation from the Khmer Rouge the population was desperate for resources of any kind, and it is widely reported that significant numbers of grave robberies occurred, as it was known that people had hidden gold and jewels in the hems and seams of their clothing. The government apparently issued a decree in the early 1980s to halt exhumations, but most graves are far from any form of surveillance, and must surely have remained vulnerable to robbery.

Animals, especially cows and pigs, pose a particularly big threat as they eat the bones for their calcium, and some visitors have been known to take skulls away with them, either as souvenirs or for memorialization in another place. As our

Figure 9.3 Memorial remains at Trapeang Sva, c. 1981, published as the cover photo on *Svaing Rok Kapet* (*Searching for Truth*), no. 8, August 2000, monthly magazine of the Documentation Center of Cambodia (photographer unknown)

teams have made return visits to some memorial sites, they have noticed a stark reduction in the number of remains to be seen. In Trapeang Sva, Tonle Bati, a site quite close to Phnom Penh (Cambodia's capital), a photograph from 1981 shows a memorial arrangement of remains in a covered hall (Fig. 9.3) – on what was probably the stage of the assembly hall in the former teachers' training college that had been used as a prison during the Khmer Rouge rule. In September 1995 we photographed remains numbering some hundreds of skulls, and by this time the building itself was severely damaged, probably from scavenging building materials, and it had no roof and only partial walls, so the remains were subject to rain and sun and to easy access by animals and people. In April 2000 there were no human remains left in the assembly hall; most have presumably been destroyed or taken, but perhaps fifty skulls had been rescued and moved to a new *stupa* built in mid-1999 to honour their memory. This is a new phenomenon. Since Buddhism was restored as the official religion of Cambodia, with the adoption of a new constitution in

1989, *stupas* have been built in various *wats* around the country to house the remains of those who died during the Khmer Rouge regime, and the honouring of these remains has become incorporated into the religious life of the community.

A special *stupa*, not inside the precincts of a *wat* (Buddhist temple), was constructed at Choeung Ek and inaugurated on 7 January 1989 on the occasion of the tenth anniversary of the overthrow of the Khmer Rouge regime. This is considered to be the national memorial, and ceremonies are organized here by the Phnom Penh Municipality Department of Culture in conjunction with the Cambodian People's Party several times a year, most notably on *Phchum Benn* (the traditional period, held in September or October, for honouring one's ancestors) and on 20 May, the day marked to commemorate those who died during the Pol Pot regime.

A *stupa* was constructed inside the grounds of Tuol Sleng Genocide Museum in the early 1980s, and the *Phchum Benn* and 20 May ceremonies were held here up until the time the Choeung Ek memorial was constructed. The Tuol Sleng high school compound is quite small and could not accommodate the large crowds that attend the Choeung Ek ceremonies. The Tuol Sleng *stupa* collapsed around 1990, though there are plans to seek funds to construct a new one. In the meantime, however, it has been replaced by a souvenir shop intended to provide salary supplementation to the staff, most of whom earn less than US$20 per month – providing a graphic illustration of the conflicting values and tensions that surround any project of memorialization.

What to do with the remains of the Khmer Rouge victims became a contested issue in 1994 when the recently reinstated King Norodom Sihanouk proposed that they be cremated, as is the normal practice in Cambodia. His proposal was abandoned after meeting with a huge wave of public protest organized chiefly by the Cambodian People's Party. More than a million people signed petitions objecting to destroying potential evidence of the Khmer Rouge crimes, at least until after some internationally recognized process of legal accountability had taken place.

Clearly there are differing views regarding the effort that should be made to maintain the genocide sites as they deteriorate in the face of both natural and human activity. In Wat Phnom Pros, on the outskirts of Kampong Cham town, in October 1995 several hundred skulls had been placed inside a small brick and cement structure not far from the mass graves. In May 2000 this building had been renovated for use as the library for the *wat* and the remains had gone. After some time looking around, we found about fifty skulls lying smashed on the ground intermingled with rubbish and weeds in a derelict structure nearby. It is possible that some of the remains have been moved to another *wat* not far away that does have a memorial but, in any event, there is now no memorial at this *wat,* nor are there signposts or guides to any of the other parts of this site that relate to the terrible sufferings that took place here some twenty years ago. At the same time, considerable money is being spent at this *wat* on building a large new sanctuary and concrete decorative entrance way.

Several years ago the Documentation Center's mapping team learned of a plan by one of Cambodia's biggest businessmen to construct a cement factory in Kampot province, right on top of one of that province's biggest mass graves, which we had recorded in 1995. In the end it seems he decided not to proceed with the project, but this incident illustrates the threat that is posed to the genocide sites by everyday development decisions in a situation without even a national map of sites, let alone a national policy on custodianship and preservation.

As I was writing this chapter on 2 June 2000 an event happened that throws more light on the shifting complexities of genocide sites in today's Cambodia. Some workers were digging foundations for a new structure in the grounds of a house located about two blocks from the Tuol Sleng Genocide Museum, and they smashed through the top of a grave containing the remains of about eight people, including what was assumed to be one Westerner from the size of the bones and skull. It appears that the grave had been located in 1979 and had a sheet of glass placed over it so it could be shown to visiting delegations, including those who attended the 1979 People's Revolutionary Tribunal. Some time thereafter, it was evidently considered unnecessary to maintain, and was covered over with earth. The present owners of the house said they had no knowledge of its presence until its accidental discovery.

The owners' immediate reaction was to erect a small shrine and burn some incense in memory of the dead. Shortly thereafter press photographers and journalists appeared on the scene together with researchers from the Documentation Center and also a military attaché from the US Embassy, who returned to take away samples of the bones of the supposed Westerner for analysis (it was quickly determined that the bones were not those of a Caucasian). Within hours the owners had decided to fill in the grave and remove the shrine – perhaps because they did not want to be the centre of attention, and perhaps risk being prohibited from going ahead with their planned construction. Although this site is close to and presumably was a part of the precinct of the Tuol Sleng prison during the Khmer Rouge period, the present management of the Tuol Sleng Genocide Museum (which is under the Department of Museums of the Ministry of Fine Arts and Culture) appears to have no active interest or responsibility for the site, leaving the decision as to whether to cover it over up to the owners of the house.

These few examples show the numerous risks being faced by Cambodia's genocide sites at the very time that legal accountability for the crimes that they represent and manifest seems at last likely to be pursued. During the 1980s the provincial Departments of Culture had responsibility for constructing and maintaining the memorials (following a Ministry of Information and Culture decree issued in October 1983), but the now Ministry of Fine Arts and Culture does not seem to place a high priority on this work and, to my knowledge, there is neither any currently effective policy on conservation of the genocide sites, nor a clear delineation of custodial responsibility at local, provincial or national level. However, largely as a result of the work carried out by the Documentation Center and CGP to publicize the existence of the sites and their precarious state, in December 2001 the Royal Government of Cambodia was drafting a decree to mandate their documentation and preservation.

CONCLUSION

Cambodia's bitter recent past has left many scars on the landscape and on human memory. One means to heal the psychological scars is to recognize the material scars, acknowledging incontestably that the wounds were real; another is to call those responsible to account for their crimes. It is to serve these ends, as well as to assist people to trace their missing family and friends, that the CGP and the Documentation Center were established to record and document the material evidence of one of the darkest episodes of our time. From its inception, the CGP has devoted considerable resources to the systematic recording of all its findings, in a wide range of media, and to harnessing new information technologies in an effort to make its results publicly available in a form that facilitates access and retrieval. Since going online on the Internet on 7 January 1997, we have reached a diverse audience – students, academics and researchers (both inside and outside Cambodia); travellers to Cambodia who want to be further informed; other advocacy or holocaust memorial organizations; and local and international non-governmental organizations. The work of the CGP and the DC-Cam may serve as a model for the documentation of other genocides and systematic human rights abuses as well as for a broader range of social phenomena.[4]

ACKNOWLEDGEMENTS

The mapping component was initiated by a small grant of A$24 300 awarded by the Australian Department of Foreign Affairs and Trade for 1995–6; and then supported by the Netherlands government with US$130 000 for 1997, which was renewed for 1998, 1999 and from the US State Department in 2000. The Documentation Center's mapping work has been directed by Phat Kosal, with many field trips led by Sin Khin, former Director of the National Archives of Cambodia.

NOTES

1 In late 1994 the Center for International and Area Studies at Yale University in the United States established the Cambodian Genocide Program (CGP) to undertake research, documentation and legal training relating to the violations of human rights that took place in Cambodia from 17 April 1975 to 7 January 1979 under the Khmer Rouge regime known as Democratic Kampuchea (DK). The CGP has partnership and contractual arrangements with the Documentation Center of Cambodia (DC-Cam) in Phnom Penh, where documents are collected, catalogued and preserved, and with the University of New South Wales, where the databases have been designed and developed. The principal funding for the CGP has come from the US State Department, with support also given from the governments of Australia, The Netherlands, New Zealand, Norway and the United Kingdom, and from a number of international organizations, non-governmental organizations, private organizations and individuals. The CGP and the Documentation Center express their appreciation for this ongoing support, manifested both in financial and in other terms, including a large number of volunteers. For a summary of their

evolution and the role they can be expected to play in the trial, see Cook (2000); Kiernan (2000); and UN (1999).

2 To manage the material we selected UNESCO's CDS/ISIS, and its Windows interface Winisis (http:// www.unesco.org/webworld/isis/isis.htm). This is a micro-computer-based information retrieval software package, used quite widely throughout the world, particularly in the developing countries. It is available from UNESCO free of charge, which is one of its major attractions. It can run in different languages and indeed in different scripts. CDS/ISIS is a very powerful and flexible package, particularly suited to the complexities posed by a wide and ever-growing multiplicity of data types and formats, and for the challenge of handling material in at least two different languages and scripts. For more details on the database designs see Cross and Jarvis (1998); and Jarvis and Loomans (1997). All research findings of the CGP and DC-Cam are publicly available, whether in their original form at the DC-Cam office in Phnom Penh, or in electronic format presented via the Cambodian Genocide Databases on the Internet or on CD-ROM. All our databases are searchable directly over the Internet (see http://www.yale.edu/cgp/) while individual province maps for the geographic database have been generated and printed with help from Yale University's Center for Earth Observation and Institute for Biospheric Studies, and are loaded on to the CGP Internet site as static images (http://www.yale.edu/cgp/ceomaps.htm) to supplement the dynamically interrogable CGEO database using the ArcView Internet Map Server at UNSW's School of Geomatic Engineering, which requires users to have JAVA enabled on their client local computer. CGDB is also published on CD-ROM, available from DC-Cam and UNSW at a cost of US$100 (address orders to Dr Helen Jarvis and Ms Nereida Cross, SISTM, UNSW, Sydney NSW 2052 Australia). See also the Documentation Center's website http://www.welcome.to/dccam through http:// www.camnet.org.kh. In addition to the provision of access to the databases, the CGP and DC-Cam have embarked upon publication programmes to make various aspects of their findings available in a more synthesized and analysed form as research monographs in hard-copy print format and/or on the Internet. Several items have already been published on the Internet (http:// www.yale.edu /cgp/translate/index.htm) and several are in press. In January 2000 DC-Cam embarked on an ambitious programme of publishing a monthly Khmer language magazine, *Sveng Rok Kapet* (*Searching for the Truth*), which is being distributed free throughout Cambodia. An English language version is now available.

3 For the structure of the bibliographic database we adopted UNIMARC, developed in 1977 by IFLA (the International Federation of Library Associations and Institutions) as an international standard format for exchange of bibliographic data, able to cope with multiple languages and scripts and different cataloguing rules, and compliant with IS02709 (http://www.ifla.org/VI/3/p1996-1/unimarc.htm). It was necessary to supplement UNIMARC with additional fields from USMARC (http:// lcweb.loc.gov/marc) (at that time the USMARC Archival and Manuscripts Control (AMC)) to cater for the archive and manuscript material, both print and non-print (including articles, handwritten reports, petitions and confessions). We have had to determine codes for the identi-fication of specific classes of items dealt with in the material. These include human rights violations, for which we have adopted a range of the Huridocs Standard Formats for the Recording and Exchange of Bibliographic Information Concerning Human Rights 1993 (http:// home.iprolink.ch/~huridocs/standard.htm), and geographic places, for which we are using codes developed for each and every village in Cambodia by the Geography Department in Cambodia and for provinces, for which we are using a Cambodian extension of the MARC Geographic Area Codes.

4 Adaptations of the CGDB have been prepared to assist in documenting human rights abuses in Bougainville and East Timor (1999) and Indonesia's 1965–6 massacres (2000). For further inform-ation on these projects, please contact the author.

REFERENCES

Chandler, D. (1999) *Voices from S-21: Terror and History in Pol Pot's Secret Prison,* Berkeley: University of California Press.

Cook, S.E. (2000) 'The Cambodian Genocide Program: a [virtual] truth commission?', paper presented at Twentieth-century Genocide: Memory, Denial and Accountability, 7 April, at University of California, Berkeley.

Cross, N. and Jarvis, H. (1998) 'New information technology applied to genocide research: the Cambodian Genocide Program', in Chen, C. (ed.), *NIT '98: 10th International Conference on New Information Technology,* West Newton MA: MicroUse Information, pp. 19–26.

DeNike, H., Quigley, J. and Robinson, K.J. with Jarvis, H. and Cross, N. (2000) *Genocide in Cambodia: Documents from the Trial of Political Pot and Ieng Sary,* Philadelphia: University of Pennsylvania Press.

Jarvis, H. and Loomans, R. (1997) 'The Cambodian Genocide Program (CGP) 1997', in *Proceedings of the Second New South Wales Symposium on Information Technology and Information Systems (SITIS '97),* 21 February 1997, Sydney: School of Information Systems, UNSW.

Kiernan, B. (1996) *The Pol Pot Regime,* New Haven: Yale University Press.

Kiernan, B. (2000) Cambodia: justice delayed, *Bangkok Post,* 17 April.

Riley, C. and Niven, D. (1996) *Facing Death,* Santa Fe: Twin Palms.

Sliwinski, M. (1996) *Le génocide Khmer Rouge: une analyse démographique,* Paris: L'Harmattan.

United Nations (1999) Identical letters dated 15 March 1999 from the Secretary-General to the President of the General Assembly and the President of the Security Council, transmitting the Report of the Group of Experts for Cambodia established pursuant to General Assembly resolution 52/135 (A/53/850 and S/1999/231, 16 March 1999).

10 Tell the truth: the archaeology of human rights abuses in Guatemala and the former Yugoslavia

REBECCA SAUNDERS

Historical archaeology can be said to have become a bona fide sub-discipline in anthropology with the establishment of the Society for Historical Archaeology in 1967. The contributions of an historic sites archaeology to the larger disciplines of archaeology, anthropology and history are still debated in both the academic literature (see for example the Annales approach – Bintliff 1991) and the popular literature (for example Chippindale 2000; Lowenthal 2000; Wiseman 2000). Most of us, however, accepted the CRM-derived cut-off date for a historic site at fifty years before present, and have devoted both our research programmes and our methodological refinements to sites dating before this time.

Within the last fifteen years or so, another application of archaeology has arisen; one that applies to the very recent past. Archaeological field techniques have been employed in a number of regions around the world to document human rights abuses. This documentation has served:

1 to counter government or military denials of human rights abuses
2 to provide evidence in litigation against high-ranking individuals under whose direction human rights abuses took place
3 to confirm or correct survivors' accounts (oral histories) by detailing site taphonomic processes
4 to excavate the remains of victims and to discover, through physical anthropology and associated artefacts, the cause and manner of death
5 to identify the victims by comparing physical anthropological data to an ante-mortem database containing physical characteristics of known victims
6 to notify families so that some closure can take place, and ultimately
7 to deter future human rights violations by demonstrating that the actions of the past are recoverable.[1]

Below I will discuss the genesis of the involvement of the two organizations – the American Association for the Advancement of Science (AAAS) and the United Nations (UN) – most committed to an archaeological approach to documentation of human rights abuses and the exhumation of remains. In addition, I present some examples from excavations in Guatemala and the former Yugoslavia; excavations in which I have been personally involved. The different problem-orientations of the two organizations have resulted in different final results; these will be briefly discussed as they arise.

THE GENESIS OF AAAS INVOLVEMENT IN HUMAN RIGHTS ABUSES

In 1970, the AAAS appointed a Committee on Scientific Freedom and Responsibility to 'examine the conditions required for scientific freedom and responsibility and to prescribe criteria and procedures which would enable the Association to respond to reported abuses of scientific freedom ...' (Stover and McCleskey 1981). The findings of this committee were published in 1975 (Edsall 1975). The committee urged that the AAAS adopt a proactive stance in defending scientists working in inhospitable sociopolitical climates. In a parallel development, in 1974, the AAAS Council resolved to promote greater AAAS involvement in promoting scientific freedom. These steps ultimately resulted in the establishment of a permanent Committee on Scientific Freedom in 1976, along with a Sub-committee on Human Rights created specifically to 'investigate the extent of abuses affecting scientists in foreign countries and to establish mechanisms for responding to these abuses.' The AAAS Clearinghouse on Science and Human Rights, which handles the documentation of such cases and provides information on items of general concerns on science and human rights, was established in 1977 (see Stover and McCleskey 1981). The first full-time staff member of the Clearinghouse was Eric Stover, whose works are referenced throughout this report.

Originally the AAAS Clearinghouse was devoted to documenting individual cases of persecution or murder of individual scientists, educators, and civil rights workers. AAAS involvement in more widespread abuses originated in Argentina (see Joyce and Stover 1991 for a more detailed account of the founding of the Argentine Forensic Anthropology Team). In 1983, newly elected president Raúl Alfonsín set up what would come to be known generically as a 'Truth Commission', in this case CONADEP (National Commission on the Disappeared). The function of CONADEP was to investigate the fate of the over 10 000 people who had been 'disappeared' during the preceding seven years of military dictatorship (following the ousting of President Isabel Perón in 1976).

The strong desire of Argentinian families to know the fate of their relatives led to CONADEP-sponsored, but hasty and uncontrolled, excavations of several of the NN (no-name) gravesites that had proliferated in Buenos Aires and elsewhere in the country. Realizing that much important information was being lost in these excavations, Ernesto Sábato, a novelist and chair of another commission investigating the disappeared, wrote to Stover in 1984,[2] requesting that the AAAS recommend someone with forensic expertise to supervise more controlled, scientific excavation of graves. Stover called the National Academy of Forensic Scientists, who recommended Clyde Snow as a physical anthropologist with the expertise to oversee the excavations (Stover, personal communication 2000).

Snow and his colleagues visited Argentina first in 1984 for a ten-day fact-finding tour (see Joyce and Stover 1991). Recruiting a small group of dedicated individuals, predominantly students, Snow's first excavations took place during that trip. Snow returned to give his embryonic team formal training in physical anthropology and forensic examination in February 1985. That team still functions, and the work in Argentina has been duplicated in Guatemala, Peru, El Salvador and Honduras; various team members have also participated in excavations in Haiti, Kurdistan, Rwanda and the former Yugoslavia. The Latin American teams remain small and depend on funding from disparate outside sources including (for the Guatemalan team) AAAS and AGAPE in the US; MISEREOR in Germany; CECI.FDD in Canada; the Norwegian Human Rights Fund; and PRODECA and DANIDA in Denmark.

GUATEMALA: LAND OF ETERNAL TYRANNY

In the name of counter-insurgency, Guatemalan government security forces and their paramilitary auxiliaries (PACs) made kidnapping, torture and murder a fact of everyday life from the 1960s into the early 1990s. Indeed, PACs gave the military a scapegoat on which to pass off its own atrocities, either by forcing patrollers to carry out their own agenda, or by claiming that military executions were the work of over-zealous PAC units (Simon 1987: 18). The disappeared included a host of scientists, medical doctors and students. In the highlands, hundreds of thousands of Maya lost their homes and their lives to government policies of relocation and genocide. A tenuous peace was established at the end of 1996, but the peace accord included a partial amnesty for war-related crimes (although acts of genocide, torture and forced disappearances were specifically excluded from this amnesty). A Truth Commission (formally the Historical Clarification Commission or CEH), which began functioning in 1997, reported in 1999 that 200 000 individuals had been disappeared. The CEH found that of the atrocities reported, state security forces and paramilitary troops were responsible for 93 per cent of the cases, the insurgents were responsible for 3 per cent, while another 4 per cent could not be attributed to a specific group (Jonas 2000: 154). Other statistics include an additional 1 million internally displaced persons, with 70 000 Mayas living in 'model villages' more like prison camps than communities, and thousands of homeless living and scavenging in the vast Guatemala City dump or in cardboard boxes in the city slums (Simon 1987: 14, 205).

AAAS confronted the Guatemalan situation in 1992, when, once again under the direction of Clyde Snow, it funded the training of the EAFG (Equipo de Anthropologia Forense de Guatemala; now FAFG) through the excavation of five grave sites in the area of San Pacho de Lemoa. The excavations were done in one of the most brutalized regions, Quiché, in an area not far from the tourist destination of Chichicastenango (Figure 10.1). Surviving villagers told investigators of a night in February 1982 when the men of Lemoa were detained, interrogated and beaten, and then marched away by a PAC unit, never to be seen again. At Lemoa, as in many cases, remains of the victims were disposed of in small clandestine graves excavated

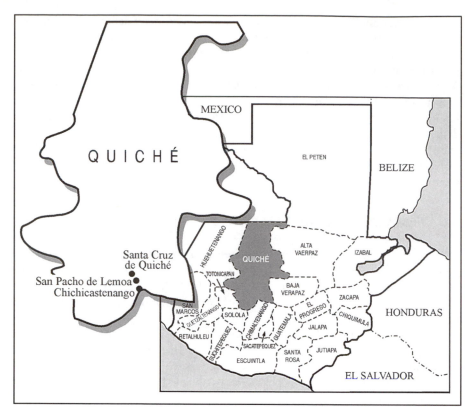

Figure 10.1 Location of Lemoa, where excavations took place; Santa Cruz, where physical anthropological analysis took place; and the tourist destination of Chichicastenango

into narrow platforms on the sides of the steep *barrancas* (ravines) surrounding the village centre. Villagers knew the locations of these graves and, in four of five sites, had been tending them, leaving small offerings of *copal* and fresh flowers.

In the early 1990s, the process of exhumation was set in motion by a request for excavation; such requests were generally made by families to a judge, who then ordered the exhumation. At Lemoa, the exhumations were overseen by the Judge of the Second Instance or his secretary and all materials removed from the graves were recorded by the judge or his representatives. There is generally less judicial oversight of excavations today.

The same methods that were developed for the Argentine excavations were applied in Guatemala. These methods included the development of an antemortem database derived from interviews with relatives. These data provided a means of identifying specific individuals, and included an account of the clothing and other personal items such as rings, watches or other jewellery worn at the time of the disappearance. The database also included physical anthropological data like handedness, past trauma (for example broken and healed bones that would be evident on examination of skeletal material in the morgue) and dental characteristics. Hair samples were taken from maternal relatives to be used for mitochondrial DNA (mtDNA) analysis should the ante-mortem database be insufficient to identify or discriminate between certain individuals.[3] One mandibular molar was retained from each burial to provide comparative mtDNA. This portion of the project was a qualified success (Boles *et al.* 1995).

Excavation methods were held constant for all five sites. Upon arrival, and prior to the removal of undergrowth or any surface alteration, the area was surveyed for surface artefacts or other information that might indicate manner of death. Photographs were also taken of each site area prior to any disturbance. Once these photographs were taken, shrubbery was removed and, if necessary, some levelling of the site was done to provide space for a staging area and for excavation. Once the work area was prepared, the surface of each grave was cleaned. In each of these five cases, removal of surface soils exposed the grave outline, which was mapped and photographed. An arbitrary datum was established at each site and used to measure depth below surface of skeletons, artefacts, or other features within the grave. Small, hand-held GPS devices were just becoming widely available at the time, and one was used to locate each grave site by UTM co-ordinates.

Excavation of the grave itself usually began with an exploratory trench that bisected the grave. This technique allowed us to determine relatively quickly the depth of the burials below surface and provided a window within which to examine stratigraphy. This trench was taken down to the level at which clothing or skeletal material was encountered. Taking that depth as a rough guide, the remainder of the grave fill was removed with hoes (*acedones*) to 10–20 cm above the skeletal remains. The loose, redeposited calcareous sands of the *barrancas* and the integrity of the clothing of the burials generally made it safe to remove soils quickly, even if some parts of the bodies were higher than this level. At 10–20 cm above bone, work with the hoes was abandoned, and the remaining grave fill was removed with trowels and brushes until the top level of remains was exposed. Burials were always pedestalled above the working floor; usually this pedestalling also involved removing adjacent undisturbed soils to the same depth to provide room for excavation, mapping and photography.

All soil removed from immediately above, around, or underneath burials was screened through quarter-inch hardware cloth, and, in the case of Site 4, in which a pregnant woman was said to have been buried, eighth-inch screen.[4] In this respect, methodology (in practice if not in theory) departs from that of most US archaeological excavations in which all soils from any feature would be screened. While all artefacts encountered, such as cartridge casings, are bagged, total artefact recovery is generally not the goal. For one thing, time constraints usually do not allow the luxury of this level of investigation. In addition, materials recovered from grave fill, like any other secondary deposit, cannot be inferred to be directly associated with the events under investigation. In some instances, however, it is reasonable to assume that grave-fill artefacts were deposited as a result of the events under investigation. For instance, cartridge casings recovered from grave fill that match bullets found adjacent to or inside an individual can be assumed to have been part of the event, but recovery adds little to the information needed to address the principal goals of the excavation. In this respect, forensic archaeology is more problem-oriented than more conventional archaeological investigations.

The exposed burials were photographed and mapped, and preliminary field observations were recorded on standard forms that included information about burial depth, items of clothing, the completeness of the skeleton, and initial observations of ante-mortem, peri-mortem, and post-mortem trauma. As the cranium of each burial was removed, a tooth, usually a mandibular molar, was taken for use in the mtDNA study. This process was repeated for each ensuing 'stratum' of burials. Excavation was considered complete at the intersection of the base of the grave fill with undisturbed soils, and the excavation was backfilled.

As noted, we were led to the graves by family members, and family members remained onsite throughout the excavations. Despite the potential danger – PAC troops still roamed the countryside and it was possible that some of the same PAC members involved in the 1982 slayings were still in the area – the crowds only increased as bodies began to appear. It was not unusual for family members to recognize clothing or personal items in the grave, provoking wails and sobs from kin. The judge or his representative calmly recorded these field identifications. Remains were not released to the family at this point, however. All burials, their clothing and other personal effects, along with other associated artefacts, were taken to the morgue in Santa Cruz de Quiché for physical anthropological analysis and comparison to the ante-mortem database before release.

With the exception of Site 4, cause of death was attributable primarily to fatal trauma delivered by a sharp implement, probably a machete. This indicated to us that the bulk of the villagers had been killed by PAC squads, as PACs had little or no access to guns and ammunition. We assumed, but could not demonstrate independently of the testimony of the families, that the individuals had been marched into the *barrancas* prior to their deaths, and were killed near the grave site. Cause and manner of death for the individuals within Site 4, mentioned above, were different. There were two women (the only women recovered from this area, though women in other areas did not fare as well; see EAFG 1996) and two men in this grave. Brass cartridge casings were found on the ground surface near the grave and within the grave fill and at least one bullet was found directly associated with skeletal remains. The grave itself was a collapsed *buzon* – a concavity cut into the side of the *barranca* and reinforced with wooden side and roof beams. Cloth and two small plastic plates were found beneath the four burials at the base of the feature. While we had no independent evidence to confirm this, the *buzon* may have been a hideaway for guerillas. Entry and exit wounds indicated that these individuals were killed by trauma attributable to execution-style gunshot wounds. This indicated that the military was involved, which supports the interpretation that the feature may have been a hideout for insurgents.

The genesis of the EAFG programme (as well as its counterpart in Argentina), the stamp of character placed on it by participants, and especially the priorities of the initial team members, along with the amnesty granted by successive Guatemalan governments, and continuing governmental instability, have resulted in less emphasis on prosecution of those responsible than might be expected. Instead, the focus is on identification and return of individual remains to the families for reburial.

THE UN AND THE FORMER YUGOSLAVIA

The former Yugoslavia fragmented into divisions along ethnic lines in the late 1980s and early 1990s. Some (see for example Silber and Little 1996: 25) place most of the blame for the rise of nationalism and the subsequent fall of Yugoslavia on Slobodan Milošević's use of nationalistic rhetoric in pursuit of a 'Greater Serbia'. Others (PHR 1996: 14–15) distribute blame more equitably, noting that nationalism was on the rise in each of the Yugoslavian republics in conjunction with independence movements (especially in Croatia, Slovenia and Serbia) and in reaction to such movements (for instance the Bosnian Serbs). The first fighting occurred immediately after Slovenia and Croatia declared independence on 25 June 1991, and discord spread rapidly between the three different ethnic groups scattered throughout the former republics.

Reports of violations of international humanitarian law in the former Yugoslavia, including rumours of mass executions and mass graves, emerged soon after fighting began. The various powers denied these accusations, saying either that mass graves did not exist or that they contained soldiers killed in battle (Stover and Peress 1998: 10, 323). In October 1992, the UN Security Council established a Commission of Experts to investigate. As an appointee of the Commission of Experts, the peripatetic Clyde Snow, along with a Canadian Mountie seconded to the UN, visited the state-run farming community of Ovčara, immediately outside of Vukovar, in October 1992 (Figure 10.2). There, according to a survivor (see Stover and Peress 1998: 102–7 and Stover 1997 for an account of 'Marko's' narrative of the events), at the head of a small ravine used as a dump, 200 patients abducted from a hospital in Vukovar had been executed and buried. This happened on 20 November 1991, immediately after the fall of Vukovar. Ironically the patients were to be evacuated by the International Committee of the Red Cross on the same day. At Ovčara, Snow observed a partially skeletonized individual eroding out of a push-up pile left by heavy machinery. A second individual was found along a path into the wooded ravine and a third was barely visible in slumped grave fill about 20 cm below the surface. The site was secured and placed under 24-hour guard by the UN.[5]

A preliminary investigation of the Ovčara site was carried out in December 1992 under the auspices of the Committee of Experts established by the UN Security Council. The team was composed of Snow, the director of Physicians for Human Rights Eric Stover, Morris Tidball Binz, an Argentine physician and former member of the Argentine Forensic Anthropology Team, and myself. Our mission at that time was only to map and otherwise record surface features to determine if there was evidence of a mass execution; to dig a test trench to verify the existence and extent of a mass grave (including an estimated minimum number of individuals), and, if possible, to determine the ethnic composition of the grave. Finally,

Figure 10.2 Location of sites discussed in text

preliminary forensic data were to be prepared for the two skeletons exposed on the surface of the site. This was done on site; we did not have permission to remove remains from the site. Excavation revealed nine individuals; the areal extent of the grave, as determined by surface features and excavation, indicated that a total population of 200 was plausible.

The report of our findings was submitted to the UN Security Council. On the basis of this information, and accruing testimony of other atrocities, the International Criminal Tribunal for the Former Yugoslavia (the Tribunal) was established in May 1993.

Work carried out under the auspices of the Tribunal has as its major goal the production of evidence to use in preparing indictments or in presenting evidence against individuals in an international court of law. In addition, among the innumerable instances of human rights abuses that took place between 1991 and the uneasy peace achieved under the Dayton Agreement in 1995, the Tribunal seeks to prosecute in those cases in which individuals at a high level of command could be directly implicated. By establishing individual rather than collective guilt, the Tribunal was intended to be 'a crucial tool for ending the cycle of ethnic violence and retribution' (Stover and Peress 1998: 137).

SIMILARITIES AND DIFFERENCES

The resources of the UN and the logistics of the excavations in the former Yugo-slavia result in a very different approach to excavations than in Guatemala. In gen-eral, the mass graves tend to be larger in the Balkans than in Guatemala.[6] Because emotions still run extremely high in the Balkans, tight security, generally provided by UN peacekeeping forces,[7] is necessary. In addition, because excavations have taken place in as little as a year since the events under investigation, bodies can be well preserved, with adiposere or soft tissue remaining. Total skeletalization like that encountered for the exposed individuals at Vukovar is rare in subsurface remains. Thus, some kind of immediately accessible cold storage is necessary to maintain the integrity of the remains between excavation and examination in the morgue, which can be quite distant from the site. In most cases, all remains from a single grave were excavated prior to transport to the morgue, so bodies were stored on site for several weeks. Morgue work is also more difficult and more expensive. The preservation of tissue or adiposere necessitates the presence of a pathologist. X-ray or some other means of locating bullets within the bodies must also be pres-ent. Finally, both tissue and adiposere must be removed for the physical anthropo-logical analysis of the skeletal remains. The point here is that excavation requires a large field and lab crew and monetary resources on a scale that is not commonly available outside of multi-national forces. While figures for the cost of individual excavations are not available, the budget for the Tribunal (including litigation) was over US$94 million in 1999. According to Stover and Ryan (2001), the 1996 exca-vation of four mass graves around Srebrenica, including, after four years of contin-uous 24-hour security, Ovčara, involved 90 forensic scientists from nineteen countries.

The size of excavations, the logistical problems described above, the goals of the multi-national effort, and, to a lesser extent, the problem of the security of the site and site personnel, dictate different excavation and analysis procedures. Sites are initially selected on the basis of testimony that indicates violations as described above. US satellite imagery is generally available and if the suspected site is in a rela-tively open area, this kind of remote sensing is indispensable for an initial look at a possible site (but can be misleading, Stover and Perress 1998: 150). At this point, a reconnaissance team of one or two UN investigators is sent out to confirm the presence of a mass grave. These investigators look for surface indications of distur-bance, dig small shovel tests to verify the presence of human remains (these are backfilled immediately), and attempt to establish site parameters on the basis of surface indications and by probing.

Once the presence of a mass grave is verified, and, again, if it appears to meet the criteria of the Tribunal, excavations may be planned on the basis of the reports of the reconnaissance team. After nearly a decade of experience (and many of the same individuals participate in the various Latin American and UN excavations), foren-sic anthropology methodology has been refined. Surface and immediately subsurface artefacts are located with metal detectors and their locations, along with site topographic features, are mapped using a total station. A site datum is established and the location fixed using a GPS. Grave boundaries and the depth below ground surface of the human remains are still established with trenching. This is usually done by hand, but may also be done with backhoes. Removal of grave fill is done, unabashedly, with backhoes. The stiff, loamy, clay soils of the area preclude efficient removal by hand; the area required for pedestalling and excavation of the graves can be quite large. Obviously, some small materials, including disarticulated bone, can be lost, but the size of these excavations, the expense for forensic and security personnel, and the goals of the excavation argue against total recovery. Backhoes are monitored at all times, however, and both the driver and the monitor develop a feel for appropriate depth of each pass.

In general, there is little significant stratigraphy within a grave feature. However, on several occasions (at Ovčara, Brčko and Pilica Farms), there was either a narrative account or stratigraphic evidence of grave tampering – of combatants returning to a mass grave, excavating all or portions of the grave with heavy machinery and removing the bodies for reburial elsewhere. In these instances, the two (or more) discrete deposits within the grave are taken out separately; bone fragments and clothing in the intrusion are collected with care.

Given the size and preservation in most of the graves investigated by the Tribunal, interpretation of the cause and manner of death have been unambiguous. Remains in the four excavations in which I have been involved (Ovčara, Cerska, Nova Kasaba and Brčko; Fig. 10.2), with a total population of almost 500 persons, have been overwhelmingly male. In contrast to statements from the parties involved in the conflicts, there was no indication that the individuals recovered were combatants. All wore civilian clothes; in the case of the Ovčara grave, some individuals had hospital garb and other medical paraphernalia. In addition, almost all had wire or some other type of restraint binding the hands behind the back.

A number of factors have combined to make identification of the remains of the victims problematic. For reasons of security, family members are not allowed at the grave sites, thus derailing one of the quickest methods of identification. In addition, once the evidentiary materials are processed, and the post-mortem database is completed, the UN teams generally leave the country, turning their data over to nongovernmental organizations (NGOs) for further identification. However, the exodus of peoples from regions under attack makes locating families and gathering ante-mortem data difficult. Even with ante-mortem data, the fact is that the victims are primarily males between the ages of eighteen and forty; osteology, dentition and clothing are simply not distinctive enough to positively identify the majority of these individuals (Vollen in Stover and Peress 1998: 173–4). DNA samples are routinely taken in the morgue during analysis, but the quality of the samples, and the funding to run them, make even this independent line of evidence problematic (Stover and Peress 1998: 174).

The low frequency of identification has been frustrating to the forensic anthropologists; in particular to the specialists from Latin America, where families are more involved in excavations. This is nothing, of course, compared with the agony of the families waiting for information, and some kind of closure. (There are persistent rumours of concentration camps in Serbia, and many survivors hold out hope that their relatives are still alive in these camps). This frustration has even been translated into violence. In February 1996, hundreds of women stormed the headquarters of the International Committee of the Red Cross in Tuzla, demanding that more effort be made to find the missing. A demonstration by some 400 women from Srebrenica demanding more information took place in front of the ICRC headquarters in Sarajevo in October 1997 (Stover and Peress 1998: 195–6, 198; see also 209–15).

TELL THE TRUTH: REMEMBERING THE PAST FOR THE FUTURE

A public ceremony was held for the victims at Ovčara in February 1998 and relatives of the victims have planned a monument to the victims either at Ovčara or in Vukovar (Stover and Peress 1998: 325). Public ceremonies and reburials have also been held throughout the Guatemalan highlands (EAFG 1996) and monuments have been built on grave sites or in other areas. In both regions, these memorials sprin from grassroots movements, not from governmental initiatives. Indeed, in both areas, grassroot support groups and alliances (such as GAM Mutual Support Group), largely composed of ethnic Maya in Guatemala, and the Mothers of Vukovar in Croatia have sprung up to provide a means for survivors to interact with, and demand information from, their respective governments and other agencies like the UN or the ICRC.

It is with the survivors and their dedication to preserving the memory of the truth of what happened in these areas that the hope of the future rests. Archaeological field methods, along with physical anthropology and interviews with survivors and relatives, have made it impossible for governments or ethnic factions to claim that these recent holocausts never existed. The arrogance of reckless leaders and their henchmen, who believe that they can lie with impunity, is countered with indisputable scientific evidence. Using the tools developed for exploring the distant past to tell the truth to survivors in the present can bring closure and thus blunt the desire for revenge. We can help relegate the past to the past for a more productive future for all concerned.

NOTES

1 Since this article was written, Connor and Scott (2001) edited a Society for Historical Archaeology volume that addresses 'Archaeologists as Forensic Investigators'. A more detailed discussion of many of the points made in this article can be found in that volume. In the same interim, Hugh Tuller (2002), a graduate at Louisiana State University, was able to identify human blood protein residues from a year-and-a-half-old excavation site in Kosovo.
2 Stover was the natural choice. He had visited Argentina frequently in the past while documenting cases of the persecution of individual scientists, and had met both Alfonsín and the Abuelas de Plaza de Mayo (Grandmothers of the Plaza de Mayo).
3 The fact that the Maya of this area were willing to donate such samples is a testament to their desire

for the identification and the proper burial of their loved ones. Much local lore warns against relinquishing any body parts, no matter how superficial, to anyone, and some individuals did refuse. Six of the twelve families involved in this portion of the project appreciated the need.

4 There were two women and two men in this grave. As discussed later in the text, this grave may have been a collapsed *buzon* – a man-made cave – that served as a guerilla hideout. The association with insurgents may explain why this was the grave that was not tended.

5 The UN contingent left in charge of security was Russian. Because Russia was considered an ally of Serbians, this arrangement made us a little uneasy, but nothing came of our fears. Ultimately, the 24-hour guard, which was supposed to be a short-term solution, was posted for four years (see Stover 1997; Stover and Peress 1998).

6 This is only *generally* true. A number of sites in Guatemala have yielded over 200 individuals (EAFG 1996; Stover and Ryan 2000). Still, the fact that most of the remains in Guatemala are skeletonized streamlines handling, transport and analysis.

7 Site security was sometimes a problem (Stover and Peress 1998: 141, 148). Thus, during one excavation, forensic investigators slept on site for several weeks.

REFERENCES

Bintliff, J. (1991) *The Annales School and Archaeology*, New York: New York University Press.

Boles, T.C., Snow, C.C. and Stover E. (1995) Forensic DNA testing on skeletal remains from mass graves: a pilot project in Guatemala, *Journal of Forensic Sciences* 40(3): 349–55.

Chippindale, C. (2000) Archaeology's proper place, *Archaeology* 53(2): 67–8.

Connor, M. and Scott, D.D. (eds) (2001) Archaeologists as forensic investigators: defining the role, *Historical Archaeology* 35(1).

EAFG (Equipo de Antropologia Forense de Guatemala; now FAFG) (1996) *Anuario No. 3: 1994–1995*, Guatemala City: EAFG.

Edsall, J.T. (1975) *Scientific Freedom and Responsibility: Report of the Committee on Scientific Freedom and Responsibility*, Washington DC: American Association for the Advancement of Science.

Jonas, S. (2000) *Of Centaurs and Doves: Guatemala's Peace Process*, Boulder CO: Westview.

Joyce, C. and Stover, E. (1991) *Witness from the Grave: The Stories Bones Tell*, New York: Ballantine Books.

Lowenthal, D. (2000) Archaeology's perilous pleasures, *Archaeology* 53(2): 62–6.

PHR (Physicians for Human Rights) (1996) *Medicine Under Siege in the Former Yugoslavia, 1991–1995*, Boston: Physicians for Human Rights.

Silber, L. and Little, A. (1996) *The Death of Yugoslavia,* New York: Penguin.

Simon, J. (1987) *Guatemala: Eternal Spring, Eternal Tyranny*, New York: W.W. Norton.

Stover, E. (1997) The grave at Vukovar, *Smithsonian* 27(12): 40–52.

Stover, E. and McCleskey K. (1981) *Human Rights and Scientific Cooperation: Problems and Opportunities in the Americas*, Washington DC: American Association for the Advancement of Science.

Stover, E. and Peress, G. (1998) *The Graves: Srebrenica and Vukovar*, New York: Scalo.

Stover, E. and Ryan, M. (2001) Breaking bread with the dead, *Historical Archaeology* 35(1): 1–27.

Tuller, H. (2002) Dirty secrets: blood protein and VFA analysis of soil from excavation of grave sites in the former Yugoslavia. Unpublished Master's thesis, Dept. of Geography and Anthropology, Louisiana State University.

Wiseman, J. (2000) Archaeology and history: addressing some delusions about our discipline, *Archaeology* 53(3): 6–9.

11 Violent spaces: conflict over the reappearance of Argentina's disappeared

ZOË CROSSLAND

INTRODUCTION

In recent years debates over the politics of archaeology and ownership of 'the past' have received substantial attention in the archaeological literature. The role of forensic archaeology in present-day conflicts has however been neglected, perhaps because of the difficulties of writing about such an emotionally charged subject. Public interest in forensic techniques may be gauged by the prominence of reports in the popular media, especially during the 1990s, concerning the excavation of mass graves. The potential prurience of these reports has perhaps also contributed to mainstream archaeology avoiding the topic. However, the increasing world-wide use of forensic excavation to assess and attest to human rights violations highlights the importance of these archaeological techniques. I am not myself a forensic archaeologist, and I have no personal experience of forensic excavation techniques. My interest in this topic was stimulated by a visit, which I made in 1992, to the forensic excavations in Avellaneda cemetery, Argentina, where I was introduced to the work of the Argentinian Forensic Anthropology Team. This study demonstrates the importance of forensic archaeology to interpretive archaeologies, arguing that far from being a marginal element of archaeology, forensic archaeology engages with epistemological and ontological issues that are relevant to the discipline as a whole.

The focus of this study is the reaction to the work carried out in Argentina by the Argentinian Forensic Anthropology Team (EAAF). The EAAF was responsible for excavating the unmarked graves of people who were 'disappeared' during the military dictatorship of 1976–83. Much of their work was used as evidence in the trials of the military juntas that took place in the mid-1980s. While the majority of the exhumations that they carried out in Argentina took place during the late 1980s and early 1990s, after the restoration of democratic government, their work retains a high profile due to the widely publicized search for the children of disappeared women, who were born while their mothers were detained by the military. Additionally, the recent indictment of Chilean ex-president Pinochet has brought the issue of disappearances in the Southern Cone of the Americas back under international scrutiny.

Presented herein is a partial 'archaeography' of the excavations at the Avellaneda cemetery on the outskirts of Buenos Aires. I have chosen the neologism archaeography as I feel that this accurately describes the emphasis of the study on both the writing and practice of archaeology in this particular context.[1] Accounts of forensic anthropology usually focus on their role as providers of evidence, and the relationship of forensic anthropology to police work (Snow *et al.* 1989; Crossland 2000). However, this chapter is not a methodological study or critique. Rather, I explore the embodied aspects of the excavations; the ways in which they are incorporated into technologies of control and resistance in the context of the aftermath of the repression. I contextualize the excavations as situated practices that are part of different, often conflicting, discourses involving the disappeared. The study draws upon the inter-disciplinary common ground between archaeology, history and ethnology, and hence the term archaeography also plays on the similarities and differences between historiography and ethnography. Although all archaeography provides a partial (in all senses) narrative, this account in particular is a partial archaeography, as it is based only on newspaper reports, articles, interviews and secondary literature. This textual analysis focuses on the spatiality of the forensic excavations, as the starting point for a larger and more detailed archaeography, that will incorporate interviews and archival documentation.

HISTORICAL NOTES

The spatial readings made of the excavations were framed within the differing responses to the restoration of democratic rule in Argentina in 1983. In order to contextualize these readings, it is necessary to first provide a sketch of the violent history that lay behind the excavations. The military coup in 1976 was not unusual in terms of Argentina's history. The country had an unstable political history as, over the course of the twentieth century, recurrent military coups unseated various elected governments. In the years leading up to the 1976 coup, the economic and political situation deteriorated, as the government came under increasing pressure from both left and right, made manifest in the often violent social and political demonstrations which took place with increasing frequency. The weak government led by Isabel Perón (General Juan Perón's widow) passed a series of decrees calling on the army to put an end to the actions of 'subversive elements' in Argentina, and in March 1976 the armed forces formed a junta which took over the government of the country. Once in power the junta's actions echoed those of Perón after he took power in 1946. Freedom of speech was immediately restricted as they placed radio and television stations under state control (Simpson and Bennett 1985: 231–7). The judiciary was restructured to put more control in the hands of the military through replacing members of the Supreme Court and the attorney general. The legislature was effectively disbanded; Congress was dismissed and provincial parliaments closed. Institutions and associations perceived as a threat were also closed down or banned; these included universities, trade unions and political parties (Argentine National Commission on the Disappeared

(CONADEP) 1986: xi–vi). Although disappearances had begun under the Perón government, the largest number of disappearances took place in the first year of military government, and they were to continue throughout the entire period of military rule (CONADEP 1986: 10, 404).

People were usually abducted by small paramilitary or parapolice groups, who acted anonymously, and of whom the police and military could, and did, deny all knowledge. These actions were implemented in the name of a 'war' waged against subversion. This terminology of war was intended to legitimize the violent activities of the state, framing the actions as a necessity and therefore not an abuse of human rights. General Videla, often portrayed as one of the more moderate elements of the junta, (for example in Harvey 1980; see also Salama 1992: 33) defined a terrorist in a now infamous statement:

> A terrorist is not only the person who carries a gun or plants bombs; he is also the person who spreads ideas contrary to Western and Christian civilisation.
> (*The Times,* 4 January 1978, cited in CONADEP 1986: xiii)

As this illustrates, the definition of 'terrorism' was sufficiently nebulous that anyone could be accused. In the name of suppressing subversion, between 9000 and 30 000 individuals were abducted by clandestine commando units, under the tacit direction of the ruling juntas (Brysk 1994; CONADEP 1984). The primary targets were people who belonged to organizations, professions and religions seen as 'subversive'. These included students, trade union members, politicians, journalists, psychiatrists, Catholics, Jews and Protestants; anyone who was perceived as a threat to the values of the ruling junta (see illustration of 'the tree of subversion' in Simpson and Bennett 1985: 226, 263). However abductions were not restricted to people from these categories, as described by the Argentine National Commission on the Disappeared (CONADEP). Thousands of people were abducted simply because they were 'relatives, friends, or names included in the address book of someone considered subversive' (CONADEP 1986: 448). For the majority of those abducted there was no pretence of due process; no chance was provided for the disappeared to answer charges made against them. However, this basic violation of human rights pales beside the widespread torture and murder that were also part of the state project of disappearance.

As the junta had control of much of the news media, it was difficult for people to publicize the disappearances. Journalists were often wary of publishing material that could be construed as 'subversive', making them vulnerable to attack. However at the end of April 1977, a small group of mothers of disappeared people organized a protest in the Plaza de Mayo in the centre of Buenos Aires. This was the beginning of a powerful protest movement built by the mothers of the disappeared that would have international influence and prominence. Various commentators have noted that the emphasis on their motherhood by the Mothers of the Plaza de Mayo had the effect of undermining the junta's framing of the repression.

Indeed the cultural importance of motherhood itself in Latin America has been the source of academic interest (Stevens 1973), and has been explored in relation to women's protest movements in South America (Malin 1994; Jelin 1990). As part of its creation of a 'war', the junta stressed the protection of 'Christian' values. One of the core values that they sought to protect was the importance of the nuclear family; yet their violent breaking apart of families, sons and daughters from parents and grandparents undermined this claim. The Mothers of the Plaza de Mayo exploited these inconsistencies. By demonstrating by their presence that the military was destroying families, the Mothers not only attempted to change the way in which disappearances were framed, but also created a slightly protected space for themselves in that, according to the junta, mothers were essential to the reproduction of the 'ideal' Argentina. The emphasis on their motherhood allowed them to defy the ban on public meetings in order to demonstrate. However, they were not invulnerable to attack. In 1978, twelve of the Mothers of the Plaza de Mayo were abducted, one of whom, Azuzena Villaflor de Vicenti never reappeared. (For a more detailed history of the Mothers organization, see Agosin 1990; Asociación Madres de Plaza de Mayo 1995; Bousquet 1982; Fisher 1989.)

The military finally relinquished control of the government in 1983, pushed by the pressure of human rights groups, foreign governments and the state of the national economy, as the country's foreign debt escalated and salaries dropped, leading to strikes and mass demonstrations. Concurrently, the Malvinas (Falkands) conflict both led to, and provided an excuse for, a more visible decrease in support for the ruling junta. Following the collapse of the junta, there was a widespread call for investigations into the crimes committed by the state. The newly elected democratic government set up a commission, known as CONADEP, which would research the human rights abuses that took place during the years of military government. CONADEP was accused by some human rights groups of having no real power, as it had no authority to impound the records kept at many police stations and army and navy barracks which would have provided evidence of human rights violations. There was indeed a whole bureaucracy behind the disappearances; however, this greater part of this mass of documentation has never come to light, having been destroyed in the last months of military rule (CONADEP 1984: 263–72; Salama 1992: 36–9; Simpon and Bennett 1985: 90–1). Eventually, enough evidence was compiled that those responsible could be brought to trial.

The democratically elected government of President Alfonsín was in a politically delicate position when the investigations began. The threat of a military coup was a real possibility for the new administration. This contributed to the pressure placed on Alfonsín that led his government to enact the 1986 'full stop' legislation that put a time limit on bringing prosecutions of those not yet on trial. This movement towards leniency intensified during the late 1980s as the stability of the new government was threatened by military insurrection, such as the rebellion which erupted in April 1987 as the result of the refusal of General Guillermo Barreiro to answer charges of human rights abuses. The subsequent president, Carlos Menem, implemented a more wide-reaching series of pardons, culminating in 1990, when the last few officers remaining in prison were pardoned. As a result of the pardoning of military officers many still saw a need for protest and activism to bring those responsible to justice. Just as during the period of military rule, the most vocal criticism came from the Mothers of the Plaza de Mayo (see accounts in Fisher 1989: 27–59).

In 1983–4, as part of judicial enquiries into the human rights abuses of the juntas, excavations of mass graves were ordered by the courts. These early exhumations were carried out without archaeological or forensic consultation, leading to the destruction of the graves, and providing neither secure evidence nor skilled consultants who could identify the remains and provide evidence in court. In order to excavate the graves more sensitively, North American forensic experts were invited to Argentina by CONADEP, and subsequently the Argentinian Forensic Anthropology Team (EAAF) was established (Joyce and Stover 1991; Verbitsky 1993: 9). The forensic excavations not only provided evidence in the trials of the junta, but also focused on identifying individuals in order to return their remains to their relatives for a proper burial. However, after the team was established, Alfonsín began the enaction of the 'full stop' legislation which brought an end to the trials of those responsible for the disappearances. This meant that over time the focus of the team's work shifted as their results were no longer used to bring prosecutions of the military. Instead, the personal and emotional significance of the excavations came to dominate public understanding of their work, as they provided grieving relatives with the remains of their loved ones. The significance of this shift for the ways in which the disappeared were and are understood is explored below.

MAINTAINING ABSENCES

Perhaps surprisingly, there has been substantial opposition to the exhumation of the disappeared by many of their mothers and relatives. This opposition has sometimes been dismissed as the extremist rantings of 'las locas' (the madwomen), a name originally given to the Mothers of the Plaza de Mayo by the junta (Bousquet 1983). As Agosin notes (1987: 433), the ascription of insanity to women who are seen as a threat is a tactic that has been employed in many contexts to disempower women who are seen as 'out of place' or as acting inappropriately. In their appropriation of the traditionally male spheres of public spaces and political discourse, the Mothers of the Plaza de Mayo transgressed on both counts against the hyperconservative values held by the juntas. The Mothers have consistently chosen public spaces as the arena for their demonstrations and criticisms of both the military regime and the subsequent democratic governments.

> The Mothers never claimed to have been the only ones or the first to fight against the dictatorship, but we do claim to have been the first to have done it publicly.
>
> (from an open letter from Epelbaum, for the Mothers, to
> Dr Raúl Alfonsín, quoted in Agosin 1990: 85)

The choice of the Plaza de Mayo provides a good illustration of their co-option of public spaces for their protests (Torre 1996; Fisher 1989: 88–108). The Plaza has had a central role in Argentinian national history. Located in the political, financial and symbolic centre of Buenos Aires, this is where independence was declared in 1810; it is also where key government buildings are located, including the presidential palace. The choice to march in the middle of the week on a Thursday afternoon was also strategically selected to maximize their visibility. The public, open nature of the demonstrations, was used as a deliberate counterpoint to the secret activities of the state. In this way the Mothers made their private grief public and revealed and subverted the clandestine nature of the disappearances.

> Our battle was legitimate; that of the military was something hidden, monstrous, and illegal.
>
> (Epelbaum, quoted in Agosin 1990: 34)

Another form of protest developed by the Mothers was the placing of newspaper advertisements that criticized the regime. In this too they chose a public arena for contestation that contrasted directly with the military's clandestine operations. The Mothers' protests were given additional impact through the choice of these most public spaces for demonstration, as they challenged social expectations of where and how women, and especially mothers, should act. Through creating their protests in public space, their conspicuous presence made visible the absences of their children.

One of the slogans frequently used by the Mothers, and often quoted as evidence of their 'irrational demands' is 'aparición con vida', meaning 'appearance alive'. This slogan is not a literal demand for the return of disappeared people who are still being held illegally; rather, it is a call for accountability.

> Aparición con vida means that although the majority of them are dead, no-one has taken responsibility for their deaths, because no-one has said who killed them.
>
> (Carmen de Guede, quoted by Fisher 1989: 128)

This position has contributed to the continuing use of the description of the Mothers as las locas. Graciela de Jeger, another of the Mothers, elaborated the thinking behind the slogan.

> We knew it was very unlikely that our children were alive. At first we were hopeful, but now we can see it's impossible. But we don't want to assume responsibility for the deaths ourselves. We want them to say who killed them. This is why we speak of our children in the present tense. Aparición con vida is the most controversial of our slogans because a lot of people support us, but say aparición con vida, no. You're mad.
>
> (quoted in Fisher 1989: 128)

The forensic excavations and identification of the disappeared run directly counter to this position, documenting the reappearance of human remains rather than of living individuals. This has led to conflict between human rights groups. Some groups, particularly the Asociación de Madres de Plaza de Mayo (Bonafini–Cerrutti line) and the Asociación de Ex Detenidos-Desaparecidos, directly oppose the forensic work of the EAAF (Asociación de Ex Detenidos-Desaparecidos 1988; Asociación de Madres de Plaza de Mayo 1989; Verbitsky 1989). Others, including the Grandmothers of the Plaza de Mayo and the Families of the Disappeared and Political Detainees are supportive of the exhumations (Verbitsky 1989; Familiares de Desaparecidos y Detenidos por Razones Politicas 1990), as is the group known as the Founders of the Mothers of the Plaza de Mayo. Other relatives and mothers who are not formally aligned with any particular interest group tend to be supportive of the excavations (Verbitsky 1993). Argentina is unusual within Latin America in having a large and vocal proportion of human rights organizations opposing the forensic recovery of disappeared human remains (Verbitsky 1989: 9).

> Bonafini and her followers … didn't want exhumations. 'We the mothers of the disappeared will not be converted into mothers of the dead,' Bonifini once declared, ignoring mounting evidence that the disappeared had indeed been executed.
>
> (Joyce and Stover 1991: 254)

The common disparagement of this position fails to grasp that it is part of a coherent political strategy calling for admission of wrongdoing by those responsible. Berta Schuberoff, whose son was identified by the EAAF, spoke well of the excavations, but she explained how she saw other Mothers' perception of them.

> [They] do not accept the exhumations because they say that their sons are still living through their ideas and they will continue their struggle and will be found alive. They do not accept their surrender in a bag of bones.
>
> (Kisilevski 1990: 9, my translation)

This refusal to acknowledge the bodies of the disappeared therefore derives from separate and related political positions, held in particular by the Association of Mothers of the Plaza de Mayo, headed by Bonafini. They insist on public judicial accountability by those responsible; until then, they insist on remembering their disappeared relatives as they were in life rather than in death. Related to this position they believe that both the CONADEP inquiry and the excavations focused overly on identifying and describing the victims of the repression, rather than eliciting admissions of guilt from the perpetrators.

> We already know that thousands of *desaparecidos* were secretly murdered and buried. The exhumations don't tell us anything we don't already know …
>
> (Jeger, quoted in Fisher 1989: 128)

As a direct response to the lack of information and the misinformation and rumours spread about the disappeared during the years of the repression, many Mothers have refused to acknowledge any attempts to account for the disappeared. The opposition by the Association of Mothers of the Plaza de Mayo to the excavations is therefore part of this effort to keep their children disappeared and in this way maintain their public visibility, until full accountability has been obtained. This strategy has been discussed by various commentators (Schirmer 1993; Malin 1994), and the Chilean writer Ariel Dorfman has also explored the sentiments behind the strategy in a poem called *Last Will and Testament*, which begins:

> When they tell you
> I'm not a prisoner
> don't believe them.
> They'll have to admit it
> some day ...

The poem moves on to outline the misinformation and lies offered to the families of the disappeared. These ranged from claiming that their relatives had not been seized, but had moved abroad, to showing them signed confessions, demonstrating the guilt of those who had been taken from them. The poem persistently returns to the refrain 'don't believe them', responding with this even to assertions that appear to be self-evidently true. The poem delineates the difficult personal experiences that led to some relatives publicly refusing to trust any information that was received from or through organizations associated with the state. Dorfman finishes the poem:

> And finally ...
> when they ask you
> to identify the body ...
>
> when they tell you
> that I am
> completely absolutely definitely
> dead
> don't believe them,
> don't believe them ...

> (Dorfman 1997)

In the absence of any sure knowledge about what had happened to their relatives, the strategy of seizing the absences created by the juntas was a novel and creative way of changing the terms of the discourse about the disappearances. In order to claim the spaces left by the disappeared, the Mothers filled the spaces with embodied public representations of the disappeared as they remembered them in life. During their demonstrations in the Plaza de Mayo, which still take place, the Mothers carry photographs of their children and wear white headscarves embroidered with their names. Probably the most well-known and literal example of this claiming of the spaces left by their children is the painting of ghostly silhouettes around Buenos Aires, marked with the names and dates of people's disappearances. These first appeared in 1983 at the end of military rule, and have become a popular motif for protest since then. The silhouettes reflect the ruptures left by people's disappearances in the lives of their friends and families. In 1979 the Mothers sent a letter to the UN, the US government and Pope John Paul II in which they described the pain of disappearance.

> The families began to relate to the absent people as 'fantasmas' ... the kidnapped lacked identity, no one knew whether they were alive or dead ... [Absence is] a pain without object. It is a vacuum, total loss, the dead without body and without grave ... [2]
>
> (quoted in Salama 1992: 43, my translation)

The absences created by the seizure of people from networks of social and family relationships, were therefore used by the Mothers as a mnemonic device to remind the country that these people had been clandestinely kidnapped and that those responsible had not yet been brought to justice. The reclamation and politicization by Mothers in Argentina of the absences left by their disappeared children ascribes new meanings to the empty spaces left by a disappearance. In this way the Mothers have modified the original violent significance that resided in this absence, a meaning primarily created by those who forced this condition upon the disappeared; 'contrary to the final assurance of death, the very absence of bodies has created a *presence* for ongoing life' (Schirmer 1993). However the use of this particular strategy is not accepted by all mothers and relatives of the disappeared, as some relatives prefer to remember their loved ones in ways which do not focus on the continuing absences of the disappeared. Others attempt to retain the uncertainty of disappearance, even after receiving physical remains.

> Really, the Mothers were right not to want the bodies, because in spite of the fact I had my son's grave exhumed, I don't know it's my son. I think it's my son, but I don't know who killed him. All I know for sure is that my son isn't here.
>
> (Elisa de Landin, quoted in Fisher 1989: 130)

The public recreation of the absences of the disappeared has contributed to the disappeared often being described as 'fantasmas'.[3] Even the official CONADEP report referred to the quality of being disappeared as a 'sinister ghostly category' (CONADEP 1984: 3). Dario Olmo, one of the archaeologists involved with the excavations wrote that the disappeared are 'like ghosts, neither alive nor dead' (personal communication 1994). The limbo-like condition of the disappeared is also reflected, recreated and contested through the space of the excavations.

THE SPACE OF EXCAVATION

One of the major sites of excavation of the disappeared is at the Avellaneda cemetery on the outskirts of Buenos Aires (Salama 1992: 251–74). Sector 134, the area
where the unmarked mass graves were located, stands in marked contrast to the
rest of the cemetery. When I visited in 1992, I was struck by the profound contrast
between the main part of the cemetery and the area where the disappeared were
buried. The cemetery itself was well kept and colourful, with carefully mown
grassy avenues separating the ordered rows of graves. It contained the usual architecture of death; gravestones marked with names and dates, flowers and photographs of the people buried there. The graves of the disappeared, however, were
delimited by a walled-off area, closed by a sheet metal gate. Inside the area was
overgrown with coarse grass. The only architecture present was a dilapidated, low
concrete building, previously used as a morgue, then abandoned, and later used by
the forensic team to complete their analyses (Joyce and Stover 1991: 284). In contrast to the rest of the cemetery, no explicit symbolism had been inscribed in Sector
134. There were no tombstones providing names for the graves. Indeed there was
none of the conventional architecture of death in this apparently 'empty' zone.

The ghostlike state of the disappeared is created by, in part, their lack of temporal incorporation into the world of the dead by passing through funerary ritual
(Crossland 2000: 153–5). Equally the space of Avellaneda reinforced their lack of
spatial incorporation into the 'proper' place for the dead. Instead, reflecting this
ghostlike status, they resided in a circumscribed zone that was walled off from
both the living and the dead. It was within this ambiguous 'empty' space that the
excavations took place. Exploring the conflicting readings of the excavations in
Sector 134 exposes the intersections between the institutionalized authority of
the military, the police and law courts and the agency of the individuals and interest groups involved. The various interpretations of the excavations are constrained and created by the larger socio-political contexts, in the placing and
interaction of the graves within societal networks of control and authority over
the memories and bodies of the disappeared. However, they are also informed by
the localized configuration of the space of excavation, which frames the interpretations within the details of the spatial relationships between architectural elements and people's interactions with them. During the excavations of the
disappeared, the individual biographies of many individuals, both living and
dead, came together in Sector 134, to create alternative and conflicting readings of
the sector as a place. These differently embodied understandings of this space, in
some people's eyes, meant that the excavations reproduced the structures of institutionalized power that created the 'empty' sector in the first place. However, in
others' eyes, the excavations challenged the very same violent institutions and the
individuals who created and maintained them. As the 'empty' space of Sector 134
was excavated, so the human remains and the embodied practices of excavation
were simultaneously incorporated, both into the creation and regeneration of
institutional authority, and the challenging of the institutionalized practices
which led to disappeared people being buried there.

Even after the military relinquished formal governmental power in Argentina, disappearances continued. Some families received telephone calls from disappeared relatives during the period of transition to democratic government in 1984, yet these people never reappeared. The security services still operated with some autonomy after Alfonsín's government was elected (Fisher 1989: 127–8). This meant that to participate in the excavations was a dangerous activity for the anthropologists. One of the members of the team described this.

> I knew that … after the first exhumation I'd just be marked. … It was 1984, democracy was beginning here, and everybody was talking about a new military coup. I was worried that I could be on … the next list.
>
> (Doretti, quoted in Joyce and Stover 1991: 295)

There were similar fears in Chile after Pinochet's government was replaced by a democratic government:

> The legacy of a dictatorship is sinister, profound, leaving permanent scars. There still exists in the minds of young parents the fear that military power might revive in our country. There still exists the fear that during the night there will be a knock on the door to take us away because we are innocent youths with political beliefs and values. The Chilean dictatorship never tolerated political dialogue nor dissident ideas. It did not allow the young to make history and this legacy has scarred us.
>
> (Agosin 1993: 407–8)

The courage it took to participate in the excavations at this early date led some commentators and relatives to compare the commitment of the EAAF with the idealism and courage of the disappeared (Verbitsky 1993: 9). There is a common association between the young and idealism which is often emphasized by the Mothers when talking of their disappeared children. Renee Epelbaum, spokesperson for the 'Linea Fundadora' of the Mothers of the Plaza de Mayo noted that 'It is normal to be idealistic when you are young. If you're not, then you're already old' (Malin 1994: 195). However, the connections made between the disappeared, the anthropologists and youthful idealism also recognize that the anthropologists' work could be seen as a threat by the military and police, most of whom were still in the positions they held under the military dictatorships.

The excavations, in addition to providing evidence for the law courts, took a great deal of their symbolic force from the physical uncovering of the bodies, revealing the secret activities surrounding the disappearance and deaths of those buried there. This again made the crimes of the juntas visible and contributed to maintaining public consciousness and memories of the years of the repression, one of the key demands of the Mothers organisations. 'The collective memory says, and will continue to say: do not forget, do not forgive' (Epelbaum, Founders of the Mothers of the Plaza de Mayo 1992 newspaper advertisement, cited in

Figure 11.1 Excavations at Avellaneda cemetery, Buenos Aires. According to the account in the *Independent* magazine, from which this is taken, the men standing against the wall are police. Standing in the centre of the group of men on the right is Clyde Snow, a North American forensic anthropologist who was instrumental in establishing the EAAF

Source: Mimi Doretti

Malin 1994: 213). The excavations provided a different, but ultimately incompatible, way in which to accomplish what the Association of Mothers of the Plaza de Mayo also hoped to accomplish, the revelation of clandestine activity and the uncovering of what was meant to be left hidden. However, some of the impact of the excavations was absorbed by the space in which they took place. The very location of the excavations in Sector 134 of Avellaneda meant that they took place in the place originally created by the military for disposing of the disappeared. The excavations, although designed to challenge the military regime were played out in an arena created by those responsible. The enclosed space that held the mass graves continues to be segregated from the rest of the cemetery. This means that it was not experienced as a public space by the excavators and the relatives of the disappeared, and as such it is less available to being visibly appropriated for political protest as with the Plaza de Mayo. Additionally the private nature of the pain and death of the people buried there also contributes to a more personal and private reading of the space. This context of excavation therefore also collided with the choice of the Mothers of high-visibility public places for protest, and led in part to accusations by the Association of Mothers of the Plaza de Mayo that the focus of the excavations lay too much on those buried there rather than on those responsible for the deaths.

This was reinforced by the presence of representatives of the police at the excavations. Fig. 11.1, originally published in the *Independent*'s magazine, shows the first excavations in the San Isidro suburb of Buenos Aires. The forensic anthropologists are surrounded by observers. The men standing against the wall are described as police. The anthropologists were frequently watched by policemen while they worked and this created a threatening presence for some of them, marking the excavations as a dangerous place. Patricia Bernardi, one of the anthropologists, recounted the following:

> The police are always there and I remember a day when one of them turned to a police doctor at one grave site and said 'if we had done it right ten years ago, these people wouldn't be here now'.
>
> (Michaud 1987: 20)

Whether these particular men were involved with the disappearances cannot be established. However, the involvement of the police in the disappearances has been documented and the police therefore constituted a threatening presence, especially in the early days of the exhumations (Fisher 1989: 18–19). One of the cemetery workers at Avellaneda described helping the police bury the bodies: 'The police would call us over in the mornings after the trucks had come in with the bodies ... The soldiers told us to begin digging holes ...' (Joyce and Stover 1991: 292). The surveillance by the police of the excavations may be interpreted as marking the area as one that is and has been under their control and as such affected the ways in which the anthropologists and relatives of the dead experienced the physical space. An account that describes this interaction relates the reactions of people present after finding the probable remains of a seventeen-year-old *desaparecido*.

> ... the cluster of relatives ... take the bad news in silence ... There is a pause in the work. A couple of bullets have been found, one lying in the tangle of ribs, another lodged deep in the right hip joint. The two plain clothes policemen take an interest for the first time. They gather around the bullets, conversing knowledgeably to each other without emotions. Mimi Doretti is aware of their scrutiny: 'It is often like that. The police know about the bullets, most of them know all about the disappeared.'
>
> (Unsworth 1989: 36)

Even the spatial configuration of people's bodies may be interpreted as replaying the inequalities of institutionalized authority and knowledge of the place of excavation. In Fig. 11.1, the positioning of the anthropologists, kneeling or lying down, physically in the grave and close to the disappeared, could be seen to contrast with their observation by the nameless men, who stand and look down upon them, apparently overseeing the excavations. The gendering of the work also echoes that of the disappeared and the paramilitary groups, as the majority of the abductions were carried out by men, and those taken were young and both male and female.

This association again echoes the parallels made between the anthropologists and the disappeared by some families of disappeared people.

The surveillance of the excavations by the police and others played into the concerns of some human rights groups, especially the Association of Mothers of the Plaza de Mayo and the Asociación de Ex Detenidos-Desaparecidos. A major criticism made of the CONADEP investigation was that, although the victims of the repression were known, the murderers were still anonymous (Asociación de Ex Detenidos-Desaparecidos 1988). Indeed during the trials there was a sense that the junta still held control, in that to some of the Mothers it appeared that much of the trial was framed in terms set by the military. One of the Mothers, Carmen de Guede recalled that during the trials, the victims of the repression were described as terrorists or subversives, without supporting evidence. Those on trial were given the dignity of their military titles and allowed to be present in full uniform for their sentencing. The Mothers, in contrast, were constrained in what they wore in that they were not allowed to wear their characteristic white scarves that represent their children and symbolize their collective search for 'truth and justice' (quoted in Fisher 1989: 141).

The excavated bodies of the disappeared also contributed to this perception of control by those responsible. As they were excavated, the identity and memory of the individual could become overshadowed by the manner of their death. The bullets and injuries inflicted on these bodies are two of the most salient characteristics of the remains. The details of the person's life recede before the violent manner of their death. Even aspects of their own bodily history, their dental records, the mark left on the skeleton by pregnancy and childbirth, childhood broken bones, could be appropriated as courtroom evidence. These details were used to identify disappeared individuals to provide evidence to bring the military to trial. However, since the convictions from these trials were later quashed, many Mothers saw the use of the remains of the disappeared in the trials as in the service of forgetting the past and moving on to a new unified future for Argentina (see the advertisement placed by the Asociación Madres de Plaza de Mayo in *Página 12* for example [December 1989]). This, taken in addition to the symbolic investment that the Bonafini–Cerrutti line of Mothers have made in finding their children alive or not at all, marks the excavations for them as a place that is created by, watched and controlled by the state apparatus responsible for the disappearances. As a result the anthropological team has come under direct attack by these Mothers for appearing, in their eyes, to collaborate with those responsible for the disappearances. At one of the earliest excavations at Isidro Cassanova Cemetery, some of the Association of Mothers of the Plaza de Mayo surrounded the exhumations and refused to let anybody get close, throwing stones at anyone who attempted (account by María Julia Bihurriet, quoted in Joyce and Stover 1991: 258–9). Some human rights groups felt that the focus on the victims while the guilty were free, and in many cases still in positions of power, was a diversionary tactic, to take the pressure off Alfonsín's and then Menem's governments from the still strong armed forces.

While the Founders Line of Mothers of the Plaza de Mayo and other human rights

Figure 11.2 Protests outside the Naval Mechanics School

Source: Reuters

groups, such as the Grandmothers of the Plaza de Mayo, support and accept the work of the excavations, the Association of Mothers of the Plaza de Mayo sees the reappearance and sanctioned reburial of bodies as sapping the power from their protests. Although many see the exhumations as enabling them to come to terms with their loss through mourning and reburial, this cannot be reconciled with the views of the Association of Mothers. At the core of the Association's strategy is a demand that the charged and threatening spaces created by the disappearances should be kept as such, and should in this way be turned against those responsible. The maintenance of Sector 134 (and other burial sites) as such a threatening and dangerous space is consistent with this strategy. For these mothers, the emptying of the area, and its gradual reincorporation back into the landscape of the cemetery rids the place of its ghosts and takes away its power as a place which may haunt those responsible, and remind people that those who should answer for their violent actions still walk free.

Another instance of this friction can be seen in the recent conflict over the proposed destruction of the Naval Mechanics School where many people were detained and tortured (Fig. 11.2). Ex-president Menem suggested that the building be razed and replaced with an 'open green space and monument to national unity' (*New York Times* 1998: 15). This has led again to a clash between differing ideas of what the collective response to the years of the repression ought to be. Certainly the Association of Mothers of the Plaza de Mayo would reject any possibility of national unity while those responsible for contributing to the fragmentation of the nation through kidnap, torture and murder are still at liberty. One Mother responded to Menem's suggestion by shouting 'let us inside to claim what is left of our loved ones'. This statement then is not a literal expectation of finding remains, but rather a symbolic claiming of hidden space. The claims made on this concealed space attempt to counter the perceived attempts of the military, and the democratic government, to convert this violent hidden space into a neutral place, no longer haunted by the uneasy ghosts of the disappeared.

ACKNOWLEDGEMENTS

Thanks to Brian Boyd, Adam Smith and Javier Morillo-Alicea for helpful comments on earlier versions of this chapter; also to Penny Dransart for suggestions with translations, and Stephen Michaud for helping with references. A related presentation was given at WAC4 in January 1999; my thanks also to Paul Lane for inviting me to participate in the Subordinate Societies, Local Archaeologies session. Thank you to Ariel Dorfman for permission to reproduce part of his poem, *Last Will and Testament*, and to the EAAF, especially Mimi Doretti, for giving me permission to use her photograph reproduced as Fig. 11.1, and helping me track down the original copy. Finally, I'd like to acknowledge the help and support of Colleen Beck and Polly Osborn, who gave me much assistance in putting the chapter together in its final form.

NOTES

1 Many thanks to the members of the 'Space and Place' seminar, run by Adam Smith at the University of Michigan, for coming up with the term.
2 'Los familiares pasan a relacionarse con los ausentes que se convierten en "fantasmas" … Se debe enfrentar la ausencia, que no es un duelo común, de por sí doloroso. Es un "duelo sin objeto". Es el vacío, la pérdida total, la muerte sin cuerpo y sin entierro …'
3 According to Velázquez 1967, even the word fantasma has an ambiguous quality in Spanish. The masculine form translates as phantom or 'image of some object which remains impressed on the mind', while the feminine form translates into ghost or spirit. In present-day usage the masculine form is more current. It has broadened out to mean ghost/phantom/apparition or vision/illusion (Simon and Schuster 1997) and also has the additional meaning of *amenaza* which may be translated as a (threatening) spectre (Concise Oxford Dictionary 1996).

REFERENCES

Agosin, M. (1987) 'A visit to the Mothers of the Plaza de Mayo', *Human Rights Quarterly* 9(3): 426–35.
Agosin, M. (1990) *Mothers of the Plaza de Mayo (Linea Fundadora): The Story of Renee Epelbaum, 1976–1985*, translated by Janice Malloy, Trenton NJ: Red Sea Press.
Agosin M. (1993) 'Democracy for a ghost nation', translated by P.M. Vega, *Human Rights Quarterly* 15(2): 406–9.
Amnesty International (1987) *Argentina: The Military Juntas and Human Rights: Report of the Trial of the Former Junta Members, 1985*, London: Amnesty International.

Asociación de Ex Detenidos-Desaparecidos (1988) 'Victimas identificados, pero asesinos anonimos', advertisement, *Página 12*, March: 13, Buenos Aires.

Asociación Madres de Plaza de Mayo (1989) 'Luchamos por la vida, no los traicionamos,' advertisement, *Página 12*, 22 December: 6, Buenos Aires.

Bousquet, J-P. (1982) *Les Folles de la Place de Mai,* Paris: Stock 2.

Brysk, A. (1994) The politics of measurement: the contested count in the disappeared in Argentina, *Human Rights Quarterly* 16(4): 676–92.

CONADEP (1986) *Nunca más (Never Again). A Report by Argentina's National Commission on Disappeared People*, London: Faber and Faber.

Concise Oxford Spanish Dictionary (1996) New York, Oxford: Oxford University Press.

Crossland, Z. (2000) Buried lives: forensic archaeology and the disappeared in Argentina, *Archaeological Dialogues* 35: 146–59.

Dorfman, A. (1997) *Wertidows and Last Waltz in Santiago,* London: Sceptre.

Familiares de desaparecidos y detenidos por razones políticas (1990) 'No los traicionamos luchamos por la vida', advertisement, *Página 12*, 10 January: 6, Buenos Aires.

Fisher, J. (1989) *Mothers of the Disappeared,* London: Zed Books.

Harvey, R. (1980) Poor little rich boy. Argentina: a survey, *The Economist*, 26 January: 3–26, London.

Jelin, E. (1990) *Women and Social Change in Latin America,* London: Zed Books.

Joyce, C. and Stover, E. (1991) *Witnesses from the Grave: The Stories Bones Tell,* Boston: Little, Brown.

Kisilevski, M. (1990) Testimonio de una lucha contra el olvido y la impunidad, *Nueva Sion*, 19 January: 9, Buenos Aires.

Malin, A. (1994) Mothers who won't disappear, *Human Rights Quarterly* 16(1): 187–213.

Michaud, S.G. (1987) Identifying Argentina's disappeared, *New York Times* (Sunday colour supplement) 27 December: 18–21, New York.

New York Times (1998) 18 January: 15, New York.

Salama, M.C. (1992) *Tumbas Anonimas,* Buenos Aires.

Schirmer, J. (1993) 'Those who die for life cannot be called dead', in Agosin, M. (ed.) *Surviving Beyond Fear*, Fredonia NY: White Pine Press, pp. 31–57.

Simon and Schuster's International Spanish Dictionary (1997) 2nd edn.

Simpson, J. and Bennett, J. (1985) *The Disappeared: Voices from a Secret War,* London: Robson Books.

Snow, C.C., Stover, E. and Hannibal, K. (1989) Scientists as detectives. Investigating human rights, *Technology Review* 92(2): 43–51, Cambridge: Massachusetts Institute of Technology.

Stevens, E.P. (1973) 'Marianismo: the other face of Machismo', in Pescatello, A. (ed.) *Female and Male in Latin America*, Pittsburg: University of Pittsburg Press.

Torre, S. (1996) 'Claiming the public space: the Mothers of Plaza de Mayo', in Agrest, D., Conway, P. and Weisman, L. (eds) *The Sex of Architecture,* New York: Harry N. Abrams, pp. 241–250.

Unsworth, T. (1989) The body hunters, *The Independent Magazine,* 30 September: 32–6, London.

Velázquez de la Cadena, M. (1967) *New Revised Velázquez Spanish and English Dictionary*, Chicago: Follett.

Verbitsky, H. (1993) Identificación de una mujer, *Página 12*, 10 January: 8–9, Buenos Aires.

12 Biography of a medal: people and the things they value

Jody Joy

INTRODUCTION

The archaeology of twentieth-century conflict can seem very impersonal and detached, often involving the assessment of battlefields or military installations on the basis of standard criteria. By contrast, this chapter is very personal and highlights the significance of a single object – my grandfather's Distinguished Flying Cross (DFC) medal (Fig. 12.1) – to me, my grandfather and other members of my family. Although the medal is one of over 20 000 DFCs awarded in the Second World War (Litherland and Simpkin 1990: 54) it is important to my family and to me because of its strong association with the life of my grandfather. By charting the biography of the medal this chapter will recount how the medal has become a vehicle for remembrance and reminiscence and how it has become so firmly tied to the life and experiences of my grandfather during the Second World War.

This chapter also explores in more general terms the relationships that exist between objects and people, the divisions that now exist between them having been identified as a recent phenomenon and a product of Western thought (Appadurai 1986; Tilley 1989). In many non-Western societies people know exactly where an object has come from and who has made it, and an object derives much of its value and significance from these associations. Using the personal example of my grandfather's DFC, I will use this chapter to argue that the distinction between people and objects within our own society is not as clear-cut as we like to imagine, if we draw a distinction between the 'object' and the 'thing'. According to Martin Heidegger (1971) things are closer to us than objects. A thing exists at a particular place and time, within a particular set of relationships: a thing has come from somewhere; someone has made it – it is made of something. A thing makes sense to us because of the network of relationships of which it is a part.

This chapter then is concerned with how the lives of objects in Western societies can become tied to those of people when they become socially constituted as 'things'; how 'things' can act to store meanings and associations; how they operate to consolidate social relationships in particular ways; and how these relationships

Figure 12.1 The obverse side of my grandfather's DFC (Distinguished Flying Cross)

Source: Author

can have greater strength and significance where they relate directly to warfare. By adopting a biographical approach to objects, it will be demonstrated that from the moment the medal entered my family it began to acquire layers of meaning as different members of my family attached different meanings to it. By analysing the life of the medal, starting with its entry into my family and ending with the present day, I will show how these layers of meaning transformed a manufactured 'object' into a multi-faceted 'thing'. I will explain how an object like a medal, which supposedly has a pre-programmed meaning as an emblem of pride and achievement, can be transformed into something which can act to store meanings and associations and can become tied to the lives of people. However, materialization is a performance (Butler 1990; 1993). The example of my grandfather's medal will show that not even an object as strictly contextualized as a war medal is innately meaningful: it must be performed in action to acquire meaning and only becomes meaningful when it is socially constituted in a particular way.

TROUBLE IN THE KITE

I begin by situating my grandfather's medal in time and space and describe the particular historical context in which it was created and awarded. My grandfather, Pilot Officer Walter William Joy, was awarded the DFC after the completion of a tour of thirty missions as a tail gunner in a Lancaster bomber during the Second World War. A section of text from my grandfather's flight log gives some sense of what it was like to fly a bombing raid over enemy territory and hints at some of the thoughts and emotions going through his mind at the time.

Well, at long last this was it – when the Battle Order came out this morning we were on in T. Tommy. Was I scared? I can't really say, but I know my heart was ticking quicker than usual and my mouth felt dry all day … Out at the aircraft doing the final checks and then that seemingly never ending wait for the take off – at last we were away – no turning back now, it was like sitting in a dentist chair when he says 'this is not going to hurt' – just got to go through with it!!

Right from the take off we had trouble with the Port inner engine and had difficulty in climbing … About 70 miles from the target when we were at 18 000 ft and still had to climb another 4000 ft to do our bombing run the worst happened – that engine went completely – Chuck [the pilot] called up and asked us what we wanted to do – drop our load now so as to maintain what height we had or as we had come so far go in and drop it in on target – after a vote had been taken we went in! At 14 000 ft Leo [the bomb aimer] dropped it bang in the middle – at the same time two 30 lb. incendiary bombs from an aircraft above us crashed through our starboard wing making two large holes and damaging the undercarriage as well as bursting a tyre … It was of course the first target I had ever seen and a sight I shall never forget – I won't even attempt to describe what it looked like or the seemingly [sic] hell of bursting flak shells all around us.

As Chuck turned the kite out of the target the old crate still lost height and we fixed parachutes and got Des [navigator] to work out how long it would take to get to France as if we baled out we wanted a chance of getting back. Just out of target at about 11,000 ft I saw a ME 109 coming to attack on the port quarter down. I warned the crew and fired at him – he disappeared for a few seconds and I next saw him coming up dead astern about 300 yards away. I ordered Chuck to corkscrew and opened fire – he opened fire at the same time – just a very short burst which passed over the kite to the port. I still kept firing and he went into a very steep dive and disappeared into the cloud below – by this time we were down to 9000 ft and Chuck reckoned we had had it, when after losing another 500 ft she started to pick up again – well after a time we got to 10 000 ft and Chuck said providing we don't meet any more fighters or searchlights we might make it. Well to cut a long story short we did get back okay and made a crash landing at Woodbridge with no brake pressure and only one wheel – Chuck made a super landing and boy! were we glad to feel mother earth again after eight odd hours flying.

PS   This was the trip when I learnt to pray and mean it – I would never think of going on a trip now without saying my prayers as I believe that's what brought me through that night at least.

(Joy 1944: 1)

A BIOGRAPHY OF MY GRANDFATHER'S MEDAL

The medal started life in a factory owned by the Royal Mint. It was probably transported along with a series of other medals (most of which were sent to various
award ceremonies) and then according to my grandfather it was posted to him. It is
interesting to question what this object was before my grandfather received it: was
there any specific meaning attached to this mass-produced object of metal and
ribbon which, although engraved with the year it was awarded, was issued
unnamed (Litherland and Simpkin 1990: 54)? Potentially the medal had meaning
as a Distinguished Flying Cross; it was awarded to officers and warrant of the
Royal Air Force (RAF) for 'an act or acts of valour, courage, or devotion to duty
performed whilst flying in active operations against the enemy' (Taprell-Dorling
1960: 33) and therefore had a number of implicit values attached to it. However,
the life history of my grandfather's medal did not follow this presumed course
because of the manner in which it was presented to my grandfather: its arrival
through the post, rather than being awarded to him by a member of the Royal
Family, or at the very least his station commander, in a formal presentation ceremony. The presentation of medals is a key event in their life histories and its performance is intended to make the recipient feel proud and to reward that
individual for their actions. It also has the effect of establishing the meanings associated with a medal firmly on that performance as well as on what the recipient has
achieved. The medal and the performance of medal presentation are therefore
integral to the constitution of the medal as meaningful in the way presumed for it.
Without the performance associated with medal-giving the recipient is given an
'object' rather than a 'thing'.

Because the medal was sent to my grandfather through the post he had a very
ambivalent attitude towards it. In fact he resented it as he believed the RAF had
considered him not 'worthy' of a 'proper' presentation ceremony. As a result
between 1944 and the early 1950s the medal was not shown off but rather hidden,
in a white cardboard box along with other memorabilia from that period of his life,
such as photographs, campaign medals and newspaper clippings.

Early 1950s: where is the medal?

During the late 1940s and early 1950s my grandfather was serving in the RAF, first
in Germany and the Isle of Man, and later at Mildenhall, Suffolk, England. Presumably, wherever he moved he took the medal with him, but sometime during
the early 1950s my grandfather and grandmother noticed the medal was missing.
The case in which the medal was kept was found but the medal was not. Around
the same time my great-grandfather came, in mysterious circumstances, to live
with my grandparents. My father was never told why this happened.

The first memory my father has of my grandfather's medal is of its absence. He
can recall that when he was about five years old he saw the empty box in which the
medal used to be kept. When he asked my grandmother (Fig. 12.2) where the medal
that should have been inside the box was, she suggested that my great-grandfather

Figure 12.2 A portrait of my grandfather and grandmother as well as my Uncle William (left) and my father Patrick (centre)

Source: Author

'probably took it'. In retrospect my father tends to regard this statement as 'just one of those things you remember as a kid', believing it equally likely that the medal was lost during a house move. However, it is clear that by uttering these words my grandmother played an instrumental role in changing the meanings attached to the medal. From the moment those words were uttered, the medal became indelibly tied to my grandmother, my great-grandfather, and the conflict between them. This conflict was in part based on my grandmother's resentment of the fact that she was providing for a once rich man in his old age perhaps because of his business ineptitude. More important, however, was religious difference as my grandmother was a Roman Catholic from an Irish background and my great-grandfather was a strict Protestant and a Grandmaster of the Freemasons. This conflict began when, upon marrying a Roman Catholic, my grandfather was forced to leave the Freemasons.

From the moment my father questioned the disappearance of the medal, the empty box became a symbol of its absence. The empty box also became an emblem of my grandmother's feelings for my great-grandfather. Over the years in which the medal was missing her resentment and dislike for my great-grandfather was maintained and enhanced by the symbolic nature of the empty box. The empty box also acted to preserve a feeling within my family that my great-grandfather was somehow responsible for the medal's disappearance, suggesting in the minds of various family members that he was capable of stealing from his own son. Even after my great-grandfather's death in 1961 these thoughts remained in the memories of my father and my uncle, fostered by the medal's continuing absence.

The medal and the bunker

During the early 1950s the medal became firmly attached, in my uncle's mind, to one of his favourite anecdotes. When he was about ten or eleven years old he went to watch an air display with my grandfather. During the show two Meteor planes collided head-on and there was a large explosion. Seconds before the crash my grandfather had spotted what might happen and had rushed my uncle to the 'safety' of a nearby bunker. When they eventually emerged from the bunker they noticed what it said in large letters above the door: 'danger high explosives' – it was probably the most dangerous place on the airfield! For my uncle the medal evokes this story because at the air show my grandfather was in his RAF uniform and in passing a friend had suggested that he could have worn his medals. This story is significant to the biography of the medal because it attaches an important aspect of my grandfather's personality on to it, one that I also remember: his ability to make things worse, even though he had the best of intentions. For my uncle therefore, the medal is strongly associated with one vivid memory he has of my grandfather, which expresses a lot about his nature and personality: about who he was.

The replica

In 1981 my father arranged for a replacement, a replica medal, to be made. This time he formally presented it to my grandfather as a birthday present. In the performance of this presentation 'ceremony' the replica medal helped to generate strong links between my father and grandfather. The gift was also important to my father because it allowed him to lessen a rift in our family, one which he had experienced since childhood, and that had been constantly reaffirmed by the medal's absence. The replica medal could never replace the original, or relieve all of the family tensions caused by its disappearance (my grandmother even at this time used to hint at its theft by my great-grandfather), but it did constitute the medal in a new form, which had positive associations and meanings. Although these did not erase the earlier meanings and associations, these fresh and more immediate new meanings became layered on top of the old ones.

Following Rainbird (1999), who has suggested that the biography of one object can be transferred to another through what he calls 'biographical entanglement', it can be suggested that some of the meanings and associations attached to the 'original' medal have been transferred, first to the empty box, and second to the replica medal. However, also associated with the biography of the empty box and the replica medal are a number of other meanings and associations, which have been layered on top of those that resided in the original. Thus, the meanings and associations, which are now tied to the replica medal are by no means the same as those that resided in the original medal or indeed the empty box. These meanings have been added to and renegotiated through time, producing a number of layers of meaning.

Figure 12.3 My grandfather with his replica DFC and his operations book (*Cambridge Evening News*, Friday 25 April 1986)

Source: Cambridge Evening News

1980s: reminiscence

Throughout the 1980s the replica medal acted as a medium through which my grandfather was able to remember 1944 and his life and friends in the RAF, operating as a source of remembrance (Fig. 12.3). Despite my grandfather's indifference and even reticence towards the medal earlier on in his life, because of its reconstituted form and the positive new meanings associated with it, the replica medal became a medium of remembrance back to the war. This reminiscence was a very private one, however, and my grandfather rarely shared his thoughts or memories of the war with any other members of my family. As the description from his flight log illustrates, this period of my grandfather's life must have been a terrifying one (Joy 1944). His life was constantly in danger and all around him other people were being killed. He was also inflicting terrible suffering on others, directly by shooting down a number of aircraft, and indirectly through the bombs carried on his plane. My grandfather never discussed this aspect of the war, although I am sure the medal served as a painful reminder to him of the lives he may have taken during this period. My grandfather was a very religious man and I am not sure how he could account morally for the fact that he had been responsible for killing a person. This I believe is the reason why my grandfather never wore his medals when he attended Remembrance Day ceremonies. He was not proud of what he had to do in the war and did not want to display his medals as a symbol of pride. At the same time, however, the medal was important to him because it represented his service to his country. The replica medal then, acted as a store for the emotions and memories that my grandfather had of this period in his life.

THE AURA OF THE REPLICA

Walter Benjamin (1973) has suggested that what is lost or eliminated when an art-work is reproduced is the 'aura' of the original. Factors such as who made a work of art, signs of wear or production which it may possess, or the artwork's social and physical history, cannot be reproduced and are absent from a reproduction. Although it is by no means possible to compare an artwork, made by the hands of an individual or group of individuals, with a medal produced on a large scale using machines, Benjamin's notion of aura can be continued in the context of my grand-father's medal. Instead of losing its aura when it was lost, my grandfather's medal took on a whole new set of meanings, relations, and connections, which now reside in the aura of the replica. In contrast to what Benjamin has suggested, the medal did not lose its aura when it was reproduced; instead the medal gained an aura after its reproduction when it was constituted in the performance of giving. Because the original medal was not presented to my grandfather in a traditional medal-giving ceremony, the constitution performance was attached to the replica medal and not the original. As a result the gift of the replica medal from my father to my grandfather inferred a whole new set of values on to the medal (cf. Gregory 1982), giving it an 'aura'. The aura of a thing therefore is not intrinsic to the object itself but must be constituted in performance.

THE THIRD GENERATION

For me personally I believe the medal has acted to strengthen my relationship with my grandfather, as it was a means by which he was able to communicate some of his memories to me. Through my interest in the medal and by asking questions about it I gained a sense of what my grandfather's life had been like during the war and obtained a rare insight into some of his experiences and feelings. Most impor-tantly, however, the medal reminds me of the times my brother and I spent with my grandfather, visiting various museums and talking about my grandfather's life and experiences during the war. These are memories I now cherish and they remind me of my love for my grandfather, who died in 1991. Since his death my uncle has kept the medal, along with other objects associated with it, such as his operations book and his campaign medals. The medal still plays a crucial role in my family life today because of its strong association with my grandfather.

I have asked myself the question, without the medal would these memories I now have of my grandfather still exist? Certainly I will always remember him. However, the central role of the medal in my relationship with my grandfather has caused many of these memories and associations to be focused around and pre-served by the medal. This belief is underlined by the fact that even though I was as close to my grandmother as I was my grandfather I have few memories of her. This, I believe, is because unlike my grandfather there are very few objects that I associate with my grandmother.

THE PERSONAL AND THE SOCIAL SELF

Janet Hoskins has suggested that in Kodi society there is a category of 'biographical' objects that can be identified as being both a person and a thing (1989: 436). These objects can become imbued with the characteristics of people, acting as 'surrogate selves' and 'transgressing' the boundaries between people and objects apparent in our own society (1998: 7). Like Hoskins' category of 'biographical' objects there are several stages in the life of my grandfather's medal where it has become strongly associated with certain individuals and a specific part of their personalities.

On two occasions in the medal's biography it is connected to certain aspects of the personality of my grandfather. On the first occasion my uncle tied a childhood memory of my grandfather to the medal, one that represented an important aspect of his personality: his ability to make things worse when attempting to make them better. On the second, when the replica medal acted as a source of reminiscence, it became associated with my grandfather and his life during the war years. The medal also became associated with a number of characteristics my grandmother implied my great-grandfather possessed, when she accused him of stealing the medal: a man now always viewed with suspicion, his morals questioned because of doubts as to whether he could steal from his own son.

Although modern Western culture places a lot of emphasis on the role of the individual, it is important not to lose sight of the fact that we are social beings and that the personal and social selves are infused together (Csikszentmihalyi and Rochberg-Halton 1981: 190). As Debbora Battaglia points out, 'the acting subject is not invariably or always consciously its own source of experience or recognition of selfhood, or of a sense of herself or himself as fashioned' (1995: 4): we as individu-als are not the only people who fashion or have a sense of our selfhood. We are social beings and our selfhood also exists in the consciousness of others, who are responsible for fashioning it in a particular way. This means that a thing imbued with characteristics of the self, expresses both the personal and social selves of that person: how the self is embodied in the consciousness of the individual and how it is embodied in the consciousness of others (Csikszentmihalyi and Rochberg-Halton 1981: 191). In the case of my grandfather's medal, even though the personal selves of my grandmother, grandfather and great-grandfather ceased to exist with their deaths, their social selves live on. A consciousness of the selves of these individuals not only resides in the memories of my uncle, my father and myself, it also exists in the memories and associations tied to the medal. My grandfather's medal can be seen as a vehicle through which memories and associations of the self can be stored (Weiner 1985, 1992). The medal is able to operate in this way, not because a particular individual has attached a part of her or his self on to it, but because other people recognize particular aspects of that individual's self in the stories and memories associated with the medal.

CONCLUSION

An object only becomes a thing when it is performatively constituted as one. As the biography of my grandfather's medal shows it has been performatively constituted as a thing three times in its life history. In the first instance the absence of an appropriate performative medal ceremony constituted the medal as something quite different from that originally intended when it was manufactured. The medal was not fixed with meanings associated with my grandfather and his life during 1944, and the medal did not make him proud of his achievements. When the medal went missing, through the act of speech, my grandmother was able to performatively constitute the medal, or rather the material reality of its absence, as a means of attacking the moral integrity of my great-grandfather. The absence of the medal and the symbolic nature of the empty box were then responsible for maintaining the image of my great-grandfather taking the medal. Finally, when my father gave my grandfather the replica the performative act of giving (cf. Gregory 1982) inferred a whole new set of values on to the replica medal. It not only acted to underline and maintain strong links between my grandfather and my father, the replica also became increasingly important as a means by which my grandfather was able to remember his life in the RAF. It is only at this point in the medal's life history then that the meanings and associations attached to it were close to those originally intended when the medal was manufactured.

In each of these three cases it was the performative action of people that constituted the medal as a thing rather than anything intrinsic to the medal itself. Even objects associated with war, like a medal, which carry such strong implicit meanings, are not pre-programmed: they still need to be constituted performatively by social action. The medal was manufactured to fulfil a certain role and was made with an implicit meaning in mind. Even so, without the performance of a medal-giving ceremony my grandfather's DFC did not take on those meanings and associations. Thingness therefore is not inherent in the object but in the social constitution of that object as a thing. It is the performative acts associated with the medal which have brought it to life and given it a biography, not the metal and ribbon that constitute its physical form.

Thus, the physical differences between humans and things become insignificant. Once an object has been socially constituted as a thing it can transcend the traditional barriers set up in our own society between people and objects. Through the meanings, memories and associations attached to a thing like my grandfather's medal, and the relationships of which they are a part, we are able to interact with them just as we are able to interact with other humans. Things may not be able to speak to us; however, as the biography of my grandfather's medal illustrates, once they are constituted by performative acts they are able to communicate to us certain aspects of the personalities of dead ancestors and they can act to create and maintain particular social relationships. Things play an active role within our society, just like human beings.

ACKNOWLEDGEMENTS

I would like to thank Yvonne Marshall for her invaluable advice and encouragement; without her help this chapter would never have been written. I would also like to thank John Schofield, Patrick Joy and Bill Joy for their support and guidance.

REFERENCES

Appadurai, A. (ed.) (1986) *The Social Life of Things: Commodities in Cultural Perspective*, Cambridge: Cambridge University Press.
Battaglia, D. (1995) 'Problematising the self: a thematic introduction', in Battaglia, D.(ed.), *Rhetorics of Self-Making*, London: University of California Press, pp. 1–15.
Benjamin, W. (1973) 'The work of art in the age of mechanical reproduction', in Benjamin, W. *Illuminations*, London: Fontana, pp. 219–253.
Butler, J. (1990) *Gender Trouble: Feminism and the Subversion of Identity,* London: Routledge.
Butler, J. (1993) *Bodies that Matter,* London: Routledge.
Csikszentmihalyi, M. and Rochberg-Halton, E. (1981) *The Meaning of Things: Domestic Symbols and the Self*, Cambridge: Cambridge University Press.
Gregory, C.A. (1982) *Gifts and Commodities,* London: Academic Press.
Heidegger, M. (1971) 'The thing', in Heidegger, M. *Poetry, Language, Thought*, New York: Harper and Row, pp.163–186.
Hoskins, J. (1989) On loosing and getting a head: warfare, alliance and exchange in a changing Sumba 1888–1988, *American Ethnologist* 16(3): 419–40.
Hoskins, J. (1998) *Biographical Objects: How Things Tell the Stories of People's Lives*, London: Routledge.
Joy, W.W.A. (1944) *Operations Book*, W. Joy DFC (unpublished).
Litherland, A.R. and Simpkin, B.T. (1990) *Spinks Standard Catalogue of British and Associated Orders, Decorations and Medals, with Valuations,* London: Spink.
Rainbird, P. (1999) Entangled biographies: western Pacific ceramics and the tombs of Pohnpei, *World Archaeology* 31: 214–44.
Taprell-Dorling, H. (1960) *Ribbons and Medals: Naval, Military, Air Force and Civil,* London: George Philip.
Tilley, C.Y. (1989) 'Interpreting material culture', in Hodder, I.R. (ed.), *The Meaning of Things*, London: Unwin Hyman, pp.185–194.
Weiner, A.B. (1985) Inalienable wealth, *American Ethnologist* 12: 210–27.
Weiner, A.B. (1992) *Inalienable Possessions: The Paradox of Keeping-While-Giving,* Oxford: University of California Press.

13 Monuments and the memories of war: motivations for preserving military sites in England

John Schofield

Over the past decade twentieth-century defences, fortifications and experimental and military production sites have become an accepted part of the cultural heritage (Dobinson *et al.* 1997; English Heritage 1998; Schofield 1999; Cocroft 2000). For heritage managers, planners, archaeologists and historians this has meant coming to terms with a new vocabulary, and intricate typologies for such things as anti-invasion defences of the Second World War, radar establishments and coastal artillery. It has also meant the need for some grounding in scientific principles, particularly relevant for studying radar and Cold War facilities, as well as in artillery and ballistics. It has meant new conservation challenges, such as the practical measures for prolonging the lives of concrete structures designed to last only 'for the duration'. It has meant developing an approach to interpretation that balances the various needs of cultural tourism with the emotions these sites often provoke. And – significantly – it has meant close cooperation between heritage professionals and those amateur archaeologists and historians who have been responsible for much valuable groundwork over the last thirty years or so (Wills 1985; Morris 1998). But why has this willingness to embrace recent military heritage been taken up with such enthusiasm and alacrity? What are the motivations for conserving what are often ugly, functional and unstable buildings? And why in particular is it important that some of the buildings and structures remain when publicly available records are known to exist, and where recording prior to demolition provides a lasting archaeological record for reference and research? These related issues form the subject of this chapter, with the emphasis here on some specific aspects of the Second World War in England: the Battle of Britain in late summer of 1940; the urban Blitz of 1940–1; and the embarkation for D-Day in 1944. It is argued that monuments relating to these episodes of the war have a particular role as 'living memorials', and this reason for their retention will form the basis of discussion.

MOTIVATIONS

In England, as elsewhere, work has been underway for some years with the aim of understanding recent military remains sufficiently to provide a credible assessment of their importance and to inform options for their future management

(Dobinson *et al.* 1997; English Heritage 1998). This assessment operates at three levels: in a holistic sense, for the subject matter as a whole (that is, twentieth-century military sites); for individual monument classes (such as anti-aircraft gunsites); and – within each of those classes – for the sites themselves.

Beginning at the most general level, several considerations are relevant. A concern often cited is that retaining the fabric of recent wars only serves to delay the healing process, and prolong what are often bitter historical tensions and rivalries. Virilio (1994), for example, has noted how German fortifications along the French coast continue to provoke responses of hostility (several bunkers sporting hostile graffiti), bewilderment (passers-by rarely recognizing the bunkers as archaeological), hatred and vengeance. These last two are perhaps the most interesting of these: many installations were destroyed when France was liberated – basements were filled with munitions and blown up, the explosions 'delighting the countryside's inhabitants as in a summary execution' (1994: 13). In studying these sites during the 1970s, Virilio recalls being told by local inhabitants how they frightened them and called back too many bad memories. '[They provoked] fantasies too, because the reality of the German occupation was elsewhere, most often in banal administrative lodgings for the Gestapo; but the blockhouses were the symbols of soldiery' (ibid.).

Then there is the extent to which the past provides 'lessons for the future'; 'the same mistakes will never be made again'. Yet they are repeated, and they continue to be repeated today in the many internal conflicts and ethnic wars to emerge from the ending of the Cold War. The horrors of the Holocaust are well documented, and some of the key sites are preserved (one is a World Heritage Site). Films such as *Schindler's List* reveal the atrocities to a new generation. Yet as cinema audiences recoiled from the gruesome scenes in a Hollywood movie, the Muslim population of Bosnia was reliving them (Rupesinghe 1998: 1). In this particular instance, therefore, the preservation of concentration camps, combined with films, books and engaging museum displays such as at the Holocaust Museum in Washington DC (Weinberg and Elieli 1995), appears to have had little influence on preventing a repetition of past atrocities.

Despite these arguments, however, there is a consensus that some recent military sites should be preserved for the benefit of this and future generations, and several reasons for this are generally given. Prominent among these is the fact that the materiality of war crystallises military thought, as well as providing reference points or landmarks to the totalitarian nature of war in space and myth (Virilio and Lotringer 1997: 10). It is a part of the heritage which tells a fascinating story and as such provides a significant cultural and educational resource, illustrating the key events of the twentieth century, Hobsbawm's 'age of extremes' (1995). Even the humble pillbox can provide an opening to the experiences of war: the imminence of invasion; the scale and speed of the construction task; the nature and mobility of 'total' mechanized warfare; 'children's playful warring … after the real warring' (Virilio 1994: 15). As we'll see, purpose-built slips, from which troops embarked for D-Day, provide a focus for commemoration and remembrance services. Bomb sites like Coventry Cathedral provide a physical reminder of the scale of civic destruction, as well as a context for the act of personal and collective remembrance.

These values exist in the contrast the cathedral provides between the powerfully destructive forces of war, and the tranquility of enclosed spaces in the modern townscape. And finally control towers, which often survive as ruins on desolate airfields, stand as powerfully iconic structures of the air war, and provide a focus for the memories of veterans who continue to return to the airfields on which they served.

As a part of the heritage, therefore, war – and especially the Second World War – has educational and emotive values which give its matériel culture particular resonance. And, though not unique to this subject matter, there is the additional benefit of personal testimony. It is often difficult to present the past through personal experiences; through real people whose lives and whose involvement in world events can be closely documented. But the availability (and accessibility) of military records is conducive to detailed studies, not only of the famous (see for example Morris 1995), but also of family members and friends who served in the war in whatever capacity. In addition to these personal testimonies – some in the form of diaries written at the time, some as reflective accounts – official record books and other military records place individuals in certain contexts at specific times; while names on memorials, alongside medals and other militaria, provide an immediate and personal reference point to past events and lives (Chippindale 1997: 509; Joy this volume). This is a past with real people whose lives can be investigated through documents, testimony and places. And this potential to move beyond the impersonal has been realized in increasingly engaging ways (Schofield in press a). The Holocaust Museum, Washington DC, 'heightens empathy by making the horrific legacy intensely personal: each visitor wears the identity tag of a specific victim, a ghostly companion whose persona the visitor adopts and whose fate is disclosed, with haunting impact, at the tour's end' (Lowenthal 1997: 142). Similarly, at the In Flanders Fields Museum at Ypres, visitors are assigned real historical characters. As they pass through the museum they learn the destiny of this person. As the curator explains: 'The museum is a place of encounter – an encounter with people of 1914–18 – not only soldiers, but doctors, nurses, writers, artists and children'.

In general terms, therefore, these sites and monuments of war are of immense value, both for those involved in the events being recalled, and their memories, but for this and future generations too. The remains have cultural and educational benefit, as well as economic potential, if marketed effectively (and for it to be effective it must also be *affective*, see Schofield and Anderton 2000; Schofield in press a). But, of course not everything can be retained, and the real challenge lies in making a selection that satisfies all these needs and motivations. What follows is an example of how this issue has been addressed in England (for further details of the underlying principles relating to heritage management in England, see Startin 1993).

VALUES

In England, all legislation and non-legislative government advice relating to the historic environment currently hinges on the related issues of character (or typicality) and significance. Under the terms of the 1979 Ancient Monuments and

Archaeological Areas Act, for example, sites will be considered for statutory protection through scheduling only where they constitute 'buildings, structures or
works or the remains thereof' and where they are demonstrably of national importance. Additional sites will have value for other reasons, relating to local character
perhaps, and sense of place. Significantly, however, not all nationally important
sites are or need to be scheduled. First, scheduling is discretionary, and second,
planning guidance (Planning Policy Guidance [PPG]16, Department of the Environment [DoE] 1990), issued by the government, states that there should be a pre-
sumption in favour of in situ preservation for nationally important remains *whether
scheduled or not*. The situation for buildings is similar: to be listed it must be of special architectural or historic interest. On character, current Historic Landscape
Characterisation projects look at the modern landscape and the historic layers and
processes that have created it with a view to influencing future planning policies
and decisions at a local level. And militarization is a relevant consideration in this;
during the Cold War for example it had a major influence on the physical appearance and 'personality' of certain regions – in England these included East Anglia,
and especially Lincolnshire.

For sites, buildings and monuments, relative importance is thus key to imple-
menting conservation policies in England, while the character of some areas of
landscape betray the significant influence of a military presence. In all these
respects, the role of English Heritage is to advise the government department (currently the Department of Culture, Media and Sport) on such heritage matters, to
recommend designations through listing and scheduling as appropriate, and to provide strategic advice to the local authorities responsible for managing the heritage at
a local level. To ensure success, both with the Department, with local authorities
and in subsequent dealings with the owners and occupiers of what are predominantly privately-owned sites, the advice issued must have a sound basis, and recommendations must be sustainable given the other available conservation options.

For many monument types a long history of research has generated the sound
understanding necessary for these purposes. It is known how many Neolithic long
barrows there are, where they are, how well preserved they all are, how vulnerable
and so on. Similarly, a sound understanding of many types of industrial monument
now exists, following a national review of the subject (Stocker 1995). Recent military sites have now reached this same level of understanding and awareness (better
in fact, as we know the original population from which the surviving sample is
derived). The approach taken by English Heritage's Monuments Protection
Programme (MPP) is documented more fully elsewhere (Dobinson *et al.* 1997),
but in general terms the aim has been to provide basic information on
distribribution, typology and chronology for ten major classes of twentieth-century
military sites, as well as documenting their historic context in order to inform
owners and other interested parties of their wider historic significance.

The approach is archive led. Official documents held at the Public Record Office
are generally released, under the terms of the Public Records Act, thirty years after
closure. For the Second World War, documents were opened in bulk in 1972 but
only consulted systematically as part of the MPP's project (the work undertaken by

Dr Colin Dobinson). Contrary to what had been believed (and stated in some publications) previously, documentary sources for Britain's twentieth-century fortifications are preserved in staggering quantities (though are only accessible up to 1970 for the Cold War period). The form of material varies widely: during the war most military units maintained daily records of their activities, and tens of thousands of these, many of them extensive narratives, are preserved. In addition, all service and civil departments created paperwork covering their activities throughout the war; much of this material is preserved in its original form. The range of this material is vast (Cantwell 1993).

The MPP survey has two main aims. First, to reconstruct the full original distribution and dating of military sites in eight major categories, and representative distributions of another two whose populations of minor works were too large to reconstruct original distributions (see Dobinson *et al.* 1997 for details of the monument classes included in this survey). Second, sets of original type drawings are recovered, showing the layouts and component parts of all categories of site. Produced by military works departments and the drawing offices at higher-level headquarters, these drawings form a ready-made typology for examples surviving in the field today. Dates on the drawings also provide a *terminus post quem* for surviving examples, making it possible for the first time to offer basic dating on many structures through criteria observable in the field.

Therefore it is now possible to produce distribution maps for the first time showing, for example, the positions of anti-aircraft gun-sites at various points throughout the Second World War, and to cross-refer such things as the distribution of anti-aircraft gun-sites with that of bombing decoys (dummies, constructed in remote areas to deceive enemy bombers and detract from the intended targets, cf. Dobinson 2000). It is now known how many sites there were, what they all looked like, where they were and when they were there. It is also possible to measure the shifting scale of Britain's anti-aircraft and anti-invasion provision against political events, such as Operation Barbarossa – the German invasion of the Soviet Union. There is also a social dimension: for example at the time of Barbarossa, Britain's heavy anti-aircraft gun-sites were welcoming women soldiers for the first time, to act as instrument operators and technicians. This is significant for two reasons: first, these 'mixed batteries' could represent the first units in which women took a combatant role in the army of any modern industrialized country (Pile 1949: 194); second, it represents a landmark in Britain's increasingly deep commitment to 'Total War'. And the archaeological record tells this story: gun-site buildings were redesigned with a centrally-heated concrete command post, and revised layout (and standard) of amenities. Women were given more space per person, better buildings, more bathrooms; twin domestic camps appear for the first time.

Having consulted primary sources, a methodology was then developed for assessing which of these documented sites survive. Using staff at Aerial Survey (the work undertaken by Mike Anderton), each gazetteer entry for anti-aircraft sites, bombing decoys, radar establishments and coast batteries was checked on modern aerial photographs. Beyond the lists of sites as built, this has generated a second listing, itemizing those sites which survive and how complete they are in relation to their original form and extent (Anderton and Schofield 1999; Schofield in press b; Anderton forthcoming). The results suggest that comparatively few of the sites in the above categories survive, with their removal due to a variety of factors: urbanization, agricultural intensification and light industry are the main ones, while many coastal batteries, located predominantly on England's east coast, have succumbed to coast erosion. Future rates of coast erosion can now be accurately predicted so it is possible to establish how long the surviving examples will remain. This is essential information for assessing the sustainability of long-term protection and priorities for recording.

Other approaches have been devised for the remaining classes of monument. For airfields a combined approach has been developed, placing airfield defences within the context of airfields as a whole (see Lake, this volume). For Cold War sites an initial recording programme, designed to document exemplars representing the full range of Cold War remains in England, was completed in 1999 (Cocroft and Thomas forthcoming). The results of this survey, combined with MPP's contextual study, will be useful in establishing national importance, before economic considerations (and specifically the interests of the Ministry of Defence) play a part in determining appropriate management regimes for the key sites. For the Cold War in particular, technology provides overlap with some aspects of industrial archaeology, and as with industrial archaeology it is important for future understanding that technological processes are addressed, accepting that these often involved sites on opposite sides of the world. Rocket-testing establishments connected with Blue Streak, for instance, extend from Spadeadam in Northumbria, to the Isle of Wight (both in England), to Woomera in Australia (Cocroft 2000: 255–61).

Clearly Cold War sites will present particular difficulties, given the scale of some operations, the conservation challenge which some structures present (for example with space-related sites cf. London III 1993), and health and safety issues, not to mention classified information and access restrictions. There is also a further international dimension and the role of the protest movement to consider (Schofield and Anderton 2000), as well as the possible contradiction between what we ('the West') consider significant, and what was identified as such during the Cold War by Eastern Bloc countries (McCrystal and Higgins 1998).

Finally there are the many (perhaps nearing a million) anti-invasion defences, most thrown up in sixteen weeks during the summer of 1940 to counter an expected German invasion. Here a national initiative related to but separate from MPP's work – the Defence of Britain Project – has the aim of using volunteers to record these structures (Finn 2000), while a local initiative has already produced a quantification of surviving sites in Essex (Nash 1998). A comparison of the results from these separate studies is interesting. The Essex survey reveals that 56 per cent of pillboxes survive of the c.800 originally built in the county, while the national study has to date recorded 6245 pillboxes (31 per cent) of the estimated 20 000 built. The explanation for this discrepancy (if indeed it proves to be such) will be interesting and will no doubt reflect regional trends in post-war development. Either way the results confirm the need for selecting anti-invasion defences for protection, and ensuring that that selection has credibility in being both representative and sustainable as well as having coherence in terms of understanding how the defence provision would have worked in harmony with related natural and artificial features. Where so many – often now isolated – structures survive, group value will be a significant consideration.

From this discussion of general principles stem three specific examples of the approach taken by MPP towards monument classes associated with offensive and counter-offensive operations in the Second World War. These classes present a particular challenge for conservation, being those most directly associated with a combination of human suffering and loss of life and, in the case of the Blitz, with the destruction of cultural property and civilian losses. By briefly describing the materiality of these aspects of warfare, the role the sites play in contemporary society will be assessed.

EXAMPLES

Bomb sites

The aerial bombing of civilian targets has its origins in the First World War, but is better known as a characterizing feature of the Second World War which reached a climax with the dropping of atomic bombs on Hiroshima and Nagasaki to bring the Pacific War to a close. Between 1939 and 1945 British and German towns and cities were subject to often intense aerial bombardment: in Britain, for example, over 60 000 civilians were killed and more than 86 000 seriously injured as a result of aerial bombing alone. Many town and city centres were badly damaged, requiring planning and regeneration in the immediate post-war years.

As we have seen, the assessment of some archaeological remains associated with aerial bombing has been undertaken by MPP, covering anti-aircraft gun-sites, Diver sites (for defence against the flying bomb, 1944–5), bombing decoys (Dobinson 2000), radar, civil defence (air raid shelters), airfields and aircraft crash sites (Holyoak in preparation). Urban areas affected by damage have been assessed in the past, but only in terms of the potential for surviving buried remains within damaged areas and the opportunity that these provide for archaeological research in the conventional sense. But attention has now turned to assessing these remains as bomb sites, while exploring conservation options for this part of the historic resource. That this wasn't undertaken before 1999 is surprising given that arguments about conservation and regeneration at various notable sites were well rehearsed during the war and in the immediate post-war years. St Michael's Cathedral, Coventry was the only one of Britain's (then) 59 cathedrals to suffer badly from bomb damage. Its surviving shell became 'a symbol of the wastefulness of war' and the decision was taken to retain it next to a new cathedral. Similarly, the church of Holy Trinity, Plymouth, still stands as a ruin. After it was bombed the church authorities decided not to rebuild, or to remove the ruin as part of the city's redevelopment; it was finally purchased in 1957 by the Plymouth Corporation, 'to be preserved as a memorial to all the civilians of the city who lost their lives during the war from enemy air attacks'. This approach to the conservation of ruined structures was in fact a global response in the immediate post-war years. In Berlin, the Kaiser-Wilhelm Gedachtnig Kirche was levelled by bombing raids, except for the western spire and portal which, after some debate, were preserved as a 'memorial to peace'. In Hiroshima, the Atomic Bomb Dome, the former Prefectural Industrial Promotion Hall, is the only ruin left from the atomic bomb and forms the centrepiece of the Peace Memorial Park. In fact only days after the bombing of Hiroshima newspapers stated that '(all) ruins should be left as memorials', but only on the false premise that the city could not now be occupied for seventy years (Toyofumi 1994: 39).

As well as select bomb sites of the Second World War, more recent examples of bomb damage have also entered the debate about the relative merits of: conservation as ruins and memorials; clearance for urban regeneration; or rebuilding. This was one of the issues debated at a World Archaeological Congress Inter-Congress on 'The Destruction and Conservation of Cultural Property', Croatia, May 1998 (Layton *et al.* 2001). For example, clearance for urban rebuilding and regeneration (with archaeological conditions) is occurring in Beirut, although 308 historic structures will be restored, chosen because of their architectural, historic or religious significance (Raschka 1996).

Usually, where sites of obvious heritage merit are concerned, rebuilding is favoured, with the sites' symbolic value often being enhanced as a result. Some churches and civic structures were restored in England after World War II for example, often to act as the centrepieces of visionary post-war redevelopments (as at St Giles Cripplegate, London). Following the launch of the Northern Ireland Assembly (1 July 1998), ten Catholic churches in the Province were fire-bombed – talk was immediately of rebuilding, 'whatever the cost'. St Ethelburga, Bishopsgate is now known as much as the church rebuilt after being partially destroyed by an IRA bomb in 1993, as it is as the smallest church in London. After rebuilding, its role is as a 'Centre for Peace' (The Ecclesiological Society 1994). Finally, the Ottoman bridge at Mostar, shelled and destroyed by Croat militiamen, symbolized the idea of a multi-cultural Bosnia, but was targeted as part of the destruction of the identity of an entire people. Rebuilding the bridge was controversial, many regarding it as an empty gesture, merely recreating a checkpoint between Croatian and Bosnian controlled parts of the city: a road to nowhere. But a poll of residents in eastern Mostar – mainly Muslims – felt the bridge should be the last monument of that conflict reconstructed: 'for shame, for mourning', as one resident put it (Dodds 1998).

Attitudes to bomb damage therefore will vary, depending on social, economic, cultural and political arguments. However, in England, and in the present climate of sustainability and urban regeneration, it is those structures which 55–60 years on remain as ruins (and which to some are 'eyesores') that present a particular conservation dilemma between heritage and economic and social interests. Two points are of particular relevance here.

First, bomb sites may have been significant structures prior to being damaged, as well as now having value as memorials. Furthermore there may be sites whose main heritage interest rests in their being situated within areas of nationally important buried (and earlier) deposits. On the other hand are sites where neither of these conventional heritage values applies. What all these sites have in common, however, is the degree to which they have accumulated a *symbolic* value over the last 55–60 years, some almost instantaneously (like the Atomic Bomb Dome), and some more gradually. Some of these sites have international significance in these terms (Coventry, Berlin, Hiroshima), while knowledge of others is more locally based, such as the bombed cinema in Kingston-upon-Hull. This National Picture Theatre only came to public knowledge following a recent local campaign to see the ruin converted to a memorial garden. While no one died in the bombing it does stand as the last obvious and tangible reminder of the Blitz in one of the worst-hit cities in Britain.

Given the extent to which towns and cities subjected to aerial bombing during the Second World War were planned and redeveloped in the post-war years, it is not surprising that so few bomb sites now stand as ruins. Many town centres were cleared and redeveloped to a new plan, while others were rebuilt, with some of the ruins restored. It is estimated that in England some 20–30 buildings damaged in the Blitz, and otherwise during the Second World War, now stand as ruins. Significance can be demonstrated for all of these, first in terms of the rarity of these structures, amounting on average to less than one bomb site per major targeted city (a few more survive in London), and second in the degree to which they represent a significant episode of twentieth-century world history. It is these ruins, and not gun emplacements and airfields, which serve to reify *civilian* casualties and *civic* destruction during the Second World War. They therefore have a significant role in: the commemoration of the war and of its casualties; providing a focus for educational initiatives which can be emotional and engaging; highlighting the character and effects of 'Total War' and its impact on infrastructure and the population as a whole; and contributing to local character.

Second is the argument that regeneration of urban areas damaged by bombing is a better and more fitting memorial than hanging on to the past. This was the subject of recent debate surrounding the Hermitage site, east London where a levelled area undeveloped since its destruction in the Blitz was proposed as the site for a major Thames-side redevelopment, albeit with memorial gardens (Ramsey 1997). As was said in a meeting of survivors at Hiroshima in 1951, 'If Hiroshima rises from the ruins left by the atom bomb to become a finer and more beautiful city than any other, won't that be a great thing for the world peace movement?' (Toyofumi 1994: 54). This argument had strength when rebuilding itself was a symbol of determination to make a new start whilst defying the bombing. However, considering Hiroshima's status now as International Peace City, it is the one bomb site to have been retained – the Atomic Bomb Dome – which provides the visual link to past events, and which acts as the focus for all commemoration and tourist activity.

It can be argued that to retain these tangible reminders doesn't necessarily require conservation of entire structures, and that a facade may be sufficient for purposes of representation. But that denies the significance of space. St Mary Aldermanbury in London, for example, bombed in the Blitz, stood as a ruined shell until 1965 when it was dismantled stone by stone and transported for re-erection in

Missouri as a memorial to Churchill and his Iron Curtain speech there in 1946. Importantly, however, the site remains as open space, with the twelve Corinthian columns and part of the lower courses still *in situ,* giving the site a character in keeping with its original function, the effects of war on civic pride, urban fabric and the wartime and post-war history of the building itself. It still therefore represents a space, within an urban setting, where the effects of the Blitz can be recalled or imagined. While the ruin may contribute more to local character, the space it contains reflects better the impact of bombing, allowing the site to function as a heritage resource, a place of memory, as well as having value for other (for example nature conservation and quality of life) interests. Collectively these small enclosed spaces are an important feature of the urban scene, and are sustainable by virtue of being in scale with their close-knit townscapes.

D-Day sites

As part of MPP's wider survey of twentieth-century military remains, a study of D-Day embarkation sites was undertaken based on archive sources (Dobinson 1996). This study provided details of the 68 embarkation sites identified in historical sources representing those built specifically to serve general cross-Channel operations from 1942 and the extension to that group built to serve Operation Neptune, the assault phase of Overlord. The study also describes the political and military strategic background to Overlord: after 2–3 years of preparations:

> [T]he Operation's assault phase lasted for little over three weeks from midnight on June 6th. By 30 June over 850 000 men had been landed on the invasion beachheads, together with nearly 150 000 vehicles and 570 000 tons of supplies. Assembled in camps and transit areas over the preceding months, this force was dispatched from a string of sites along Britain's coastline between East Anglia and South Wales.
>
> (Dobinson 1996: 2)

Additional work by English Heritage and others has demonstrated that all aspects of the preparations for D-Day in England can be identified in the material record, including: the mulberry harbour construction sites; the maintenance and repair areas for landing craft and ships; the camps occupied in the weeks prior to embarkation; the widening of roads to accommodate troop and vehicular movement; training areas; supply facilities; the Pipeline Under the Ocean (known as PLUTO); and decoys to deceive enemy reconnaissance (Schofield 2001). But of all these, one aspect of the Operation merits particular mention when considering remembrance: the embarkation sites.

Embarkation sites are among the best preserved of these related classes of monument, partly a result of their having to be well designed and well built in advance if embarkation was to be a rapid and efficient exercise. (Geographically the sites had to have access to hinterlands in which large numbers of troops and supplies could be concealed from enemy reconnaissance, yet which had the road and rail networks to allow their easy movement at the time of departure. Most embarkation hardstandings (or 'hards') were built in the period October 1942 to spring 1943.) However, the principal reason for their survival was the extent to which these sites were memorialized in the post-war period.

Embarkation sites were either in modified docks, quays or harbours (such as Southampton Docks) or were constructed specifically for the purpose. Two main types of loading facility were used: LCT hards for 'landing craft, troops' and LST hards for 'landing ship, tanks'. Although LST hards were the most numerous, the two types were broadly similar. Each had: a concrete apron (solid concrete above high water, and flexible concrete matting below), and a series of 'dolphins' or mooring points; also hutting for offices, workshops and stores; fuelling facilities; electric lighting and roads and transit areas (see Dobinson 1996: 14–18 for details). Survival tends to be confined to those hards built specifically for the purpose (those in existing docks having been redeveloped in the post-war period): Torquay (Torbay), Brixham (Devon), Turnaware, Polgerran Wood, Tolverne and Polgwidden (Cornwall), Lepe (Hampshire), Stone Point and Stansgate (Essex), and the hards at Upnor (Kent) are among the best preserved.

There are obvious benefits in retaining all well-preserved structures associated with D-Day for their cultural and historic value, but in terms of remembrance and commemoration the embarkation slipways have particular resonance. These were the places from which 850 000 men embarked in early June 1944, many of whom died on the Normandy beaches. Most embarkation sites have small memorials to this effect. At Tolverne the entire site is presented as a memorial, with information and displays comprising text and contemporary photographs set out to one side of the original concrete apron. A road sign indicates the presence of this 'D-Day embarkation beach', which visitors then access along a 2–3 km stretch of the original concrete road, passing the bases of contemporary Nissen huts along the way. This is a popular spot where one learns a great deal about the scale of the Operation in Cornwall. The nearby site at Turnaware has a different atmosphere altogether. Again access is via the original concrete road, though here the site is remote, quiet and tranquil. The site has no signage and following the tracks through the trees down to the beach, examining traces of vehicle tracking in the concrete and traces of Nissen huts, the character and significance of the place is tangible. For these different reasons, both sites will be considered for protection.

However, of all these embarkation sites, the substantial concrete slipways at Torquay stand out, dominating the modern harbour. Surprisingly, they are not advertised in any way and their historical significance is not obvious to the many visitors the town attracts. In fact the men of the 77th Infantry Division, destined for Utah Beach, embarked from here, and it is here every four years that the Normandy Veterans hold a commemoration service on the harbourside at the head of the slips (Figs. 13.1–13.2). To coincide with the 56th anniversary of embarkation, on 6 June 2000, these structures were afforded protection by the Secretary of State, much to the delight of the veterans. Thus the Torquay slips now have recognition as structures of particular importance for commemorative and historic reasons.

Figure 13.1 The Torquay slipways

Source: Author

Figure 13.2 6 June 2000: Normandy veterans and members of a re-enactment group at the
D-Day commemoration service, Torquay

Source: Dr John Salvatore

Figure 13.3 The ruinous control tower on Davidstow Moor, Cornwall

Source: Author

Control towers

In recalling the air war, control towers (or watch offices as they are sometimes known) provide a focus for the attentions of enthusiasts, historians, film makers and veterans. These are the structures which arguably most reflect the character of the air war, and which symbolize the losses incurred. It was from here that aircraft movements were controlled, and therefore it was here that losses were often first registered. While Operations Rooms have a similarly symbolic role in recalling these events, the control towers have a visual appeal which makes them obvious and iconic structures in the modern landscape (Fig. 13.3); furthermore, they contribute significantly to sense of place and local identity.

English Heritage's approach to managing control towers takes this into account. In all around 450 control towers existed in England during the Second World War, some 220 of which survive in some form today. This c.50 per cent survival rate is much higher than that for most other classes of Second World War monument and is likely to reflect the commemorative values these structures imbue and have imbued since the end of the Second World War. By selecting the best-preserved structures, and those with original fittings and fixtures, only those towers which have remained in use or which have been adapted to new uses would be retained. Some of these examples will indeed be protected through listing. Many of the towers are now ruined, however, and some of these no longer bear any obvious relationship to their flying field, or other components of the airfield such as hangars. Yet in the case of Battle of Britain airfields, or those associated with the bombing campaign or the Battle of the Atlantic, ruinous and isolated towers still remain hugely significant for reasons of iconicity described earlier.

To balance these various factors, and to ensure the selection takes in good surviving examples as well as those ruins whose values are more symbolic and connected with remembrance and commemoration, a set of criteria was developed for selecting control towers for protection. In short, control towers may be identified as significant for any, or a combination of, the following reasons:

1   Where a well-preserved structure survives with original features, being exemplary of its type – and there were eighteen main types of control tower in all (Paul Francis, personal communication): for example Duxford, which now houses part of the Imperial War Museum and has an unmodified tower, acknowledged as the best of its type.
2   Where the tower stands on a site that has operational significance, such as Tangmere, with its strong ties with the Battle of Britain.
3   Where the site has historic interest, but for non-operational reasons: for instance Twinwood Farm, the station from which Glenn Miller flew on his ill-fated flight.
4   Where the control tower has an obvious and visual relationship to contemporary surviving fabric or the flying field, such as Catterick, where the relationship to the grass airfield and airfield defences can be clearly seen.

By selecting sites on this basis, some 55–60 control towers will be considered for protection. Some have continued in use and remain as control towers; others are ruinous structures (Fig. 13.3). Either way a selection will remain – to remind and inform future generations of the air war, a characterizing feature of the twentieth century; to contribute to local character; to act as the focus for remembrance and commemorative events; and, at a more personal level, to act as a catalyst for memory and remembering amongst veterans and their families.

CONCLUSIONS

This chapter has described the approach taken in England towards managing recent military remains, and the motivations for preserving a selection of sites. It has also shown how those surviving monuments provide a focus both for commemorative events, and for remembrance as well as having historical interest. Often these are places for quiet reflection, but which also have strong visual impact, providing a physical record of significant wartime events.

The Second World War is remembered in many different ways in England: by anniversaries, commemoration and remembrance services, visits to museums, in educational curricula, airshows, television broadcasts and other popular media. But what all of these also need are some of the places where these events unfolded, and which provide touchstones to the past. These aren't just historic sites, however, like prehistoric burial mounds and hillforts; these are also memorials to the events of the Second World War, and to warfare generally. As with the physical remains of First World War battlefields, for example at Vimy Ridge and Beaumont Hamel (Cave 2000), these are often sacred sites and as such should engage the visitor, and provoke emotions which bring the events of sixty years ago into sharp focus. Arguably, those sites associated directly with loss of life, personal tragedy and civic destruction to cultural property (D-Day embarkation sites, bomb sites and airfields) provide the best opportunities for engaging the events of the Second World War in this way. It is primarily for that reason that representative examples of these classes of monument are being protected or retained in England for the benefit of this and future generations.

ACKNOWLEDGEMENTS

A version of this chapter was originally presented as a paper at the World Archaeological Congress, Cape Town in January 1999, and was pre-circulated on the WAC4 website. I am grateful to Rose Malik for assistance with the section on bomb sites, and to Paul Francis for information on control towers, supplied as part of a project commissioned by MPP. Graham Fairclough, Jeremy Lake and Jez Reeve have made helpful comments on aspects of the chapter at various stages of its production.

REFERENCES

Anderton, M. (forthcoming) *An Aerial Photographic Assessment of WWII Sites Surviving in England*, London: English Heritage.

Anderton, M. and Schofield, J. (1999) Anti-aircraft gunsites – then and now, *Conservation Bulletin* 36: 11–13.

Cantwell, J.D. (1993) *The Second World War: A Guide to Documents in the Public Record Office*, London: HMSO.

Cave, N. (2000) Battlefield Conservation: First International Workshop in Arras 29 February–4 March 2000, *Battlefields Review* 10: 41–60.

Chippindale, C. (1997) Editorial, *Antiquity* 71(273): 505–12.

Cocroft, W.D. (2000) *Dangerous Energy: The Archaeology of Gunpowder and Military Explosives Manufacture*, London: English Heritage.

Cocroft, W.D. and Thomas, R.J.C. (forthcoming) *Monuments of the Cold War*, English Heritage.

Dobinson, C. (1996) 'Twentieth Century Fortifications in England. Volume 5: Operation Overlord', unpublished report for Council for British Archaeology/English Heritage.

Dobinson, C. (2000) *Fields of Deception: Bombing Decoys of World War Two*, London: Methuen.

Dobinson, C., Lake, J. and Schofield, A.J. (1997) Monuments of war: defining England's 20th-century defence heritage, *Antiquity* 71(272): 288–99.

Dodds, J.D. (1998) Bridge over the Neretva, *Archaeology* 51(1): 48–53.

DoE (1990) *Planning Policy Guidance Note 16: Archaeology and Planning*, London: HMSO.

English Heritage (1998) *Monuments of War: The Evaluation, Recording and Management of 20th Century Military Sites*, London: English Heritage.

Finn, C. (2000) Defiant Britain: mapping the bunkers and pillboxes built to stymie a Nazi invasion, *Archaeology* 53(3): 42–9.

Hobsbawm, E. (1995) *Age of Extremes: The Short Twentieth Century, 1914–91*, London: Abacus.

Holyoak, V. (in prep.) *The Archaeology of Military Aircraft Crash Sites*.

Layton, R., Stone, P., Thomas, J. and Roa, N. (2001) *Destruction and Restoration of Cultural Property*, Routledge: One World Archaeology 41.

London III, J.R. (1993) The preservation of space-related historic sites, *Journal of the British Interplanetary Society* 46: 279–85.

Lowenthal, D. (1997) *The Heritage Crusade and the Spoils of History*, Viking.

McCrystal, C. and Higgins, A. (1998) How (and where) the Russians planned to annihilate you, *The Observer*, 10 May 1998.

Morris, R. (1998) Amateurs all the way, *Defence Lines* 11: 7–9.

Morris, R., with Dobinson, C. (1995) *Guy Gibson*, Harmondsworth: Penguin.

Nash, F. (1998) 'Anti-Invasion Defences in Essex', unpublished Essex County Council report.

Pile, F. (1949) *Ack-ack: Britain's Defences against Air Attack during the Second World War*, London: Harrap.

Ramsey, W.G. (1997) Memorial to the London Blitz, *After the Battle* 96: 20–5.

Raschka, M. (1996) Beirut digs out, *Archaeology* 49(4): 44–50.

Rupersinghe, K. (1998) *Civil Wars, Civil Peace: An Introduction to Conflict Resolution*, London and Sterling VA: Pluto Press.

Schofield, J. (1999) 'Conserving recent military remains: choices and challenges for the 21st century', in Baker, D. and Chitty, G. (eds) *Presentation and Preservation: Conflict or Collaboration?*, London: English Heritage and Routledge, pp. 173–86.

Schofield, J. (2001) D-Day sites in England: an assessment, *Antiquity* 75(287): 77–83.

Schofield, J. (in press a) 'Jessie's cats and other stories: presenting and interpreting recent troubles', in Blockley, M. *et al.* (eds) *Heritage Interpretation: Theory and Practice*, London: English Heritage and Routledge.

Schofield, J. (in press b) 'The role of aerial photographs in national strategic programmes: assessing recent military sites in England', in Bewley, B. and Raczkowski, W. (eds) *Aerial Archaeology: Developing Future Practice,* 269–82, NATO Technical Handbook: IOS Press.

Schofield, J. and Anderton, M. (2000) 'The queer archaeology of Green Gate: interpreting contested space at Greenham Common Airbase', in Dowson, T. (ed.) *Queer Archaeologies,* World Archaeology 32(2): 235–50, Routledge.

Startin, B. (1993) 'Assessment of field remains', in Hunter, J. and Ralston, I. (eds) *Archaeological Resource Management in the UK: An Introduction*, Stroud: Alan Sutton/Institute of Field Archaeologists, pp.184–96.

Stocker, D. (1995) 'Industrial archaeology and the Monuments Protection Programme in England', in Palmer, M. and Neaverson, P. (eds) *Managing the Industrial Heritage: Its Identification, Recording and Management*, Leicester Archaeology Monographs no.2, Leicester: Leicester University Press, pp. 105–13.

The Ecclesiological Society (1994) *The Past, Present and Future of St Ethelburga Bishopsgate, Partially Destroyed by Bomb, April 24th 1993*, London.

Toyofumi, O. (1994) *The Atomic Bomb and Hiroshima*, Tokyo: Liber Press.

Virilio, P. (1994) *Bunker Archeology*, Paris: Les Editions du Demi-Cercle.

Virilio, P. and Lotringer, S. (1997) *Pure War* (Revised edn), Semiotext(e) Foreign Agents Series.

Weinberg, J. and Elieli, R. (1995) *The Holocaust Museum in Washington*, New York: Rizzoli.

Wills, H. (1985) *Pillboxes: A Study of UK Defences 1940*, London: Leo Cooper.

14   'So suspicious of enemies': Australia's late nineteenth- and twentieth-century coastal defences, their archaeology and interpretation

Denis Gojak

INTRODUCTION

Although the twentieth century is regarded as a century of global war, it left Australia remarkably unscathed. The colonial conquest of Aboriginal Australia had been largely completed and basic cultural survival within white society became a more pressing objective for indigenous people. Two world wars were fought mostly in other parts of the world, with only relatively minor air raids and submarine attacks having a direct impact on Australian soil. The ideological war between Communism and capitalism was fought to the north, but Australia was never a potential domino. One of the paradoxes of the Australian situation therefore is that despite the lack of a direct threat to the land during the past century Australians were so willing to volunteer to fight and die elsewhere. The resulting legacy of a century of war for archaeologists is primarily made up of war memorials (without cemeteries) and coastal defences that never fired in anger.

Presented herein is an overview of the archaeology of the coastal defence of Australia, focusing on Sydney, New South Wales. As the largest city and primary strategic port of Australia it has the most comprehensive collection of defences against enemy attack. The sites span the period from almost the start of European settlement in 1788 to the 1960s. Many have now been incorporated into the national park system that surrounds Sydney and are part of the recognized cultural heritage of the nation. The study of these remains has great potential to show the developing nature of Australia's responsibility for defence as a key aspect of its evolving independence from Britain, and to reveal how Australians saw that relationship. It also shows the way the paradox noted above informs our modern views about the archaeological remains.

The provision of defence is one of the defining purposes of nations, generally through a standing army and the safeguarding of borders. Imperial powers also project their national interest to supporting economic colonies or command of the sea or directly thwarting their opponents. The British Empire relied upon all three strategies to maintain its global position during the nineteenth century, with the Australian colonies firmly dependent upon Britain for much of that time.

The structure of Australia's defence should therefore reflect the interplay between Britain and Australia as the latter gradually developed a more independent sense of nationhood and took on the responsibility for defence that came with the creation of a nation. The prospect for historical archaeology in this situation is significant, providing an opportunity to examine how sites reflect the perceived patterns of growth and change that are largely derived from documentary and contemporary social sources. It is a separate source of information about how resources were used, designs and ideas were borrowed and adapted throughout this period. In Australia there are also significant gaps in the historical resources dealing with the development, design and use of military installations; the physical evidence is in many cases the only source of information about how Australia was defended.

The majority of defence heritage sites around Sydney are in the public domain within national parks and other reserves. Only about 10 per cent are still occupied by the military. The remains therefore are part of the public estate that agencies such as the National Parks and Wildlife Service (NPWS 1997), Interim Sydney Harbour Federation Trust (ISHFT 2000) and local councils are expected to conserve, make accessible and interpret. The last section of this discussion examines the meaning that the defences have for modern Australians; the relationship of these meanings to how the public appreciates, understands and places value; and how they reflect our understanding of the past.

AN OVERVIEW OF SYDNEY'S DEFENCE HERITAGE

Most work on coastal defences and military history in Australia is conflict- or period-specific, and relatively little looks at the large spans of time, such as the entire 170 years of coastal fortification in Australia, as a unified period worth analysing in its own right. The standard analytical tools of historical and archival research, oral history and systematic archaeological survey have been used with success in studying individual sites (see Lowry 1995; Dobinson *et al.* 1997). Excavation has been limited to date and its potential for investigating specific sites remains untested in Australian twentieth-century military contexts. The studies that have been undertaken on coastal defences in Sydney (see for example Gojak 1985, 1993, 1995; Harvey 1985; Wilson 1985; RAAHS 1997; NPWS forthcoming) provide the basis for the discussion that follows.

Through the course of the nineteenth and first half of the twentieth centuries a series of clear advances in the technological capabilities of coastal defences may be seen. These are easy to measure – the penetrative power and range of the guns, the size of projectiles and the rapidity of their fire. Less obvious but still evident are advances in the tracking of ship targets and the collation of this information to allow the integration of fire on a range of targets (Clarke 1893).

These advances are comfortably within the realm of the Industrial Revolution, particularly the late nineteenth century component, where the armaments industry was a prime instigator of research in metallurgy, chemistry, electricity and

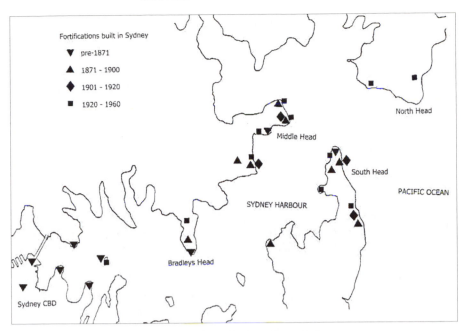

Figure 14.1 Defence sites around Sydney Harbour by period

advanced physics and mathematics (Hacker 1994). Wars were frequent enough to both justify expenditure of masses of money and to serve as a proving ground, though again the value of coastal defences meant that there were relatively few occasions where they were engaged in battle, and lessons were drawn from a very small number of instances where ships and shore defences engaged (see for example Walford 1883).

Coastal defence systems have an interesting relationship to naval design. The majority of ships' armament was used against other ships, therefore the guns were low trajectory, puncturing armoured wood, iron or steel and sacrificing target accuracy for speed. Getting into a gunfight with a coastal battery disadvantaged the ship. The static nature of coastal defences meant that they could have a clear view of lightly armoured decks, being able to lob shells, having a range of high-explosive and armour-piercing shells, and being able to be concealed or protected by massive armour or earthworks. Throughout the nineteenth century additional innovations were introduced, including electronically operated minefields, searchlights and telephone communications. These, together with constantly improving camouflage, armour, tactical planning and crew training, further advantaged coastal defences over attacking ships.

All of these changes are well understood and well represented in the heritage of Sydney's historic coast artillery and defence systems, and the interpretation of technological evolution and acceleration of change provides a very useful and very powerful explanatory device and interpretative tool for these sites. As an example, it provides a useful framework for understanding the gradual movement of defences during the nineteenth and twentieth centuries. Initially, in the first part of the nineteenth century, the defences were close around Sydney Cove, but moved to the outer harbour and coastline in the latter part, and then in the twentieth century culminated in the creation of a strategic coastal fortress system that commanded about 100 km of coastline (Fig. 14.1).

The main form of threat came from raids by ships that could hold the town to ransom or catch vessels at anchor. Because the range of their guns was short they would have no choice but to come close to the city – the only real target – to do damage. As gun range increased it became necessary to deny an increasingly large amount of harbour to enemy ships, otherwise they could fire from a sheltered cove on to the city.

Sydney had some natural advantages in this regard. Not only is Port Jackson admirably suited for defence, with elevated headlands, a usefully placed reef near the entrance and a winding channel, but the city is well away from the coast, making it imperative, at least in the nineteenth century, that any ships would need to enter. Only at the end of the nineteenth century was it necessary to put any guns on the coast, and that was because gun ranges had increased to the point that a ship could sit off Bondi and bomb Parliament House or the General Post Office. The bombardment of Sydney by a Japanese submarine lying off the coast during the Second World War for example put a few holes in suburban houses but came nowhere close to doing any serious damage. However, there are other themes that I think can be used to look at the 170-year period that provide equally interesting and useful models for archaeologists and historians interested in the interplay between physical and documentary evidence.

The twentieth century began for Australians with the federation of six colonies into a national entity on 1 January 1901. At that time troops from the colonies were fighting under British command in South Africa. The connection between nationhood and defence goes further back to the 1870s when British military advisers began to promote inter-colonial cooperation in defence as a policy that would support British imperial interests. The last three decades of the nineteenth century reveal a gradual emergence of an agreed 'national' position – even in the absence of a nation – which saw a defence alliance both for continental defence and to support British interests globally. By this time Australian defence policies were almost completely dictated by British imperial interests.

This contrasted with the situation in 1870, where the Cardwell reforms had removed all British garrison troops from Australia, resulting in a short-lived experiment of the colonies developing their own defence policies without substantial British input. The despatch of two senior military advisers was prompted by concern over the state of defences during the tensions leading to the Russo-Turkish War of 1877. Their unstated objective was to reshape Australia's defence to meet British imperial needs, not colonial paranoia.

Two interrelated themes that recur throughout the period are the 'scare mentality' and the very complex path of increasing independence of Australia from Britain. For much of their history, Australians have seen themselves as Britons on the wrong side of the planet. Whenever Britain got into hostilities or even just diplomatic argy-bargy with another power that had any sort of presence in the Pacific, Sydneysiders felt themselves likely targets for any pre-emptive attack. This was only heightened after the gold rushes of the 1850s created the self-perception of a golden goose, rather than just a sitting duck.

The archaeological signature of the scares is reasonably clear: an incident – usually somewhere else on earth – or the unheralded arrival of American warships into the port, suddenly alerts the population to their vulnerability and lack of vigilance. The newspapers fill with 'we'll all be murdered in our beds' letters. There is a hasty and poorly conceived construction programme, usually not authorized by the relevant authorities in Britain. As a result they use existing armaments that are old if not obsolete, fail to consult military authority and place the defences where they will reassure the population rather than be effective militarily. The scare soon passes and the money runs out, leaving a half-finished (often half-baked) gun battery sitting alone on a cliff-top somewhere.

There are a substantial number of fortifications around Sydney Harbour that fit this model. They tell us something about the technology of the day, but more clearly they tell us something about the psychology of Australia in times of crisis. Examples that clearly fit this model are the 1839 fortifications on Bradleys Head, Pinchgut (Fort Denison) and elsewhere, generated by the unheralded arrival of (friendly) American warships one night, the first 1851 phase of military construction in the lead-up to Britain's involvement in the Crimea, the major works programme initiated in response to the Cardwell reforms and the works initiated around September 1939 and again in late 1941.

The other linked theme is the gradual search for independence from Britain during the nineteenth and early twentieth centuries. If we accept that defence is both a responsibility of government and likely to reflect its robustness and perceptions of threats then the defences should chart the changing nature of the relationship between the Australian colonies and 'mother' Britain. This relationship was both complex and dynamic when examined through conventional historical sources. However, the responsibility for coastal defence, and other forms of defence, accurately reflects the nuances of that relationship over the course of the entire period.

Although it is a complex scenario when taken over the course of 170 years, the following schematic structure applies, along with the physical evidence represented.

1788–1870 Britain responsible for colonial defence with garrisons and Royal Navy presence until 1870. Barracks and other military installations and military personnel closely integrated with civil administration and society.

c.1850 From the 1850s pressure for the gold-rich colonies to pay a subvention to support the costs of maintaining the garrison, and later subsidising Royal Navy contingents. British control and institutions continue. Greater civil control, although professionals from Royal Engineers used extensively in civil works. Defence reserves identified on most harbour headlands.

1870 Cardwell reforms of the British Army result in withdrawal of Australian

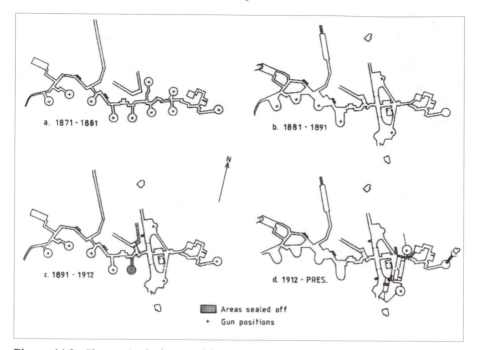

Figure 14.2 Changes in the layout of the Outer Middle Head batteries 1870–1911

garrisons. A Select Committee of NSW Parliament develops a defence scheme for Sydney. The British at this stage had completely walked away and said that sole responsibility for defences was a colonial problem. 1870–1 defence scheme for Sydney results in innovative modular design for gun batteries and installations within Sydney Harbour (Fig. 14.2).

1877   The British are being drawn into the Russo-Turkish War. The colonies have been constructing fortifications of questionable effectiveness, and failing to create the sort of secure coaling port that the Royal Navy needed to guarantee naval dominance in the Pacific. As a result military advisers Jervois and Scratchley are sent out to 'assist' the various Australian colonies and New Zealand with their defences (Trainor 1994). While these were technically much better, their main purpose was for imperial rather than colonial defence. Immediate rectification of critical faults in 1870–1 gun emplacements, and longer term replacement of them.

1877–1900   Colonial defences upgraded and integrated into imperial defence strategy. New gun emplacements built, reflecting advances in armament technology. Replication of British defence designs. Colonies seen as a major market for the products of arms manufacturers.

1900–14   From Federation to the outbreak of the First World War there was a consolidation of the organisation of the garrison units into the national army. There was little change in their operation or layout, save that which resulted from gradual cost-cutting and running down as the emphasis for national defence shifted to a land army and a new navy (Meaney 1994). Assessment of colonial installations of this period revealed that many were obsolete and were subsequently shut down.

1914–18   During the First World War the coastal defences were initially put on to alert and their operability increased, but this did not last long, once it became clear that there was no effective German threat remaining in their Pacific possessions. Posting to a coastal battery became an assignment in boredom. One unit is recorded as lowering a piano into one of the gun emplacements around Sydney to alleviate the tedium ('Fronsac' 1929). Other evidence of lots of time being available comes from the elaborate engraving of unit crests into sandstone bedrock, extensive landscaping and garden planting around the gun batteries.

1919–1930s   Following the First World War, there was a general degradation in the armed forces, and the neglect of coastal defences continued. Left to itself Australia would probably have allowed the running down to continue unabated; British strategic planners had however begun to rethink the operating requirements for the Royal Navy in the immediate post-war period. As in the 1880s there was a recognition that British sea power was what mattered most to the effective defence of Empire, and this could only be achieved through a network of secure ports and refuelling stations. Australia's inadequate defences were to be upgraded, and an integrated system of fortress defence was to be introduced around the key ports, closely modelled on British examples (Fullford 1994; Lowry 1995).

1930s   The fortress system integrated coastal artillery of various sizes with radio communications and sophisticated ballistic calculations to provide for layered defence of a strategic port. The core of the system was a series of counter-bombardment guns, generally of 9.2-inch calibre or greater. These could engage the largest battleships while they were still well out to sea. The guns relied upon positional information that came from a series of observation posts placed along the coast. Target information came back to a battery command post where it was triangulated. The information on location was adjusted to reflect the speed and direction of the target, the state of the tide, wind and weather and the wear on the barrel. If these variables could be accounted for, then the expectation was that every shot would be a hit. In an exchange of gunfire a battleship could be expected to fare worse than a coastal battery. The battleship would be an unstable platform for guns, aiming at a target that was concealed, dispersed and heavily protected. Ship guns are primarily designed to fire high-velocity armour-piercing shells against other ships, and lobbing high explosives at a distant target is not an optimal use. The coastal battery would be lobbing shells to fall on to the less-armoured decks of the battleship, bringing accurate target location to bear with every shot (Hogg 1974: 9; Fullford 1994).

The archaeological representation of the fortress system is, ideally, of a series of observation posts, command posts and supporting facilities, with a hierarchy of gun batteries from the largest (9.2-inch or larger), to the anti-ship guns (6-inch) and close defence guns against fast torpedo boats or raiders. Around Sydney a few buildings and vacant gun emplacements are the main remnants.

1939–45   The defence system around Sydney was largely operational on the eve of war, and only required minor extension initially. Entry of Japan into the war

Figure 14.3 Vietnam War period 'tiger cages' in the disused engine room at Outer Middle Head, used to train Australian troops to withstand interrogation

Source: Author, copyright NSW NPWS

meant there was greater risk of aerial bombardment and pre-emptive landings, making revision of close defence, anti-air defence and beach defences necessary (Fullford 1994). The archaeological evidence reflecting this is largely through changes in fabric of individual buildings following construction and the abandonment and repositioning of small guns for close defence.

Because British supplies had to be directed to home defence, Australia had to import large amounts of American coastal defence equipment during the war (Kidd and Neal 1998). Although not used around Sydney these represent only the second time that Australia broke with an exclusive reliance upon British armaments and tactical doctrine, the other being 1870. Not coincidentally it was at this time that Prime Minister John Curtin made his statement that the future destiny of Australia lay with the United States rather than Britain.

1945–70 The coastal defences were abandoned by 1968. These twenty-five years saw the revegetation of cleared areas, squatting in buildings and the general degradation of the fabric of the military installations.

The last use of the coastal defences following their decommissioning was of an altogether different character. During the early years of the Vietnam War Australia agreed to send a force of military instructors to assist the South Vietnamese government. The abandoned defences at Middle Head were used as a training ground to prepare the Australian Army Training Team to withstand torture if Communist Vietnamese forces captured them. Corrugated iron cages in imitation of the North

Vietnamese 'tiger cages' were built and inductees were put through a period of psychological torture and punishment (Fig. 14.3). An account of the training speaks of standing for extended periods waist-deep in water, rooms with loud volume 'white noise' blasting from radios, and constant broadcasts of propaganda interspersed with periods of interrogation (Petersen 1988).

This schematic outline demonstrates that there were considerable variations within the relationship between Australia (colonially and federally) and Britain. While the general trend was towards increasing independence being sought by colonial governments, and generally by British governments seeking to reduce the costs of keeping what were otherwise economically self-supporting colonies, there were strong countervailing factors. These included the reluctance of Australian colonies to see themselves abandoned by Britain, manifested as scares such as in 1870. There was the gradual rise in the perception of the United States as an alternative global power that could replace the protective role that Australia sought from Britain. Each of these twists in the narrative is reflected closely in the archaeology of the period, showing that the historical archaeology of defence as a national institution provides a close model for broader national relationships and perceptions.

THE MEANING OF THE DEFENCES

How are the coastal defences seen and understood by the people of Sydney? They are reasonably visible – particularly Fort Denison, which is a defended island near the Sydney Opera House. Many are visited on guided tours operated by the National Parks and Wildlife Service, and nearly all those that are not still operational military or naval bases can be easily visited. Few are interpreted in any way except for tour guide commentaries.

The harbour headlands where these sites are located embody a number of competing values for the public. As a result of the abandonment of military activity and separation from suburban development, the sites have now revegetated and form important quasi-natural ecological communities in the centre of Sydney. Activists who are seeking to ensure there is no further development of former defence land have given the presence of these natural areas a high premium. To passers-by on ferries and cars the green bits are just that: parts of Sydney Harbour National Park (NPWS 1997). Only relatively few people know about the presence of defence sites, and fewer know how to access them. This has been a deliberate strategy by the NPWS to reduce the visitation and discourage impacts on the natural and cultural heritage. The consequence has been that much of the public discussion of the future of land that the military has vacated is couched in terms of managing it only for its natural values and removing evidence of human interaction (see for example Uren 1999, 2000).

The story of Aboriginal use of the headlands has generally been neglected but is also very important in documenting human presence in Sydney for at least 20 000 years. The most recent phase of Aboriginal history following European settlement includes several significant contact sites that helped to shape relationships between

the races. The meaning and presence of these sites is also masked by the predomi-
nance of the natural heritage argument, and features by omission in technologically
driven discussions of the military heritage of the harbour lands (Bickford *et al.*
1999).

Australia managed to be little affected by war in the twentieth century on its continental landmass. Bombing raids on northern Australia, midget submarine raids
on the eastern seaboard and torpedoed merchant shipping is as close as we came to
attack in the last century. This sense of security operates in opposition to the very
real sense of fear and vulnerability that characterizes the scares that were equally
present in the period.

The role of coastal artillery in ensuring national defence is summarized in a
recent history as 'We stood and waited' (Fullford 1994). The passivity that the
phrase implies has, because of the lack of military action that it can be seen in context against, been assimilated in such a way that the defences have essentially been
denatured. While there is recognition of their military origins and their function,
they are for many Australian visitors almost completely disassociated with either
specific wars or war in general. They cease to represent 'war' except in a very general and undefined manner.

This is a specific reflection of a broader consideration of war in the Australian
psyche. Despite contemporary accounts of conflict between Aboriginal people and
European settlers being described in terms of wars and battles, most Australians
would hold the view that all of our wars happened overseas. Only recent military
historiography has begun to place the European occupation in a context equating it
to Australia's foreign wars (Grassby and Hill 1988; Grey 1990). The interpretation
of European settlement as a process involving war and violence is still a current
political debate.

The same ethos prevails in the material culture of war memorials. Australians
went overseas to fight. The remains of the dead were buried in war cemeteries on
the battlefields themselves. The war memorials that were erected in towns and
institutions throughout Australia during the two world wars and later conflicts are
different from those elsewhere in the world in that they do not just record the
names of the fallen, but also of those that served and returned. Ken Inglis (1998),
the key historian of these war memorials, considers that this is a reflection of the
unique nature of Australia's foreign contingents – they were all comprised of volunteers, not conscripts, until the Vietnam War. The memorials also reflected the
ambivalence of the community to the prevailing notions of sacrifice in war as being
in some way honourable. War memorials strengthen the notion of war as being
something that happened overseas and in other countries.

The disassociation of the coastal defences with war is further strengthened by the
gradual community distancing from war as a noble or virtuous or even necessary
role for society. This manifests itself in a number of ways, including questioning
that any interest in military heritage is inherently militaristic or supportive of war
(see for example Courtney 2000: 27).

When the remains of the coastal defences are interpreted to the public consideration needs to be given to the question of what to interpret. As has been shown they

are more than a narrative of technological change over the past two centuries. Interesting and informative as the processes of industrial change are, they must be secondary to the message demonstrated about how closely the defence heritage documents Australia's gradual national evolution. There are other types of site which serve to demonstrate national institutions in their physical form, but none do so with as much fine-grained correspondence to the entire political narrative over 170 years. The fortifications chart each of the major changes in a way that can be read from visible physical evidence.

The second issue in interpretation is to counter the disassociation that has taken place between these sites and the military context within which they were created. As shown above, this denaturing of the coastal defences reflects a more prevailing denial of the physical and psychological impact of war upon Australians. 'It all happened overseas' denies not only the process of European settlement and Aboriginal resistance that was often bloody, but also the consequences of war upon those who returned. As Uzzell (1989) argues, the 'hot' interpretation of war, which focuses upon the human impact of conflict rather than the technological accompaniments is not only a powerful presentation strategy, it also does what good interpretation should do – challenge the viewer and make them think about themselves differently. Potentially most evocative are the tiger cages, being on a more personal scale and more recent in experience than the defences. The argument can also be couched in terms used by Carman (1997), who argues for more consideration of the potential of the 'moral voice of archaeology' to focus concern on the nature of war and its impact on humans.

CONCLUSION

The physical patterning of Sydney's defences is a detailed reflection of the shifting relationship between an increasingly independent Australian nation and its 'mother' Britain, and the economically dominant United States. The archaeology of the institution of defence is therefore a legitimate source of information about the nature of these national relationships, and serves to chart it in detail. It also provides the ability to question the way that these relationships are seen from other contemporary sources and from a modern vantage. While the physical does not have primacy over other sources of evidence it extends the range and nature of questions that can be asked. The caveat is that, as with all historical archaeology, the relationship between the sources is not fixed but is reactive and reflective, prompting re-examination and testing using the full range of sources.

The interpretation and presentation of Sydney's defences has to compete with alternative emphases. The lack of conflict with other national powers, and the downplaying of conflict within the colonial settlement process, has served to rob the coastal defences of a key part of their associative value. They are seen less as an expression of military thought and process than as anomalous and frivolous functionalist architecture. Any interpretation of the defences needs to strongly consider the reversal of this perspective, and to place them firmly within their military and broader political context. To denature the defences by partial or selective interpretation does not just result in a misreading, it perpetuates the message that Australia was morally, as well as physically distant from war.

The quotation in the title of this chapter, from Anthony Trollope's 1873 visit to Australia, reflected his surprise at the perceived belligerence of the colonial Australians, when he read the evidence of a tour of the gun batteries and defences of Sydney Harbour (Trollope 1873). By reading the same physical evidence today we can interpret it less as belligerence than a combination of trepidation and unease during the gradual development of an Australian nation.

ACKNOWLEDGEMENTS

The original survey work that is represented in this chapter was funded by the NSW Heritage Assistance Program administered through the (then) Department of Planning, with additional funding for publication by the Australian Army History Research Grants Scheme. A large number of NPWS staff contributed to the formulation of this chapter, including Joan Kent, Jennifer Carter, Bronwyn Conyers, Rob Newton, Miriam Stacy and Neville Burkett. Other people who generously provided information, site knowledge or simply let me earbash them include the late Matt Croser, the late Roy Harvey, Dave Pearson, Helen Dawson and Grahame Wilson. I am especially indebted to Colleen Beck for her efforts in dragging this chapter out of me, and her patience when she had every reason not to be.

REFERENCES

Bickford, A., Brayshaw, H. and Proudfoot, H. (1999) 'Middle and Georges Heads Model Interpretation Plan and Application', unpublished report to NPWS, Sydney.

Carman, J. (1997) 'Giving archaeology a moral voice', in Carman, J. (ed.) *Material Harm: Archaeological Studies of War and Violence*, Glasgow: Cruithne Press, pp. 220–39.

Clarke, G.S. (1893) *Textbook on Fortification and Military Engineering* Part II: *Permanent Fortification, Historical Development, Siege Works, Coast Defence*, London: HMSO.

Courtney, P. (2000) The historical archaeology of war: some recent developments in Europe, *Society for Historical Archaeology Newsletter* 33(4): 26–7.

Dobinson, C.S., Lake, J. and Schofield, A.J. (1997) Monuments of war: defining England's 20th-century defence heritage, *Antiquity* 71: 288–99.

'Fronsac' [pseudonym] (1929) *Garrison Gunners*, Tamworth: privately published.

Fullford, R.K. (1994) *We Stood and Waited: Sydney's Anti-Ship Defences 1939–1945*, Manly: Royal Australian Artillery Historical Society.

Grassby, A. and Hill, M. (1988) *Six Australian Battlefields*, Sydney: Allen and Unwin.

Grey, J. (1990) *A Military History of Australia*, Cambridge: Cambridge University Press.

Gojak, D. (1985) 'Sydney Harbour Fortifications Study Stage II. Archaeological Survey', unpublished report prepared for the NPWS, Sydney.

Gojak, D. (1993) 'NPWS Defence Heritage Study', unpublished report prepared for the NPWS, Sydney.

Gojak, D. (1995) 'Defending the indefensible: an archaeological approach to Sydney's historic coastal defences', paper presented to the First Military Archaeology Conference of Australasia and the Pacific, Albury.

Hacker, B. (1994) Military institutions, weapons, and social change: toward a new history of military technology, *Technology and Culture* 35: 768–834.

Harvey, R. (1985) 'Sydney Harbour Fortifications Archival Study: Final Report Part 2', unpublished report prepared for the NPWS, Sydney.

Hogg, I. (1974) *Coast Defences of England and Wales 1856–1956*, Newton Abbot: David and Charles.

Inglis, K. (1998) *Sacred Places: War Memorials in the Australian Landscape*, Carlton: The Miegunyah Press.

Interim Sydney Harbour Federation Trust [ISHFT] (2000) *Reflections on a Maritime City: An Appreciation of the Trust Lands on Sydney Harbour*, Mosman: Interim Sydney Harbour Federation Trust.

Kidd, R. and Neal, R. (1998) *The 'Letter' Batteries: The History of the 'Letter' Batteries in World War II*, Castlecrag: the authors.

Lowry, B. (ed.) (1995) *20th Century Defences in Britain: An Introductory Guide*, London: Council for British Archaeology Practical Handbooks in Archaeology 12.

Meaney, N. (1994) 'Ministerial policy-making and the defence of Australia', in Eddy, J. and Nethercote, J. (eds), *Towards National Administration: Studies in Australian Administrative History*, Sydney: Hale and Iremonger, Royal Institute of Public Administration Australia, pp. 127–42.

National Park and Wildlife Service (1997) *Sydney Harbour National Park Plan of Management*, Sydney: NPWS.

National Park and Wildlife Service (forthcoming) *Sydney Harbour National Park – Middle and Georges Heads Fortifications Conservation Management Plan*, Sydney: NPWS.

Petersen, B. (1988) *Tiger Men: An Australian's Secret War in Vietnam*, South Melbourne: Macmillan.

Royal Australian Artillery Historical Society [RAAHS] (1993) 'New South Wales World War II Fortification Study – final report', unpublished report prepared for the NPWS, Sydney.

Trainor, L. (1994) *British Imperialism and Australian Nationalism: Manipulation, Conflict and Compromise in the Late Nineteenth Century*, Cambridge: Cambridge University Press.

Trollope, A. (1873) *Australia and New Zealand*, London: Chapman and Hall.

Uren, T. (1999) Don't sell off our precious harbour land. Opinion column, *Sydney Morning Herald*, 27 May 1999.

Uren, T. (2000) Wanted: a park not tricks. Letter to the editor, *Sydney Morning Herald*, 3 July 2000.

Uzzell, D.L. (1989) 'The hot interpretation of war and conflict', in Uzzell, D.L. (ed.) *Heritage Interpretation:* Volume 1: *The Natural and Built Environment*, London: Belhaven Press, pp. 33–47.

Walford, N. (1883) The effects of the bombardment of the forts of Alexandria, July 11, 1882, *Journal of the Royal United Services Institution* 27: 145–204.

Wilson, G. (1985) 'Sydney Harbour Fortifications Archival Study: Part 1', unpublished report prepared for the NPWS, Sydney.

15   Historic airfields: evaluation and conservation

Jeremy Lake

> He sat smoking on the bench in the well-remembered crew room, fascinated by the weather-stained poster still fluttering on one damp wall. The door, which had never closed properly, now swung to and fro in the whistling wind, groaning on its single rusty hinge. There had once been laughter as well as tragedy in these ghostly surroundings and life had been simple; in four years the sense of purpose sustaining aircrews, ground crews and a whole people behind them had withered.
>
> (Boyle 1955: 282)

This passage describes a visit to a deserted aerodrome in Yorkshire by Leonard Cheshire who, as leader of 617 Squadron, had demonstrated the effectiveness of precision bombing in a celebrated series of raids. The opening scenes of Anthony Asquith's film *The Way to the Stars* (1945) explored in similar fashion the thoughts of a veteran returning to another deserted airbase, as a ploughshare pulled by a horse team returned to agriculture land formerly used for waging aggressive war.

These two images have relevance as, since 1989 and the consequent rationalization of Britain's Defence Estate, many of those airfields retained for military use during the Cold War have been earmarked for disposal and a variety of new uses (Blake 1995). It was this process, in addition to a growing awareness of the need to evaluate the historical importance of twentieth-century military sites, that prompted English Heritage to undertake a review of surviving sites with the objective of identifying the most significant examples for protection. The aim of this chapter is to explore a range of challenges and issues arising from this survey, through a discussion first of the contextual significance and interpretation of military airfields and then the criteria for evaluation that have underpinned the selection of key sites and structures in England for protection.

BACKGROUND

As befits a century riddled by paradoxes – Hobsbawm's *Age of Extremes* (1994) – awareness of the civilizing and even peacemaking potential of powered flight contrasted with a growing realization in the inter-war period that it was the most effective means of bringing 'total war' to civilian populations. This was a process considered to be both the end product of a Clausewitzian philosophy which regarded warfare as the continuation of political means (Keegan 1993: 20, 370) and by others to be both enabled by the industrialized fragmentation of responsibility and the remoteness (Hobsbawm 1994: 49–50; Glover 1999: 69–88). The core of parent bomber stations – augmented by wartime satellites – which launched the Royal Air Force's (RAF) Strategic Bomber Offensive against Germany was planned from 1923, initially under General Sir Hugh Trenchard, the period's most strident advocate of the doctrine of offensive deterrence (Deighton 1993: 342–5). During the Second World War the country's total of 150 airfields expanded to 740 (Dobinson 1997: 1), many of the new airfields having concrete runways (Betts 1996) for the four-engined bombers that were 'the visible expression of the RAF's determination to make a contribution to the war independent of the two services' (Hastings 1979: 58). They thus had an immense impact upon the landscape (see for example Blake 1989), the scale of construction at some of these sites being immense:

> In order to construct each Type A or similar size airfield [the standard operational airfield of 1942–5], about 600 acres had to be requisitioned, cleared and levelled, and access roads and sometimes branch railway lines built [...] 130 000 tons of hardcore, cement and tarmacadam were needed to lay the 40 000 square yards of runways, taxiways, hardstandings, roads and pathways. This, plus about 50 miles of pipes and conduits, went into the self-contained small township that would rise out of the British countryside.
>
> (Willis and Hollis 1987: 3)

The establishment of training and maintenance bases behind an eastern front line facing Germany sustained the bomber offensive that until the invasion of northwest Europe in 1944 provided the Allies' primary means of waging aggressive war against Germany. Both aircraft and the munitions they delivered formed an integral element of the *Materialschlacht* – the battle of materials – which had characterized the First World War and which in the Second World War ensured that Allied aircraft production outstripped that of Germany (Deighton 1993: 411). By 1940, as some contemporaries and later historians have argued, the presence of the British bomber deterrent in fixed bases had been accomplished at the expense of fighter defence and the development of ground-unit support that was a feature of the German advances in the early stages of the conflict. In contrast, the swift movements of mechanized units that characterized the campaigns waged across the desert landscapes of North Africa and the steppes of Russia called for the rapid construction of improvised airfields. Similarly, although traces remain of the airfields constructed in association with the Pacific War, from the Aleutian Islands of Alaska (Murphy and Lenihan 1998) to Micronesia (Haun and Henry 1993; Cleghorn 1996), and noting the decisive role of air power launched from carriers in the Battle of Midway – 'the turning point battle of the Pacific War' (Keegan

1995: 66) – only minor archaeological traces will survive here in the form of terrestrial airfield sites (Dudley 2000).

Nevertheless, the deployment of airfields within their international context, and in relation to the shifting geography of military campaigns, is as worthy of proper study as that of land fortifications. In Britain, new bases under construction in the Second World War were sited in reaction to the German occupation of northwest France, in support of the Strategic Bomber Offensive in eastern England and the Advanced Landing Grounds sited in southern England in support of the Allied invasion of northwestern Europe (Dobinson 1997: 175–95). The 'Atlantic Gap', beyond the reach of land-based air cover, was the prime killing ground in the Battle of the Atlantic, a factor which drove the establishment of airbases in Iceland, Newfoundland, Nova Scotia and later Greenland. Shore-based aircraft accounted for 41–45 per cent of U-boat losses, and their effectiveness increased in tandem with aircraft technology from the 500-mile range of the Hudson, Wellington and Whitley bombers to the 1100-mile range of the Liberator (in service from 1943). May 1943 is generally acknowledged as the turning point in the conflict, shore and ship-based aircraft then accounting for two thirds of U-boat losses (Terraine 1985: 238–50, 413–60). The airfields associated with the Battle of Britain of 1940 include historic sites and fabric stretching from those used by the RAF (Lake and Schofield 2000) to those used by or built especially for the Luftwaffe – Paris Le Bourget (Smith and Toulier 2000: 114) and Deelen in The Netherlands (Vossebeld 1997).

The construction of airfields around the world was also closely linked to the productive capacities of military-industrial complexes – at first the American and European core of populations, with 'a long history of literacy, metal machinery and centralized government' (Diamond 1998: 417), soon joined by Japan and other powers. Indeed, just as the naval technology which projected British power overseas in the eighteenth and nineteenth centuries was buttressed by the engineering expertise and the industrial output of the world's first industrial power, so the dominion of the air that characterized the *Pax Americana* of the late twentieth century was sustained by the post-war economic dominance of the United States. The investigation of the levels of investment and adaptation of those bases under development by both sides during the Cold War period would certainly make a contribution to the argument sparked by Paul Kennedy's *The Rise and Fall of the Great Powers* (1988), that argued for a close link between the economic strength and military prowess of particular states. Even a casual observer of those German airbases that now straddle the former Iron Curtain will be struck at how the Warsaw Pact's low investment in base infrastructure contrasted with the successive remodelling and multi-phased character of NATO bases.

In terms of their planning, therefore, the vast range of building types[1] and the 'stratigraphy' of airfield development and evolution, airfields merit consideration as highly complex sites that contain evidence for a wide range of factors from social distinctions to technological development and state resources. Airfield size, for example, is closely related to technological development, a survey of Lincolnshire airfields having established that whereas the average size of airfields in the 1914–18 period was 167 acres, this had increased during the 1930s to 400 acres and by 1945 to 640 acres (Blake *et al.* 1984: 210). Airbase planning also demanded the integration of a wide range of requirements. These ranged from housing communities of flyers, technicians, administrators and their families to accommodating the functions of a technology-based service. The war journalist Martha Gellhorn, who stood with the 'Bomber Boys' in the 'flat back emptiness' of an aerodrome as their ground-staff colleagues prepared their machines for another raid (Gellhorn 1959: 97), graphically conveyed to her readers the fact that the warriors trained to fly the machines accommodated on these bases took up a small proportion of their populations. It has been estimated, for example, that in 1945 82.5 per cent of the personnel on British airbases were support and maintenance staff, the remainder (just 17.5 per cent) being aircrew (Terraine 1985: 4–5).

Building design, similarly, manifested a wide range of considerations, from defence against attack to the imposition of social order and corps discipline. The latter is evident in the planning of the earliest military air stations, representing a continuation of the dynamics that underpinned the planning of barracks since the sixteenth century (Douet 1998: xi–vi). Netheravon, under development from late 1912 as the second new site built by Britain's Royal Flying Corps and the first new squadron station selected by their Military Wing, was planned with a clear separation between domestic and technical sites. The planning and architectural elaboration accorded to individual buildings on the domestic site also respected its subdivision into areas occupied by personnel of different ranks (Dobinson 1998). From 1923, airbases were planned on dispersed principles, the result being a diversity of building types and the planning of hangars on arcs and mess buildings in linked compartments in order to minimize losses to machines and personnel. The gas decontamination centres and protected operations blocks which appeared on RAF bases from 1937, along with the flat roofs widely introduced in the same period, were designed in order to counter the effects of incendiary bombs and bomb fragmentation (Francis 1996a: 186–93).

By the 1930s, the issue of airbase design had become inextricably bound with that of national identity. For example, the International Style was chosen in Finland as a means of 'underlining the modernity and progressiveness' of a newly independent nation (Makinen 1994). Streamlined Moderne styles were also chosen for some of the bases of the *Regia Aeronautica* in Mussolini's Italy, where Futurist-inspired art and Moderne architecture served as the voice of Fascist ideology (Ranisi 1998a and b). In Britain, and in contrast to the manner in which those municipalities commissioning terminal architecture looked to the rest of Europe and America for inspiration (Voigt 1996; Smith and Toulier 2000: 16–25), the planners for the post-1934 expansion of the RAF were enjoined to soften the impact of new bases on the landscape by politicians mindful of public concerns over the issues of rearmament and the pace of environmental change. In 1931, the Air Ministry had been instructed by government to consult on airbase design with the Royal Fine Arts Commission (Dobinson 1997: 142), all of whose consultant architects and planners had cut their teeth in the late Victorian period: one of their number, Sir Reginald Blomfield, was an outspoken critic of modern architecture and its threatened erosion of regional traditions (Stamp 1988: 9) and another was the distinguished country house architect Sir Edwin Lutyens. The result, for the first generation of bases constructed after 1934, was a curious blend of Garden City planning and architecture for married quarters, neo-Georgian propriety for the barracks and other domestic buildings, and a watered-down Moderne style for the technical buildings. The facing of the training base at Hullavington in Wiltshire in local limestone provided the most marked example of Air Ministry reaction to local concerns, most probably voiced by the Council for the Protection for Rural England (Dobinson 1997: 142).

Both the dynamic modernity conveyed by the International Style and the traditionalism of historicist styles were thus considered to represent national ideals and considerations. In Hitler's Germany, despite the establishment of a neo-classical 'National Socialist style' as early as 1933 in Ernst Sagebiel's Berlin Air Ministry, the 'Blood and Soil' ideology of the National Socialist regime rejected the International Style of Mies van der Rohe and the other architects of 1920s Weimar Germany as degenerate art. The adoption of traditional regional styles, in continuation of the manner in which the Domestic Revival of late Victorian Britain had made a deep impression on German architecture, was seen as a way of reinforcing and deepening the party's power. The designers of some Luftwaffe training bases made considerable use of local architectural styles and detailing, through the use for example of sgraffito decoration in Bavaria (*Der Baumeister* 1937). The Luftwaffe engineers' practice of varying standard-type plans drafted by Organization Todt was also exported to key bases in the occupied countries of western Europe, providing a style in marked contrast to the manner in which the moulded plastic forms of 1920s German Expressionism lent potency to the Atlantic Wall fortifications designed under Todt and later Speer (Anderson Bo 1994). At Deelen in The Netherlands, under construction from as early as May 1940 (Vossebeld), the 55-cm concrete walls of the station buildings were clad in brick finished with steeply-pitched crowstep gables and their windows ornamented by traditional-looking (but steel) shutters that mirrored the traditional architectural style of the region. The various operational zones of the site are dispersed across the landscape, and camouflage was undoubtedly a factor in the choice of style, as in the hangars disguised as traditional 'stolp' barns.

CONSERVATION

Architectural considerations have hitherto been foremost in the assessment of the importance of structures associated with the history of flight. It was in France, Italy and Germany, as one might expect in view of their leadership of innovative forms of construction in concrete, that the most innovative aircraft hangars were built. Pre-eminent amongst the structures already given statutory protection are the shell-domed hangars constructed in 1917 by the Munich-based company Gebruder-Rank at Friedrichsfelde (Karlshorst), now on the eastern outskirts of Berlin (Czymay 1999).

One obvious consequence of our sudden familiarity with air travel has been a reticence to evaluate airfield sites and structures for their historical significance. Indeed, a recent editor of a collection of aviation literature considered that 'aviation has developed so quickly, too fast for it ever to become a stable fact of life, for us to put our finger on its significance before it has moved on again' (Coster 1997: x). As befits the birthplace of powered flight, America's National Parks Service has completed the most advanced work aimed at the protection of historic aviation properties through registration on the National Register of Historic Places. Thus, besides the sites and structures associated with the early career of the Wright brothers, the Red Barn near Seattle, purchased by William E. Boeing in 1910, is noted as a landmark in early development and production (Milbrooke 1998). Military sites have been subject to several analytical studies (see for example Brown 1990) and those now designated by the National Parks Service include the six seaplane hangars of 1916–18 at Pensacola Air Station in Florida and the training base at Randolph Field in Texas, under development from 1928. Also protected is the Full-Scale Tunnel under development from 1931 at Langley Field; here, NASA's forerunner, the National Advisory Committee for Aeronautics, established in 1915, developed key civil designs such as the DC-3 in addition to the B-17 bomber in 1935, this latter being 'the forerunner of all modern subsonic bombers' (Milbrooke 1998: II, 4). The simultaneous development of the B-52 bomber and the 747 airliner by Boeing (Bowers 1989) is but one reminder of the symbiotic relationship between civilian manufacturers and military planners that has sustained the world's largest military-industrial complex.

Research and development sites such as Langley typically absorbed a high proportion of national defence budgets (Edgerton 1991: 35). Protection accorded to similar wind tunnel buildings constructed for the European powers at Farnborough (England), Meudon (France) and Adlershof (Germany) now provides recognition of the fact that these are some of the most spectacular manifestations of what Bernal, as far back as 1939, had termed the 'Scientific-Technical Revolution' (Teich 1996: 29). They demonstrate through their engineering and design the great inter-war advances in aeronautical research, including aerodynamic theory, construction, fuels and engines that paved the way for the monoplane fighters, four-engined bombers and first jet aircraft of the Second World War. A recent European project, which has aimed at achieving a consistency of approach towards the evaluation of the civil airport terminals of the 1930s (Smith and Toulier 2000), is also now providing the basis for the international comparisons that are critical to an evaluation of the importance of military sites. This is clearly demonstrating the layered history of those civil sites also with a military past. Berlin Templehof is remembered by Berliners for the critical role it played in NATO's first decisive encounter – the Berlin Airlift of 1947 – but its immense scale also embodied Hitler's unrequited dream of a greater Germany; it functioned as an aircraft factory in the Second World War and retains evidence of the Red Army's advance in 1945, and its use in the Cold War. All these phases, down to even the characteristic brown paint used by the Americans for the radar control room, are included in the conservation plan now being drawn up for the site, which must also face the difficult and controversial issue of the conservation of the airfield (Jockeit 2000).

Work on recording military airfield sites is most advanced in Britain (Francis 1996a), The Netherlands (Kuipers 2000) and Germany. The *Nederlandse Federatie voor Luchtvaartarchaeologie* has pioneered recording of Luftwaffe and RAF sites in The Netherlands, and its research has served to underpin the designation of Deelen, a decision by the Dutch monuments service (ibid.). In Brandenburg the completion of survey work by Johannes Bruns and an analysis of hangar types by Andreas Skopnik has underpinned the selection for protection of concrete hangars and barracks buildings at Werneuchen, which functioned as a nightfighter station during the Battle of Berlin and later as a Soviet fighter airfield close to the NATO border. France has an exemplary documentary-based survey of aviation architecture (Dumont 1988) which will soon form the basis of an evaluation of surviving sites. Italy's *Regia Aeronautica* has also been the subject of a comprehensive study (Ranisi 1998b). It is to work in England however that this chapter now turns.

AIRFIELDS IN ENGLAND: AN ASSESSMENT

The recent completion of English Heritage's assessment of military airfield sites has been based on a full process of documentary research and fieldwork.[2] A balance has to be struck between understanding the entire resource and the identification for protection of those sites and structures which will most graphically inform present and future generations. It is now considered that the identification of key sites will constitute the most effective and historically valid method of protecting standardized building types which are otherwise well represented in other, more altered or less significant contexts. Outside these key sites, it is only groups and individual structures of strong intrinsic historical or architectural importance which have been recommended for protection. A site-based approach also brings with it the need to address the full range of statutory and non-statutory options for protection, including listing for the most significant buildings, and scheduling for bomb dumps and the earthworks and pillboxes associated with airfield defence in the Second World War. Conservation area designations for key groups and sites are also being actively explored, together with guidelines for management, agreed between all parties and which aim to assist in the daily operation of designated sites (English Heritage 2001).

The following factors, in addition to the degree of completeness of individual buildings or groups, have been judged to have critical importance to an evaluation of the relative significance of military airfields in England (Lake 2000):

- Identification of sites which, as a consequence of events on the world stage, military imperatives or varying degrees of public and political support, reflect the development of military aviation from 1910 to 1945. (Cold War aviation forms part of a separate though related study by English Heritage's Monuments Protection Programme.)

- Identification of the sites which are most strongly representative of functionally distinct airfield types. These ranged from bases built or adapted for the purposes of training, maintenance and repair to operational use (seaplanes, fighters and bombers) and the storage of reserve aircraft.
- Identification of buildings and sites which have strong associations with key historical episodes of the Second World War, principally the Battle of Britain, the Battle of the Atlantic and the Bomber Offensive.
- Innovative site and building plans.
- The relationship of built fabric to the flying field, its character and development.
- International context.

The available evidence indicates that sites that meet these criteria are extremely rare both in England and in Europe. For example, Schleissheim, sited just to the north of Munich and established in 1912 as the base of the Royal Bavarian Flying Corps, is the only survivor of 87 aerodromes in existence in Germany by August 1914 (Czymay 1999). In England the survival of a key group of sites in the Salisbury Plain area dating from before the First World War is equally rare. The surviving hangars of 1910 at Britain's first military airfield at Larkhill formed the core of a series of civilian schools where army officers received their first flight training, collaborating with the War Office in army manoeuvres on Salisbury Plain. It was one of a series of flying schools built for Sir George White, who had adapted the workshops of his Bristol tramway empire at Filton for his British and Colonial Aeroplane Company in 1910 (South Parker 1982; Wessex Archaeology 1998). Half of all pilots who qualified in 1911 were Bristol-trained and flying schools on the Bristol pattern were established in Spain, Germany and Italy in 1912. The War Office then determined that Upavon – under development from 1912 as the Central Flying School – and Netheravon also offered ideal hilltop positions for military flying. All the mess buildings and other structures from the domestic camps on these two sites dating from before 1914 are recommended for protection. The group of timber hangars at Montrose in Scotland, built from late 1913 close to the naval base at Rosyth, is the most important pre-1918 group of hangars to have survived in Britain. Besides Montrose, seven hangar groups (of three or more structures) have survived, all in England, out of 301 bases occupied by the RAF in November 1918 (Lake 2000). Such suites of hangar buildings exemplify their aviation use more clearly through their plan and form than isolated survivals of domestic or technical buildings. Whilst the latter merit protection in the context of the formative Salisbury Plain sites, examples dating from the First World War period are generally only recommended for protection where they relate to key hangar groups and thus can be interpreted as part of recognizable aviation sites.

Most (271) of the 301 sites occupied by the Royal Air Force at the end of 1918 had been abandoned by 1920 (Dobinson 1997: 16), and a similar fate awaited those sites constructed during the Second World War. These sites merit study as transient settlements, whose archaeology has affinities with other classes of monument such as contemporary prisoner-of-war camps (Hellen 1999), Napoleonic militia camps and the navvy camps associated with the railway construction programmes of the nineteenth century. In contrast, the bases of the inter-war period were built with the capacity for long-term survival, where the inter-relationships of buildings as part of planned groups or as a reflection of their functional diversity can still be clearly read and interpreted. The eligibility of inter-war bases for protection is closely linked to the nature and intensity of post war use. Kemble, for example, provides the most outstanding example of the twenty-four Aircraft Storage Units constructed from 1936 and planned and built by the Air Ministry for the storage of vital reserve aircraft in the period 1936–40. The Junkers-Corporation designed Lamella sheds (Allen 1999) and the parabolic-roofed concrete hangars used on these sites comprised the Air Ministry's most advanced hangar designs, clearly related to contemporary experimentation elsewhere in Europe. Bicester, another one of Trenchard's Oxfordshire bomber bases, is the best preserved of the bomber bases constructed as the principal arm of Sir Hugh Trenchard's expansion of the RAF from 1923 based on the philosophy of offensive deterrence. It retains, better than any other military airbase in Britain, the layout and fabric relating to both pre-1930s military aviation and the development of Britain's strategic bomber force in the period up to 1939. The grass flying field still survives with its 1939 boundaries largely intact, bounded by a group of bomb stores built in 1938–9 and airfield defences built in the early stages of the Second World War. Duxford near Cambridge, now occupied by the Imperial War Museum, is likewise the pre-eminent example of a fighter base representative of the period from 1918–45. Duxford has retained the best-preserved group of First World War hangars and associated technical buildings in Britain, in addition to fabric dating from both inter-war phases of expansion and relating to the expansion of the base for American fighter pilots in the Second World War.

The exceptional levels of documentation relating to the phases of use at sites like Duxford (Francis 2001) can be clearly read on the ground, and serve as a reminder of how historical significance and the development of air power in its national context can be read into their layered history. For example, until the onset of perimeter dispersal from the late 1930s all the aircraft of an operational airfield would be accommodated in its hangars.[3] However, an early deceleration in Trenchard's programme – the result of events on the world stage and political and financial pressures at home – meant that only two of the proposed six 'A-type' hangars for the projected three-squadron station at Bicester were built (Fig. 15.1a–c). The next major phase of building formed part of the post-1934 Expansion Period, which had been prompted by the collapse of the Geneva disarmament talks in 1933. The increase in the number of aircraft at Bicester was thus marked by the completion of new C-type hangars in 1937. The building of a new control tower in 1938 reflected the belated importance given by the Air Ministry to the need to control movement with the defined zoning of serviceable landing and take-off areas (Francis 1996b; Lake 2000).

Some airfields have significance for their strong association with specific aspects of the war effort. For example, besides Duxford – the most southerly of 12 Group's sector airfields during the Battle of Britain and later a USAAF base for long-range

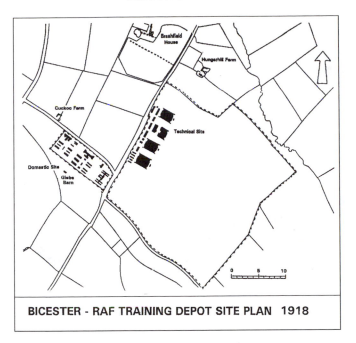

BICESTER - RAF TRAINING DEPOT SITE PLAN 1918

Figure 15.1a The layered archaeology of military airbases is illustrated by these successive plans relating to RAF Bicester; none of the Training Depot Station of 1918 has survived

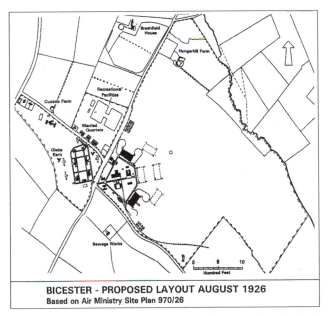

BICESTER - PROPOSED LAYOUT AUGUST 1926
Based on Air Ministry Site Plan 970/26

Figure 15.1b The airfield had expanded by the time that this plan for the bomber station was made in 1926

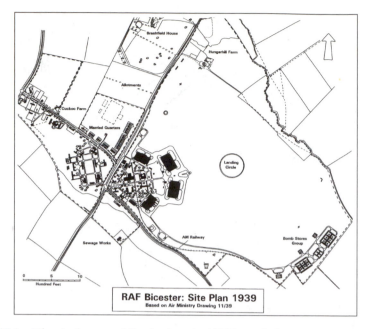

Figure 15.1c The site has now fallen back on its 1939 boundaries

fighter escorts (Ramsey 1978: 72–6; Ramsey 1996: 198–211) – significant station fabric has remained from the Battle of Britain. Dowding's grading of Fighter Command airfields in order of importance placed the sector stations of 11 Group (which bore the brunt of the Luftwaffe assault in August and September 1940), as well as Duxford and Middle Wallop, in the most strategically important category: a total of eight sites (Deighton 1977: 206). Of these, Biggin Hill is commonly regarded as the most historically significant, more enemy aircraft (1400, including the first thousand by 1943) having been destroyed by squadrons based here than any other airfield, for the loss of 453 aircrew. It is significant that few buildings have been demolished on the technical site since 1945, and that the existing lacunae on the site date from the Luftwaffe raids in summer 1940. Fighter Command ensured prior to the Battle of Britain that the 11 Group airfields built around London were provided with runways, perimeter tracks and fighter pens, of which Kenley survives as a uniquely complete landscape (Lake and Schofield 2000: 236–8). Its importance as a battlefield site is thrown into sharper relief when it is realized that it was subject, on 18 August 1940, to one of the most determined attacks by the Luftwaffe on a sector airfield. During this raid, three personnel were killed and three hangars and several aircraft destroyed (Price 1979: 74–80). Its scars can still be read in the form of postwar repair work to the officers' mess, the most impressive surviving building dating from the rebuilding of the station between 1931 and 1933 and prominently sited on the west side of the aerodrome.

The operational infrastructure put in place by Sir Hugh Dowding – in command of Fighter Command during the Battle of Britain – from March 1936 facilitated the incisive and economic marshalling of fighter squadrons during the battle. Thus Chain Home radar stations and Observer Corps posts were linked by telephone and teleprinter to Fighter Command Headquarters, the operations rooms controlling the Groups into which Dowding had subdivided the country, and finally, within each Group, those operations rooms on the principal sector airfields which controlled the fighter squadrons. From the underground operations room at RAF Uxbridge, built in 1938, as Churchill witnessed during his visit on the vital 15 September, Air Vice Marshall Keith Park commanded the deployment of squadrons within 11 Group. 'All the ascendancy of the Hurricanes and Spitfires would have been fruitless but for this system of underground control centres and telegraph cables, which had been devised and built before the war under Dowding's advice and impulse,' wrote Churchill (1949: 293–7). It could be said, indeed, that 'Dowding controlled the battle from day to day, Park controlled it from hour to hour, and the 11 Group sector controllers from minute to minute' (Wood and Dempster 1969: 84–90). As a consequence of their historical importance, surviving examples of sector operations rooms within 11 Group (at Debden and Northolt) have been recommended for statutory protection, as have the examples at Duxford and Uxbridge (Lake 2000).

The cover provided by shore-based aircraft of all three Commands proved to be a decisive factor in the Battle of the Atlantic, aided of course by the decryption of Ultra and the development of radar. Only a handful of sites with important fabric associated with the battle have survived, including the Sunderland flying boat hangars at Pembroke in Wales. Dunkeswell in Devon survives as the pre-eminent example of a purpose-built site associated with the battle, more complete even than Limavady in Northern Ireland (Lake 2000). The airfield, begun by the contractor George Wimpey in 1941, was occupied by US air force and navy Liberator bombers whose task was to patrol the sea areas traversed by U-boats en route between their bases in France and their hunting sites in the North Atlantic. The bulk of the airfield site, with its runways, perimeter track and hardstandings for the dispersed parking of aircraft characteristic of Second World War bomber stations, has survived as a very rare example of a substantially complete Second World War airfield site. The historical and landscape importance of this site has underpinned recommendations to protect key fabric, notably the operations block, a complete hangar with its associated hutting and the control tower group.

Because the Strategic Bomber Offensive of 1942–5 involved such a large number of bases in a shared purpose, combined with the fragmentary condition of wartime airfields and the generally high levels of adaptation on those permanent bases retained for use in the Cold War period, opportunities for statutory protection are very limited. The exceptions to this general rule are the bases associated with the most famous precision-bombing raids of the war. The full complement of four C-type hangars at Scampton, a bomber station begun in 1936, survive: the newly formed 617 Squadron achieved fame under the command of Guy Gibson with its raid on the Ruhr dams in May 1943. This raid pioneered the long-distance control by squadron commanders of precision operations converting, in the words of one historian, Bomber Command's tactics from those of 'a bludgeon into a rapier' (Terraine 1985: 540). It captured the imagination of the press and public at a critical moment in the war, making national heroes of Guy Gibson and his crews. It pro-vided a huge boost to Bomber Command's morale and enabled Churchill, in Washington with his chiefs of staff for a meeting with Roosevelt, to both silence American critics and boost confidence among the Canadians who were contribut-ing increasing amounts of aircrew to Bomber Command (Morris with Dobinson 1994: 184–6). Otherwise, the diffused nature of the campaign is matched by the terrible loss of life both wrought and endured by the teams of highly trained men – 'individually treasurable comrades' (Coster 1997: xv) – who took the bomber offensive to Germany. Sir Arthur Harris's own estimates put Bomber Command's fatalities – out of 125 000 who entered its units during the war – at 50 000, a figure matched by USAAF losses (Glover 1999: 76). There is thus a case for the protection of selected control tower buildings, both for their iconic importance as operational nerve centres and as memorials (Schofield, this volume). One example is that at Bassingbourn, opened as a medium bomber base in March 1938 and noted from 1942 for its role as the USAAF's flagship station. The control tower, a 1934 design, was extended in association with the remodelling and extension of the airfield in 1942, prior to the arrival of the 91st Bomber Group in October – known as the 'Ragged Irregulars' this Group was chosen as the subject of Wyler's celebrated colour film of an American bomber crew, known to millions for their association with the 'Memphis Belle' (Lake 2000).

CONCLUSION

The deployment, design and construction of military airfields are, therefore, reflective of many key aspects of twentieth-century history: from 'total warfare' to the political and military dynamics operating both within and between nation states. Their study is relevant to understanding twentieth-century archaeology in its full historical context, and is a critical factor in underlining recommendations for protection and setting out future research agendas that can ensure sites do not go unrecorded. There are practical issues, however, which set limits to a sustain-able policy of protection. Many of the bases built 'for the duration' of the First and Second World Wars did not have the potential for long-term beneficial reuse, while many of the 'permanent' stations built during the 1920s and 1930s, which comprised nucleated settlements of some hundreds and even thousands of people[4] formed the backbone of the RAF's infrastructure during the Cold War period. Upper Heyford – which was the test-bed for the planning of Trenchard's Home Defence Scheme stations – was still in the process of being remodelled for the USAAF with hardened shelters for F-111s in 1989.

Against the background of government policy which favours sustainable devel-opment, local authorities in Britain have envisaged a wide range of new uses for redundant bases, from reversion to agriculture to housing and industrial estates (Bell *et al.* 2000). Military airfields have, indeed, provided a considerable stimulus to local economies and a catalyst for place evolution, such as San Francisco Bay (Hall 1998 : 430–3). In England, many airbases have been developed as industrial or business parks, as at Greenham Common,[5] or for new communities on sustainable lines with their own schools, shops and amenities. Rouse Kent's development at West Malling, an historically important fighter base, is a case in point. It is also the subject of some recommendations for listing resulting from English Heritage's evaluation of military airfields, notably an officers' mess and barracks now used as offices and a control tower, which will probably be developed as a community centre: the tall concrete anti-aircraft tower, which now stands sentinel at one entrance to the site, will be considered for scheduling. The English Heritage survey has also, crucially, identified eighteen key sites (1.5 per cent of those sites in existence in 1945) where buildings are recommended for listing and fighter pens and defences for scheduling. These range from museum sites (Duxford), those earmarked for further development for civil flying (Biggin Hill), public amenity and gliding (Kenley), sites identified for mixed-use development with open space provision (Bicester) to ongoing military use (Netheravon, Scampton). English Heritage's survey has provided the baseline from which credible and sustainable decisions can be taken on these significant historic sites, setting heritage interests alongside social and economic considerations. The task is not an easy one, and conflict between these interests cannot be avoided in all cases. There will also be the inevitable pressure to protect sites and buildings which do not fulfil national standards for selection. Conservation must, therefore, be seen as part of an overall strategy of understanding the significance and archaeology of airfield sites, one that extends from clarifying the limitations imposed by designation to a promotion of their research potential in an international context.

ACKNOWLEDGEMENTS

My thanks to Marieke Kuipers and Rene Vossebeld for information about Deelen. Colin Dobinson lent copies of *Der Baumeister* and Leonard Cheshire's biography, used in this chapter. My thanks also to Paul Francis for permission to reproduce his drawn plans of Bicester.

NOTES

1 In Britain, there were at least 250 different types of structure or comparable structures serving different functions (Francis 1996a).

2 A thorough statistical analysis of what has survived, comparison with original populations and a critical analysis of importance or otherwise in a typological and national context, has been compiled by Paul Francis. Archival research (Dobinson 1997) has been published as Volume IX of the *Twentieth Century Fortifications in England* series, otherwise commissioned by the Monuments Protection Programme as a key element in English Heritage's evaluation of defence sites of this period. A summary report (Lake 2000) has compressed this data and presented a list of recommendations for protection placed in their national and international contexts.

3 Their construction took up a considerable part of the overall cost for a new site, the six hangars at
   Upper Heyford taking up 30 per cent of its total budget.
4 Henlow near Bedford, considerably rebuilt and extended in the early 1930s, accommodated over
   7000 personnel during the Second World War.
5 The airfield is being restored to heathland, while the cruise-missile shelters (the GAMA Site) are
   under consideration for scheduling.

REFERENCES

Allen, J.S. (1999) A short history of 'Lamella' roof construction, *Transactions of the Newcomen
   Society* 71: 1–29.
Anderson Bo, P. (1994) *Le Mur de L'Atlantique en Bretagne, 1944–1994*, Rennes: Editions
   Ouest-France.
Bell, P., Gallent, N., and Howe, J. (2000) New uses for England's old airfields, *Area* 32(4):
   383–94.
Betts, R.A. (1996) *The Royal Air Force Construction Service, 1939–1945*, Ware: Airfield Research
   Publishing.
Blake, R. (1989) 'The development of military and civil airfields in the United Kingdom
   since 1909, with special reference to land use', PhD thesis University of London.
Blake, R. (1995) 'Alternative strategies for the restoration and reuse of abandoned airfields',
   in *Proceedings of the International Symposium on the Environment and Defence*, NATO/ CCMS
   Report no. 211, Brussels.
Blake, R., Hodgson, M., and Taylor, B. (1984) *The Airfields of Lincolnshire since 1912*,
   Leicester.
Bowers, P.M. (1989) *Boeing Aircraft since 1916*, London: Putnam Aeronautical Books.
Boyle, A. (1955) *No Passing Glory: The Full and Authentic Biography of Group Captain Cheshire*,
   London: Collins.
Brown, J.E. (1990) *Where Eagles Land: Planning and Development of US Army Airfields, 1910–
   1941*, Westport: Greenwood Press.
Churchill, W. (1949) *The Second World War. Volume II: Their Finest Hour*, London: Cassell.
Cleghorn, P. (1996) *Draft Archaeological Investigations at Kagman Airfield, Kagman Saipan*, report
   prepared for US Army Corps of Engineers.
Coster, G. (ed.) (1997) *The Wide Blue Yonder: The Picador Book of Aviation*, London: Picador.
Czymay, C. (1999) 'Aviation architecture in Germany', unpublished paper delivered to
   Europe de l'Air conference in Liverpool.
Deighton, L. (1977) *Fighter: The True Story of the Battle of Britain*, London: Pimlico.
Deighton, L. (1993) *Blood, Tears and Folly: An Objective Look at World War II*, London:
   Jonathan Cape.
Der Baumeister (author not given) (1937) Die Deutsche Luftwaffe Baut! *Der Baumeister* 35(5):
   137–77.
Diamond, J. (1998) *Guns, Germs and Steel*, London: Random House.
Dobinson, C.S. (1997) *Airfield Themes*, unpublished report for English Heritage Thematic
   Listing Programme.
Dobinson, C.S. (1998) *RAF Netheravon: A Short Structural History*, unpublished report for
   English Heritage Thematic Listing Programme.
Douet, J. (1998) *British Barracks, 1600–1914: Their Architecture and Role in Society*, London: The
   Stationery Office.

Dudley, W.S. (2000) *The Battle of Midway. Maritime Archaeology and History of Hawaii and the Pacific*, 12th Annual Symposium, Hawaii.

English Heritage (2001) *Historic Airfields: Guidelines for Management*, London: English Heritage.

Edgerton, D. (1991) *England and the Aeroplane: An Essay on a Militant and Technological Nation*, London: Macmillan.

Francis, P. (1996a) *British Military Airfield Architecture*, Sparkford: Patrick Stephens.

Francis, P. (1996b) 'RAF Bicester', unpublished report for Cherwell District Council.

Francis, P. (2001) 'RAF Duxford: Historical Appraisal', unpublished report for Imperial War Museum, Duxford.

Gellhorn, M. (1959, reprint 1993) *The Face of War*, London: Granta.

Glover, J. (1999) *Humanity: A Moral History of the Twentieth Century*, London: Jonathan Cape.

Hall, P. (1998) *Cities in Civilisation*, London: Weidenfeld and Nicolson.

Hastings, M. (1979) *Bomber Command*, London: Michael Joseph.

Haun, A. and Henry, J. (1993) *Historic Context: US World War II Development of Airfields on Saipan July 1944–August 1945*, Hawaii: Paul H. Rosendahl.

Hellen, J.A. (1999) Temporary settlements and transient populations. The legacy of Britain's prisoner of war camps, *Erdkunde (Archive for Social Geography)* 53(3): 191–211.

Hobsbawm, E. (1994) *Age of Extremes: The Short Twentieth Century, 1914–1989*, London: Abacus.

Jockeit, W. (2000) 'The Conservation Plan for Templehof', unpublished paper delivered to the Europe de l'Air Conference, Berlin.

Keegan, J. (1993) *A History of Warfare*, London: Hutchinson.

Keegan, J. (1995) *The Battle for History: Re-fighting World War II*, London: Hutchinson.

Kennedy, P. (1988) *The Rise and Fall of the Great Powers: Economic Change and Military Conflict*, New York: Random House.

Kuipers, M. (2000) 'The Protection of Historic Aviation Sites in The Netherlands', unpublished paper delivered to the Europe de l'Air Conference, Berlin.

Lake, J. (2000) 'Thematic Survey of Military Aviation Sites and Structures', unpublished report for English Heritage Thematic Listing Programme.

Lake, J. and Schofield, J. (2000) 'Conservation and the Battle of Britain', in Addison, P. and Crang, J. (eds) *The Burning Blue: A New History of the Battle of Britain*, London: Pimlico, pp. 229–42.

Makinen, A. (1994) 'Hygiene, Technology and Economy: The 1930s Architecture of the Finnish Defence Forces', in *Docomomo Conference Proceedings*, Barcelona: Docomomo, pp. 135–40.

Milbrooke, A. (1998) *Guidelines for Evaluating and Documenting Historic Aviation Properties*, Washington DC: US Department of the Interior (National Park Service).

Morris, R. with Dobinson C.S. (1994) *Guy Gibson*, London: Penguin.

Price, A. (1979) *The Hardest Day*, London: Cassell.

Ramsey, W.G. (ed.) (1978) *Airfields of the Eighth*, London: After the Battle.

Ramsey, W.G. (ed.) (1996 (5th edn)) *The Battle of Britain: Then and Now*, London: After the Battle.

Ranisi, M. (1998a) *L'Aeroporto Italiano. Dalle Origine al Secondo Conflitto Mondiale* (2 volumes), Rome: Aeronautica Militare.

Ranisi, M. (1998b) *L'architettura della Regia Aeronautica*, Rome: Aeronautica Militare.

Smith, P. and Toulier, B. (eds) (2000) *Berlin Templehof, Liverpool Speke, Paris Le Bourget. Airport Architecture of the Thirties*, Paris: Edition du Patrimoine.

South Parker, N. (1982) Aviation in Wiltshire, *South Wiltshire Industrial Archaeology Society Monograph* 5.

Stamp, G. (ed.) (1988) *Britain in the Thirties*, London: Architectural Design, Profile 24.

Teich, M. (1996) The 20th-century scientific-technical revolution, *History Today* 46(11): 27–33.

Terraine, J. (1985) *The Right of the Line: The Royal Air Force in the European War, 1939–1945*, London: Hodder and Stoughton.

Voigt, W. (1996) 'From the Hippodrome to the Aerodrome, from the Air Station to the Terminal: European Airports, 1909–1945', in Zukovsky, J. (ed.). *Building for Air Travel: Architecture and Design for Commercial Aviation*, New York: The Art Institute of Chicago, pp. 27–49.

Vossebeld, R. (1997) *Luftwaffe in Nederland, Achtergrondaspecten*, Arnhem: Nederlandse Federatie voor Luchtvaartarchaeologie.

Wessex Archaeology (1998) *Stonehenge Military Installations*, unpublished report for English Heritage.

Willis, S. and Hollis, B. (1987) *Military Airfields in the British Isles, 1939–1945*, Newport Pagnell: Enthusiasts Publications.

Wood, D. and Dempster, D. (1969) *The Narrow Margin*, London: Tri-Service Press.

16 Social space and social control: analysing movement and management on modern military sites

MICHAEL J. ANDERTON

INTRODUCTION

Following the end of the Second World War in Britain, military sites came under pressure from several directions. Some sites continued in use as military bases, while others became agricultural stores or light-industrial workshops; the majority were destroyed by human forces, while further sites were removed by natural processes such as coastal erosion (Anderton forthcoming). Those sites which were left to decay are now few in number when compared with their original populations, though a small proportion have survived in a reasonable enough condition that they can be recorded, and in some cases preserved, through current heritage legislation and planning controls (Anderton forthcoming; Schofield this volume). These remaining sites have taken on a new cultural significance in recent years extending beyond the realms of their previous, immediately post-war roles as subjects for research among dedicated enthusiasts (see for example Wills 1985) or as children's playgrounds. During and beyond the celebrations for the fiftieth anniversary of D-Day in 1994 and VE Day in 1995, military sites in Britain began to enter the national psyche as they took on a wider cultural and political significance as symbols of our past for the future. This is an element of the history of these monuments that is familiar to those who analyse similar sites in other parts of the world, and one widely and eloquently discussed elsewhere in this volume. However, what isn't considered to the same extent is how these sites operated as entities within a nation at war. How much did they reflect the nation's contemporary social, political and cultural attitudes and aspirations during the Second World War?

While being viewed as symbols of history and current philosophies in a wider, modern, realm, these sites are only likely to be seen as the shells of buildings – albeit of varying shape and form – when conducting a conventional archaeological recording survey. Is there more that can be done; can the contemporary nature of these sites be assessed using archaeological techniques? In this chapter, primarily using anti-aircraft batteries as examples, I will consider whether we can use theoretical techniques which have been successfully employed elsewhere in archaeology to analyse the contemporary use of space and social approaches at these sites.

SPACE, STRUCTURE AND MEANING: ARCHAEOLOGY
AND SOCIAL LANDSCAPES

Archaeology has, in recent decades, made good use of anthropological, sociologi-
cal and psychological theories to examine the social meanings of space and structures in earlier societies and cultures. From the macro through to the micro level
of analysis archaeologists have proposed ways of understanding how both societies
and individuals defined their *place* within the *spaces* they occupied, and it is now
judged that 'space is both a reflection of cultural codes and meanings [as well as] a
reflection of practical activities and functional requirements' (Engelstad 1991: 50).
The physical landscape has become more than just a series of humps and bumps
across which the quality of land might vary; whole areas can now be seen as part of
a complex element in the journey through spiritual and secular life. Groups of
buildings are defined by observable rules regarding the way in which they are
approached and utilized by individuals and communities, and within individual
buildings family, social and gender hierarchies can be observed. These relationships can be examined at various levels.

At the macro level of study, landscape analysis can reveal complex arrangements
between physical and mental entities; arrangements that create the narrative within
which an individual and a society or culture-group perform or act out their daily
actions in the long term. Earlier monuments are very often reused as cultural signifiers for later generations, although they are not always used in the way that they
were originally intended (Barrett *et al.* 1991). The key point here is the fact that they
are still part of the narrative which defines the social dynamic for societies and individuals alike. The work of Roymans (1996) is an example of how this kind of
approach can map a social landscape. He shows that, within the southern Netherlands and northern Belgium, an ideological ordering of the landscape developed to
form an inner and outer circle of areas that defined aspects of social activity. Within
the inner circle were the more essential, living elements of social and cultural activity such as houses, cattle, meadows, fields and humans; in the outer circle were gal-
lows, pagan cemeteries, forests, heathlands and moors concentrated upon more
ethereal, darker elements.

Analysing anthropological evidence at the middle level of social space Lyons
(1996) has shown how the domestic structures in Déla, northern Cameroon,
reflect more than just the culture of a singularly identifiable social group. Buildings
in the area comprise a mix of round and rectilinear structures; and at first glance
there would appear to be little indication that either type had any particular cultural
significance. However, when statistical analysis is carried out on the families who
dwell in these structures a clearer picture of cultural groupings within Déla comes
to light. Four ethnic groups can be identified within a single community, each
being visible through their use of a particular style of building. For example, the
Mura group are equally divided in their choice of building, while the Wandala
group are firmly in favour of rectilinear structures.

At the individual level much information can be gained about social space, the
connection with family and social units and the way in which their roles are

developed and defined through the otherwise invisible rules which constitute the narrative of daily life. It has been shown by Møjberg (1991) that within the Inuit winterhouses of Greenland, social and gender groupings are visible in the limited number of material remains excavated from these structures. An important element in this study was the knowledge that these 'houses' were used on an irregular, cyclical basis and were cleaned out prior to each new occupation – presenting a single, identifiable layer of material prior to the structure's final abandonment. This cleaning process, and the fact that the winterhouse was known to have last been inhabited in the first half of the twentieth century, meant that some of the original occupants could be interviewed in order to examine the validity of the analysis of excavated material. Questions could be addressed such as the extent to which material left behind reflects the individuals who resided, or the activities that took place, within that particular area of the structure.

ANALYSING MILITARY SITES

These examples represent a small selection of the plethora of studies now available which have provided a means of interpreting earlier cultures. What has not been asked is how these types of study fare when used to analyse modern military sites. At present when this form of analysis is undertaken for modern sites and structures, reliance is placed on the work of social psychologists and architects to achieve results. While such studies have proved useful to a degree in interpreting human interaction at the wider scale, the study of shopping arcades (Shields 1991), Victorian psychiatric hospitals (Bartlett 1994) and twentieth-century domestic building plans (Brown 1990) does not necessarily provide the ideal raw material for the more intimate level of understanding of social and cultural discourses which the study of modern military sites requires.

At the landscape scale, the work of Roymans (1996) shows how landscapes may be viewed by archaeologists as symbolic entities, but it is difficult to see how this approach contributes to understanding the distribution of recent military sites. Primarily laid out with operational and topographical needs in mind, there is little to suggest that these sites developed any form of specific social symbolism in their original lifetime (beyond their obvious practical, protective function). It is only more recently in the UK, and particularly during the celebrations for the fiftieth anniversaries of D-Day and VE Day, that these military sites took on a new, culturally significant role. In a similar fashion to the way in which earlier monuments were used by later generations as cultural signifiers in the prehistoric period (Barrett *et al.* 1991), so these military sites were reinvented as symbols of an island nation that 'would never surrender to invasion from Europe': this is generally the line taken by the popular press in documenting approaches to the conservation and recording of modern military structures (cf. Finn 2000).

In examining contemporary site plans, and using the example of Lyons' (1996) work in Cameroon, is it possible to gain insight into how military sites operated and to define the social and cultural approaches of their occupants? Can a modern archaeological survey of the surviving buildings provide the necessary level of detail for such an enquiry or can it only be undertaken using contemporary plans and accounts? Recent surveys of Second World War anti-aircraft batteries in Britain are groundbreaking in terms of the level of detail and accuracy given over to military structures, but they do only concentrate on the extant buildings and structures themselves, particularly as the project brief for such work will, typically, dictate this approach (Oswald and Kenney 1994; Riley 1995; Brown and Pattison 1997). In other words, a great deal is written about the fabric of each site's surviving compo-nent parts, but no attempt is made to gain any insight into the contemporary social life of these sites. However, if surveys were undertaken with this objective in mind, and drew upon the examination of contemporary documents and plans, then the level of detail necessary for the application of appropriate theoretical analysis could be achieved.

A vast number of contemporary records are held in the Public Records Office, London (cf. Dobinson 1996), ranging from complete camp, airfield and station plans through to the minutiae of individual lavatory facilities. While the latter, more individual designs contained within documents such as the 'Barrack Synopsis (War)' (Dobinson 1996: 177) do not reveal a great deal beyond the mind of the designer's desire for uniformity, the labelled plans of the camps and their building layouts prove more useful sources. Just as the labelled plans of houses constructed prior to the Second World War give an indication of social hierarchies in terms of their functionality and allocations of space (Brown 1990), insight into forms of mil-itary control (and thus social orders) may be gleaned through the examination of contemporary layouts of military sites and the buildings shown on site plans. While many Second World War military sites have been demolished and others now lack all of their component parts, these drawings provide us with the scope for examin-ing the use of space in many forms. Studies can now range from examining con-trasts in the space and settings available within such areas as officers' and sergeants' messes through to the level at which the ordinary soldier, sailor or airman was con-trolled within his immediate surroundings.

Good examples of this latter point can be seen in the analysis of anti-aircraft and coastal battery plans where the guardroom and the officers' quarters are located close to the site entrance; while the soldiers' quarters were located near to the oper-ational centre of the site (that is, close to the artillery weapons). That the guard-room was located at the entrance is militarily self-explanatory, but locating the officers' quarters at the entrance provides a clear example of contemporary social control. No soldier entering or leaving the site would have been able to do so with-out being visible to the officers, thus emphasizing the officers' authority and supe-riority over the soldier in both a military and a social sense. The soldiers' journey through social narrative was reinforced with images of the contemporary hierarchi-cal status through the prominent location of the officers' quarters.

In addition to the above, the location of the soldiers' quarters near the guns could be seen as a sensible location: the men were thus 'ready for action' at a moment's notice. However, the guns were often in action for long periods and placing the sol-diers' accommodation further away would have been ideal for them (particularly in terms of rest and quiet). Unfortunately, doing this would also have resulted in a huge renegotiation of the social narrative at the site (and within the military order as a whole) as the huts would have been located opposite the officers' quarters. The new location would have equalized the soldiers' position, both physically and mentally, with that of the officers. This would have broken contemporary norms of social structure and appears not to have been considered.

Apart from the analysis of the layout of military sites from plans, and the social information this provides, a further option is to examine the testimony of individuals involved in the daily operations of these establishments. Individual accounts were used with great success by Møbjerg (1991) in her corroboration of the excavated remains of Inuit winterhouses in Greenland, and the application of this approach to military sites will now be examined.

While there is always some concern that individual testimonies may be biased – contemporary accounts may be influenced by the subjective atmosphere that prevailed at the time, and later accounts can be subject to the vagaries of time that may include such problems as memory loss or adjustment – as long as this is borne in mind a great deal of information can be gained in this way. One particular account of life in an anti-aircraft battery, for example, provides enough material to warrant analysis using theoretical techniques. Examining the account of Vee Robinson (1996), using the concepts of social laws and interactions as part of a wider form of narrative discourse, there is a great deal to be learnt about these military sites.

The concepts related to social laws and interactions are based upon the premise that while there is a main text of social norms to be read as a surface narrative, below it are many subtexts and alternative discourses. In essence, life is not one long, uncomplicated string of dialogue between people, a straightforward division between classes, genders or cultures. Individuals generally, and often without being conscious of it, operate on a more subversive level, constantly challenging and reinterpreting the social norms by which they are surrounded.

The image of anything military is one of a homogenous fighting machine, wheeling and standing to attention at the bark of an order (Fig. 16.1). However, this narrative does not recognize that the whole is made up of a substantial number of parts; and that these parts are human beings. In particular they were human beings from many different backgrounds drawn together for one purpose, and one purpose alone – to fight for their country for the duration of the war. That said, the higher classes still remained at the top, becoming officers, with the remainder being expected to abide by the external, civilian social system that this division perpetuated.

Robinson emphasizes the way in which individuals were, from day one, indoctrinated into this social narrative with recruits being 'inspected, injected, tested and physically graded' (1996: 12) (Fig. 16.2). She does, however, go on to stress how the Royal Artillery's attempt to turn recruits into 'khaki robots' (ibid.: 24) did not always succeed: 'underneath the khaki we were still very much individuals' (ibid.). It was this 'individuality' which came to the fore on numerous occasions, and emphasizes how a social subnarrative operated within the wider discourse of the contemporary military system (Fig. 16.3).

Figure 16.1 Keeping on the straight and narrow: military discipline at the pedestrian level

Source: Imperial War Museum (photograph H41360)

Robinson's account of life within anti-aircraft batteries emphasizes that military norms were only maintained to a certain degree. Individuals were very much involved in creating subnarratives within the system. For example, uniform in the military is, to all intents and purposes, exactly what it purports to be. It is designed to promote a homogenous, uniform, herd-like feel which inspires the notion of teamwork. Individuals being what they are, however, alternative actions are deemed necessary. As Auxiliary Territorial Service (ATS) personnel, rather than Royal Artillery Regiment staff, the women manning anti-aircraft batteries were not entitled to wear the insignia of the Artillery Regiment (white lanyards and grenade-flash badges). Many of the women did just that, however, breaking the strict homogeneity that is military rule. In addition, many of them wore officer-issue ties (a finer quality product) (cf. Kerr 1990: 57–8; Robinson 1996: 45). This may seem a trivial fashion statement, but it can also be interpreted as an attempt at breaking down the social divide.

Other efforts to create an alternative narrative to the social order were carried out by groups of individuals in the name of the collective body. Two examples stand out from Robinson's accounts. The first concerns the ordering of two ATS women to clean the accommodation of two male sergeants. This was not an ATS duty and it was felt that the women should make a stand to prevent this happening again. Subsequently, the hut (which accommodated two men in a space which twelve soldiers lived in: a social statement in itself) was transformed from the pigsty it resembled when the work began, into a veritable palace. Wild flowers were placed in shaving-mug 'vases', the floors were scrubbed and the beds exceptionally well made. But the

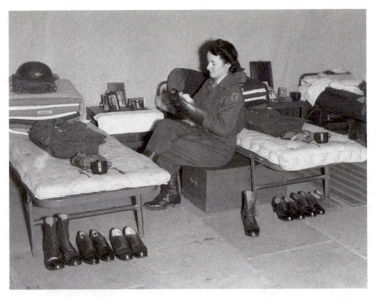

Figure 16.2 The Khaki Robot at work: homogenous, uniform and herdlike, but with personal touches visible

Source: Imperial War Museum (Photograph H41356)

Figure 16.3 The Khaki Robot at rest: a Des Res barracks. Individuality within the system?

Source: Imperial War Museum (Photograph H41358)

women also added some 'personal touches' to their work: the arms and legs of pyja-
mas were sewn up and the beds were 'apple-pied' (the sheets folded in half underneath the covers) and leaves and dirt were placed within the folds of the sheets (Robinson 1990: 97–8). Safe to say that no ATS personnel were ever asked to tidy up a
sergeant's quarters again. The result: Alternative Discourse 1 – Military Discipline 0.

In the second incident, the visit of a high-ranking officer required a great deal of
spit and polish around the camp in order to impress the visitor – cleanliness equating to efficiency in the Royal Artillery. Unfortunately the visit came at a time when
our Russian allies were suffering heavy losses during the Battle for Stalingrad.
Resentment was running high amongst some people that not enough was being
done to help the Russians. As the parade was mustered and brought to order one
gunner decided to voice his resentment, declaring that 'Britain blancos while
Russia bleeds' (Robinson 1996: 121). This expression of sentiment was very much
against the normal discourse that was supposed to prevail in the military, and as a
result the parade sergeant ordered the culprit to step forward for suitable punishment. What happened next shows how a collective response can subvert the 'traditional' narrative. Three male gunners immediately stepped forward, to be followed
seconds later by the whole parade. No response was given by the sergeant in charge
and the parade was dismissed without any individual being punished. Alternative
Discourse 2 – Military Discipline 0.

CONCLUSION: FUTURE DIRECTIONS?

The analysis of contemporary social approaches on military sites during the
Second World War can only be achieved through archaeological examination
combined with testimonial and documentary sources – though the level of information retrieved will vary according to the approach used. At the wider level of
landscape analysis, the contemporary nature of the sites' placement was very much
subject to the military need for operational efficiency and its location took no
account of prevailing agricultural, religious or other socio-cultural needs. It is only
during the post-war years, and particularly over the last two to three decades, that
these sites have become more than functional sites: they have been redeveloped as
cultural signifiers for a new generation. This aspect is not revealed through standard archaeological examination of the sites themselves (the 'bare-shell' syn-
drome); it requires the reading of more modern cultural texts.

Social evidence may be observed when the layout of a site is analysed, though this
is best carried out through the examination of contemporary plans. A survey of surviving buildings without the plans will merely reveal a series of comparable empty
structures from which the lack of artefacts will not reflect the complexity of their
former use. Even though only a few decades have passed since the building and
occupation of these sites, their analysis will be difficult without the benefit of contemporary documentation.

Personal accounts, such as those of Robinson (1996), provide a way into individual as well as collective social narratives. These accounts, however, are few and far

between, and more work needs to be done with first-hand accounts to establish how individuals and groups used their space, both within buildings, and across the site as a whole. Some work has already been conducted, and veterans of both world wars have been interviewed by the Imperial War Museum, London, for their oral history archives. These archives provide a wealth of information regarding technical operations and general day-to-day military life, but the interviews have failed to address the questions we as archaeologists would find pertinent in understanding social interaction within military bases and their buildings. Questions regarding domestic layouts within huts, living space per individual, domestic hierarchies in huts and so forth would provide the sort of material needed to turn building plans and empty, concrete shells into living, breathing cultural artefacts that reflect the contemporary social culture in which they were erected. An archaeologically driven oral history programme would be a valuable exercise, and is urgently needed. The effective integration of documentary sources, first-hand accounts and archaeological investigation (for example of artefact deposition across sites) could then combine to create an integrated methodology which could satisfy all the needs of a modern interpretation of military structures and sites, moving beyond the fabric to the social lives and order they once constrained.

ACKNOWLEDGEMENTS

Thanks go to the Imperial War Museum for their permission to publish the photographs in this chapter; and also to Bob Bewley and John Schofield without whom this military odyssey would never have begun in the first place.

REFERENCES

Anderton, M.J. (forthcoming) *An Aerial Photographic Assessment of World War II Military Sites in England*, London: English Heritage.
Barrett, J., Bradley, R. and Green, M. (1991) *Landscape, Monuments and Society: The Prehistory of Cranborne Chase*, Cambridge: Cambridge University Press.
Bartlett, A.E.A. (1994) 'Spatial order and psychiatric disorder', in Parker Pearson, M. and Richards, C. (eds) *Architecture and Order*, London: Routledge, pp.178–95.
Brown, F.E. (1990) 'Analysing small building plans: a morphological approach', in Samson, R. (ed.) *The Social Archaeology of Houses*, Edinburgh: Edinburgh University Press, pp. 259–76.
Brown, M. and Pattison, P. (1997) *Beacon Hill Fort, Harwich, Essex*, Cambridge: RCHME Survey Report.
Dobinson, C. (1996) *Twentieth Century Fortifications in England Volume 1.1: Anti-Aircraft Artillery, 1914–46*, York: Council for British Archaeology.
Engelstad, E. (1991) 'Gender and the use of household space: an ethnoarchaeological approach,' in Grøn, Ø., Englestad, E. and Lindblom, I. (eds) *Social Space: Human Spatial Behaviour in Dwellings and Settlements*, Odense: Odense University Press, pp. 49–54.
Finn, C. (2000) Defiant Britain: mapping the bunkers and pillboxes built to stymie a Nazi invasion, *Archaeology* 53(3): 42–9.

Kerr, D.B. (1990) *The Girls Behind the Guns*, London: Robert Hale.

Lyons, D. (1996) The politics of house shape: round versus rectilinear domestic structures in Déla compounds, Northern Cameroon, *Antiquity* 70: 351–67.

Møbjerg, T. (1991) 'The spatial organisation of an Innuit winterhouse in Greenland: an ethnoarchaeological study', in Grøn, Ø., Englestad, E. and Lindblom, I. (eds) *Social Space: Human Spatial Behaviour in Dwellings and Settlements*, Odense: Odense University Press, pp. 40–8.

Oswald, A. and Kenney, J. (1994) *Second World War Anti-Aircraft Batteries at Bowaters Farm, Thurrock, Essex*, Cambridge: RCHME Survey Report.

Riley, H. (1995) *Brean Down, Brean, Somerset: An Archaeological Survey*, Exeter: RCHME Survey Report.

Robinson, V. (1996) *Sisters in Arms*, London: Harper Collins.

Roymans, N. (1996) The South Netherlands Project – Changing perspectives on landscape and culture, *Archaeological Dialogues* 3(2): 231–45.

Shields, R. (1991) 'Reading the Built Environment: 150 years of the shopping arcade', in Grøn, Ø., Englestad, E. and Lindblom, I. (eds) *Social Space: Human Spatial Behaviour in Dwellings and Settlements*, Odense: Odense University Press, pp. 60–78.

Wills, H. (1985) *Pillboxes: A Study of UK Defences 1940*, London: Leo Cooper.

17 The differing development paths of Second World War concentration camps and the possibility of an application of a principle of equifinality

JOHN G. BEECH

Although evidence of the existence of Nazi concentration camps had been placed before the Allies during the war, it was not until liberation in the spring of 1945 that the full extent of what had been happening became public knowledge. Initially the camps continued to hold their inmates, ostensibly for medical reasons, but soon they were released. Some camps were then abandoned, but others found new uses, typically as detention camps for Nazi detainees. Westerbork, in The Netherlands, was used for approximately twenty years to house displaced persons from the former Dutch colonies (Land-Weber 1998). One camp – Neuengamme – continues in use as a prison today.

It was only in the 1950s that plans to commemorate those who had suffered and died in the camps were drawn up. Two issues were implicitly addressed under the general umbrella of continuing to recognize their former function:

1 A 'remembering' function – typically a monument or a garden of remembrance, designed more for the needs of the survivors and the families of those who did not survive (Stein and Stein 1993).
2 A 'not forgetting' function – the preservation of what remained in terms of infrastructure, designed more for general societal needs.

In both cases the need for 'site management' arose, as the site had become, in a loose but literal sense, a visitor attraction. At this point the interest of two academic strands meet. One strand takes in archaeology and heritage interests; the other management, tourism and business interests. They meet under the heading Modern Heritage Site Management.

As unconventional tourist attractions, some of the camps are attracting large numbers of tourists and are becoming 'must-sees' in their particular localities. Auschwitz is arguably the most developed as a tourist attraction, and it is depressing to note that a shopping centre has been proposed within yards of the site (Edmonton Jewish Life 1996). Equally contentious has been the opening of a McDonald's fast food outlet a short distance from the Dachau camp visitors' car park (Jewish Defense League 1996).

In earlier papers (Beech 1998; Beech 2000), the author highlighted the two-part aspects of Buchenwald concentration camp as a tourist attraction (Table 17.1) and

Table 17.1 Two-part aspects of Buchenwald concentration camp as a tourist attraction

Location	Remains of camp	1950s memorial
Origin	Historical; a construct in its own right.	Memorial; dependent on the original construct for its meaning and symbolism.
Function	Debatable – 'lest we forget' or 'inherent historical interest'? Inherently concerned with both history and heritage. No longer an intentional function.	Reflective; respectful. Overtly concerned with heritage. Above all, intentional.
Symbolism	In the mind of the beholder but not in the mind of the originator.	In the mind especially of the originator and also the beholder.
Typical engendered emotions	Revulsion; anger; puzzlement; discomfort.	Attraction; peace; understanding; comfort.

the bipartisan nature of its visitors. The camp meets the needs of two groups of visitors with totally different motivations. The distinction lies in the connection, or lack of one, between the individual visitor and the camp: those who suffered personal loss as a result of what happened at the camp are clearly not tourists other than in a narrow technical sense, but on a personal voyage; those who lack a personal connection are, by any definition, either excursionists or tourists, depending on how long they are away from home.

This inherent dissonance is, Tunbridge and Ashworth argue, 'universal in that it is a condition, whether active or latent, of all heritage to some degree' (1996; 21). The balance between the two functions of the camps today and the two types of visitor must inevitably change over time.

As a final consideration in this introduction, the existence of the camps today as a focus for a much wider heritage of atrocity commemorated by the victims of the holocaust should be noted. Tunbridge and Ashworth (1996; 127) point out that it is the very success of the extermination policies that has resulted in the fact that the largest communities sharing the heritage lie well away from the sites of the atrocities. For them, a sense of 'pilgrimage' envelops a visit to the sites, making the distinction between the two kinds of visitor – an irony indeed that the segregation of the Nazis, the enforced divide between the two communities, has become self-perpetuating.

HISTORICAL BACKGROUND

The first concentration camp established by the Nazis was at Dachau in 1933. Its establishment was noted in local newspapers, but subsequent camps were not publicly acknowledged. The early role of the camps was to detain perceived opponents of the regime. Buchenwald, which was opened in 1937, was originally intended for 'political opponents of the Nazi regime, separatists, so-called social misfits, Jews, Jehovah's Witnesses and homosexuals' (Haertl 1996). In fact the first inmates included German political prisoners, habitual criminals and Jehovah's Witnesses (Lüttgenau 1995). By the summer of 1938, large convoys of Jews, Sinti and Romany gypsies and homosexuals had begun to arrive. The opponents of the regime ultimately included the politically and racially unacceptable, the criminally unacceptable (for whom the camps provided a small-scale alternative to prisons), and, in some cases, the physically unacceptable: disabled people, homosexuals and those considered to be psychologically unacceptable – people suffering from mental illnesses.

Although Germany began military operations in 1938, annexing first Austria and then Czechoslovakia, it was not until the following year that opposition was encountered, in Poland, and a formal state of war began. As the war progressed, the camps began to take on one of three functions: transit camp or holding centre; forced labour camp, associated with production of goods to support the war effort; and extermination camp.

From January 1943, they were classified into three types (Austrian Home Office 1997) with increasingly harsh regimes:

- Camp Category I: 'for all detainees charged with misdemeanours and relatively improvable as well as for special cases and prisoners in solitary confinement' (e.g. Dachau, Sachsenhausen and Auschwitz I);
- Camp Category II: 'for detainees charged with a felony but nevertheless educable and improvable' (e.g. Buchenwald, Flossenbürg, Neuengamme and Auschwitz-Birkenau);
- Camp Category III: 'for accused felons, incorrigibles and at the same time hardened criminals and asocial individuals, in other words, hardly educable detainees' (uniquely the Mauthausen concentration camp).

They remained essentially civilian detention centres in spite of the war, although there are a few examples of Allied prisoners-of-war (PoWs) being detained in forced labour camps – examples are Buchenwald and Mauthausen – as a result of persistent attempts to escape from PoW camps.

The progression of the war resulted both in individual camps changing (Buchenwald, for example, which originally held only German nationals, was holding only 5 per cent German nationals by April 1945), and in new camps being built. Following the Wannsee Conference of 1942, the extermination camps began to operate at Auschwitz-Birkenau, Belzec, Chelmno, Majdanek, Sobibor and Treblinka, all in pre-war Poland. As the Red Army pressed forward from 1944, the most easterly camps – Belzec, Chelmno, Plaszow, Sobibor and Treblinka – were liquidated and the Nazis attempted to hide evidence of their existence. Similar action was taken at Natzweiler in France, where the Allies were approaching from the Mediterranean coast. In the final days of the war the Allies came upon the awful truth as they liberated the camps listed in Table 17.2.

Table 17.2 Liberation of the camps

Camp	Liberated by troops of
Auschwitz–Birkenau	USSR
Bergen–Belsen	UK
Buchenwald	USA
Dachau	USA
Dora/Mittelbau	USA
Flossenbürg	USA
Gross-Rosen	USSR
Majdanek	USSR
Mauthausen	USA
Neuengamme	UK
Ravensbrück	USSR
Sachsenhausen	USSR
Stutthof	USSR
Terezin/Theresienstadt	USSR
Westerbork	Canada

Development since the war

Let us initially view the camps in a generalized form in order to establish a possible archetype for development following liberation. Broadly, the following stages of development were passed through, although not every camp will have followed this exact progression:

1   Immediate post-liberation: Because of the medical condition of any inmates still on site, it was necessary to provide medical treatment and to make some attempt to relocate them. The kind of counselling that one might expect today was not available.

2   Allied occupation: Occupying forces made use of the camp in some way for large groups of people. This continued an earlier practice in a few cases – Mauthausen and Theresienstadt had been Austro-Hungarian PoW camps in the First World War. The nature of the use depended on the political inclination of the occupying power. The Soviets tended to use the camps as detention and punishment centres for captured Nazis, and the deaths not only continued, but, in the case of Buchenwald, the death rate actually increased. The Western powers tended to use the camps for displaced persons.

3 Abandonment: In the early 1950s the requirement for continued use dimin-
   ished and the camps were generally abandoned. Those that were small
   tended to be demolished. The first plans for memorials were formed, initiated largely by survivors and especially Jewish survivors.
4 Memorial: Memorials were dedicated and sites developed to emphasize
   remembrance. No great emphasis was placed on conservation or on active
   remembrance. Visitors were those who had direct connection with the specific camp, either as survivors or as relatives of survivors.
5 Active remembrance, conservation and interpretation: There was, on the one
   hand, an increasing sense of awareness that 'we must never forget' and yet, on
   the other hand, a sense of distancing from the events that had taken place
   because of the passage of time. This led to a realization that, however uncomfortable it may be, however unpleasant to recognize, it was necessary to accept
   the concentration camps as part of – at least – the victims' cultural heritage. It
   was therefore essential to preserve what survived and to begin the task of
   offering some formal on-site interpretation and facilities.
6 The beginnings of impersonalization and normalization: As the time distance
   increased and the events of the Second World War began to become less
   immediate in the public psyche, the camps which had memorials, and especially those with preserved infrastructure, started down the road of becoming
   more conventional tourist attractions. The socio-political environment saw
   the fall of Communism, the rise of neo-fascism (arguably as a backlash) and
   the heightened awareness of identity among world Jewry. All of these factors
   mitigated towards vastly increased numbers of visitors to concentration
   camps, albeit for widely differing motivations. A new type of visitor began to
   appear: the student of the holocaust (Gilbert 1997). Some of the sites developed as almost conventional tourist attractions (Terrance 1999), albeit in the
   genre that has become known as dark tourism (Foley and Lennon 1997).

The variables

Some flaws in the presentation of a general model are already apparent from the
above – the differing scenarios in Eastern and Western Europe, for example. It is
therefore necessary to identify the variables which might lead to differing development paths and to consider their impact in such paths.

1 Camp location with respect to pre-war Germany. While the earlier camps were
   by definition in pre-war Germany, most camps constructed after 1938 were
   built in occupied territories. Particularly noticeable as a trend is that the extermination camps were built in Poland rather than Germany. In Second World
   War terminology, they were built in the General Government area rather than
   in the part of *Grosses Deutschland* which had been part of pre-war Poland. The
   greater atrocities were thus committed outside the old Reich borders.
2 Camp location post-1948.[1] The ambient regime seems to have had a strong
   influence on development paths. In contrast with those in the West, Eastern

Bloc camps have been a focus for commemoration of the triumph of Communism over fascism. In the 1950s and even the 1960s camp sites were used for annual military parades to commemorate liberation. In addition, they have been used as educational sites. In the Eastern Bloc camps, school parties have been regular visitors, with children being taught their heritage from the current regime's perspective. The tendency in the West has been to ignore their existence, although efforts that have made to educate the new generations of Austrians about Mauthausen (Wyman 1996: 503; Haunschmied 1998). The two camps that are located not only outside the former Eastern Bloc but also outside the German-speaking world enjoy almost total anonymity in the UK for example: a straw poll of the author's colleagues revealed total ignorance of Natzweiler, in France, and Westerbork, in The Netherlands.

3   Role and category of the operational camp. Here there are stark differences in public perception, at least from the Western non-Jewish perspective. Of the extermination camps, Auschwitz-Birkenau and Treblinka are well known, Sobibor is known to a few, but Belzec, Chelmno and Majdanek are virtually unknown other than to those with a personal connection. The two well-known camps are those with clearly the highest number of deaths, but lower down such a scale the correlation breaks down – Belzec, for example, saw the perpetration of more than 600 000 deaths, compared with Treblinka's 800–900 000 and Sobibor's 250 000. The author can offer no explanation for how Belzec, where over half a million people were murdered, is so little known. The number of deaths is the quantitative measure of inhumanity in each camp, but there are qualitative factors as well, notably the inhumane treatment of inmates of the forced labour camps. The death tolls, although significantly lower than in the extermination camps, are surprisingly high if viewed in the cold light of attrition rates of a workforce. Mauthausen, responsible for 120 000 deaths, does not share the notoriety of, for example, Buchenwald (former East Germany) with 60 000 deaths, or Dachau with roughly 30 000 deaths.

4   Current status: degree of conservation and commemoration. The list of camps which today have both memorials and some preserved infrastructure includes all the well-known camps, and also a few less well known. They are Auschwitz, Birkenau, Buchenwald, Dachau, Flossenbürg, Gross Rosen, Majdanek, Mauthausen, Natzweiler, Ravensbrück, Sachsenhausen, Strutthof and Terezin/Teresienstadt. Those that have a memorial but no extant buildings are Belzec, Chelmno, Dora/Mittelbau, Sobibor, Treblinka and Westerbork and include only one well-known camp. This suggests that the preservation of buildings has been more crucial in sustaining popular interest and recognition than the erection of a memorial, although the presence of extant buildings does not in itself constitute a precondition for the development of holocaust visitation, as the presence of holocaust centres in North America demonstrates. The only major camp with no memorial or extant building, Plaszow, is today scarcely known.

CONCLUSIONS

The suggestion that a general evolutionary model of development can be advanced is thus too simplistic. The major variables which influence the development of concentration camps as visitor attractions, including some which pre-date the war, offer a bewildering variety of inputs which make generalized conclusions seriously flawed because of the multitude of exceptions.

Since the fall of Communism in the early 1990s, however, one major variable has become constant. This socio-political revolution has resulted in the opening up of tourist markets and a great increase in East–West tourist traffic. Prior to this, tourist traffic had been largely confined to travel within each bloc – the quantity of international traffic within the old Eastern Bloc should not be underestimated. Other factors are historically based, for example the position of the camp with respect to Third Reich frontiers, and are therefore of diminishing influence. If any principle of equifinality might be applicable, then this is the era when it is most likely to work.

The equifinal outcome might be imagined as a tourist attraction not entirely dissimilar to visitor centres associated with earlier sites of war and brutality. Memorials and visitor centres to mark twentieth-century military devastation and carnage are increasingly familiar. The Menin Gate, for example, and the Arc de Triomphe are tourist attractions: few seem to question the acceptability of the 'triomphe'. Many city tours include stops at war memorials and tombs of the unknown warrior; the tour of Cambridge includes a visit to the war graves of the USAAF personnel who died bombing Europe.

The trend then is clear. As time distances the personal contact and the number of visitors with personal sensitivities to be respected diminishes, we move towards an era when the concentration camps will be sites of education, warning and remembrance, but no longer places where the heritage hurts quite so much. In the further future, what are the prospects for concentration camps as tourist attractions? Two factors are likely to determine outcomes: the inherent 'attractiveness' of the site to tourists and the marketing skills with which it is presented.

In the former case, the evidence of two surveys of web presence, conducted using the Alta Vista search engine on 19 September 1998 and again on 5 June 2000, argues reasonably strongly for equifinality, especially if a restricted view of which camps are under consideration is taken. Of all the variables discussed, the only one with any real hint of affecting the outcome was whether there were extant buildings. In the long term, these will be the 'attractive' camps rather than those with only memorials. Memorials do not constitute sufficient visitor interest to be stand-alone attractions – they only attract as part of some wider city tour, for example. Buchenwald and Dachau are near enough to city centres to fall into this category had they not had extant buildings. The shorter term evidence of the web survey does not support a case for the identification of clear strands, however. With the exception of Strutthof, where a tiny interest has actually declined, there has been mostly significant growth. Auschwitz offers an example of lower-than-average growth of interest, which might suggest reaching saturation. The five camps which have shown the greatest growth of Internet interest are, in decreasing order: Treblinka, Majdanek, Buchenwald, Mauthausen and Sachsenhausen, and do not offer any entirely consistent pattern, although all but one were formerly under Communist regimes.

In the case of marketing skills, there is clearly the full potential for equifinality. With the fall of Communism, the level of local marketing skills at each site is becoming very similar. The only significant difference at the present time is the willingness to use those marketing skills or not, a decision that seems to be determined by the geo-political context of the camp. The former Eastern Bloc countries continue to promote the sites, though more for economic than political reasons perhaps. The German-speaking world still has to come to terms fully with the Third Reich and it may well be many years before the 'distance' is sufficient for the camps to become domestic destinations as well as international ones. In the case of France and The Netherlands, there is still a reluctance, born of political correctness or imagined sensitivity, to promote the camps, but again time will inevitably bring the necessary distance.

While many will deplore the coldness of the argument which suggests equifinality will appear through marketing the camps, this is indicative of both the scale of the horrors committed (and our perception of them) and the still relatively short time distance from such horrors. But to assume that the horror will not diminish with time and that the curiosity which we have for horror will not grow is to assume that human nature will change. For this, there is sadly no evidence.

NOTE

1 The reason for choosing 1948 as a marker is twofold:
   * the liberators of camps were not necessarily the commanding power in the post-war era. Buchenwald, Dora/Mittelbau and Mauthausen were liberated by Western Allies but within a very short period were handed over to Soviet control. Mauthausen returned to the Western Bloc in 1955 with the re-establishment of an independent Austria, but the other two remained under communist regimes until the early 1990s;
   * the imposition of communist governments did not follow Soviet occupation immediately, Czechoslovakia, for example, not becoming a communist state until 1948.

REFERENCES

Austrian Home Office (1997) *Mauthausen Memorial*, available: http://www.mauthausen-memorial. gv.at/engl/Geschichte/menu-o.01.03.html (5 June 2000).

Beech, J. (1998) 'Buchenwald Concentration Camp as a tourist attraction', in *The Third Annual Cambridge Heritage Seminar: Heritage That Hurts* (unpublished), Cambridge University Department of Archaeology, Cambridge.

Beech, J. (2000) The enigma of holocaust sites as tourist attractions – the case of Buchenwald, *Managing Leisure* 5(1): 29–41.

Edmonton Jewish Life (1996) *Auschwitz Development Project on Hold*, available: http://www.compcocity.com/ejl/april/AUSCHWITZ.htm (5 June 2000).

Foley, M. and Lennon, J. (1997) 'Dark tourism – an ethical dilemma', in Foley, M., Lennon, J. and Maxwell, G. (eds) *Hospitality, Tourism and Leisure Management*, London: Cassell, pp. 153–64.

Gilbert, M. (1997) *Holocaust Journey*, London: Weidenfeld and Nicolson.

Haertl, U. (1996) *Buchenwald Memorial*, Weimar: Buchenwald Memorial.

Haunschmied, R.A. (1998) *KZ Mauthausen-Gusen*, available: http://linz.orf.at/orf/gusen/index.htm (5 June 2000).

Jewish Defence League (1996) *JDL Protests (You Can Too): Close McDonalds at Dachau!* Available: http://www.jdl.org/mcdonalds.html (18 September 1998).

Land-Weber, E. (1998) *Westerbork*, available: http://www.humboldt.edu/~rescuers/book/Bochove/bertlinks/wbork.html (5 June 2000).

Lüttgenau, R.G. (1995) *Buchenwald Concentration Camp from 1937 to 1945 – Explanatory Booklet for the Historical Exhibition*, Weimar: Buchenwald Memorial.

Stein, S. and Stein, H. (1993) *Buchenwald – A Tour of the Memorial Site*, Weimar: Buchenwald Memorial.

Terrance, M. (1999) *Concentration Camps: A Traveler's Guide to World War II Sites*, Parkland: Universal.

Tunbridge, J.E. and Ashworth, A.J. (1996) *Dissonant Heritage – The Management of the Past as a Resource in Conflict*, Chichester: Wiley.

Wyman, D.S. (1996) *The World Reacts to the Holocaust*, Baltimore: Johns Hopkins University Press.

18   A many-faced heritage: the wars of Indochina

P. Bion Griffin

> The MIA team had uncovered a vast family of forgotten members of their regi-
> ment, dead under the mantle of the warm jungle. The fallen soldiers shared one
> destiny; no longer were there honorable or disgraced soldiers, heroic or cowardly,
> worthy or worthless. Now they were merely names and remains.
> Those who survived continue to live. But that will has gone, that burning will
> which was once Vietnam's salvation. Where is the reward of enlightenment due to
> us for attaining our sacred war goals?
>
> Bao Ninh (1993: 25, 47)

Call it La Sale Guerre, the Vietnam War, the American War, the First and Second
Indochina Conflicts, as you will.[1] The wars in question in that part of Southeast
Asia still most easily called Indochina, or Indochine, ran their violent courses from
the final days of the Second World War through to 1975. Of course, the whole
region has been at war for some 2000 years of record. Conflicts have continued
from 1975 through AD 2000, first with the victorious armies of the Socialist
Republic of Vietnam flowing with unexpected ease to Phnom Penh and beyond,
and most recently with the ever-vigorous Hmong of northern Laos resisting the
alleged exploitation by the Lao People's Democratic Republic.

Clearly, when thinking of the archaeological and cultural landscapes of
Indochina and of the heritage of war, we have many points of view to consider.
And, unlike the legacy of the First and Second World Wars, there are few battlefields of the traditional sort. Post-Second World War Indochina was a war of rice
paddies, jungle hillsides, peasants' hamlets and occasionally urban streets. Remnants of the wars include tunnel systems and physical sites of conflict now denuded
of most material culture, as well as abandoned and then commandeered airfields,
port facilities and administrative buildings. The battlefields, or battlegrounds most
visible and most remembered, are few and are those in which the foreigners either
suffered devastating defeat or got out by the grace of God and overwhelming technology. Indeed, the marking of heritage has largely gone to the victors, and their
cultural and touristic views are as interesting and important as is a focus on the
return of the non-native.

The archaeology of the Indochina wars is, strictly speaking, non-existent. An archaeological view of the heritage, of its landscape and material remains, and the role of both heritage management and heritage tourism is, however, of immediate concern and importance. As indicated in the present volume, the heritage management of war – the representation of the past and the construction of national memory – is big business. Tourism may be the single largest domain of the world economy. Considering Vietnam, domestic and international tourism is growing rapidly, in spite of the relative difficulties of entrance to the country. Monuments and museums abound, ranging from facilities with large exhibits in Ho Chi Minh City and Hanoi to small displays such as at the village of My Lai, where busloads of Vietnamese visitors mingle with the international crowd. The return of American military personnel who once served in-country dominates the foreign war-heritage visitor community. The interests of these few will dominate foreign interests in site management for two or three decades, but a larger and more inclusive view must soon be addressed.

Here, five principal countries and their interests will be considered: Vietnam, Laos, Cambodia, France and the United States of America. A competent archaeology researches remains within each of the five. France is most removed by time, but retains military bases, museums, and memorabilia of its various colonial sites, and of the military action therein. Never a country or a culture prone to lose interest in its soldiers' heritage, France and the French are, as will be noted below, returning to Vietnam as tourists of the war and as tourists in the former Francophone world. The United States, with its post-Second World War warrior generation, more visibly displays the symbols of the war. The Vietnam Veterans' Memorial in Washington DC, and travelling (as well as Internet) displays are incredibly important. Since memorials and materials are a significant part of war heritage, the Washington Memorial, the most frequently visited national monument, is especially germane, with its tens of thousands of gift offerings by surviving veterans and families. Our thoughts on the war's heritage begin with the memorial and its offerings, sacred offerings really, pouring out the hearts of the donors for the dead, and providing the symbolic essence of the war's American meanings (Palmer 1987; Allen 1995). These offerings, all secured by government personnel, have even been used in a Smithsonian Institution exhibit. The offerings are at the heart of archaeological material culture, representing not only the dead, but also the losses of the living. Combat boots, teddy bears, American flags: all the true memorabilia of human loss and sacrifice are the 'archaeological data' left at the memorial, and while each piece's individual meaning is lost, the cultural pattern remains for us to understand.

Indochina, while full of the stuff of archaeologically translatable heritage phenomena, is not abundant in heritage as seen from the two world wars. As noted, battlefields are few, though the few are especially of interest. Fortifications are minimal, facilities much modified and the daily stuff of war – tanks, planes, firearms of all sorts and sizes, even expended rounds – has been largely recycled. The monuments and displays are those of the victors: on occasion captured hardware, at other times the machinery of the NVA, or North Vietnamese Army – more properly named the PAVN, or People's Army of Viet Nam. Two heritage landscapes are especially worthy of heritage understanding: those of armed conflict and those of facilities supporting the military. The former may in turn be divided into two types: the scenes of major battles and the terrains representative of the nature of the war. For example, today's Khe Sanh valley and rice paddies in a monsoon downpour evoke different but powerful images and emotions to both former actors and the informed visitor. A survivor of the Northern army may (and surely will) bring different values and emotions, but these landscapes are central to the marking of all heritage.

The town of Angkor Borei, Cambodia, in the upper Mekong Delta and about 8 km upstream from the border with Vietnam exemplifies this multi-faceted and equivocal view. Angkor Borei was heavily bombed by American airmen and was the site of action by ARVN (Army of the Republic of Vietnam), American and Royal Cambodian Army soldiers against Viet Cong. As one former American soldier recently put it,

> I was sitting on those walls you archaeologists study, listening to Nixon assure Americans that the United States would never invade Cambodia! And even more ridiculous, when the ARVN and Cambodians were not killing Viet Cong, they were killing each other!
>
> (Shaughnessy, personal communication)

Yet in 1995, when I asked about the remnants of an interesting concrete building, the locals at Angkor Borei stated that Lon Nol bombed it. The next year they confessed that they had mis-stated, concealing the American bombing to save us embarrassment! Today there is no local heritage of the war, only memories of dying from the late 1960s through the destruction by the Khmer Rouge in the late 1970s. Instead, they speak of the heritage of Angkor Borei as the true Kok Thlok, the place at the beginning of history where the Khmer people were created and civilization began 2000 years ago. Tourists too come to look at ancient remains, and have yet to be educated about the Pol Pot-built canals and the bombed-out town.

The two present foci in heritage tourism in Vietnam itself are aimed at its citizens and their memory and appreciation of the American war, and at American veterans returning for reunion, reconciliation and relief from the 'Vietnam' war. Interestingly, both foci favour an integration of war heritage tourism and cultural tourism, or an appreciation (and monetary expenditure) for the beauties of the natural, cultural and historic environments. The Vietnamese hosts and officials realize that the country's military conflict sites may briefly draw visitors, but without the country's beauty, sights, smells and sounds, the contact will be cursory and fleeting. Indeed, most returning veterans wish a flavour of the whole sensory experience, I believe, but sites of conflict are critical to those who lived them.

Dien Bien Phu, Ia Drang and Khe Sanh valleys represent three of the battlefield landscapes that are of special interest here. All were sites of protracted action and serious loss of life for both 'sides', and were symbolically critical in the war efforts. Two of the three remain favoured battlefield tourism sites. Battlefield tourism and

pilgrimage (Lloyd 1998) both characterize the motivations of present visitors to
Indochina battlefields, and both seem interwoven with sacred, symbolic and voy-
euristic behaviours and rationales.

Dien Bien Phu[2] is a remote valley in northern Vietnam, very close to the Lao
border, and a favoured destination for a small number of French visitors. Dien Bien
Phu saw the siege and battle that ended the French colonial occupation that had
been resumed after the Second World War. In 1953 some 16 500 Legionnaires and
others under General Henri Navarre fortified the valley. The Viet Minh, under Vo
Nguyen Giap, surrounded the French with more than 49 000 soldiers, assisted by
about 200 000 civilians who dragged artillery and other weaponry up into the
mountains overlooking the valley. After letting the French wait, Giap attacked on
13 March 1954. On 7 May 1954 the French surrendered, and the surviving soldiers
were marched to captivity (Giap 1962; Fall 1966; Simpson and Karnow 1994). Less
than fifty years later, French citizens singly and in tour groups visit the battlefield,
reflecting on its loss and on the changed colonial world. While remote, difficult and
without amenities, Dien Bien Phu is the premier battlefield heritage site, one that
archaeological heritage managers may well consider for development. It is the one
site in Vietnam whose significance easily speaks to the entire post-Second World
War era, and to all of the combatants – winners and losers.

Ia Drang is neither a typical battlesite nor a significant tourist destination, but still
may symbolize problems marking the war's heritage. Ia Drang, in the Central
Highlands of southern Vietnam, witnessed an especially bloody series of battles in
which both 'sides' lost an inordinate number of men and signaled to some observers the unlikelihood of a southern victory. Beginning in October 1965, a 34-day
campaign, most violently fought on the 14th through to the 20th, ended in the 1st
Air Cavalry Division losing over 200 men and the PAVN over 1500. Both armies
claimed victory; both might today visit the desolate area as a marker of both valour
and futility.[3] At the same time, the valley's remote location and less-than-spectacu-
lar-scenery make it an improbable heritage battlesite.

Khe Sanh Valley is arguably the most recognized battlesite of the war, and the
heritage site most visited in recent years, at least by Americans. Many remember the
77-day 'siege' of January to April 1968 (Marino 1999) as the heroic stand of the 9th
and 26th Marine Regiments, in which 205 Marines were killed in action and 852
were wounded (Stanton 1981). Khe Sanh was, in fact, first reached by American
forces in July 1962, eventually saw an airstrip and the KSCB (Khe Sanh Combat
Base) major support facilities built, and the eventual deactivation (abandonment)
coincident with escape route road construction by 23 June 1968. General Giap,
whose forces suffered losses in the thousands due to heavy aerial bombardment,
considered the victory his. General Westmoreland, the architect of the Khe Sanh
operation, found victory in defeat. Looking at it today, both forces of warriors
fought with great skill, courage and honour.

Minority tribesmen today again inhabit Khe Sanh Valley. The surrounding hills
and the valley are largely bereft of buildings, and may be best viewed as an archaeological landscape.[4] As with many sites of armed conflict, the current Vietnamese
government has installed a plaque commemorating the 'victory'. In fact, the

plaques tend to be dynamic in their placement and messages, somewhat softening their exultation as American veterans increase their visitations. Khe Sanh arguably is one of the best heritage battlefields for preservation and development. Although still distant from resort developments and the luxurious accommodations many foreigners expect, facilities are now basic. As tour traffic increases both infrastructure and site interpretation may proceed apace.

Khe Sanh is best seen as comparable to the Little Big Horn Battlefield National Monument, at least in potential. Certainly the battle was not the Marines' last stand, nor a wipe-out by the NVA. Public imagination coupled with the variation in the landscape, the ground disturbance now archaeologically observable, and the deep supply of historical data, suggest that a monument to the entire military history of the valley seems appropriate.

Other cultural landscapes, some natural draws for all stripes of tourists, exist in both northern and southern Vietnam. The famous Cu Chi tunnel system just outside Ho Chi Minh City is the most notable, although other tunnel systems exist, awaiting restoration and visitation. Beginning in about 1948, assorted forces opposing the South Vietnam government and eventually the Americans built the Cu Chi tunnels. Viet Cong (the VC or the Liberation Army), local supporters and northerners constructed vast underground tunnel systems that hid and housed hospitals, sleeping quarters, schools, food facilities and armaments depots. From concealed and hardened entrances, guerrilla fighters moved out on their missions. Partly due to their exotic nature, their great successes and their proximity to the amenities of former Saigon, the tunnels are perhaps the most popular war tourism destination in Vietnam. A morning trip from the city suffices the casual tourist. The tunnels now open have been restored, widened to accommodate bodies larger than the average Vietnamese. The bulk of the tunnels remain closed, with restoration possibilities should a greater quantity be warranted. And the tunnels are aimed at the general tourist, including Vietnamese, as opposed to the former warriors, who seek out sites of personal memory, and the war buff, who is interested in the wider range of cultural and archaeological landscapes.

A number and variety of less obvious heritage sites come to mind. Can Ranh Bay and its naval facilities are, of course, still utilized: occupied by the Russians after the American departure, it now has a multiplicity of uses (including consideration for return by the United States Navy). The infamous Hanoi Hilton, which once housed PoW aviators, has largely disappeared in the flurry of development in Hanoi; only a remnant survives, largely ignored or seen as a piece of the war best removed from heritage considerations. Still, the museums of Hanoi might well be supplemented by the locations of citizens' activities during the bombardments. Given the relative lack of economic gain seen, however, in northern heritage site memorializing, few of the war's activities will be marked 'in concrete'. Old French fortifications do dot the landscape, not unlike the concrete bunkers found in such disparate places as Hawaii's coastline and European sea cliffs. These French fortifications add an easily seen and marked depth of history to the war heritage. Post-1975 military sites could include facilities build up to resist the Chinese invasion as well as the conquest of Khmer Rouge Kampuchea.

A primary destination for heritage tourists is Hue, the former capital and imperial city, cultural centre, and location of the central battle of the Tet Offensive in 1968. The old palace, once destroyed, has been partially rebuilt. A sense of the glory of pre-French colonial Indochina may be glimpsed at Hue, and the war tourist may still appreciate the battle that shocked the western world via television. And, not least, Hue is about two hours drive to numerous bases and battlesites, including Khe Sanh, Quang Tri and Con Thien. The tunnels of Vinh Moc and its killing zones are also within striking distance. Da Nang, known to many Americans, markets itself as a heritage destination for war veterans as well as those interested in traditional archaeology and art history. The Cham kingdom, which paralleled the Khmer kingdom of Cambodia, existed from roughly the fourth through to the thirteenth centuries; Cham architectural remains, coupled with those of the Imperial City of Hue, make cultural tourism a natural match-up with war tourism. The Ho Chi Minh Trail is another planned tourist destination; already adventuresome backpacking tourists have travelled portions of the trail which extends outside Vietnam's borders. The trail is an outstanding example of the mix of adventure, war heritage and eco-tourism.

Other sites that exemplify the war effort outside Vietnam are important, if less striking. The air base at Long Tieng in the north Central Highlands of Laos, deep in Hmong tribal territory, was an important CIA base, the HQ of the Hmong General Vang Pao, and the strip from which the Ravens (a secret Air Force unit) flew as FAC (Forward Air Control) observers (Wetterhahn 1998). Today little remains of the once booming community except the defunct landing strip and the torn-up landscape. This is exactly the landscape an archaeologist finds useful when studying and interpreting a more distant and fragmentary past. The nearby Plain of Jars, an ancient archaeological landscape, saw much action, and remains dangerous because of unexploded ordnance. Another striking example of the interfacing of ancient sites and modern war scars is seen at the seventh–eighth century capital of the Khmer empire, Sambor Prei Kuk, in Kampong Thom, Cambodia. Here among beautiful brick temples and an open forest are the depressions resulting from lines of bombs dropped from American B-52s. Indeed, as with France and the two world wars, large parcels of the Lao People's Democratic Republic are still handicapped by landscapes full of bomb craters, ordnance and land mines. These represent what is potentially an entirely new and novel location to critically memorialize the war.

The significance of the sites of the Indochina wars vary markedly according to the centrality of their functions, the passions that even a small group of adherents bring to a site and the nationality of the viewers. The development of heritage sites, therefore, is exceedingly difficult. Clearly recent conflicts over the proposed and aborted exhibition of the Smithsonian's Enola Gay, the B-29 that dropped the first atomic bomb on Hiroshima (Harwit 1996) and the ongoing criticisms of the presentation of the Arizona Memorial introductory film show that the development of interpretive materials for sites will be difficult. Renaming the Custer Battlefield Site the Little Big Horn Battlefield, and bringing forth 'what the Indians did right' that day long ago brings to mind the greater difficulties in the reconciliation of battlefield heritage marking. Khe Sanh would be an especially interesting location to mount an exhibition that told the multiple stories of its battles. A polyvocality in interpretation would seem to invite ongoing reinterpretation and a constantly renewed contextualization.

Doubtless interpretation cannot be objective, given different cultures and individuals' passions, nor should it be. With the building of heritage sites the multiple voices will argue through what should be presented on location, with compromise reached. The pains of loss – of life, of national pride, of 'the war' and the nostalgia of victory as well as its diminishing importance among the young, who post-date the war, all conspire to force a re-thinking of the sites of war. Americans, with difficulty, will realize that in spite of continued economic dominance they cannot call the shots, determining the interpretation of these sites and in the serving of their political ends. And, while maintaining pride of accomplishment, the lure of the tourist dollar will continue to influence the style of site presentation.

Landscape and heritage archaeology can and must play a pivotal role in the rescue, building and promotion of the sites of the wars in what may be called Indochina. Khe Sanh and Dien Bien Phu are no longer facilities, but are landforms with the scars of human activities. These scars are the stuff of archaeology. They permit both physical marking of human activities and the opportunities for excavation of new evidence that complements that of the military historian. Archaeology cannot work alone, however. Anthropologists exploring the memories of the surviving participants, ferreting out the information, values, ways of thinking, personal judgements and the inevitable contradictions, must work with the archaeologists. Historians, exploring archives, will tap the richest database of any war period, learning from the written and film records in ways that complement archaeology and anthropology.

What cannot happen, I am certain, is an attempt at interpretive dominance by Americans, now as ever so committed to memorializing their heritage. The Vietnamese never fully understood what the Americans thought they were doing in Vietnam (Jamieson 1993: 348). As Americans return to Vietnam, Laos and Cambodia in ever increasing numbers, one sees the same efforts at cultural dominance again – a view that through the power of money and certainty of purpose, a new heritage orthodoxy may be created. This did not work in the past, and will not in the future. Still, the strange but real mutual attractions, the bonds of battles fought, may yet create a new archaeology of the war.

> At camp, together in an idle hour,
> they talked about those squalid days gone by.

> Whenever he remembered Keiu's ordeal,
> he wept and felt a tightened knot inside.

> Nguyen (1983: 119, 147)

ACKNOWLEDGEMENT

Richard Rohde provided invaluable assistance through advice, the loan of his extensive book and video library and by offering encouragement. Steve O'Harrow and Annie Griffin provided critical input.

NOTES

1 The literature on the Indochina war and on specific battle locations is voluminous. The present chapter cites only those sources deemed most relevant to the task at hand. For further works a good place to begin is the 'Vietnam War Internet Project' at www.lbjlib.utexas.edu/shwv/shwvhome.html. Web sites of recent visits by veterans to various locations in Vietnam may be linked here or found through related searches. *Vietnam* magazine also is valuable for specific articles and points of view.
2 See especially Fall (1967) and Simpson and Karnow (1994).
3 The Ia Drang episode may be quickly seen from the American perspective by reading Smith's (1967) account, originally in the *Saturday Evening Post* and now found at http://mishalov.com/death_ia_drang_valley.html. See also Moore and Galloway (1992).
4 Views of the battle site – KSCB - are found in many publications. Perhaps the first source to examine is at the Khe Sanh Veterans Homepage http://www.geocities.com/Pentagon/4867/. Photographs of the area today are also available at this site.

REFERENCES

Allen, T.B. (1995) *Offerings at the Wall: Artifacts from the Vietnam Veterans Memorial Collection*, Atlanta: Turner.

Bao, N. (1993) *The Sorrow of War: A Novel of North Vietnam*, New York: Riverhead.

Fall, B.B. (1966) *Hell in a Very Small Place*, Philadelphia: Lippincott.

Giap, V.N. (1962) *Dien Bien Phu*, Hanoi: Editions en langues etrangeres.

Harwit, M. (1996) *An Exhibit Denied: Lobbying the History of Enola Gay*, New York: Copernicus.

Jamieson, N.L. (1993) *Understanding Vietnam*, Berkeley: University of California Press.

Lloyd, D.W. (1998) *Battlefield Tourism*, Oxford: Berg.

Marino, J.I. (1999) Strategic crossroads at Khe Sanh, *Vietnam* December: 38–46.

Moore, H.G. and Galloway, J.L. (1992) *We Were Soldiers Once, and Young: Ia Drang – The Battle that Changed the War in Vietnam*, New York: Random House.

Nguyen, D. (1983) *The Tale of Kieu*, New Haven: Yale University Press.

Palmer, L. (1987) *Shrapnel in the Heart: Letters and Remembrance from the Vietnam Veterans Memorial*, New York: Random House.

Simpson, H.R. and Karnow, S. (1994) *Dien Bien Phu: The Epic Battle America Forgot*, Washington: Brassey.

Smith, J.P. (1967) Death in the Ia Drang Valley, November 17–18, 1995, *Saturday Evening Post*, 26 January, www.mishalov.com/death_ia_drang_valley.html.

Stanton, S.L. (1981) *Vietnam Order of Battle: A Complete, Illustrated Reference to the US Army and Allied Ground Forces in Vietnam, 1961–1973*, Washington DC: US News Books.

Wetterhahn, R. (1998) The Ravens of Long Tieng, *Air and Space/Smithsonian* 13(4): 51–9.

19 Evaluating and managing Cold War era historic properties: the cultural significance of US Air Force defensive radar systems

MANDY WHORTON

The Cold War (1946–89) was a global conflict that prompted the construction of increasingly complex military technological systems spanning large geographic areas. In the early 1950s, the United States constructed an aircraft early-warning radar network across Alaska that extended east along the arctic perimeter of Canada and Iceland. By the end of the decade, when the threat of aircraft carrying nuclear bombs was replaced by the threat of missiles armed with thermonuclear warheads, the United States began constructing a ballistic missile early-warning network to detect inter-continental ballistic missiles launched from the polar regions. In the 1970s, in response to the threat of sea-based ballistic missiles, the United States constructed another radar warning system with coverage for the Atlantic, Pacific, Gulf and Caribbean coasts. The design, construction and operation of all of these radar systems represented important technical accomplishments for the United States and contributed significantly to the strategies and outcomes of the Cold War.

In the mid-1990s, the US Air Force began to evaluate the historic significance of these defensive aircraft and missile warning systems and to explore cost-effective ways of preserving their legacies. This chapter describes these systems, the process and context used to evaluate their cultural significance, and the actions the US Air Force has taken to document their historic contributions.

HISTORICAL BACKGROUND AND CONTEXT

In the late 1940s and early 1950s, the United States developed several Arctic-region aircraft warning radar systems to detect polar flights by Soviet Union bombers. These radars were some of the first technical systems developed and deployed during the Cold War, and they represented an important strategic shift. The initial confrontations between the Soviet Union and the United States in Europe between 1946 and 1948 were left behind, and a more global nuclear stand-off characterized the remainder of the era.

During the Second World War, the US Army had developed and deployed radar stations in Alaska: the stations were concentrated in the Aleutian Islands to support the Pacific Campaign. At the end of the Second World War, the threat to America switched from the Pacific to the Arctic North, and the Alaskan military was reorganized around what became known as the 'polar concept' – prioritizing air defence along the 'polar approaches, namely the North Atlantic and Alaska' (Schaffel 1991: 58). Most bases in the Aleutians were dismantled and equipment and personnel were moved to bases in Alaska's interior. Using Second World War era equipment, five radar stations were established on the Alaskan mainland. These stations provided very limited coverage, were subject to frequent outages and were linked by inadequate communication systems. The one closest to the Soviet Union, St Lawrence Island, tracked ships rather than aircraft. These shortcomings rendered the system virtually useless. In early 1947, the US Air Force began planning for a comprehensive radar warning network to provide strategic air defence of North America. At the time, Congress was reluctant to fund an upgraded or expanded network because of costs and doubts about the effectiveness of Second World War era radar equipment. However, when the Soviet Union exploded its first atomic bomb and developed an intercontinental bomber in late 1949, well ahead of American predictions for these capabilities, Congress quickly appropriated money for the Aircraft Control and Warning (AC&W) System in Alaska.

Construction contracts were issued in early 1950 for ten permanent Alaskan radar sites, including five coastal surveillance sites, three interior ground control and intercept sites, and two control centres. In June 1950, following the attack on South Korea, the US Air Force put air defence systems on around-the-clock operation. Defence appropriations from Congress increased significantly in the wake of the Korean attack, and the US Air Force was able to accelerate completion of the AC&W system and the installation of new radar equipment. The ten original sites became operational between 1952 and 1954. Two additional sites were selected in 1951 to expand radar coverage in the interior; these sites became operational in 1954. Six additional sites were added in 1958, which brought the total number in the network to eighteen.

Each AC&W site consisted of a complex of ten to fifteen wood-frame buildings connected by enclosed passageways (Fig. 19.1). The buildings included radome towers, operations, administration offices, dormitories, a power plant and other facilities. The permanent sites were initially equipped with the AN/CPS-6B radar, which was quickly upgraded to the AN/FPS-6, and other new radar systems that provided better coverage than the types used in the Second World War (for example AN/CPS-5).

Even as the AC&W System was under construction, plans were being made to improve and expand air defence coverage with better radar and more stations located throughout the polar region, including Alaska, Canada, Iceland and Greenland. A joint United States–Canadian initiative, the Pine Tree Line, became operational in 1954. More than thirty installations, very similar in design to the AC&W installations, were located along the United States–Canadian border. Canada developed its own warning system, known as the Mid Canada Line, to fill the gaps left by the Pine Tree Line in Canada's interior along the 55th parallel. This system relied on simple Doppler radar and was prone to numerous false warnings (Schaffel 1991; Neufeld 1996). Soon, the Distant Early Warning (DEW) Line was

Figure 19.1 Murphy Dome AC&W station, January 1966

Source: US Air Force

constructed by the United States and operated by the North American Air Defense Command (NORAD), a joint United States–Canadian command formed in 1957. Planning and testing for the DEW Line began in 1953; it was completed in 1957. It was the most ambitious, expensive and comprehensive system to be developed for aircraft control and warning.

The DEW Line consisted of a series of radar stations located near the Arctic Circle (at the 70th parallel) to provide several additional hours of warning and interception time. In 1954, largely in response to advances in Soviet air power, construction of the DEW Line became the US Air Force's highest priority (Shaffel 1991). The US Air Force contracted with General Electric to design and construct 57 DEW Line installations spaced about 160 km apart, from the northwestern tip of Alaska to Cape Dyer in eastern Canada. In addition to the main receiver stations, unmanned transmitters were located between the posts (Buderi 1996). Construction began in the spring of 1955 and was completed by early 1957. In 1958, at a cost

Figure 19.2 Modular buildings under construction for DEW Line station

Source: US Air Force

of over US$1 billion and after remarkable engineering construction achievements, the DEW Line reached initial operating capacity.

The DEW Line stations employed new, longer-range radar with autowarning capabilities (Buderi 1996). These radars not only provided better coverage but they also required significantly less manpower to operate. Unlike the Pine Tree stations, which required more than 200 radar personnel, DEW Line radar could be operated around the clock with as few as ten men (Neufeld 1995).

The DEW Line buildings also incorporated improvements on the earlier aircraft warning networks. Rather than constructing separate buildings interconnected through utilidors (enclosed passageways), the DEW Line buildings were modular structures that fitted together as in a train (Fig. 19.2). Modular buildings were pre-fabricated then shipped and assembled on site to meet the requirements of the particular installation. Intermediate stations consisted of five modular buildings, auxiliary stations had twenty-five buildings, and main stations required fifty buildings. Because of the extreme weather conditions and geographic isolation of the sites, large supplies of heating oil and other supplies were needed; consequently, large tanks and warehouses were present at all of the DEW Line installations.

The North American air defence networks operated from the 1950s until the end of the Cold War. However, they declined in importance after the emergence of intercontinental and submarine-launched ballistic missiles (ICBMs and SLBMs).

The Soviet Union first tested an ICBM and launched its first satellite, Sputnik, in 1957. From that time forward, resources in both countries were focused on missile delivery and warning systems (Levine 1994).

Although missile defence had been considered as early as 1952, it did not receive serious support until after the launch of Sputnik. Five days after the launch, Congress made missile defence a top national priority and approved US$1 billion for the construction of the Ballistic Missile Early Warning System (BMEWS). This called for three northern radar installations located in Alaska, Greenland and the United Kingdom. By the summer of 1958, construction was under way at the first two sites, which became operational in 1961. The site in England became operational in 1963.

The BMEWS consisted of two types of radar. The first type used massive detection radar screens, each measuring 123 m by 50 m (larger than an American football field on end) and weighing more than 900 metric tons. The second type of radar used a parabolic dish tracking antennae, which was modeled after an experimental radar developed at Millstone Hill, Massachusetts, by the Lincoln Laboratory and others. Scanning equipment located in buildings in front of each radar screen fed radar signals to the screen through two rows of feed horns located on the exterior face of the building. The screen projected two radar beams and collected a continuous echo. An object piercing the lower fan signaled the alarm. The position and velocity of the object were measured. Seconds later, as the object passed through the upper fan, position and velocity were measured again, and computers determined whether the object was following a ballistic trajectory. If an object was determined to be a missile, a second tracking radar locked on to the missile and tracked it to impact. Each site had a different configuration of these two types of radar.

Climatic conditions presented challenges for the BMEWS project. Although the US Air Force and Army had experience with construction in Arctic climates with the aircraft radar sites, the scale and weight of the BMEWS equipment required the development of new construction techniques. Climatic conditions, at the Thule site in Greenland, where permafrost was present at less than 2 m and temperatures could drop to 50°C below zero, were most challenging. For instance, the heat from a building constructed on the surface would melt the permafrost and cause the building to sink, which created a special problem for the scanner buildings, which had to be extremely stable. To accommodate these conditions, thousands of feet of pipe were incorporated into the building foundations. The pipes were left exposed on the sides of the buildings and were fitted with covers that could be opened and closed. In the winter months, these pipes were left open to circulate cold air beneath the buildings and to freeze the ground above the permafrost. In the summer, the pipes were closed. The theory was that the heat from the building foundations would melt the ground above the permafrost without compromising it. The foundations sagged slightly, but for the most part, this system was effective.

Although the BMEWS sites continued to function extremely reliably throughout the Cold War, the 1950s technology became increasingly expensive to support, and new technology outpaced some of the BMEWS capabilities. Consequently, in the 1980s, the US Air Force began upgrading the BMEWS network with phased-array radar, which is electronically steered and much faster (see PAVE PAWS

Figure 19.3 Upgraded radar facility at Thule Air Base, Greenland

Source: Author

discussion below). Construction began on the Thule upgrade in 1984. After the upgraded radar became operational in 1987, the original screens were dismantled; the remaining buildings are awaiting demolition. The new radar was built atop an existing transmitter building, largely as an attempt to ward off Soviet complaints that the upgrade represented the deployment of a new radar and was a violation of the Anti-Ballistic Missile (ABM) Treaty (Fig. 19.3). In 1991, the third site at Fylingdales Moor in the United Kingdom was also upgraded to phased-array radar. The new facility is the only three-faced phased-array radar in the United States network and provides 360° of coverage. Site II in Alaska is undergoing upgrading (scheduled to be completed in 2002) but remains operational with its original radar equipment.

The development in the 1970s of sea-based missile delivery systems brought about the need for a new warning system and a new technology. The widespread deployment of advanced nuclear submarines equipped with multirange SLBMs in the 1970s, coupled with an expansion of Soviet naval forces, prompted a major strategic shift from the polar concept on which BMEWS was based (Watson 1982; Moore and Compton-Hall 1987; Catudal 1988). Rather than being confined to attacking the United States from ground-based sites in the USSR, SLBMs gave the Soviet Union a mobile missile force capable of attacking from off the US coast.

In the early 1970s, the United States constructed a conventional radar detection and tracking system for SLBMs. The system consisted of seven AN/FSS-7 radar sensors located along the coastal perimeters of the United States. The radars were deployed on the east coast at MacDill Air Force Base (AFB) (Florida), Fort Fisher Air Force Station (AFS) (North Carolina), and Charlestown AFS (Maine); on the west coast at Mount Hebo AFS (Oregon), Mill Valley AFS (California), and Mount Laguna AFS (California); and on the Gulf Coast at Laredo AFS (Texas). All sites became operational in 1971 (Pretty 1980).

Throughout the 1970s, the USSR continued to improve the designs of and deploy in greater numbers SLBM-equipped nuclear submarines. The newer submarines ('Delta' Class) had a significantly longer range and were equipped with long-range (nearly 7000 km) SLBMs, which could strike targets from nearby coastal waters, and, in some cases, from their homeports. During 1971–80, the USSR systematically deployed nuclear submarines off the US coasts in an effort to reach parity with US capabilities (Watson 1982: 29–35).

As the USSR developed and deployed a more advanced SLBM-equipped submarine fleet, the conventional AN/FSS-7 radars became obsolete. Each of these radars, which were designed by Avco Electronics Division, Massachussetts, had a parabolic antenna that performed, in conjunction with automated computer controls, both search and tracking functions. The radars had limited ranges (1300 km), moved mechanically, and could only track single objects.

To guard against the more advanced Soviet submarine fleet, the US constructed a more advanced ground-based missile early-warning system, the PAVE (US Air Force programme name) PAWS (phased-array warning system), to cover the Atlantic and Pacific coasts. The PAVE PAWS radars were complemented by satellite surveillance which allowed detection of an SLBM launch from heat plumes (Burrows 1986). Construction of the first two PAVE PAWS sites at Otis AFB in Massachusetts and Beale AFB in California began in 1978. The sites became operational in 1979 and 1980, respectively. The AN/FSS-7 radars were dismantled when these PAVE PAWS units became operational.

PAVE PAWS utilizes phased-array radar technology, which integrates thousands of individual antennae into a radar face on the side of a radar building. The US Army and Raytheon Corporation developed this technology in the 1960s for use with an ABM system. It was first deployed at Eglin AFB in Florida for use in space tracking (still operational), and then at the Safeguard ABM Complex in North Dakota. The Safeguard System was dismantled in 1975–6, but the Perimeter Acquisition Radar (PAR) Facility was retained as a complement to the north-pointing BMEWS for use in early warning. Both of these facilities have single-array faces. Raytheon designed the first twin-faced phased-array radar facilities for PAVE PAWS.

In the mid-1980s, the PAVE PAWS network was expanded to cover the South Atlantic and Caribbean, with the addition of sites in Georgia and Texas. These facilities became operational in 1985 and 1987, near the end of the Cold War. They are very similar to the first two sites but incorporate some technical advances that expand their coverage and discrimination capabilities. The Texas site was partially dismantled in 1999, and its radar elements were shipped to Alaska for use in the upgrade of the Alaskan BMEWS facility. Since 1993, the Georgia site has been in 'caretaker status', meaning that the facility is not operational (that is, radar

Figure 19.4 Cobra Dane, Shemya Island

Source: Author

equipment has been disconnected, and the computer equipment has been removed) but is being maintained should it need to be reactivated.

Additional facilities complemented the primary missile early-warning network consisting of BMEWS and PAVE PAWS. These included: the PAR facility in North Dakota; the Spacetrack facility at Eglin AFB; satellites; and the Cobra Dane radar facility, which was deployed on Shemya Island in the Aleutian chain primarily to collect data on Soviet missile tests off the Kamchatka Peninsula and as a secondary mission to provide SLBM and ICBM tracking capabilities (Fig. 19.4). All of these facilities are still operational at reduced levels.

MANAGEMENT OF AIRCRAFT AND MISSILE WARNING SYSTEMS AS HISTORIC PROPERTIES

The National Historic Preservation Act of 1966, as amended, requires US federal agencies to inventory cultural properties and evaluate them on the basis of a standard set of criteria to determine which, if any, are eligible for the National Register of Historic Places (NRHP), the nation's official list of cultural resources worthy of preservation. Federally-owned properties eligible for the NRHP require some form of treatment as historic properties.

Because historical perspective is enhanced by the passage of time, sites and facilities less than 50 years old are not generally eligible for the NRHP unless they possess 'exceptional importance' (Sherfy and Luce 1989). However, the end of the Cold War and subsequent downsizing of American military bases and properties prompted the widespread consideration of properties that achieved historical significance during this period (1946–89), most of which are less than 50 years of age.

The US Department of Defense (DoD) began a broad evaluation of its Cold War era properties in 1991. Downsizing, realignment and base closures create an urgency to complete evaluations before important properties were unintentionally altered or destroyed without documentation. The US Air Force, itself a creation of the Cold War, owns numerous properties built during this era. Over the past ten years, the US Air Force has inventoried a variety of installations to determine which of its thousands of Cold War era properties are historically significant.

Both bomber and missile defence systems were critically important to the Cold War. As a result, the US Air Force determined that the AC&W network, the DEW Line stations located in Alaska, the BMEWS installation in Alaska, the PAR Facility in North Dakota, the PAVE PAWS network, and Cobra Dane on Shemya Island are eligible for the NRHP and require management as historic properties. How the properties will be managed varies, depending on their condition and current use.

That these properties are associated with significant events in American history is clear. What is less apparent, because of the unique nature of radar, is what story the physical remains tell and how the preservation of the remains might further our understanding of history. The radars themselves were changed, upgraded or dismantled throughout the Cold War. Sometimes these changes were visible, but often, however, they resulted in the modification of very small components of the equipment not perceptible to the general observer. As technology improved, fewer radars were needed and fewer personnel were required to maintain and operate them. These improvements affected ancillary structures as well. The sites evolved throughout the Cold War, and many continue to do so in their post-Cold War missions. Preservation strategies have been designed on the basis of the condition of the remains of the structures and on the practicality and utility of their physical preservation.

For the most part, these properties are part of specific technological systems that are not easily adapted to other uses. Further, many of the properties are in remote locations that are not easily accessible by the public for educational purposes, and they are extremely costly to maintain because of arctic climate stresses. Generally, those that are not in active use are being documented and dismantled. Those in active use are being documented and upgraded to meet new mission requirements and to take advantage of technological improvements – some details follow.

Most of the original AC&W network was abandoned in the 1970s. All of the original radar equipment was removed; many of the buildings were demolished or abandoned. Abandoned wood-framed buildings exposed to arctic conditions quickly fell into disrepair and now represent safety hazards and eyesores. The US Air Force plans to demolish the remaining buildings and withdraw personnel from the sites. (In the mid-1980s, some of the installations were upgraded to minimally attended radar with a mission of ensuring air sovereignty over Alaska. These radars can be operated remotely and do not require on-site personnel.) Before demolition occurs, the US Air Force is committed to recording the network through the compilation of a systematic history and the photographic and architectural documentation of one representative site. In addition, the US Air Force will prepare a brochure describing the historical significance of this system. The historical documentation will be supplemented by oral histories of veterans who served at the locations.

The DEW Line installations were closed in the late 1980s, but much of the infrastructure remains. Photographic documentation and collection of as-built drawings for two of the sites – Bullen Point in Alaska and BAR-1 in Canada – have been completed. The US Air Force intends to document the history of the DEW Line in a brochure and to identify materials from the system to be archived for future historical research. Final decisions regarding the structures have not been made: in two locations, it is possible that individual buildings could be transferred to and used by the local Alaskan village.

The BMEWS network was significantly modified at the end of the Cold War. Only one site, Clear Air Station in Alaska, retains its historical integrity. In the near future, the Air Force will construct a new phased-array radar to replace the original BMEWS equipment. Treaty restrictions require that the original property be demolished after the upgrade. The US Air Force has committed to preserving the history of this important system. It will fully document the site with photographs and drawings; prepare a brochure interpreting the historical importance of BMEWS; and curate some of the key equipment and set up an interpretive display in a US Air Force museum. The original BMEWS site in England was photographed by the Royal Commission on the Historical Monuments (England) prior to demolition and the subsequent construction of the new phased-array facility.

The PAR Facility is the only operational component of the former Safeguard ABM System. The Safeguard System was determined eligible for the NRHP, and the US Army completed documentation of the Safeguard remains, including the PAR Facility, in 1996. Documentation consisting of a historical narrative, architectural drawings, and large-format photography was submitted to the Historical American Engineering Record (HAER) Program (Walker 1996). The US Air Force continues to operate the PAR Facility for missile warning and space tracking.

The PAVE PAWS network will also be preserved through documentation. The two later sites, which became obsolete after the end of the Cold War, have been documented with photographs and drawings. The first two sites are still operational and are subject to continual modifications, some of which may alter features of the facilities that are unique to their Cold War missions. To preserve the Cold War history of these buildings, the Cape Cod site was documented in the summer of 1999; the Beale site will likely be documented in the coming years. In addition, a systematic history is in preparation.

Cobra Dane remains operational. The US Air Force is finalizing an agreement with the Alaska State Historic Preservation Office that outlines how the US Air Force will balance historic integrity of the facility with its ongoing military mission, including regular maintenance and upgrades. Changes that might affect the historic character of the facility – replacement of built-in equipment, changes to the radar configuration, and structural modifications to the exterior – would be mitigated through documentation. Because of cost, the Air Force is unlikely to undertake these types of major modifications except to support essential mission requirements.

CONCLUSION

Aircraft and later missile radar early-warning stations played a significant role in the Cold War. They are associated with important technological, social, political and military themes and are worthy of preservation. The scope and scale of these systems make physical preservation impractical, but the US Air Force programme of historical evaluation and documentation of these systems will provide valuable information to future generations studying this historic period. The memories of Cold War veterans, technicians, and scientists will provide insight into the construction and operation of these systems and will ensure that their significance is preserved for the benefit of future generations

ACKNOWLEDGEMENT

Argonne National Laboratory work was supported by the US Air Force under a military inter-departmental purchase requisition from the US Department of Defense through the US Department of Energy contract W-31-109-Eng-38.

REFERENCES

Buderi, R. (1996) *The Invention that Changed the World*, New York: Simon and Schuster.

Burrows, W.E. (1986) *Deep Black: Space Espionage and National Security*, New York: Random House.

Catudal, H.M. (1988) *Soviet Nuclear Strategy from Stalin to Gorbechev*, Atlantic Highlands NJ: Humanities Press.

Levine, A.J. (1994) *The Missile and Space Race*, Westport CT: Praeger Press.

Moore, J.E. and Compton-Hall, R. (1987) *Submarine Warfare Today and Tomorrow*, Bethesda MD: Adler and Adler.

Neufeld, D. (1996) 'BAR-1 DEW Line Radar Station, Ivvavik National Park, Cultural Resource Description', CD-ROM produced for Parks Canada with funding from the US Air Force Legacy Program, Yukon Archives, and the MacBride Museum.

Pretty, R.T. (1979) *Jane's Weapon Systems 1979–80*, (10th edn) London: Jane's Publishing.

Schaffel, K. (1991) *The Emerging Shield: The Air Force and the Evolution of Continental Air Defense 1945–1960*, Washington DC: Office of Air Force History.

Sherfy, M. and Luce, W.R. (1989) *National Register Bulletin 22: Guidelines for Evaluating and Nominating Properties that Have Achieved Significance within the Last Fifty Years*, Washington DC: US Department of the Interior, National Park Service.

Walker, J. (1996) *Stanley R. Mickelsen Safeguard Complex, ND*, Vols 1 and 2, Washington DC: National Park Service HAER Number ND-9.

Watson, B.W. (1982) *Red Navy at Sea: Soviet Naval Operations on the High Seas 1956–1980*, Boulder CO: Westview.

20 *Archaeological examination of Cold War architecture: a reactionary cultural response to the threat of nuclear war*

WILLIAM GRAY JOHNSON

Fear was probably the single most important characteristic of the Cold War. It drove nations to unprecedented spending on defence, fuelled ideological battles and, for the first time in human history, threatened the very existence of our planet. As much as it was a placeless war, its effects are now everywhere. We, in the historical sciences and preservation community, are just beginning to review and assess these effects on material culture. Examination of the remains from atomic weapons tests provides a stark contrast between science and engineering capabilities and cultural reaction to the threat of nuclear annihilation.

COLD WAR REMAINS AT THE NEVADA TEST SITE

Starting in 1991, the United States (US) Department of Energy's Nevada Operations Office (DOE/NV) took a bold step in the direction of historic preservation of the remains from nuclear weapons testing at the Nevada Test Site (NTS). In recognition of the exceptional importance of the historic value of two properties associated with the Cold War, DOE/NV initiated historical evaluations of the Underground Parking Garage and BREN Tower under Section 106 of the National Historic Preservation Act.

The BREN Tower was used in a non-explosive nuclear weapons programme where the US government studied the effects of radiation on survivors of the Hiroshima and Nagasaki bombs. BREN is an acronym for Bare Reactor Experiment, Nevada in which an open reactor was placed on a hoist car and mounted on the tower. Japanese-style analog houses, outfitted with moveable dosimetry devices, were placed 686 m from its base. Systematic exposures from the bare reactor provided dose calculations for each victim to understand and treat the health consequences of radiation from those weapons.

The Underground Parking Garage was built for an atmospheric nuclear weapons test, called Priscilla, to determine which types of edifices had the best chance of surviving a nuclear detonation. Tests of this type were known as Civil Effects Tests, the purpose of which was to establish the ability of a typical urban structure to protect the civilian population in the event of nuclear attack.

In 1992, DOE/NV provided funding to complete a preliminary inventory of the buildings, structures and objects which are potentially eligible for the National Register of Historic Places. The 1996 Nevada Test Site Historic Structures Survey provides DOE/NV with five historic contexts related to the Cold War period, identification of buildings, structures and objects associated with those contexts and recommendations for historic districts, conservation efforts and other management actions (Beck *et al.* 1996). The scope of the report is NTS-wide and includes information on Cold War properties associated with the development of nuclear-powered rocket engines, storage of radioactive materials and sites associated with studies of the effects of radiation on the environment as well as properties associated with atmospheric and underground nuclear weapons testing.

As an archaeologist, I am trained to research material culture at specific locales, assess their significance against specific criteria (especially for their research value) and compare and contrast material remains at one location with material remains at other locations from the same time period. Generally, I use a materialist strategy to define the parameters of my research and any insights gained. For the most part, my goal is not to develop models that allude to broad generalizations of motivators but rather to describe, with as much accuracy as is possible, the fundamentals of the material remains under study. Indeed, the broadest statement I may make is one that affects an understanding of a particular cultural history. In this chapter, however, I depart from my norm to focus attention on what I believe to have been a motivator of human behaviour. Leone's (1973: 136) belief that archaeologists should study how material culture affects the culture using it is apropos; I therefore draw your attention to the civil effects programmes as the material remains have comparable and contrastable counterparts in the civilian world.

CIVIL EFFECTS PROGRAMMES

The civil effects programmes were spearheaded by a federal government agency called the Federal Civil Defense Administration (FCDA). It was organized to teach the US population how to survive a nuclear weapon assault. Broad in its approach, the FCDA was given authority to conduct research on the effects of atomic and hydrogen weapons on simulated civilian settings and disseminate information about the results. Transportation, communication, utilities, industry and residential simulations were created and subjected to blast, thermal and radiation effects of nuclear bombs. Pamphlets, brochures, news stories and documentaries were used to inform the population of the latest survival techniques. Local offices of the FCDA were installed in major metropolitan areas to prepare the US for nuclear war.

At the NTS, the remains from these civil effects tests include residential-type structures, industrial facilities, a variety of bomb shelters and transportation devices. The residences include two-storey houses (Fig. 20.1), single-storey ramblers (a one-storey house typically with a low-pitched roof and an open plan) and a utility-type shelter. Many of these were outfitted with mannequins (Fig. 20.2) set around furnishings including television sets, sofas, dining-room tables and

Figure 20.1 Two-storey house on NTS subjected to atomic test

Source: US Department of Energy

Figure 20.2 Mannequins in test

Source: US Department of Energy

Figure 20.3 Priscilla nuclear weapon test detonated at the NTS on 24 June 1957

Source: US Department of Energy

kitchens stocked with food. Industrial facilities include the previously discussed parking garage along with hangars, offices and a bank vault. The latter was located only 350 m from the Priscilla ground zero (Fig. 20.3) and was subjected to 70 pounds per square inch of overpressure. According to documents, the items stored inside survived the blast. However, some of the nearby bomb shelters did not fare as well. These included domes and semi-subterranean structures. Of the domes, those created of cast aluminum fared the worst with complete collapse of structural integrity. The mannequins placed in the semi-subterranean structures were relatively unscathed. Transportation devices included train trestles and automobiles.

The lessons learned and disseminated to the American people were simple: nuclear war is inevitable; survivability depends on cover. The greater your ability to cover yourself with reinforced, concrete and earthen enclosures, the greater survivability for yourself, your family and your neighbours.

Praxis of this message is best observed in non-civil effects structures utilized to house instrumentation for performance and yield of the nuclear weapons tests. A series of bunkers are located near numerous ground zeros on the NTS. These semi-subterranean structures housed racks of oscilloscopes attached to photomultipliers and photodiodes via coaxial cable. They have at least 0.6 m-thick

Figure 20.4 Miss Atomic

steel-reinforced concrete walls with sealable blast doors. There are no windows. Many, if not all, were used for multiple detonations. Surrounding these structures are numerous underground vaults that housed electrical and communication equipment.

Concern for blast effects and thermal damage is also evident at the Control Point. Although located at a distance not expected to be affected by such destruction, thick-walled, windowless structures dominate this group of buildings.

COMPARING AND CONTRASTING CIVILIAN STRUCTURES

At only 105 km from the NTS, the city of Las Vegas served as the host city to America's atomic weapons testing programme. It was, apparently, the ideal city for hosting it as Las Vegas was not only tolerant; it adopted the programme with enthusiasm (Fig. 20.4). The populace celebrated with atomic cocktails, mushroom-cloud hairdos and before-and-after displays of atomic-scarred mannequins.

Figure 20.5 Architectural rendering of the Sands Hotel and Casino in 1952

Even today, the atomic liquor store is still open under the same name and one of the stained-glass windows in the Catholic Cathedral depicts the 1963 Las Vegas skyline featuring a nuclear symbol in the background.

Many of Las Vegas's long-time residents recall witnessing the flash of atmospheric tests. For some, the announcement of an upcoming test was reason for a family outing. Angel Peak, at 41.6 km northwest of town and 2700 m high, was a favoured destination for viewing.

This enthusiasm was probably not expected by the federal government. A great deal of concern had been expressed by federal officials about locating a test site anywhere in the continental US. Approval of the site by US President Harry Truman expressed this concern as he is quoted as saying to proceed 'without fanfare, and very quietly to advise the key officials in the area of the plans we had for the testing area' (Shelton 1988: 4–12).

Thus, in many ways, the city of Las Vegas was not the typical American city. Casino-style gambling, legalized prostitution and 24-hour liquor laws provided an almost heretical atmosphere at the gateway to the nuclear age. On the other hand, the built environment mirrored much of the style and design occurring elsewhere in the US. The following examples feature a resort, government complex, a commercial property and a residential structure.

The resort is the Sands Hotel and Casino that was located on Las Vegas Boulevard (Fig. 20.5). A 1952 architectural rendering depicts what is known as the distinctive suburban style. The expansive porte-cochere with angled legs provides an open, airy elegance that speaks of high, late-modern luxury. The floor-to-ceiling

Figure 20.6 Automobile dealership dating to 1962

plate glass windows enhance natural lighting for the lobby and express minimal separation between the indoor and outdoor environments. This is a structure built purposely around the automobile. It is fast, sleek and bold.

The Clark County courthouse in downtown Las Vegas was designed in the late 1950s. The complex features narrow, closely-spaced shades providing filtered sunlight through floor-to-ceiling plate-glass windows at the street level. The linear towers with rectangular, patchwork windows are reminiscent of the Moderne movement within art deco. Cool blue pastels soothe the hot desert environment.

The roof-lines of an automobile dealership feature spectacular, Polynesian-style angles (Fig. 20.6). Folded plate attachments shade walkways on either side. This 1962-built space has floor-to-ceiling window panes to capture morning sunlight on the showroom floor. The image was considered to be both smart and sassy.

A 1963-built house emphasizes open-frame, thin-walled, rambling ranch-style architecture. It follows the splayed A-frame design of late-modern, suburban style. Molded glass windows dominate the upper half in the front. The back repeats the pattern on top of four 1.3 m-wide sliding glass doors. Built for a view, the house overlooks a golf course and the Las Vegas Valley. The style was called swanky.

DISCUSSION

Needless to say, the message from the FCDA was not only ignored but appears to have been castigated. The adoption of the suburban style is the antithesis of the brutish, survival-minded lessons taught by civil effects testing. Excepting the proliferation of bomb shelters in suburban backyards and fallout shelters in downtown areas, the acceptance and, indeed, preference for open, thin-walled buildings with huge glass windows speaks volumes about a population faced with an apocalyptic future. In order to explain this apparent incongruent behaviour, a little-known philosophical trend that developed at the same time is examined.

IGY, as named by Donald Fagan (1982), was a semi-utopian philosophy that was based principally on advances in science and engineering. Its basic assumption was that limitless energy was going to provide health, wealth and justice for all. Fagan's parody, named after the International Geophysical Year which took place between July 1957 and December 1958, speaks of solar energy that powers our cities, travel by undersea rail that connects New York and Paris in 90 minutes, the expansion of leisure time for artists everywhere, and the expectation that eternal freedom and eternal youth will become standard for all.

This ideological development is coupled with the adoption of suburban-style architecture to capture what is best described as a reactionary response to a threat that never materialized. The population may have been frightened but, rather than run for cover, the behaviour and ideology appear to reflect courage. Adjectives that have long been used with the suburban style include avant-garde, proud and heroic. The aftermath of the Second World War, especially the devastation wrought on Hiroshima and Nagasaki, coalesced into an anti-Communist, xenophobic, extremely patriotic cultural landscape in America. The population exploded in what is now called the baby boom and the economy grew at an unprecedented rate. These changes fortified the American people into a sense of imperviousness that allowed the deliberate adoption of an architectural style least likely to withstand the effects of atomic war.

CONCLUSIONS

Leone (1973: 140) argues that the management of the physical environment has direct effects on behaviour. Today, over fifty years since the only combat use of atomic weapons, I argue that a reactionary cultural response was adopted to neutralize fear. American culture focused on affluent, suburban, married white families to the exclusion of all others while this reactionary response flourished. I believe that this rigid cultural focus formed a paradigm that stabilized the population during the darkest days of the Cold War. Neutralized fear supported and strengthened the paradigm.

ACKNOWLEDGEMENT

The author wishes to thank DOE/NV for providing the funding and management opportunities to research Cold War-era properties on the NTS. It was that research that allowed me to develop this line of reasoning. The views expressed herein are solely those of the author and in no way reflect a position of the US Department of Energy nor any other government agency.

REFERENCES

Beck, C.M., Goldenberg, N., Johnson, W.G. and Sellers C. (1996) *Nevada Test Site Historic Building Survey*, Las Vegas: Desert Research Institute, Quaternary Sciences Center Technical Report no. 87 (prepared jointly with Carey and Company for the Department of Energy, Nevada Operations Office), also available through the Office of Scientific and Technical Information, Oak Ridge, TN.

Fagan, D. (1982) 'IGY', in Fagan, D. (ed.) *The Nightfly,* Track 1, Los Angeles: Warner Brothers.

Leone, M.P. (1973) 'Archaeology as the science of technology: Mormon town plans and fences,' in Redman, C. (ed.) *Research and Theory in Current Archaeology*, New York: Wiley and Sons, pp. 125–50.

Shelton, F.H. (1988) *Reflections of a Nuclear Weaponeer*, Colorado Springs: Shelton.

21   The Berlin Wall: an archaeological site in progress

GABI DOLFF-BONEKÄMPER

PROLOGUE

Early in the year 2000, I asked friends and colleagues in Berlin where they felt the most lively memory of the Berlin Wall. The answers differed surprisingly: for some, it was places where the authentic material substance had survived best, that is, the actual concrete border-wall topped with the asbestos tube, the death-strip and hinterland-wall, lanterns and watchtowers. These were the places our Historic Buildings Preservation Office had listed in 1990/91 and more or less preserved since then. I call this the 'archaeological approach'. Others said, on the contrary, that they felt the Wall's presence most strongly where no material remains are visible, for instance at the Brandenburg Gate where it interrupted the main axis of the whole of Berlin – a scandal, blocking the central entrance to the old city. This could be named the 'image of remembrance' approach. Others replied that the most interesting places were those where the former borderline is still present as a gap in the urban landscape, but everything else is changed, overgrown or developed, artistic interventions of the less heavy and dramatic kind showing that the history is past and that Berliners of the new post-Cold War city are allowed to laugh about the Wall. The former Checkpoint Charlie on the Friedrichstrasse (Fig. 21.1) or the rebuilt Oberbaumbrücke crossing the Spree between Kreuzberg and Friedrichshain can be named as examples. I felt myself inclined to the last way of thinking. I call it the 'let the present/future take over' approach.

But then, in March 2000, I visited for the first time the recently cleared area of a former merchandise railway station, the Güterbahnhof der Nordbahn between the districts of Mitte (East) and Wedding (West), now lying deserted and bare (Fig. 21.2). Here were the traces of an historic railway landscape, overlaid with the remains of the border landscape, with some large parts of the hinterland-wall and spontaneously grown birch trees. Here I found once more what had been essential to me in the year after the Wall had been torn down: this emptiness, a promise of future in the air, where the debris of the past was standing free, in a vacant space, still without a newly-set order. Part of my memory of those images was a hint of nostalgia about the fact that this state, containing future and past in such an incomparable way, was not

Figure 21.1 Artistic intervention at the former Checkpoint Charlie on Friedrichstrasse –
Frank Thiel's lightbox portrays a Russian and an American soldier, looking
into the sector their forces used to observe; we see the Russian soldier facing
south, behind him appear the new buildings in the former eastern sector

Source: Author, 1999

Figure 21.2 The historic landscape of the Wall: the former Nordbahnhof, overlaid by the
borderland with parts of the Hinterlandmauer

Source: Leo Schmidt, 2000

Figure 21.3 The Wall as the end of the world

Source: Landesdenkmalamt's archive; date, site and author untraceable

conservable and never would be. So I recently met with an echo of my own feelings of 1990/91, when I first started to work on the preservation of some parts of the Berlin Wall as a monument of history.[1]

WHEN THE WALL BECAME A MERE MONUMENT OF HISTORY

The Berlin Wall has been for many years the place where the inhabitants and visitors of the western part of the city could touch the geopolitical division of Europe with their own hands, while in the East, people were kept from approaching the frontier at all by additional barriers, prohibited zones and controls (Fig. 21.3). In spite of political agreements on passage passports and the possibility of visiting relatives, the Wall became an impenetrable border. Buildings that overlooked it from the other side seemed unreal – as if on another planet.

After the 9 November, when general freedom of movement for all the citizens of the GDR was officially announced, the Wall was soon no more than a gigantic obstacle to traffic, its systematic demolition only a question of time. During the summer of 1990 Berliners celebrated the opening of the Wall enthusiastically and mayors of East and West Berlin districts shook hands above reconnected streets and bridges. The freedom to move everywhere created an incomparable feeling of liberation and serenity; everywhere the view widened up.

Immediately after the opening of the Wall the discussion about a possible strategy for its preservation began. It was, no doubt, a monument of history of the greatest national, even international, importance. We conservators of historic buildings in Berlin thought at first it would be enough to reconnect the interrupted streets and to tie together the urban relations that had been torn apart. The Wall with all its elements, in our opinion, could be left to decay slowly. We thought it would be impossible to restore such a structure.

The aim to keep the whole Wall more or less untouched and leave it to rot away slowly proved impossible and quite inappropriate. An overwhelming majority of Berliners wanted the building to disappear completely and as soon as possible. To preserve only parts of the fortifications in a few significant places was more realistic. Later generations would thus find at least some original matter in situ and not dispersed all over the world. This was hard enough to achieve. In 1990/91 legal protection of the Wall had to come up against the opposition of local authorities and politicians, who claimed for Berliners the right to no longer see the Wall wherever they looked, in however short or small sections. In the end, four sections and two watchtowers were protected:

- A part of the border-wall on Niederkirchnerstrasse, between the area known as the 'Topography of Terror', where the Gestapo Headquarters were situated on one side and the former ministry of the air (Reichsluftfahrtministerium), a big building of the Nazi period and the refurbished neo-baroque Prussian Landtag, now the house of the Berlin Parliament, on the other.
- A long strip – 1.3 km – of the hinterland-wall on the side of the River Spree on Stralauer Strasse in Berlin-Friedrichshain, that was painted on its northern (politically: Eastern) face by artists in 1990 (the 'East Side Gallery').
- A shorter strip of the hinterland-wall on the eighteenth-century Cemetery of the Invalids on Scharnhorststrasse in Berlin-Mitte, a foundation dating back to the days of Frederic II of Prussia (1743), where some beautiful baroque and classical tombstones have survived.
- A 210-m section of the border-wall on the Bernauer Strasse, including the death-strip, the hinterland-wall, several lamps, the narrow tarred road for the borderline-troops and remains of a transformer for the electric wire.
- Two watchtowers: one at the Schlesischer Busch in Berlin-Treptow, listed in 1992, and one on the Kieler Strasse in Berlin-Mitte, listed in 1995.

THE MEMORIAL AT BERNAUER STRASSE

The Bernauer Strasse was a significant place in a very particular sense. Here, the frontier ran at the foot of the houses on the eastern side, which means that the houses belonged to the Russian sector in the East, while the sidewalk belonged to the West, to the French sector. In August and September 1961, the street became famous in a dramatic way: while the doors and the windows below were walled up, the inhabitants of the upper floors dared to jump out of the windows, which was dangerous and for some fatal. Others tried to climb the Wall in one of the blocked-up streets in the neighbourhood. For the first weeks, the GDR authorities gave orders to shoot into the air only, but then orders were changed and people got killed.

The walled-up houses became the fortification. Later, the houses were pulled down and only the outer walls of the basements and first storey were kept as 'the Wall'. Finally the border works were built, with a 3.6-m high border-wall, topped with an asbestos tube, a 2.5 m high hinterland-wall, a 50- to 60-m-wide death-strip in between, electric wire, anti-tank barriers, a tarred road for the guards, high and strong lamps and numerous watchtowers. To keep the death-strip clear and bare, it was raked and occasionally sprayed with anti-plant chemicals.

The German Historic Museum (Deutsches Historisches Museum) had worked for the preservation of the site in 1990 and wanted to use it as a combination of an open-air exhibition, a museum and a memorial. One part of the preserved strip was to become a 1:1 reconstruction, the Museum proposing to complete it with authentic pieces from its own collection, to show what the Wall was really like. This was problematic. A ready-made image that pretends to give answers to all questions will more easily obscure personal memory and experience than stimulate it. Authentic dread cannot be caught in such an installation because the terror was not bound to the objects but to the system. And, moreover, the dread belongs to those who experienced it – it is neither conservable nor can it be simulated. The Historic Buildings Conservation Office (Landesdenkmalamt Berlin), following its own understanding of the term authenticity, wanted nothing more or less than to keep the material remains and traces on the site and, if possible, slow down its ongoing decay.

In spring 1991, opposition against the museum exhibition scheme and against the legal protection took shape. The Wall on the Bernauer Strasse had been erected on a part of the Sophien cemetery, the Sophien community being located in Berlin-Mitte, formerly East Berlin. Now the community claimed its rights to the land they had been forced to sell to the state. In their opinion, the continued existence of the border works and especially its complete reconstruction, as well as the use of the land for a memorial, represented a renewed profanation. People who had lived on the western side of the border declared that the remains still hurt their feelings. They found support with politicians of the Berlin Parliament. Only a few would accept the remaining part of the Wall as it was, bruised by the wall-peckers, gaily coloured with old and new graffiti, as a monument of its overcoming, a keepworthy reason of joy.

Under the impression of these stormy controversies, on 13 August 1991, the thirtieth anniversary of the Wall's initial construction, the Berlin Senate took the decision to strive for the building of a memorial in any case. A compromise with the involved representatives of the church was achieved: the preserved 210 m of the border works at the Bernauer Strasse were to be cut into three sections. One part would be left as it was, as a monument but without any reconstruction (70 m), one part would be used to build a memorial (60 m) and one would be given back to the Sophien community (80 m). The last part would be demolished; the fate of the middle part would depend on what came out of a planned competition for artists and landscape architects.

The Conservation Office had to accept this decision, otherwise it would have been impossible to keep anything at all. The community consented to tolerate the memorial if the Senate would support its claim for the legal ownership of the whole territory. The actual owner was the federal state, who inherited the borderland from the GDR Ministry of Defence. The Senate promised support, feeling responsible for finding a place where the division of the city and its victims could be properly commemorated.

The perspective of an artwork somehow appeased the opponents and art unfolded its culturally integrating effect. Individuals could now hope that an artwork would capture and transform the spirit of the site with all its ruptures and contradictions in *their own* sense. It took three years to prepare the competition. In the meantime, the Wall was not touched, except for a treatment of the concrete (*Hydrophobierung*) to stabilize the border-wall's crushed surface. No one saw a reason to insist on the immediate accomplishment of the three-divisions compromise.

The competition brief's inherent contradictions and the short distance to the actual events impeded the artist's imagination instead of giving it wings. In October 1994, the jury chose no first prize but three second prizes. But only the project of Kohlhoff and Kohlhoff from Stuttgart had a real chance to get on, because it alone respected the compromise. Their scheme frames the border works on a length of 60 m with two Cor-Ten steel walls, rusty outside, polished inside, a cut into the endless border. The space inside – the former death-strip – is cut off, inaccessible. The rest of the still wholly-preserved border works – 150 m – were to be given up and demolished.

All the debate could have ended here and we would have definitely lost most of the original monument at the Bernauer Strasse. But in 1995, when the construction of the Kohlhoff project was planned, higher authorities suddenly declared the monument would become too small and would not represent the real horror of the Wall. It was proposed to put a watchtower from the Museum's depot into the cut-off Kohlhoff space to strengthen the impact. This was a significant change of direction. First, we had to defend the few remaining pieces of the wall against demolition, because they were too hurtful. Now we had to fight against a different scheme because the same remains, or what was to be left after the building of the memorial, were felt to be not hurtful enough.

Indeed, since 1991, the partly decayed border works had lost a lot of their sharpness, as vegetation became stronger every year. The border at the Bernauer Strasse no longer looks frightening. The feeling of being in a no-man's land, a dead land, used up in history, cut off from the space and life around, has faded. Visitors must imagine control and deadly threat in their own fantasy. Should we have stopped this slow, mildening process to keep the site raw? This would have asked for continuous intervention, as in the GDR period, with rakes and anti-plant spray. If nobody had intervened at all, and the site had been left alone, it would already be overgrown by spontaneous vegetation, and, in 150 years, become a stable forest.

With the site's slow transformation came a transformation in the local people's perception and interpretation of the Wall. The growing distance not only promoted oblivion but encouraged the willingness to remember as well. Some of the strongest opponents to the monument and memorial could now – in 1997 – accept the view of the Wall in their neighbourhood. Thus, the three-divisions compromise became obsolete as did the artwork.

It is hard to understand how and why, in the end, the Kohlhoff memorial was built. The Berlin Senate's administrations of culture and building took over all responsibilities, and our objections to the whole and to the details – for instance the complete resurfacing of the border-wall (*Torkretierung*) that looks new since blotting out the traces of the wall-peckers who worked at it in 1990 – were not taken into account. Inauguration was on 13 August 1998. Discontent with the memorial was obvious. The 'real' monument, the remains of the Wall, looks small and insignificant against the big steel-panes; visitors have to peep through a very narrow horizontal gap in the reconstructed hinterland-wall to see the inaccessible space between the panes. Its very emptiness is disappointing, no explanation is given and no strong abstract form invites imagination or self-projection.

The Sophien community got its land back and started to rebuild the churchyard wall in red bricks as it was until 1961, but only a short section adjacent to the rusty side of the memorial's steel-pane on Bernauer Strasse has been finished. Several elements of the remaining border-wall were taken away, because they were standing on a mass grave of the Second World War and this could no longer be tolerated. The elements are still kept on the former death-strip, and there is still a long section of the border-wall in situ, waiting for further decisions. So we see bits of everything, or, better, nothing of everything (*von allem nichts*), as the Berlin journalist Detlev Lücke put it in an interview with the author. The site no longer tells the story of the Berlin Wall as a frontier between the two blocks of power or between the two halves of the city. It tells the story of the quarrels about the Wall after its fall, and tells it impressively well.

But Bernauer Strasse was not the only site of dispute about the Wall. Quarrels accompanied the preservation of the other listed parts too, conservation policy colliding with the redevelopment of the borderland and with the understandable wish to establish a new kind of spatial order, to put an end to the chaos of the last ten years. All the protected sites have changed considerably since 1991, some in a more purposeful way than others. In all cases, the pieces of original matter, still preserved, aged quickly and became, in less than one third of a generation, archaeological vestiges as if of a remote period. This does not mean that they are already falling apart. The concrete has proved, on the contrary, quite solid up to now. It is the political and spatial system of the border that faded away so fast. The preserved bits, listed or not, now appear completely out of context, like disconnected items on an excavation site.

THE EAST SIDE GALLERY

The longest open-air gallery, as it has been called (1.3 km), has suffered a lot since it was listed in 1991. This is partly due to weather impact and to traffic, especially during periods of frost, when salt and dirt are sprayed up from the nearby street. In

Figure 21.4 East Side Gallery, Mühlenstrasse: Birgit Kinder's 'Test the Best', second version, covering the heavily damaged original that had been painted during the campaign of summer 1990

Source: Wolfgang Bittner, 1997

1990, the Wall's surface was painted without any preparation which also created problems, the paint coming off the concrete and conventional restoration techniques being difficult to apply. A project to protect the gallery with a roof was abandoned. In 1995, the most popular painting, 'Fraternal Kiss' (Dimitri Vrubel), showing Breshnev and Honecker kissing, was cleaned and secured. But the effect did not last: graffiti-sprayers could not be brought to respect the integrity of the work.

We had to accept two points. First, that it is practically impossible to make the East Side Gallery last for a very long time. Second, that our professional notion of authenticity of material and form are not applicable in this case. If we want to keep the material untouched, the original paintings will soon have completely disappeared. If we want to keep the images, they'll have to be repainted. If we want the gallery to be a living artistic reflection of our own time, new 'original' paintings must be allowed, covering the old originals.

So the decision was taken to ask the artists who had created the most famous and most often reproduced paintings, like the above-mentioned 'Fraternal Kiss', 'Test the Best' (Fig. 21.4), showing the proverbial GDR Trabant car breaking through the Wall (Birgit Kinder) and the big heads (Thierry Noir), to make a replica of their original work, on the same segments of the Wall that were cleaned and refurbished and smoothed to prepare a longer life for the new versions. This was done in 1998. The general effect was not too bad, but somewhat clumsy and slightly anachronistic;

probably the painters could no longer identify with their own overjoyed optimistic mood of 1990, nor can the beholders. Another part of the gallery was treated in the same way in 2000. As some of the painters do not want to repeat their ten-year-old works and others have left Berlin, space is set free for new artists and new works.

THE CEMETERY OF THE INVALIDS

The cemetery is situated on the northwestern rim of the old Prussian town, on the eastern bank of a canal, the Berlin–Spandauer Schiffahrtskanal, through the middle of which ran the frontier. There was no need for a border-wall here as this was achieved by the canal. The hinterland-wall was put up some 30 m from the bankside, transforming the outer part of the burying ground into the death-strip. The cemetery is a listed garden monument, with remains of the original eighteenth-century structure, several very old trees and a large number of very high- quality sculpted tombstones and monuments, like Karl Friedrich Schinkel and Christian Daniel Rauch's Monument to General Gerhard von Scharnhorst (1823). The place was in use until the 1930s. The German Wehrmacht General Udet, model for 'The Devil's General' in Carl Zuckmayer's drama, is buried here. Surviving relatives of the dead whose graves had been damaged or dislocated by the GDR authorities requested restoration. The site was treated like a garden monument: the lost alleys were replanted, the walkways reshaped, sepulchral monuments restored, the decrepit old wall of red bricks above the canal rebuilt, grass was kept short to become a green carpet; in springtime blue flowers cover the ground. The hinterland-wall, interrupted by several gaps for practical reasons, is still hard and solid, but not at all aggressive. It is reduced to the status of a fabric in a park, telling an old story that is already sunken in history, like the graves of the dead of the eighteenth-century Silesian wars.

THE NIEDERKIRCHNERSTRASSE

The border-wall on Niederkirchnerstrasse is the best preserved part of the Wall in Berlin. During the months that followed the opening, wall-peckers were particularly busy in this area (Fig. 21.5), hewing fragments out of the concrete and reducing them to bigger or smaller bits that were sold to tourists for cash (from 1 DM for a small fragment up to 50 DM for a larger piece). Visitors could even rent a hammer and hit at the Wall themselves; no wonder the Wall is all holes and gaps and crushed surface. But nevertheless, it is still there, surprisingly durable in its damaged state. The team that works on the adjacent 'Topography of Terror' put up a fence against further wall-pecking on the street-side and adopted responsibility for the site. Thus, except for the steel-bars set loose by the peckers and which had to be cut off, for many years no conservation has been necessary. The trouble began when the fence, a razor-sharp metal fence from GDR provisions, was replaced by a prettier and lower one in 1999. The result looked ridiculous, like a monument behind a garden fence. As the fence

Figure 21.5 Wall-pecker at work in Niederkirchnerstrasse, a listed part of the Wall that runs along the area of the 'Topography of Terror', former centre of the Gestapo

Source: Author, 1990

was judged inappropriate, it was taken away and for a time nothing at all protected the street-side of the wall. Only a sign told visitors that it was forbidden and dangerous to approach. Now a simple, mobile, high metal fence for building sites has been put up.

No projects for redevelopment will endanger this part of the Wall. The 'Topography of Terror' that became a world-famous site of memory and history in the 1980s and 1990s, will remain what it is and where it is. But there is still no solution to the problem of how to stabilize the concrete in its damaged state.

THE WATCHTOWERS

The whole border was scattered with watchtowers of different types and sizes. The two protected ones (built in 1963) are both of the same type, originally designed for the Russian–Chinese frontier, comprising technical installations in the basement, a toilet and an arrest-cell on the first level, a staff room on the second level and a roofed platform on the third. The tower on Kieler Strasse, not far from the Cemetery of the Invalids, overlooked the whole area of the cemetery and canal. But the site has been redeveloped for housing, and a group of six-storey buildings now surrounds the watchtower. One side was left open, so that it is still possible to see the tower from the canal and vice versa, the bankside being integrated as a nautical element in the new landscape scheme. The tower looks shabby and banal, like a leftover of the last clearing.

The watchtower near the Schlesischer Busch in Berlin-Treptow has had a somewhat better fate. It is still standing alone, in a newly landscaped green space, and has been used since 1990 by an initiative called '*Das Verbotene Museum*' – the forbidden museum – originally meant to show the work of artists who were not admitted into the official GDR art world. The work of the initiative has been supported by the Senate, but is now in danger because of a lack of public funding. Practical things like heating and plumbing had to be refurbished but no major preservation problems arose.

UNPROTECTED REMAINS AND TRACES

Almost eleven years after the opening of the Wall (at the time of writing), it should be easier than before to give a professional judgement on the historic and monumental value of the existing remains of the border works that have hitherto escaped our perception. But, strangely enough, this is not at all the case. The criteria of selection seemed to be obvious: the most complete, the most authentic, the best preserved, the easiest to understand, the most significant sites were to be protected; authentic witnesses of the Wall as it was. But now, I am no longer sure. Does authenticity depend upon the quantity of matter and upon its immediate understandibility for visitors? Couldn't smaller things become more important now, items in a narrative that has to be reconstructed anyway and from diverse points of view, Western and Eastern? This does not mean that every single piece has to be listed by the Conservation Office. We may be the experts for evaluation and it is certainly our task to create a public interest in the less spectacular remains, but we cannot – and should not – manage the preservation and memory of the Wall alone. It has to be shared by others, in private and public functions, politicians, planners, architects, landscape architects, academics, artists and journalists.

Polly Feversham and Leo Schmidt's bilingual survey and reflection on the Wall *Die Berliner Mauer heute/The Berlin Wall today*, published in November 1999, has pointed out assets until then unnoticed by the public and the Conservation Office. A lot of material is scattered around, indeed, and has to be registered, such as a metal gate on a plot on Chausseestrasse that once gave access to the death-strip, topped with barbed wire tilted to keep off the people from within, not the supposed enemy from without the GDR territory. Or a piece of white and yellow paint on a sidewalk that marked the real borderline between East and West, the border works being always entirely built on the eastern territory. Or the hinterland-wall on the wasteland of Nordbahn Merchandize Station. Last but not least, there is the whole landscape of the border, its spatial definition as a gap in the built environment, the forty-year-old spontaneous vegetation on the former western side of the border-wall, the ten-year-old vegetation on the death-strip, with trees and bushes, grass and flowers. This is an historic landscape and has to be taken into consideration as such, even though it may be materially and legally impossible to protect as an historic landmark

– like most of the other above-mentioned objects and circumstances. The landscape is in itself transitory; its time will be over when property reattribution will set the plots on the borderline free for new construction. The post-Cold War fight about their reprivatization is still going on, the federal state insisting on its ownership, inherited from the GDR authorities. The expropriations of the 1960s are considered legal because the owners received an indemnity. This was hard to accept for surviving owners or their heirs, who would not buy their former property back from the federal state. The legal insecurity is the condition for the long-lasting provisional state of non-intervention on the borderland, except for places like Potsdamer Platz or Brandenburg Gate.

Thousands of tourists look out for remains of the Wall every day. But, except on anniversaries – 13 August, 9 November – it is no longer a topic of public debate. It was replaced by other sites and buildings that serve as the catalyst of dissensus between East and West. The Palace of the Republic, the East Berlin house of culture and parliament of the 1970s, maintains its position as the most (un)popular building to argue about, its contamination with asbestos being the very welcome pretext for ten years of neglect. The quarrel is heated by the project to replace the Palace with a reconstruction of the Berlin Schloss, blown up in 1951.

The remains of the Wall as a monument of contemporary history have lost, for the time being, their function as 'sites of dispute' and might now become 'sites of memory'. I propose to introduce the term 'sites of dispute' = *'lieux de discorde'*[2] as a complement to Pierre Nora's *'lieux de mémoire'*.[3] It allows one to make a difference between consensual and dissensual situations and to accept a monument's capacity to create dissensus – or to make it visible – as a positive quality, a social value. A monument that is argued about becomes precious *because* it does not embody cultural and social consensus on historic or present events. Of course, we would like to win in the end and convince our adversaries that preservation is justified. There is no reason to give this up. But we need not necessarily persuade the adversaries to share the same interpretation. If we reach an agreement on the fact that dissent may be accepted as a part of the matter, the monument may remain ambivalent, which will be one more strong reason to preserve it.

In the future, the controversial debate will become part of the monument's history, one more layer of meaning. But we should not forget: a 'site of memory' always carries the potential as a 'site of dispute'; both are inseparable, like the two sides of a coin. And who knows when a monument of the past will become once more a site of dispute, because it serves as a catalyst for new controversies in actual political and cultural life. There is nothing like a finally-appeased patrimonial status: cultural heritage will always include political and social conflicts, inscribed on the substance and history of its objects – monuments, literature, artworks, artefacts. One day it may be useful to dig up those historic conflicts to see more clearly what happens in the present. This is when a monument's capacity to create dispute or to make it visible will be precious once more. I am quite sure we will still need the remains of the Wall for future quarrels.

NOTES

1 Being involved as an actor and a witness myself, I took most of the information out of my own and my office's dossiers and my own experience. I felt no need to put this into detailed endnotes. My article, though based on solid facts, should be read as a personal narrative.
2 In German: *Orte des Dissenses.*
3 *Lieux de mémoire* is the title used by Pierre Nora for a series of essays representing a kind of inventory of assets of French national identity and memory. He chose the term *lieux de mémoire* as an analogy to the patterns of the *ars memorativa*, a mnemotechnique used by the antique orator: each argument is laid down in a specific house or temple or tied to a part of it. Thus, the sequence of the *loci memoriae* (*lieux de mémoire*) represented the order of the speech (Nora 1990, p. 7 [Vorwort/preface: pp. 7–9]) – *Lieux de mémoire* points to objects and locations in space and time in a very concrete way. Sites of memory appears to me the most equivalent English term, more appropriate than 'realms of memory' chosen by the English translation of Pierre Nora's books.

SELECT BIBLIOGRAPHY

Deutsches Historisches Museum (Hrsg) Gedenkstätte Berliner Mauer in der Bernauer Straße, architektonisch-künstlerischer Wettbewerb, Ausschreibung (April 1994), Vorprüfungsbericht (Oktober 1994), Protokoll (Oktober 1994). *(Unprinted material about the artists' competition for the memorial on Bernauer Strasse.)*

Feversham, P. and Schmidt, L. (1999) *Die Berliner Mauer heute: Denkmalwert und Umgang/The Berlin Wall Today: Cultural Significance and Conservation Issues*, Berlin: Verlag Bauwesen. *(A richly-illustrated thorough study of all theoretical and practical issues concerning the Wall.)*

Flemming, T. and Koch, H. (1999) *Die Berliner Mauer. Geschichte eines politischen Bauwerks*, Berlin: be.bra verlag. *(Tells the story of the Wall's construction, richly illustrated with historic photographs.)*

Haspel, J. (1995) 'Die Berliner Mauer – das Beispiel East-Side Gallery', in *Denkmalpflege nach dem Mauerfall* (Beiträge zur Denkmalpflege in Berlin, Heft 10), Berlin: Verlag Schelzki und Jeep.

Möbius, P. and Trotnow, H. (1990) *Mauern sind nicht für ewig Gebaut. Zur Geschichte der Berliner Mauer*, Frankfurt: Propyläen-Verlag. *(Contains photographs that show Bernauer Strasse before, during and after the building of the Wall.)*

Nora, P. (1990) *Zwischen Geschichte und Gedächtnis/aus dem Französischen von Wolfgang Kaiser*, Berlin: Wagenbach (Kleine kulturwissenschaftliche Bibliothek; 16). *(German translation of some of the essays out of Les lieux de mémoire. With a foreword by Pierre Nora for the German edition.)*

Nora, P. (1996) *Realms of Memory: Rethinking the French Past*, under the direction of Pierre Nora, edited and with a foreword by Lawrence D. Kritzman, translated by Arthur Goldhammer, revised and abridged translation in 3 volumes, New York, Chichester: Columbia University Press, c.1996–c.1998 (European perspectives). *(The English editor chose 'realms of memory' to translate 'lieux de mémoire'. I prefer the translation 'sites of memory' in the sense of a concrete location.)*

Riegl, A. [1903] 1982 'The modern cult of monuments: its character and its origin', in *Oppositions* 25: 21–50, translation by K. Forster and D. Ghirardo of *Der moderne Denkmalkultus: Sein Wesen und seine Entstehung*, Wien und andere: Braumüller, 1903. A new translation by K. Bruckner and K. Williams: 'Alois Riegl, The Modern Cult of Monuments: its essence and its development', in Price, S. *et al*, (eds), Historical and Philosophical Issues in the Conservation of Cultural History (1996), 69–83. Los Angeles: the Getty Conservation Institute. *(The most fundamental contribution to conservation theory, introducing a system of terms that allows the evaluation of monuments past and present. The translation represents a shortened version of Riegl's original text.)*

22 Managing heritage in District Six, Cape Town: conflicts past and present

ANTONIA MALAN AND CRAIN SOUDIEN

INTRODUCTION

District Six, Cape Town, is South Africa's foremost site of forced removals. Set on the slopes of Devil's Peak, District Six commands imposing views of the sea and Table Mountain and covers a substantial area (approximately 150 ha) of prime inner-city real estate (Fig. 22.1). In February 1966, the then Minister of Community Development, P.W. Botha, declared District Six a 'white' group area. Over 60 000 people of colour were evacuated and much of the District was physically destroyed. Soon after the evacuation the state set about reinscribing District Six as

Figure 22.1 District Six, Cape Town, 2000

Source: Antonia Malan

Figure 22.2 Artwork at the Sculpture Festival, 1997, by James Mader and Brett Murray

Source: District Six Museum

a 'white' group area. An old-age home and a police barracks, both for whites only, were built. In 1979 architects were appointed to design a consolidated campus for the segregated Cape Technikon, which, by the early 1980s, came to dominate the District Six skyline. By the early 1980s, when the last residents were removed, almost two-thirds of the area had been appropriated and reused by the apartheid state. Significantly, however, the remaining third was still not developed by the end of 2000 because of popular protest and other reasons. It is estimated that of the approximately 50 ha that remain undeveloped, 38 ha are considered developable; 28 ha of this land belong to the government and 10 to the Municipality of Cape Town (District Six Redevelopment Project 1997: 6).

After the evacuation of District Six, both the landscape and its memory became the subject of intense struggle as ex-residents, local and national governments, archaeologists, historians, artists and other scholars debated and wrestled with each other over the issues of restitution, conservation, memorialization and development. Several symbolic reappropriations have been made by former residents and citizens of Cape Town. In 1995 the District Six Civic Association organized a large public festival in the area, uncovering the old streets and kerbstones of the District in the process. In 1997, with the assistance of the District Six Museum, almost 100 artists came together and 'inhabited' the landscape with artworks (Fig. 22.2), which recalled and celebrated the memory of the area (see Soudien and Meyer 1997).

When Tom Mitchell, the well-known American scholar of public art, visited the District in 1997, he commented, '[i]t is unprecedented … that a community would have such a powerful cling to a site … It seems when buildings are torn down the erasure of memory is pretty much complete. I don't see [that] … loss of memory … [that] loss of community here' (Bedford and Murinik 1998: 13). The memories to which the community clung were indeed powerful. Against the apartheid order, which sought to define people's identities in the narrow vocabulary of race, people found in District Six the social resources to live across the limiting boundaries of colour, class and religion. The area was and still is a source of spiritual and moral sustenance for its people, signposted by its religious diversity, its colour and exuberance, and its capacity for taking in the poor, the weak and the indigent. So emblematic is District Six that District Sixers have difficulty in separating their identities from the sheer physical presence of the place. For instance, almost twenty-five years after having been evicted from her parental home in District Six, Ngcelwane Nomvuyo (1998) talks of the almost sensual pleasure she derived from just tripping off the names of the various streets of District Six.

The landscape, however, has also come to represent a development opportunity as government, civic groups and commerce have argued the need for using the valuable real estate for housing and commercial development. The land is currently the subject of a complicated process of restitution and compensation. In terms of the Restitution of Land Rights Act (no. 22 of 1994), which established a Land Commission to oversee the process of compensating victims of the Group Areas Act, property owners and tenants, whose properties and occupancy rights were removed, are entitled to restitution and compensation. In District Six this process has been disputatious as the City Council, a body called the Beneficiary Trust (consisting of ex-residents including many tenants) and another body called the District Six Traders' Association, have haggled over how to manage the process of restitution and compensation. At the heart of the disputes have been differences of opinion about preferential rights to property – for example, do property owners have prior claims over specific properties to their tenants? – and about the kind of redevelopment which is to take place. Following a large public ceremony where the President formally 'restored' the rights of the dispossessed, many ex-residents who missed out on the legal protocols in the restitution process came forward to complain of being left out.

While the legal battles over the area appear to be over, it is clear that there are widely divergent expectations of what will become of District Six. Hence, even as the lines of opposition around the area have been somewhat reconfigured, with the emergence of new partnerships such as that between the state and civil society, what becomes of District Six – its physical remains and its soul – continues to inflame passions. Symbolically, within the reconstruction and renewal processes currently under way in South Africa, the area holds emblematic status for issues and causes such as forced removals, restitution, racism, reconciliation and reconstruction. While there may be communities where more egregious experiences may have been recorded, none has the singular cachet of District Six. Its very material presence remains the country's foremost symbol of its past, its present and its future. That it continues to be struggled over is almost to be expected. As this chapter will show, strong claims are being made for the use of the land primarily for housing purposes. Having been told that rebuilding is imminent and expected to begin in early 2001, many former residents are anxiously awaiting the opportunity to come back and live in the area. Large property owners also have hopes of utilizing their land for, inter alia, developing new offices and commercial properties. Conservationists have taken another view and are arguing for the development of integrated frameworks for managing the redevelopment process in the area.

Within these contestations for the District, particular sites have emerged as holding especial significance, such as places of worship, schools and the original topography and street-grid. In places remains of the pavements and kerbstones, and even the original cobbled streets, are to be found immediately beneath a surface layer of grass or topsoil. One such site that has been the focus of attention and study from a range of disciplines is Horstley Street. What is to be done in Horstley Street – its management as an important archaeological and social resource – provides an opportunity for significant cross-disciplinary work.

This chapter summarizes the issues and problems involved in the identification, excavation (and further excavation) and future management of the physical remains of Horstley Street. It examines the debates around the management of the archaeological heritage of Horstley Street and through a review of the debates concerning the future of District Six, suggests ways in which partnerships involving scholars, civil society and government might be developed. The chapter sketches the contours of the debate, showing how the different interests of development on the one hand and conservation and memorialization on the other, have crystallised as contending discourses for the District. The chapter begins with a discussion of the significance of Horstley Street and then moves to a consideration of the debates around it.

THE CONTEXT AND SIGNIFICANCE OF HORSTLEY STREET

Horstley Street was an important connective thread in both the physical and social make-up of District Six. Banking steeply from the upper reaches of Upper Ashley down towards Hanover Street (Fig. 22.3), it tied together a number of disparate parts of the District. For organizations such as the Hands Off District Six! (HODS) Committee, a coalition of churches and mosques, civic organizations, schools and other cultural bodies formed in 1987 (see Soudien 1990: 173) against the encroachment into the area by big business, it represented one of the last visible reminders of the District. The HODS declared District Six 'salted earth' and declared a 'people's moratorium' on development, speculation and physical work, including archaeological investigation, in the area. It was not until the watershed year of 1992, when it became clear that the apartheid government was on its way out, that what was only too obviously the most extensive archaeological site in Cape Town could be considered as a site for archaeological endeavour.

The choice of Horstley Street for the first excavation was significant on a number of levels. The founders of the District Six Museum (an institution formally

Figure 22.3 Looking down Horstley Street towards Table Bay, early 1970s

Source: Noor Ebrahim

established in 1989 as a direct result of a campaign to save the memory of key institutions in the area), many of whom had come out of the HODS era, needed to identify both a symbol and a physical place to represent the larger memory-scape of the District. Because Horstley Street had already been the focus of historical research, oral history, film (such as *The Last Supper in Horstley Street* made by Lindi Wilson) and artistic themes (many of the residents of Horstley Street featured in a mural 'Res Clamant' painted by artist Peggy Delport), it seemed sensible to extend its role.

Two important events followed. The District Six Museum convened a series of public meetings in 1992 and 1993 out of which emerged the idea of and a public commitment to the development of a memorial park in Horstley Street. On the basis of discussions with members of the community through the museum, an architect and trustee of the museum, Lucien Le Grange, was commissioned to design the park. Le Grange prepared a proposal and model 'to remember District Six's destruction within new developments in the future' and to provide a 'sense of place' within the city. His proposal covered the whole area between old and new Constitution Streets, a big area high up on the slope of Devil's Peak 'so the link between sea and mountain is remembered'. Part of the plan comprises an outdoor interpretation centre situated on the platforms of old houses, which can also be used for sitting on. A mound symbolizes the result of bulldozer actions, and screens

Figure 22.4 Looking up Horstley Street towards Devil's Peak and Table Mountain, probably 1950s

Source: Jagger Library Manuscripts and Archives, University of Cape Town (Photo BZE 92/2 (88A))

off the Technikon from view. Blocks of stone contain the mound and provide an opportunity for 'inscriptions on a wall of memory'. Overall, Le Grange suggests, the park should have a feeling of neglect and forlornness, 'with weeds and wind'.

Le Grange recommended that if the memorial park were to become a reality, strategic excavations within its precincts would be commissioned to expose selected house foundations and street features. A conversation about the archaeological remains of District Six was thus begun and out of this, Martin Hall, historical archaeologist at the University of Cape Town (UCT), was invited to search the area for a suitable site for excavation. Hall was both teaching and practising a politicized ('critical') archaeology – working with the material culture of colonialism – in which the history of the effects of apartheid on places like District Six formed a significant chapter in the long story of colonial dispossession and resistance (Hall 1998; 2000). In 1992, Hall, in conjunction with the District Six Museum Foundation, selected a site in upper Horstley Street for excavation.

By inspecting a sequence of aerial photographs and then combing the rough terrain on foot, preliminary surveys of the Horstley Street area confirmed that the uppermost section of Horstley Street was most feasible for archaeological intervention. The remains of the cobbled street and a kerbside drain were still visible so that the exact houses that had once stood there could be located on historical maps and photographs (Fig. 22.4), and in other records (Hall 1993). The excavations were carried out in 1993 as part of the Archaeology Department's undergraduate fieldwork programme under the direction of the Archaeology Contracts Office (ACO).

Numbers 73 and 75 Horstley Street were exposed, a pair of mirror-image units that were part of a row of nine dwellings built in 1897 on a small subdivision of a portion of land that had once been the farm Zonnebloem.

The gradual reconstruction of the history of Horstley Street is progressing as a haphazard but cumulative process. Archival and archaeological research into sites in District Six has begun to reveal the spatial and textural past from documented and material remains (ACO 1996a; ACO 1996b; Clift 1996). Mementoes, visual and remembered, are accumulating in the museum's archives.

The very early days of the development of the District were tracked through research into the Tennant Street site, when housing for freed slaves and European immigrants spilled over the old boundaries of the town during the 1840s. The large rural estate of Zonnebloem was divided into market gardens, brickfields and lime works; streets and lanes were demarcated and lined with houses, 'cottages' and stores. Then, dense rows and terraces of dwellings and tenements, shops and businesses were crammed in between. The buildings reflected the identities of the owners and the occupants – from substantial villas to rooms shared by whole families – and the prevailing architectural styles, from late eighteenth-century Cape vernacular town architecture to globally recognizable British Empire 'Victorian' (van Heyningen and Malan forthcoming).

Horstley Street developed later, at the end of the nineteenth century, and in a different context. The first record of Horstley Street appeared in the Cape Almanac of 1865, when only three residents were recorded. By 1888 straight lines of houses had crept up the slope of Devil's Peak, starting at the lower end with relatively spacious dwelling units, some double-storeyed, and ending at the upper end with tiny, flat-roofed rows of houses. Ownership of the properties in upper Horstley Street passed through the hands of various absentee landlords, and the dwellings were occupied by a diverse succession of tenants from different racial, religious and occupational backgrounds.

The larger context of the architectural history of working class housing in District Six remains under-researched. There are two valuable survey plans of the city – by Snow in 1862 and Thom in 1898 – which record the footprints of structures and certain amenities (water, for instance). The absence of any municipal building regulations until 1872, and then a lack of enthusiasm in enforcing them, enabled developers to build without plans or to minimum standards. From the 1930s, however, all building plans had to be approved by the City Council, so some records still exist (for instance lower down Horstley Street). A series of surveys of the built environment were hastily commissioned by the Department of Community Development in 1967 before the District was demolished but these were not systematic and were based on the researcher's personal assessment of significance (Fransen 1977).

Legally proposed building plans and alterations, of course, had little connection with what actually took place on the premises. Modifications to individual dwellings were often associated with activities at the back of the properties or to interiors. Yards were roofed, rear services were roughly inserted, sheds, walls and doorways were broken through. As an example, council memoranda record that O.M. Parker illegally inserted an inter-connecting door between his two houses, and Louis Spolander was ordered to remove unauthorized roofing over his yard. At number 75 Horstley Street, archaeological excavations revealed layers of linoleum extending from the kitchen into the yard, which must have been roofed. Backyard activities included the raising of livestock and small business activities. At the Stuckeris Street site archaeologists found evidence of boot and shoe repairs (ACO 1996b; van Heyningen and Malan forthcoming).

Archaeological and oral evidence are complementary. While some meaning can be derived from the spatial context of Horstley Street, the excavated artefacts from numbers 73 and 75 are mostly remarkable for their mundane nature and an archaeological context that defies interpretation. Most of the assemblage was excavated from unstratified deposits beneath the floorboards of number 75. The artefacts represent things that were broken or lost in the house, rather than general household refuse. For the more recent past, oral testimonies are the source of interpretation of the material culture of the households. For example, the description of an Eckard Street interior – recreated in a period room in the museum – can be linked to the objects excavated from numbers 73 and 75 Horstley Street, showing how and where they were used.

In upper Horstley Street the buildings were designed for the poorest of tenants. There were no decorative architectural elements such as front stoeps or small gardens. The stoep, a paved area in front of a dwelling often raised above ground level, is where family members gather in the evening and at weekends; it forms a link with the outside world through interaction with passers-by and visitors. In August 1900, only three years after these houses were constructed, a piece in the *Cape Argus* described conditions in Horstley Street as 'unfit for beasts'. The subject of this article was an outbreak of plague that reached epidemic proportions in 1901. The homes to which the article referred were amongst thirty in Horstley Street (out of 428 in the whole of District Six) where reported cases of bubonic plague were located.

Especially significant about these dwellings is that they housed a large number of African people who were the subjects of severe discrimination. Having been stereotyped as dirty and as being responsible for the spread of the disease, they were removed from District Six and herded off to a camp on the outskirts of the city, a forced removal carried out at five o'clock in the morning by an armed guard of fifty men. 'All had fixed bayonets,' reported the *Cape Argus* on the clearing of Horstley Street, 'and the mass of aborigines, variously estimated at from 700–800, was soon closely fringed by the glitter of steel.'

PUBLIC ARCHAEOLOGY IN DISTRICT SIX

The main focus of the Research Unit for the Archaeology of Cape Town (established in 1995) was directed toward the archaeology of nineteenth-century Cape Town, and in particular District Six. After 1996, however, no further excavations were carried out in District Six. Instead, the Unit turned to 'dissemination of information' to achieve its aims (Hall 1999: 8–9), although detailed results of the archaeological excavations and archival research in District Six remain largely unpublished. On a broader scale, a conservation plan for District Six, and negotiations for its implementation, are yet to be commissioned by the authorities. A powerful new Heritage Resources Act, which is discussed below, appears to be almost unenforceable due to both confusion and dissension about the future of District Six and a lack of capacity at all levels. So what will happen to the archaeology of District Six?

In 1999, in the context of a new exhibition called 'Digging Deeper', the District Six Museum provided archaeologists (including one of the authors) with another opportunity for engaging with the challenges posed by Nasson (1990: 49–50) in his question of what a 'people's history' of District Six ought to be about. Initially, the brief for the exhibit was open-ended and interpreted by archaeologists as a welcome invitation to expose archaeology to the public by using a dense display of the archaeological resources and techniques used to build the history of Horstley Street. The room in which it was to be erected was separate from the main exhibit hall. The proposed display was presented as a teaching resource and site of debate and discussion about issues such as critical use of documents, possession and dispossession, the non-static changing face of District Six, and so on.

The thread of the detective process in recording Horstley Street ran through horizontally, and the contexts in which the street was created and destroyed were added above and below. At the end, an open interactive space was planned, in which new material, dissenting views and different perspectives could be added and altered. This model follows that described by Carol McDavid:

> The use of context – spatial, cultural, historical, and geographical – enables information about artefacts to become information about past human behaviour. A public interpretation must reveal the importance of archaeological context – otherwise it is boring and appears to be uncontestable 'truth'. Present-day social contexts give the interpretation relevance, even if discord and debate ensues. The community's understandings of its own past are important.
>
> (McDavid and Babson 1997: 1)

A series of meetings ensued which substantially refocused the concept of the exhibit. The first event was in the form of an invitation to previous inhabitants of Horstley Street to view the exhibit and to exchange information about the street. This workshop resulted in a clear recommitment to the idea of a memorial park. For many the story of Horstley Street, its exposed foundations, its artefacts and memories, typified the full complexity of the District Six experience.

The second meeting was between museum interpretation and display staff and archaeologists, the first event at which everyone involved in the exhibit over the previous two years came together. The cobbles of Horstley Street were assessed as highly significant. Already represented in the flooring of the exhibit room, the image was now to be carried up the wall in a large photograph of the street. The style and tone of the exhibit were to match the rest of the displays in the museum where the stories and voices of the ex-residents run both literally and figuratively through the images. The density of written and graphic information was dramatically pruned to create more visual immediacy and impact. What remained unresolved, however, was how to take the process of conserving the remains of Horstley Street forward. In the section that follows, the debate around the conservation and development of District Six is reviewed.

CONSERVATION AND DEVELOPMENT

What the discussion in the preceding section has foreshadowed are the outlines of the various discourses around the future of District Six and of significant sites such as Horstley Street. In the last few decades since the removals these discourses have emerged in various forms, addresses and accents and have brought with them various forms of authority and power (see Soudien and Meltzer 1995; District Six Redevelopment Project 1997). While these feelings, enunciations and statements are by no means always distinct, separate and even representable, and often do not amount to full-blown theories or paradigms, one can, essentially, discern two major ways of conceptualizing how the urban space of District Six might be used. These we call discourses: a discourse, in Foucault's (1972: 21) terms, is an organizing arena which coheres theory and practice in shaping principles of classification, normative rules and so on. The first discourse around District Six is that of conservation, memorialization, retrieval and recovery and the second is that of development (see Pinnock 1989: 150).

The first discourse involves the recovery of subjected memory and forgotten artefacts and their deployment. Memory and artefact betoken a past rich with emotion, of lives carefully nurtured and protected, of families broken and trampled on. Memory and artefact in this discourse operate as allegories. They remind and warn of, and draw attention to, good and evil. When the discourse of conservation is invoked in meetings by District Sixers, they do so mindful of how socially and economically impoverished their lives have been made by apartheid. In wanting to hold on to their memories of District Six, they hope that their lives might one day become better than they currently are. They know that, awful as District Six was, it contained the possibility of living with some measure of dignity in the city. It contained, within itself, a model of what Le Grange (1996: 15) called urbanity: mixed-land use, streets as community spaces, a sensitivity of the street layout to the natural topography of the area and so on. Conservation of memory and artefact in this sense is not an act of conservatism, but profoundly one of learning from the past for generating a better future. Archaeology practised in this way is primarily a principle of engagement with urbanity.

The second discourse is that of development and emerges out of the debates around urban planning. At the heart of the discourse of urban planning in Cape Town was an obsession with rationality and order. Building on the ideas of architect and urban planner Le Corbusier and his vision of the totally planned urban space, the intention of much of the urban planning which emanated from the City of Cape Town was to improve everyday life by removing the disorderly, the unplanned and the serendipitous. Norman Hansen, speaking at the Town Planning Congress in Johannesburg in 1938, said:

> We must concentrate our first activities at the city's centre, so that freedom of movement, accessibility and breathing space can be restored where they are vital. It is possible to achieve this radical re-organisation by drastic methods only, by a fresh start on cleared ground […] This ruthless eradication directed towards a re-vitalising process we, following Le Corbusier's lead, named the surgical method […] through surgery we must create order.
>
> (quoted in Pinnock 1989: 156)

This discourse was evident in the approaches taken to the re-planning of Cape Town well before the District was razed to the ground. Severe modifications were inflicted on the landscape. In terms of this approach, it was deemed that the old city and particularly District Six had nothing worth preserving. The construction of shoreline thoroughfares (rail and road) and industrial sites in the 1920s (Worden *et al.* 1998: 64) started the process of filtering access between District Six and the sea (Woodstock beach), and between people's places of work and recreation. Motivated by an interest in slum clearance, the Cape Town City Council played a key role in the drafting of the 1934 Slums Act (Barnett 1993: 36). This act enabled the authorities to consider dealing with social and street layout problems, such as in District Six, 'by a complete replanning of the whole area […] with allowance for commercial interests' (Bickford-Smith *et al.* 1999: 147), and through demolition and relocation of inhabitants to 'a garden city'. While the city authorities lacked the will to see through the plan, their vision of a clean slate upon which to build a new city remained.

Part of this vision was realized with a succession of plans that emerged for the city after the Second World War. The implementation of the 1947 'foreshore plan' set in motion the building of wide boulevards to replace much of District Six and the 'Malay Quarter' (Bo-Kaap) and to create a 'circle of beauty' round the 'mother city' of South Africa, a 'sentinel town of the globe'. This plan was based on changes in forms of transport, to cater for passengers from large ships and motor cars. The result was that:

> From 1959, and with the opening of De Waal Drive and Table Bay Boulevard, dual carriageways and flyovers made their contribution to dehumanizing the built landscape. In 1968 the Eastern Boulevard cut a swathe through the newly condemned District Six and ten years later the Western Bypass, complete with missing section, became a further visual and physical barrier between city and sea. […] Town planning continued to display a neat dovetailing between racial and spatial ideology.
>
> (Bickford-Smith *et al.* 1999: 152)

After the 1980s the process of 'renewal' continued with the building of the Cape Technikon in District Six, now officially renamed Zonnebloem, at the insistence of national government. The Technikon has slowly and insidiously encroached on the open slopes of the District. At the same time new streets were marked out on the ground, then tarred and edged in concrete by the City Council – and perhaps most significantly, Hanover Street was realigned and renamed. This new streetscape effectively (and deliberately) sought to reinscribe the District.

MANAGING HERITAGE: THE FUTURE

What these developments draw attention to is the management of the landscape of District Six. Central to the issue is how the future of the area can be managed in a way that acknowledges the District in Cape Town's history and is simultaneously sensitive to the memory of the built and natural heritage of District Six in continuing archaeological and other forms of research.

In managing this process it is clear that some former District Six residents do not want to come back to live, but they do want to come back to visit a memorial space. The space is where, 'things should be kept and memory associated with them recorded – trees, drains, corners, and so on – respect for every remnant, including space around buildings [...]; a living museum' (Vincent Kolbe, personal communication July 2000). Many people remember Nelson Mandela's visit to the area and his promise that: 'Not a stone should be moved from Horstley Street.' Many wish a memorial park to be used for visits with their children and families; to be a place where there will be benches, 'places to rest', places from which to see Table Mountain and Table Bay, places where 'you feel that the southeaster still blows the same'!

At a meeting of former Horstley Street residents, the emotion in people's memories was almost palpable. Surprising, considering one's general mind-picture of a teeming, densely-packed built environment, was Latifa Hendricks' description of her strongest childhood memory being the open fields on Horstley Street – 'you could smell the grass and flowers'. Another resident spoke of her grandmother (who lived at number 87 Horstley Street next to an 'open field') who used the steep cobbles as a playground – tobogganing boards were greased with soap or candlewax. Frances Titus' family, at number 43, learned to appreciate aromatic curries from their Indian neighbours, while the street's sewers provided the perfect hiding place for 'shebeen stuff' (illegally-sold alcohol) when there was a raid. James Semple Kerr includes such 'sensory heritage' in his seminal guide to conservation planning and assessing the significance of places (Semple Kerr 2000).

Equally clearly, on the other hand, is that there is strong pressure to develop the area for meeting the city's housing backlog. Current development plans emphasize the need for using the land primarily for housing purposes. The Draft Contextual Framework (District Six Redevelopment Project 1997: 3) places the need for housing at the top of its list of what it calls Development Principles. This view is shared by many of the residents who wish to return to the District. Spokespersons for the

District Six Beneficiary Trust have also expressed an impatience with environmental and heritage impact assessments which have identified new heritage sites in the area. A point of view crystallising in the Beneficiary Trust is that an agreement brokered between former residents and the authorities, including local government, for the restitution for the area overrides all legal regulations governing the physical environment, including the new National Heritage Resources Act (no. 25 of 1999) that requires the prior execution of impact assessments for any new development.

Meanwhile, and independent of District Six Museum initiatives, the City is preparing a new document, a Draft Conceptual Framework for an 'integrated development plan', including developments in District Six, linked to a budget for the forthcoming 'Unicity' to implement. There are many considerations in the integrated plans. Tourism, for example, features as a crucial factor in assessing the significance of a new District Six. (Ironically, however, the District Six Museum has received little support for its initiatives in promoting tourism.) Thus, though Horstley Street may well become the site of a memorial park, the process of bringing it into being will require further workshops and the establishment of a systematic and cooperative partnership between the District Six Museum and various authorities such as the new 'Unicity'. Part of the Museum's role is to facilitate the proposal, 'to help the process work smoothly and fairly – not to be prescriptive' (Crain Soudien, personal communication, July 2000).

What these different desires for the District serve to do is to realign the stakeholders for District Six in complex and sometimes contradictory ways. In terms of the desire for development some ex-residents and the City Council find themselves working alongside each other, a new development in the normally racially-polarized politics of the city. While the debate has not yet expressed itself in adversarial terms, this development position is counterpoised to a position occupied by residents and stakeholders who favour the need for memorialization. For the former group what is at stake is a notion of improvement that hinges around the maximum use of the landscape. Currently they work together in a formal structure called the District Six Steering Committee. The latter sees the past as an integral component of any form of redevelopment. Improvement for them is inconceivable without a consideration of the lessons of the past. In reality, as representatives of the City Council make clear (interview with Peter de Tolly, 12 October 2000) and as members of the Beneficiary Trust have argued, the current approach of the City and those ex-residents who seek to prioritize housing, development is not inconsistent with the interests of those who seek to remember the past. It is towards a consideration of the modalities for managing this discussion that the chapter turns.

Recently introduced legislation (National Heritage Resources Act, no. 25 of 1999) places powerful protection over identified significant heritage sites, and the South African Heritage Resources Agency (SAHRA) acknowledges the area of District Six as significant. However, the procedures, implementation, responsibilities, funds and decision-making processes are still to be established. In general, both private and public sectors show a lack of crucial skills and competence in drawing up conservation plans (policies) and subsequent heritage management plans (impact assessments, recommendations for implementation), and a limited understanding of the broadened criteria on which cultural significance is assessed (Semple Kerr 2000).

What are the most significant directions for the archaeology of Horstley Street? In 1996 the Archaeology Contracts Office and the University of Cape Town were commissioned by the Transitional Metropolitan Substructure of Cape Town to conduct a Phase 1 archaeological assessment of state land available for development in District Six (ACO 1996a). The study focused on determining the degree of preservation of below-surface structures and the original street-grid system. Some disturbing comments were made in their report (ACO 1996a):

> Besides the human tragedy associated with the demolition of D6, this study has shown that a significant amount of Cape Town's built heritage was destroyed without any kind of formal assessment or prior documentation. These include industrial structures, commercial buildings and large numbers of residential buildings from the late 19th century and early 20th century. Unique terrace housing dating to the early British period at the Cape as well as a number of Dutch colonial period buildings were also destroyed.
>
> (ACO 1996a: 5)

In a section on 'Post Demolition Damage', the report states boldly that archaeological remains from the core historic portion of District Six (between Hanover and Ekhard Streets and Ekhard Street itself) no longer exist. New street alignments, property development and the Techikon are the culprits, with modern parking lots adding to the destruction. Interestingly, though, they reported that '[t]he effect of the demolition method [after removals] resulted in many of the streets being left intact. The most serious damage to the street layout seems to have taken place in the years following the demolition.' They also referred to inappropriate renaming of modern streets with old names but in different locations, because '[c]ontext, especially in terms of the community memory of an area and streets, is very important' (ACO 1996a: 6).

The archaeologists recommended that streets and their names should be re-established along their original alignments and that where possible kerbstones, cobbles and stone gutters should be retained or reclaimed. They concede that 'it would be unreasonable and unfeasible to expect that all preserved archaeological material should be excavated before redevelopment of the area takes place. For this reason, areas for future testing will have to be prioritized in consultation with interested and affected parties' (ACO 1996a: 12).

In some areas of District Six there is extensive preservation of the foundations of structures and probably other kinds of archaeological deposit which may be equally interesting. The archaeological approach is based on comparisons: it is a truism that a single artefact or a single site constrains interpretation. For comparative purposes, therefore, a range of sites should be strategically earmarked for excavation as part of the memorial park project. For instance, diverse Horstley Street households (identified by ex-residents or by size) and the potentially artefact-rich areas behind the houses may produce stratified deposits and chronological sequences. Possible projects could focus on diet and cooking, table and kitchen wares, building design and techniques, disease and medicines, and so on.

Also interesting for archaeologists is the relationship between the public domain of the street front and what went on behind Horstley Street, on the undeveloped land alongside the watercourse. Maps and plans are idealized records – it is the manipulation of the material world by individual actions that results in subversion of the intended purpose of social housing. While the streetscape may have remained virtually unchanged until it was demolished, the back parts were areas of movement: informal visits, short-cuts, cooking, workshops, ablutions, dumping of refuse, unregulated building alterations and integration of fowls, livestock and draught animals into the city.

However, there is always the lurking danger of prescription. In a recent broadside aimed at 'official archaeology' and 'an elite of self-accredited practitioners', Neil Faulkner (2000: 21) suggests that 'heritage should be an active process of creation belonging to the people whose past it is' through means of an alternative archaeology, 'archaeology from below'. He proposes that 'fieldwork is rooted in the community, open to volunteer contributions, organized in a non-exclusive, non-hierarchical way, and dedicated to a research agenda in which material, methods and interpretation are allowed to interact.' In this way 'knowledge creation replaces standardized data-accumulation' and heritage is 'something living, growing and changing in the hands of the people to whom it belongs.' He provides some guidelines and suggestions (ibid.: 30–2):

- Sites should be dug (not necessarily preserved)
- Low-budget projects can be 'organically' resourced
- Projects should be community based
- Hierarchy should be minimized
- There is no single correct method in research.

To a certain extent, this is already happening in District Six, but has not been clearly articulated: for example the RESUNACT Schools Project at Tennant Street (Clift 1996). Future 'public archaeology' projects – 'deeply and professionally concerned with the interpretation and management of the past in the present' (Ascherson 2000: 1) – could certainly be linked to the proposal that Horstley Street becomes the site of a memorial park. These decisions will emerge from a combination of community and academic opinions, such as those represented at a workshop held on 15 July 2000. Though a conservation plan has not yet been drawn up, many of the requirements of 'mapping culture' are already being met.

CONCLUSION

While the processes for bringing the Horstley Street Memorial Park into being are potentially in line with much of what Faulkner (2000) suggests, it is clear that the relationship, and the management of the relationship, between conservation and development remain fragile. While development discourse will increasingly gesture towards and even on some occasions embrace conservation, as the new Heritage Resources Act shows, how people in actual conflict or in struggle resolve debates over those things they hold dear falls entirely outside of a preordained script. Embedded in the complexity of their struggle will always be dissonant and incompatible logics. Sometimes these logics will harmonize, but often they will not. When they are set against each other, they each appropriate morality, correctness, and justice in different ways. In the case of District Six what is at stake is an understanding of the relationship between the past, the present and the future, the place of morality and justice within the past, present and future and who exactly will take responsibility for determining what aspects of the past need to be carried forward into the future. The way in which public historians, archaeologists and scholars present themselves and their work to the community of District Six – in identifying memory, artefacts and remains that speak to justice and morality – is key. They will have to convince the people that their interests coincide, and that development is inconceivable without an understanding of the past. And they can only do so, as Faulkner (2000) suggests, by working with the people.

REFERENCES

Archaeology Contracts Office (ACO) (1996a) 'Phase 1 archaeological assessment of open state land in District Six', report prepared for the Transitional Metropolitan Substructure of Cape Town.

Archaeology Contracts Office (ACO) (1996b) 'Excavations in District Six: a residential property at the corner of Stuckeris and Roger Streets', report prepared for M. Hall, RESUNACT, University of Cape Town.

Ascherson, N. (2000) Editorial, *Public Archaeology* 1: 1–4.

Barnett, N. (1993) 'Race, housing and town planning in Cape Town, c. 1920–1940, with special reference to District Six', unpublished MA thesis, University of Cape Town.

Bedford, E. and Murinik, T. (1998) 'Remembering that place: public projects in District Six', in Soudien, C. and Meyer, R. (eds) *The District Six Public Sculpture Project*, Cape Town: The District Six Museum Foundation: pp.12–22.

Bickford-Smith, V., van Heyningen, E. and Worden, N. (1999) *Cape Town in the Twentieth Century*, Cape Town: David Philip.

Clift, H. (1996) 'Excavation of a spoil heap in District Six' (RESUNACT Schools Programme), unpublished report prepared for the National Monuments Council.

District Six Redevelopment Project (1997) *Draft contextual framework*, Cape Town Community Land Trust, District Six Development Forum and the Municipality of Cape Town.

Faulkner, N. (2000) Archaeology from below, *Public Archaeology* 1: 21–33.

Foucault, M. (1972) *The Archaeology of Knowledge*, London: Tavistock.

Fransen, H. (1977) 'District Six Survey', unpublished report prepared for the Cape Town City Council by the Vernacular Architecture Society of South Africa.

Hall, M. (1993) 'Horstley Street, District Six: an archaeological trace', unpublished report prepared for the District Six Museum Foundation.

Hall, M. (1998) 'Memory as cultural property: Cape Town's District Six', paper presented at Inter-Congress of World Archaeological Congress, Croatia.

Hall, M. (1999) Archaeology of Cape Town, *CSD News*, March 1999.

Hall, M. (2000) *Archaeology and the Modern World: Colonial Transcripts in South Africa and the Chesapeake*, London and New York: Routledge.

Le Grange, L. (1996) 'The urbanism of District Six', in Anon. *The Last Days of District Six*, Cape Town: The District Six Museum: pp. 7–15.

McDavid, C. and Babson, D.W. (1997) In the realm of politics: prospects for public participation in African-American and plantation archaeology, *Historical Archaeology* 31(3): 1–4.

Nasson, B. (1990) 'Oral history and the reconstruction of District Six', in Jeppie, S. and Soudien, C. (eds) *The Struggle for District Six: Past and Present*, Cape Town: Buchu Books, pp. 44–66.

Nomvuyo, N. (1998) *Sala Kahle District Six: An African Woman's Perspective*, Cape Town: Kwela Books.

Pinnock, D. (1989) 'Ideology and urban planning: blueprints of a garrison city', in James, W.G. and Simons, M. (eds) *The Angry Divide: Social and Economic History of the Western Cape*, Cape Town: David Philip: pp. 150–68.

Semple Kerr, J. (2000) *Conservation Plan* (5th edn), New South Wales: National Trust of Australia.

Soudien, C. (1990) 'District Six: from protest to protest', in Jeppie, S. and Soudien, C. (eds) *The Struggle for District Six: Past and Present*, Cape Town: Buchu Books, pp. 143–84.

Soudien, C. and Meltzer, L. (1995) 'Representation and struggle', in Maurice, E. (ed.) *Image and Representation: District Six*, Cape Town: South African National Gallery: pp. 8–13.

Soudien, C. and Meyer. R. (1997) *The District Six Public Sculpture Project*, Cape Town: The District Six Museum.

van Heyningen, E. and Malan, A. (forthcoming) 'Twice removed: Horstley Street in Cape Town's District Six, 1865–1982', in Mayne, A. and Murray, R. (eds) *The Archaeology of Urban Landscapes*, Cambridge: Cambridge University Press.

Worden, N., van Heyningen, E. and Bickford-Smith, V. (1998) *Cape Town: The Making of a City*, Cape Town: David Philip.

23 In small things remembered: significance and vulnerability in the management of Robben Island World Heritage Site

KATE CLARK

> What is Robben Island like, that dreaded prison we have heard so much about?
> What is the island really like?
>
> > (Naidoo and Sachs 2000: 48)

> The prison is above all punitive, it operates to break the human spirit, to exploit human weakness, undermine human strength, destroy initiative, individuality, negate intelligence and process an amorphous, robot-like mass. The great challenge is how to resist, how not to adjust, to keep intact the knowledge of society outside and to live by its rules, for that is the only way to maintain the human and social within you. …
>
> > Nelson Mandela (quoted in Hutton 1994: 55)

INTRODUCTION

Robben Island, the place where Nelson Mandela and his colleagues were imprisoned, is perhaps one of the best-known cultural heritage sites in the world today (Fig. 23.1). On 1 December 1999 at a meeting in Marrakesh, the island was inscribed as a World Heritage Site[1] in recognition of its outstanding universal value to mankind, having already been designated as a national monument. Designation and inscription are only the beginning of a management process, however, which poses the dilemma of how best to conserve the place in a way which retains its significance and yet at the same time caters for the hundreds of thousands of people, both local and international, who want to visit. More imporantly, in the longer term, sites such as Robben Island may force us to re-examine traditional models of heritage management which have been developed in Europe.

Significance lies at the heart of this heritage project. Robben Island is an extremely complex place in heritage terms because it represents a mosaic of significance to many different people at different levels and for different reasons. On the one hand, it is of international significance for its association with Nelson Mandela and his colleagues; on the other it is typical of a number of prison islands – Alcatraz, Rottnest off Freemantle, the isthumus of Port Arthur, St Helena – which are of

Figure 23.1 Visitors to the island enter through the prison gateway

Source: Author

heritage significance. Although the prison is perhaps the reason that the island is well known, the site includes internationally-significant flora, wildlife, a marine reserve, maritime archaeology, earlier buildings and a generally complex archaeological record. The prison is not just a set of buildings, but a landscape and associated community. There is also an important spiritual dimension to the island for the local Muslim community.

Inevitably these numerous values will generate debate and potentially conflict. Buildings which are very ordinary pieces of architecture become outstanding for their associations. The urge to look forward in the new South Africa conflicts with the difficulty of remembering. And those different values pose questions: is it more important to repair the prison buildings or the landscape? Is it worth keeping the original boats in commission when new ones are cheaper and faster? Are penguins more important than the graves their nests destroy? Should the buildings associated with the prison warders be conserved?

Such questions are more than academic niceties because, in the short term, the answers will set priorities for the allocation of scarce resources, while in the long term they will determine the landscape of the future. What we value, we try to maintain and to keep. What we do not value – or see as being of lesser value in relation to something else – will be vulnerable. Already the island is under pressure. To the archaeological eye, that pressure is resulting in quiet, cumulative and insidious alteration to the landscape. This is not deliberate destruction at all – it is the type of minor alteration, usually done for extremely good reason and in response to genuine public pressure, which will nevertheless over time gradually and irrevocably change the place.

More importantly, some 500 000 people have visited the site since it opened to the public on 1 January 1997 and by 2003 some 400 000 visitors per year are expected.[2] The requirements of visitors to any site – facilities such as shops, catering, toilets and accommodation; transport and access; interpretation and education – all have the potential for creating conflicts with the integrity and significance of the site.

Many important sites face similar pressures. Robben Island is no different and no less sensitive or vulnerable than Stonehenge, Chichen Itza or Uluru. In order to address such pressures the Operational Guidelines for the Implementation of the World Heritage Convention stipulates that natural sites should have a management plan (para. 44(b)(v)) as well as 'adequate long term legislative, regulatory or institutional protection' (para. 44(b)(vi)). For cultural sites, the requirement is that sites 'have adequate legal and/or contractual and/or traditional protection and management mechanisms to ensure the conservation of the nominated cultural properties or cultural landscape' (para. 24(b)(ii)). This is increasingly demonstrated by the preparation and implementation of a management plan, an activity which is underway at Robben Island at present. A methodology for World Heritage Site Management Plans is set out in Feilden and Jokilehto (1993). However for a place like Robben Island – where significance is complex, multi-layered and indeed multi-vocal, and where as a result there is great potential for conflict between types of significance – it may be necessary to refocus the contents of the standard World Heritage Site Management Plan.

THE HISTORY OF ROBBEN ISLAND

Human intervention on Robben Island dates back many thousands of years, and possibly to the Middle Stone Age. When European explorers arrived, they used the island as a source of food and refuge from the Khoisan living on the mainland. The island was plundered for its seals and wildlife to provide supplies for sailors, and in the 1600s sheep were introduced to supplement the diminishing natural resources.

Robben Island was used as a political prison from the mid-seventeenth century, initially for local people who were perceived to be causing problems for the Dutch: for instance, Krotoa, a bilingual Khoisan woman who acted as an intermediary between the Khoisan and the Dutch. The Dutch later used the island to imprison other political prisoners opposed to Dutch rule in Southeast Asia. Today the Robben Island Karamat – an Islamic shrine – stands on the site of what is probably one of the graves of the eighteenth-century Muslim prisoners.

The British continued the tradition of using Robben Island as a prison during the nineteenth century, and later extended this to provide housing for the sick, the poor, the mentally ill, and people with leprosy. During the conflict between the Xhosa and British known as the Hundred Years War, important tribal leaders were also held there. The political prison closed in the late nineteenth century but the island remained a hospital until 1891 and a leper colony until 1931. During the Second World War, Robben Island became a military base, with up-to-date weapons, gun emplacements, training camps and arms store, workshops, roads, harbour, landing strip, bungalows, messes and a power station.

The National Party came to power in South Africa in 1948 and its policy of apartheid led to discriminatory laws affecting almost every aspect of life for the majority of the population – school, work, business and families. In response to these harshly enforced laws, the African National Congress (ANC) and Pan-African Congress (PAC) formed armed wings. Nelson Mandela and colleagues Walter Sisulu, Andrew Mlangeni, Elias Motsoaledi, Raymond Mhlaba, Dennis Goldberg, Govan Mbeki and Ahmed Kathrada and others, were founder members of one of these armed wings – Umkhonto we Sizwe – and were arrested in 1963, and sentenced to life imprisonment. Robben Island had been reopened as a prison in 1960 and these political prisoners were subsequently transferred there.

The Soweto uprising of 1976 led to another clampdown, and a further wave of arrests; many of these prisoners were also sent to Robben Island. In the early 1980s, various organizations united to call on the people to make South Africa ungovernable. Repression intensified and in July 1985 a state of emergency was declared. Again, hundreds of people were detained further increasing the prison population. However, change was in the air and talks with the government were initiated in 1986, leading ultimately to the first democratic elections held in South Africa in 1994.[3] The prison was finally closed in 1996.

UNDERSTANDING THE PLACE

> The long drawn-out wail of a siren. Stage-lights come up to reveal a moat of harsh, white light around the cell. In it the two prisoners … mime the digging of sand […]. It is an image of back-breaking and grotesquely futile labour.
>
> (Fugard 1993: 195)

> I see the gardens of the Island in my mind: patches of lawn, rockeries, flowerbeds: everything produced by our patient labour. What arguments we used to have about those gardens: some saying it was wrong to beautify the Island, making it a showpiece; others replying that we were doing it for ourselves, our own dignity, we had a right to see beautiful things, it was up us to to transform the Island in terms of what we wanted, not what the warders said.
>
> (Naidoo and Sachs 2000: 248)

Atholl Fugard's play, *The Island*, reminds us that to be imprisoned on the island was not just to be confined to a prison building (Fig. 23.2). The prison is as much about a landscape of 'back-breaking and grotesquely futile labour' as it is about the buildings of the prison. On the other hand, Idres Naidoo touches on the importance of beauty in adversity. It is clear from these accounts that what might seem today a fairly bleak island landscape is, in fact, one on which a huge number of events and memories have been imprinted. Robben Island is not just a prison or the site of a series of important events; it is a cultural landscape, a network of

Figure 23.2 Although the prison buildings are the focus of attention on the island, it is important to remember that there is a 'prison landscape' which is as significant but which poses many management challenges

Source: Author

human intervention imprinted on and interacting with the natural landscape. That intervention is as apparent in details such as a small rubbish dump, an initial carved on a stone as it is in the major buildings either in the settlement or the prison.

The first step in producing a management document for a place like Robben Island is to understand it as a whole, and in particular to understand what it is that we have inherited. Understanding in this context means having a clear idea of what survives today – whether buildings, landscapes, archaeology or ecology – and what factors have shaped what survives. Understanding, in turn, provides the basis for assessing significance.

There have already been several surveys of the island, including surveys of buildings and archaeological sites in 1986, 1992 and 1998 and of the wildlife in 1993 (Riley 1992; 1993; Robinson 1996: 156; Le Grange and Baumann 1998; Archaeology Contracts Office 1998). These in turn draw upon a considerable amount of academic research (Deacon 1996). Each of these surveys has been conducted to a high standard by a different professional. They have used slightly different systems of numbering and a different basis for selecting what to describe and why. This situation is common to many important heritage sites, and as a result the site manager – who may not be a specialist – is inevitably left with a large heap of documents, full of useful information which nevertheless may be difficult to find. As a result, there is a real risk that such documents are often left unused on a shelf, whilst critical decisions are made without them. In order to make the decisions needed to manage a place like this, it is vital to have ready access to integrated data which bring together our understanding of the place with what we see today, whether it is a road, a building, a row of trees or a shipwreck.

However, a site such as Robben Island forces us to ask whether conventional survey approaches are appropriate. This is not heritage in the conventional sense – most of it is neither old nor grand; instead it may be about the marks left by ordinary people as they went about the numbing routine of prison life. The place does not divide neatly along professional lines into architecture, archaeology, landscape or ecology. The island is also distinguished because of its rich oral history; many of the people who were imprisoned there are still alive and their memories are a vital part of the story of the island. It is thus a mosaic of memories and things, in which the prison is both buildings and landscape, while the earlier history – whether of illness, imprisonment or defence – underlies and shapes what is seen today.

Surveys for sites such as this need to be extended in a way which is sensitive not just to the buildings, but to this network of ephemeral remains in the landscape which in turn places them in their context, and identifies the links and patterns they represent. The implication is that professional barriers between for example, architectural historian and archaeologist, ecologist and oral historian, need to be broken down so that data can be collected in an integrated way.

We also need to begin to question the structure of survey data. Current classificatory mechanisms can often hinder understanding. Rather than classifying sites as prison buildings, housing, services, etc., it could be more useful to record the imprint of the daily life of a prisoner on the landscape (the cell, the route to the quarry, the lunch area, the narrow view from a cell window) or the routine of life in the leper colony. The political prisoners lived within a landscape inherited from others – the fragmentary remains of the burnt-out leper colony and hospital, the more brutal concrete of the Second World War emplacements. How did the two interact – were the prisoners oblivious of the past?

Robben Island is a place where prisoners were denied freedom. They were separated, controlled and ordered; a routine of work, meals and confinement was imposed. In mapping the site, this landscape needs to be approached afresh, if possible without the prejudices of either archaeological or conservation architectural mind sets. It requires openness, cultural sensitivity and flexibility. A survey in the traditional mould of archaeology or architectural history cannot do justice to a place like this. As part of the management plan, staff on the island and consultants are currently pioneering a new approach to collecting site data, which will integrate oral history and historic environmental evidence (Deacon and Baumann, personal communication).

SIGNIFICANCE AND VALUE

Significance lies at the heart of all heritage management. If the aim of conservation is to pass on to future generations what we value, then it is essential to articulate those values as part of the management process. Equally, if conservation means, in effect, declaring a public interest in private property, and as a consequence, potentially depriving an individual or group of their ability to exploit that property without restrictions, then that public interest must be made clear and substantiated.[4]

Most people working in cultural heritage today will be used to dealing with a relatively narrow bandwidth of value. In England, for example, the legislation for ancient monuments selects sites which are of 'national importance' or in the case of buildings, 'architectural and historic interest'.[5] The source and authority for these values tends to be academic scholarship, and the scale of values hierarchical. There is less scope for dealing with other values within the legislation, such as community, spiritual or local values. Commemorative values can also be problematic in such systems.

Traditional designations also tend to be mono-valent; thus in England a site may be a Site of Special Scientific Interest for its ecological interest, a Scheduled Monument for its archaeological interest or a Listed Building for its architectural interest. Such systems tend to mitigate against an integrated approach to value, or to values which fall outside the fairly narrowly-prescribed criteria. Site management approaches also tend to be segregated along these lines.

In practice, as at Robben Island, most of the values associated with heritage sites are multi-valent and non-hierarchical. Traditional value systems do not work. For example, the political prison buildings on the island are of little or no traditional architectural value, representing standard government buildings, yet they are of universal significance for their association with individuals. But even that association is complex. Within the buildings are many cells, of which the main focus of interest is one: Nelson Mandela's cell. An ordinary prison cell, no different from its neighbours, but special because of the association with an individual. Yet each of the other cells was occupied by people with stories to tell, some of which are set out in the present interpretation.

And whilst we may be shown the cell where Mandela or his colleagues were kept, it is less easy for the visitor to plot the daily routine of the prisoner. Where is the place where seaweed was collected? Which road did he and his colleagues take to the quarry? Where is the tennis court which was so painfully built with handfulls of quarry material, brought back each day. Again, a stretch of road, a patch of scrub or a bit of worn tennis court may have little conventional heritage value, but here they gain a new significance.

The stories told by prisoners are an essential part of understanding and valuing the buildings and landscape of Robben Island (Fig. 23.3). Yet this in turn raises the question of whose stories. The island was at the same time a common law prison. Are the stories of the common law prisoners less significant? And what about the warders? The houses, shop, pool and facilities provided for them survive on the island. Should we value these places as well as the prison? Antje Krog (1999) writes movingly of the aftermath of apartheid, of guilt, responsibility and understanding, and most of all, of the importance of telling the story and knowing what happened through the Truth and Reconciliation Committee. The story of the warders may not be palatable, but for many white people there is a reminder of complicity represented by these buildings.

Figure 23.3 Today, ex-prisoners take visitors around the site. Their stories and experiences are an important part of the significance of the site

Source: Author

There are many other values on the island. The island acted as a crucible for the consolidation of the Muslim faith in South Africa in the late seventeenth and eighteenth centuries; the role of the island as a place of resistance to state oppression dates back to before the period of the political prison; the place illustrates attitudes to medical care of the mentally ill. It also played a strategic role during the Second World War in protecting Allied war efforts and an extraordinary collection of military items remain (Le Grange and Baumann 1998: 8). Many local people have relatives who are buried on the island, in marked or more commonly unmarked graves. There are also conventional heritage buildings – a fine collection of colonial buildings, including church, school, Commissioner's House and club house – as well as a large collection of shipwrecks of international significance.

The inscription for Robben Island is based on the significance of the buildings as an 'eloquent testimony to its sombre history', and the fact that 'Robben Island and its prison buildings symbolize the triumph of the human spirit, of freedom, and of democracy over oppression'. However, although Robben Island was inscribed as a World Heritage Site primarily for its association with the fight against apartheid, it is clear that the place embodies a much greater range of values which, whilst perhaps not deserving World Heritage inscription in their own right, nevertheless contribute directly to what makes the place so special. In managing the island it is easy to focus only on the prison, or even Nelson Mandela's cell, at the expense of the wider prison landscape around it, or indeed of the deeper and more complex history which has shaped what we see today.

The process set out in the Australian Burra Charter (Australia ICOMOS 1999) provides a useful framework for considering places such as Robben Island where values are complex and multi-layered by emphasizing the centrality of the definition of significance to the cultural heritage process. At Robben Island, such approaches will be vital if the complex significance of the place is to be articulated in such a way that responsible management decisions can be taken.

A VULNERABLE LANDSCAPE

Another reason for ensuring that we have articulated value as widely as possible at a site like Robben Island is simply that what is not valued or understood is potentially vulnerable. Caring for heritage sites implies that we try to prevent unnecessary damage or harm. Yet it is frighteningly easy to damage historic places. That damage may be major – the demolition of key buildings, inappropriate new development – but more often it is minor but cumulative. Small losses in a landscape, the lack of maintenance of buildings, incidental damage by tourists, all of which may be minor in their own right, yet when taken cumulatively over say fifty years, can result in significant loss. Most of this damage is not deliberate; it is usually done because we have other priorities in mind and are not aware of the consequences. Often it is also the result of competing values.

Helao Shityewete describes the limestone quarry as follows:

> We were sent to work in the two lime quarries, chipping away at the rock-face with only picks, shovels and spades. It was very hard work, and a dazzling glare came off the white rocks when the sun shone – as we had no sunglasses, the eyesight of many of us was damaged.
>
> (quoted in Hutton 1994: 57)

Today, the stone of the limestone quarry has been blackened by the fumes from the buses taking tourists there. One set of values – the need for visitor access to the site – is competing with another set of values: the experience of the prisoner as reflected in the landscape.

> The dyke entered the sea and curved round to form a breakwater with a road on top. [...] wherever one looked, hammers could be seen flying up and down,

beating the hard stones, wheelbarrows carrying little mountains of sand to the Nipline, fourteen-pounders cracking into the rocks and bringing down huge slabs of granite which landed with a mighty crash.

(Naidoo and Sachs 2000: 86)

With no prison labour to strengthen it, the dyke (or bund) separating the quarry and the sea is now eroding rapidly. It is likely that one or two bad storms will breach the bund and carry it away, thus flooding the quarry. An estimate of 5 million rand has been provided for the cost of the repair to the bund (island staff, personal communication). Here the question concerns the significance of the quarry; island managers must decide whether to find the resources to repair the bund – most likely at the expense of other work such as interpretation or perhaps basic maintenance of the prison buildings – and thus retain the quarry. Behind all of these decisions are fundamental assumptions about value and significance.

When we arrived at Cape Town harbour the truck pulled in right next to a little passenger boat called Diaz, and, still handcuffed and chained – many of the prisoners had never seen the sea before, let alone been on a boat – we were taken on board and placed in a hold below deck [...]. It was frightening for many of the prisoners, especially as the waves hit the portholes and as we felt the chains heavy on us, trapped in the hold.

(Naidoo and Sachs 2000: 48)

The traditional boats which took prisoners across to the island have been supplemented with a modern ferry imported from Australia. The old boats are expensive to maintain, slow and carry few passengers. The new ferry enables more tourists to visit the island, creating a business opportunity for a group of people to act as tour guides, some of whom were previously imprisoned on the island and otherwise have no income. The boats are clearly a significant part of the story of the island. Site managers will have to make a difficult decision about what priority to place on the retention of the boats.

Elsewhere on the island the story is the same (Robinson 1996: 159–60) – items are removed as souvenirs by visitors, buses drive over a stone carved with somebody's initials, a walkway to help visitors see penguins has been dug through a tramway. This is not deliberate damage at all, but small actions, taken with other priorities in mind, which over the next fifty years will accumulate to erode the character of the place.

All heritage sites are vulnerable in this way. Therefore part of the process of managing them has to be an understanding of how and why this occurs. We need to know what has happened to it in the past, what is happening now and what may happen in the future if we continue with the present regime. The idea of vulnerability does not mean that management is failing; it is part of responsible management to accept that almost everything we do to a site has the potential to damage it. It is better to acknowledge and anticipate such damage rather than to pretend that it does not exist.

Figure 23.4 It is always difficult to reconcile the needs of visitors to the island with the significance of the site

Source: Author

At Robben Island the critical vulnerabilities are to do with visitors and resources (Fig. 23.4). People want to visit the site; they will need facilities such as water, somewhere to eat and toilet facilities. Most will want some form of transport to get around the island. They will expect interpretation of the site and of the landscape, and places for educational events and seminars. There are already demands for overnight accommodation on the island. All of these activities have the potential to put aspects of the site at risk.

At the same time, in common with most heritage sites, resources are scarce. The costs of running a site such as Robben Island are high; the costs of maintaining and managing buildings must be met on top of the costs of managing visitors and providing facilities for them. Visitor income rarely covers the full cost of caring for a place such as this, and revenue must be found from elsewhere or visitor numbers increased.

More visitors may mean more resources, but they can also put the significance of the site further at risk. Part of the process of understanding the site may involve setting limits – how much can be lost before the island loses its character? How many coaches can the landscape absorb? How many people can the island realistically support? How many visitors can the island afford before the visitor experience comes to dominate the experience of the prison?

In such circumstances a proactive approach to managing the site requires managers to define limits of acceptable change, in other words, the maximum limit of damage or wear that is acceptable, and also to establish what action will be taken if that limit is reached. Such limits are usually defined through indicators or physical parameters.

This approach to the resource is more common in the conservation of the natural heritage than it is in the cultural heritage, and there is already a resource strategy in place for the natural history on the Island (Davies, personal communication). In England, programmes such as the Monuments at Risk Survey, or English Heritage's Buildings at Risk strategy (English Heritage 2000) have begun to quantify the loss of heritage resources as a basis for setting priorities for action, but unfortunately the heritage world is only just beginning to develop more systematic indicators for patterns of loss in the historic environment. Nevertheless, it is possible to apply the ideas of indicators and limits to the management of an individual site such as Robben Island, through, for example, modelling the impact of predicted visitor numbers or documenting the loss of features through time. Sustainable development asks that we consider the implications of our actions, and if necessary set limits; it is time to begin to do this for cultural heritage resources as well as for natural history.

The UNESCO Operational Guidelines rightly ask countries to monitor the state of World Heritage Sites, reporting regularly on problems, although these reports tend to identify only major issues. At a more detailed level, the idea of 'vulnerability' is implicit in World Heritage Site management planning, but has been explicitly incorporated into the process of Conservation Planning, an integrated approach to conservation which draws upon World Heritage Site Management Plans, but also a variety of other conservation approaches (Clark 1998; Semple Kerr 2000). Sites such as Robben Island further emphasize the need to be clear about both significance and vulnerability as part of the management planning process.

CONCLUSION

Robben Island is a place which threatens some of the most basic assumptions of the heritage industry. Whilst part of the island is old, it is the heritage of the past twenty years which has most meaning; parts of the island are indeed beautiful, but it is the grim grey prison buildings that attract visitors in thousands; while the wildlife makes the site internationally important in ecological terms, the management of 'natural' ecology potentially conflicts with the traces of the introduced human landscape, planted by prisoners and others who lived there. And where in the present heritage canon of national and international importance, archaeological and architectural significance, is there a category for the prison cell of someone who in some eyes would be called a terrorist?

The genuine dilemmas raised by the management of Robben Island are of relevance to anyone involved in managing a modern heritage site whose significance centres on *streitwert* or 'discord values' (Dolff-Bonekämper, this volume), whether a prison, a monument to or site of war, or a place associated with difficult events.

It is easy to tame and to tidy such places, to make life easy for the visitor through elegant rapid boats, a comfortable bus journey, interpretation that is not too challenging and the provision of whatever facilities are needed. Yet in some way we need to reconcile hospitality – for that is what good manners demand that a heritage site provide for its visitors – with a care for the significance of the place which was, in itself, inhospitable.

Those who manage sites such as Robben Island will have to reconcile these very different priorities. In order to do this, decisions must be based upon an open and imaginative understanding of what survives, as well as a broad articulation of what is significant and why. Western European sites have been able to rely upon a limited range of values – old, aesthetic – established by academic experts. Sites such as Robben Island challenge such values, and the methods by which they are established and given authority. And by challenging values, they also call into question assumptions about management. We need new ways of understanding sites, and need to listen to new voices as part of the process of articulating significance which is fundamental to all heritage management. We also need to realize that vulnerability goes beyond the choice of conservation techniques, to include a far wider range of issues.

The new South Africa is a challenging context for the management of the cultural heritage (see Soudien and Malan, this volume). In a country where expectations of the government are high and resources are short, and where health needs and the provision of basic services such as clean water and education must take priority, it is easy to ask 'why conserve sites?'. Yet culture is important; and no government can, in the long term, improve the quality of life without recognizing that at least part of the quality of life involves caring for cultural values. Overcoming poverty and respect for cultural heritage are not mutually exclusive activities; indeed as international agencies are learning, social programmes which work with cultural values are likely to be more successful in the long term than those which do not.

Robben Island is a place of outstanding cultural value, at local, national and international levels. It will attract tourists, and indeed must do so to survive, but this need not happen at the expense of a significant and fragile place. The island is in a position to set a new standard in heritage management, which recognizes the multiple and complex values of a diverse heritage, and integrates those values into practical management approaches.

Whatever meaning is now or has been attributed to those remains, history shows us that it is likely to change. What we value today may not be what we value tomorrow. Our responsibility is to hand that fabric on to future generations, cared for as best we can with as open a mind as possible, in order to enable our successors to make up their own minds and to draw their own meaning from the past.

ACKNOWLEDGEMENTS

This chapter began life as a presentation to the Cambridge Seminar entitled 'Heritage that Hurts' in 1997. Following that I was invited to help facilitate the preparation of the Robben Island Conservation and Management Plan. Many of the ideas set out in this chapter were discussed during seminars on the island, and benefited from the expertise of island staff members and consultants.

NOTES

1 The site was inscribed under the Convention Concerning the Protection of the World, Cultural and Natural Heritage, adopted by UNESCO in 1972.
2 Heritage Day Festival Leaflet given to visitors on 24 September 2000.
3 For a full history of the site, see Deacon 1996. Published first-hand accounts of life on the island include Sachs and Naidoo 2000, as well as Mandela 1996 and Alexander 1994. Hutton 1994 provides a popular overview.
4 Carman 1996 provides a useful overview of significance within British archaeological legislation; Bruier and Mathers 1996 do the same thing for the United States.
5 An overview of heritage management legislation in six European countries, including the UK, undertaken as part of the Herein project can be found on the Council of Europe website at european-heritage.net.

REFERENCES

Alexander, N. (1994) *Robben Island Prison Dossier 1964–1974*, Cape Town: UCT Press.

Australia ICOMOS (1999) *The Burra Charter: the Australia ICOMOS charter for places of cultural significance*, Canberra: Australian Heritage Commission.

Bruier, F.L. and Mathers, C. (1996) *Trends and Patterns in Cultural Resource Significance: An Historical Perspective and Annotated Biography*, Evaluation of Environmental Investments Research Programme: US Army Corps of Engineers IWR Report 96-EL-1.

Carman, J. (1996) *Valuing Ancient Things, Archaeology and Law*, Leicester: Leicester University Press.

Clark, K. (1998) *Conservation Plans in Action*, London: English Heritage.

Deacon, J. (ed.) (1996) *Monuments and Sites South Africa*, Sri Lanka: ICOMOS.

English Heritage (2000) *English Heritage Register of Buildings at Risk 2000*, London: English Heritage.

Feilden, B.M. and Jokilehto, J. (1993) *Management Guidelines for World Cultural Heritage Sites*, Rome: ICCROM.

Fugard, A. (1993) *The Township Plays*, edited with an introduction by Dennis Walder, Oxford: Oxford Univeristy Press.

Krog, A. (1999) *Country of My Skull*, New York: Viking.

Hutton, B. (1994) *Robben Island, Symbol of Resistance*, Johannesburg: Sached Books/Mayibuye Books.

Mandela, N. (1996) *Long Walk to Freedom*, London: Abacus.

Naidoo, I. and Sachs, A. (2000) *Prisoner 885/63, Island in Chains: Ten Years on Robben Island*, London: Penguin.

Robinson, L. (1996) 'Robben Island: a case study in contemporary conservation practice', in Deacon, J. (ed.) *Monuments and Sites South Africa*, Sri Lanka: ICOMOS, pp.151–62.

Semple Kerr, J. (2000) *The Conservation Plan* (5th edn), Sydney: National Trust of New South Wales.

UNPUBLISHED SURVEY REPORTS

Archaeology Contracts Office, University of Cape Town (1998) 'Base line archaeological assessment of Robben Island', Environmental Risk Services.

Le Grange, L. and Baumann, N. (1998) 'Robben Island: survey of the built environment', Robben Island Museum.

Riley, P. (1992) 'Robben Island: survey and inventory of existing sites and structures', National Monuments Council.

Riley, P. (1993) 'Conservation survey of Robben Island', National Monuments Council.

24 Troubling remnants: dealing with the remains of conflict in Northern Ireland

Neil Jarman

INTRODUCTION

All conflicts leave physical scars on the landscape as well as on the people who fight and suffer in them, but diverse styles of conflict leave diverse forms of material remains. Wars of invasion fought out by professional armies will create different remnants from conflicts between a guerrilla army and the state; rural and urban conflicts will each produce their own distinctive traces. The nature of the material scars will be different as a result of a short but intensely violent conflict from those left by a long, slow-burning dispute. The time frame will affect both the breadth and variety of remains. A long-running conflict might be expected to generate a much wider and deeper sample of remains but this will also be subjected to considerable change as defences are built and rebuilt and earlier structures replaced with new. This may seem no more than stating the obvious, but the recognition of the nature of the conflict and the acknowledgement of the full range of participants will in turn affect the remains that are accepted as part of the archaeology of war. Furthermore the scale and nature of violent disputes has changed over the years such that many recent and contemporary conflicts do not fit so easily into classical categories of war. Therefore, one must accept that the nature of the material remains will vary and to a great extent the remains will reflect the form and scale of the conflict that generated them. The nature and scale of the conflict will also affect how the physical remains are dealt with, how long they are preserved, how quickly they are removed, and how or whether they might be conserved as a memorial. The nature of the resolution and ending of the conflict may also affect the possibility of their preservation as mimetic devices, whether they can be converted into tourist or educational resources, or whether their physical presence will be razed and their memory erased in an attempt to move forward and reconcile past combatants. All such factors will affect the work of those people and institutions whose interest is in preserving or restoring, or more simply recording and documenting, the remains of military and paramilitary conflicts.

Many of these questions are particularly significant in the case of Northern Ireland as it slowly emerges from thirty years of violent conflict. Northern Ireland is an example of the less readily classifiable form of contemporary conflict. It is seen by some as a war, by some as a national liberation struggle, while to others it is nothing more than a violent and vicious terrorist campaign. The conflict is known locally as the Troubles, a somewhat understated term for a violent campaign that has continued for over a generation. The name also disguises the fact that there is little agreement about the nature of the conflict, the reasons why it began or the reasons why it has ended. As a consequence there is little agreement about the status of the physical remnants of the war, and public consideration of how one should approach the material remains has not yet emerged as a factor in the debate about the transition to peace. Yet at the same time, destruction of military and security installations, perhaps the most sensitive and therefore the least accessible or documented of these artefacts, has begun apace as the British state attempts to illustrate its commitment to peace. The period of negotiation and debate about the nature of the future state is therefore proceeding in parallel with the removal and destruction of many of the more overtly militaristic physical remnants of the conflict. In spite of attempts to establish a new start many of the underlying tensions between the two main communities have not been resolved and feelings of mistrust remain strong. The military conflict may have come to an end with the declaration of paramilitary cease-fires but low level sectarian conflict continues. In particular disputes over the right to parade have ended in rioting on a number of occasions and the issue has, more than once, threatened to provoke a return to full-scale armed conflict (Jarman and Bryan 1996; Jarman 1997). The consolidation of the peace is therefore proceeding in a somewhat staccato manner and political moods oscillate between optimism and gloom.

    This has led to a similarly uneven response to the physical structures constructed in response to the Troubles. Some installations were rapidly removed; for example, all border crossings were reopened in the first year of the peace process and a wide variety of physical barriers were therefore removed or destroyed. A number of military structures around the border and even in Belfast have also been taken down. This is not an entirely new process, as much of the security architecture imposed on the commercial centre of Belfast has been steadily removed since the 1980s (Jarman 1993), but the pace of change and normalization has increased in recent years. However many facets of the architecture of conflict remain a necessary part of the moves towards peace. New security structures continue to be built, rebuilt, redesigned, strengthened and extended at the same time as others are being removed. The categorization of a structure as a product of the military conflict does not therefore mean that its use has come to an end because the conflict has come to an end. In this chapter I want to cast a wide-ranging exploratory eye over the physical products and remnants of the conflict, in particular those in Belfast, in order to try to classify and categorize some of the key remnants. I also want to make some initial points about how the differing types of remains are being treated and why they provoke varied responses, and finally to consider how perhaps they should be dealt with in the immediate future.

    Part of the problem is in trying to define what should be considered as constituting the military archaeology of the Troubles. From one perspective one might take a fairly narrow and prescriptive frame and focus on the formal military and security installations of the British army and the Royal Ulster Constabulary and other agencies of the state. On the other hand one could take the maximal position and include all physical installations that are in some way a product of, and response to, the violence. This could perhaps be problematic in terms of deciding whether something should be considered a military product in the strictest sense while the diverse and lengthy nature of the conflict might be expected to produce a diverse and varied range of responses. Including the widest range of material artefacts, architectural structures and physical constructions within the remit also draws attention away from the machismo of technologically complex armies and refocuses it on the wider constituency of paramilitary and civilian parties to the dispute. This in turn means that the process of analysing and categorizing material remains demands that our conceptions and expectations of the nature, scale, style, form and complexity of modern warfare must be expanded. It requires a move beyond the view of war as a conflict between sovereign states to include intra-state militarized disputes involving a complex variety of paramilitary organizations fighting for a diverse range of social, political, ethnic and financial interests.

SECURITY STRUCTURES

State military and security structures are prominent across Northern Ireland. There is no discernible regional variation in form, scale, structure or style. All police stations are highly fortified and highly distinctive. They have lookout posts, which are protected by metal grills placed to deflect missile attacks; they are defended by blast walls and bounded by bollards designed to prevent vehicles from being driven too close in case they contain explosive devices. They are overlooked by a range of CCTV cameras and they are physically dominated by masts which contain a plethora of aerials and panoptical devices. The main military barracks have a similar appearance. However, whereas the British army has remained content with a somewhat brutal façade of military-green steel cladding, the police stations have been subjected to a gradual aestheticization in the process of reconstruction and enlargement. The two most recently completed police stations in Belfast are defended by elaborate multi-coloured brick walls with painted steel palings incorporated into their design. In one case this has created something of the appearance of a post-modern medieval castle. Older stations have defensive walls that were built on to existing structures and could therefore be relatively easily removed in order to reflect a more 'normal' political situation. In the newer structures the defences appear as more integral features and clearly suggest a long-lasting need for high-level security.

Military bases and police stations are only a small facet of the security architecture of the city. Probably the most distinctive features are the numerous 'peace-lines' or interface barriers that separate many of the working-class Protestant and Catholic areas (Fig. 24.1). Most residential areas have long been dominated by one community rather than being mixed or equally balanced; churches are obviously segregated but so too is the

Figure 24.1 The peace-line between the Falls and the Greater Shankill areas of Belfast

Source: Author

school system, many work places as well as sports and social clubs. Most people therefore are born, grow up, live, work, socialize and are buried amongst their own kind.
The two working-class communities have lived relatively segregated lives since the
early expansion of the city in the nineteenth century (Heatley 1983), but over the thirty
years of conflict these patterns of segregation have hardened. When the violence
erupted in 1969 much of it took the form of inter-communal rioting at the boundaries
of the many distinctive enclaves, at the very places where the two ethnic groups maintained a tenuous and fragile relationship. The families who lived in the streets that connected the Catholic Falls Road and the Protestant Shankill Road were in one of the
most vulnerable locations and were subjected to extensive rioting and violent intimida-
tion. The already divided communities were further polarized and a no-man's land was
established as a boundary zone after people moved away from the interfaces and further into the heart of their community. Initially improvised barricades or rolls of
barbed wire segregated the two sides. Soon these were enhanced by more solid sheet-
steel fences and then further strengthened by a two-tier steel fence so that the barrier
reached some 6–7 m in height. The dividing wall between the Falls and Shankill was
also steadily extended in length so that now the barrier extends from the boundaries of
the city centre to the foothills of Divis Mountain some 3 km away. The rebuilding,
extension, strengthening and consolidation of the boundary wall at the westerly
extreme of the divide began the day the Irish Republican Army (IRA) declared their
cease-fire in August 1994 and was completed early in 1998. This Falls–Shankill barrier
is the longest interface between the two communities but is only one among many
such structures. In North Belfast there are a dozen such barriers and others can be

found in the east and the south-west of the city. The war has left Belfast a heavily fragmented and divided city.

The barriers take a variety of forms and these have changed and developed in form and style over the course of the Troubles. Walking the length of the Falls–Shankill reveals not only the scale of the division between the two communities but also something of the variety of aesthetic approaches to segregation. Closest to the city centre, where there has been little redevelopment, the barrier is at its most stark and brutal. Grey steel cladding faces on to derelict land on the Protestant side while the fence backs close on to the houses on the Catholic side; here some houses have also protected their backyards from missile attacks by building a wire-mesh structure from the guttering to the back wall. But as one follows the route westwards the styles change. A recently redeveloped area is bounded by a 3-m high cream-and-red brick wall fronted by a metal fence. This fence protects an array of trees and shrubs, incorporated as part of the Northern Ireland Office design, and which it is hoped will help mask the barrier as they grow in years to come. Adjacent to this residential area is an engineering factory and the land next to this is earmarked for a new university campus. In both instances the idea is that both communities can use the resources but at the same time these will also provide a substantial buffer zone rather than the more blatantly formal physical barrier. The next section of the boundary is marked by houses, which have metal grills over their windows to protect them from stones and other missiles. This is then followed by a zone where the row of houses fronting on to the main road has been demolished. Once the buildings had been removed the land was planted with a dense bed of trees and shrubs to hide and protect the houses behind. At the beginning of the final section, where the barrier makes a 90° turn, a new state-of-the-art police station, heavily fortified with blast walls, iron bollards and fortified lookout posts has recently been completed.

Along the route a number of roads intersect the barrier. At the lowest level of security the road is barred by a low-level gate, which is permanently locked but allows pedestrian access at any time. At the next level the roads have been permanently closed to traffic but have a gate which is opened during the day to permit pedestrian access to shops and other shared facilities. The two major roads connecting the Falls and Shankill areas remain open but one has low-level gates which can be manually closed, while the main intersection can be controlled by 3-m high solid gates, electronically controlled from a local police station and which are regularly closed at the first sign of trouble.

Across the city people live with barriers on a daily basis. Small enclave estates are enclosed behind their barrier walls like miniature walled towns. Some people have 5-m high barriers at the bottom of their garden, segregating them from their neighbours. Houses are often demolished and land is allowed to remain derelict in the vicinity of barriers; elsewhere buildings are left derelict as a no-man's land is created when two walls are built 50 m apart to restrict the flow of missiles from one community to the other. People have to take extensive detours to get to shops or public transport because connecting roads are closed. Movement is therefore restricted, and facilities and resources become claimed by one side or the other. Perhaps the strangest and most melancholy peace-line of all is in Alexandra Park in the north of the city. In recent years the park had become a regular site of 'recreational rioting' between rival Protestant and Catholic youths (Jarman and O'Halloran 2001). To stop the fighting a steel fence now divides the park in two. The war may have ended but it has been replaced by an uneasy and nervous peace. Trust and mutual understanding between the two communities have been serious casualties of the Troubles. There is no indication that the fear and suspicion each side feels for the other has yet begun to be ameliorated.

Attitudes to these diverse structures and installations vary. The pure military remains, such as army bases, observation posts and lookout towers have been removed fairly rapidly in recent years, as Northern Ireland moves towards peace. They are regarded by many in the nationalist community as emblems of the British occupation of the north and their removal is seen as an indication of the political goodwill on behalf of the British government. The government on the other hand is using the opportunity for their removal as confidence-building measures and to create pressure on the IRA to give up their weapons. In many areas the army occupied land that was already in use, thus depriving the local community of a resource. In Crossmaglen, in South Armagh, the army occupied the Gaelic football pitch and local people have long campaigned for its return. In Belfast the main army base in the west of the city occupies land that was once a local industrial estate and the announcement that the base would close was welcomed by local people who argued that the land should be returned to its original use. Calls have also been made for the main base in the north of the city to be closed and the land made available for housing for the adjacent Catholic communities, while a local school has also made claims on the site. Any announcement that a military installation is to be closed is generally welcomed and there are few dissenting or questioning voices. On one occasion a local nationalist politician suggested that a military lookout tower in South Armagh might be preserved as part of a tourist initiative rather than demolished. But he was derided by other members of his community who see the removal of all army installations of any kind as part of the general process of demilitarization (*Irish News* 7 October 1998). Nationalists are therefore encouraging the rapid removal of military architecture and while unionists want to ensure that security installations are not withdrawn too swiftly; no one has raised arguments for the preservation of physical structures except on military grounds.

Unlike the military structures, the heavily fortified police stations are considered a permanent feature of the landscape. The police are acknowledged as a necessary presence. Even though the size, scale, structure and symbols of the future service are subject to argument and debate, their presence in some form or other is not challenged, nor is the future of the police stations in general. They continue to be built and rebuilt albeit with aesthetic refinements which attempt to soften and disguise the defensive requirements through design and colour (Fig. 24.2). But old and ageing police stations are treated without sympathy. Installations and structures that are no longer required are removed and their sites cleared and levelled as new buildings are constructed without any thought for recording what buildings there were or what state they might have been in. This process has received a general sanction from the Patten Report into the future of policing in Northern Ireland which

Figure 24.2 The new RUC station on Lisburn Road, Belfast

Source: Author

recommended a wholesale evaluation and rationalization of the Royal Ulster Constabulary (RUC) estate and the disposal of properties where possible to raise capital for further redevelopment. There has been no suggestion to date that any of the security architecture of policing should be preserved in any way for future generations.

The peace-lines have a somewhat anomalous status. Most people deplore their presence while at the same time acknowledging that they are a necessary evil. People who live in the interface areas want the barriers and feel safer with them, but at the same time they express hope that it will be possible to remove them at some future time. However peace-lines continue to be seen as a prime means of dealing with ongoing low-level conflict. Three new barriers have been erected in north Belfast since the first cease-fire was declared and there are recurrent demands for new barriers to be installed at a number of contentious interfaces. Several other barriers have been rebuilt as part of recent redevelopment; still more are going to be reconstructed, strengthened and extended as part of planned future redevelopment work. No interface barrier has been removed to date. The peace-lines will be a part of the Belfast landscape for the foreseeable future.

(IN)FAMOUS SITES

Alongside the general category of security sites, there are a small number of individual buildings that have a special significance in the history of the conflict in the north but which are at, or coming to, the end of their useful lives. Three in

Figure 24.3 Crumlin Road Prison (with paramilitary graffiti), Belfast

Source: Author

particular are noteworthy: Crumlin Road Prison, Crumlin Road Court and HM Prison The Maze (Long Kesh). Crumlin Road Prison (Fig. 24.3) was used to house paramilitary prisoners held on remand and who were moved through a tunnel under the Crumlin Road to be tried in the court opposite. The prison was closed in March 1996 and the court closed in June 1998. Since this time there has been considerable uncertainty over their future although a number of suggestions have been made about possible uses. These include utilizing them for government offices, converting the prison site to industrial units, demolishing both buildings or converting one or the other into a museum of the Troubles. Both buildings are listed (and thus have a degree of statutory protection) and government policy is to dispose of surplus buildings provided their status is respected. At one time it seemed likely that the Public Records Office Northern Ireland would move into part of the prison site but that no longer seems probable. The neighbouring Mater Hospital has expressed an interest and a number of local groups have lobbied to have part of the building set aside for a development that would benefit the local community. The Courthouse was sold to a property developer for a nominal sum, but there are no evident plans for redevelopment. In both cases it seems that there would be considerable local support for an imaginative plan that conserved the existing structures while utilizing the space in a way that would benefit the local area in a positive way. As yet no one has taken the initiative to formulate such a proposal.

The Maze prison is one of the most famous sites of the Troubles. At the beginning of the conflict paramilitary prisoners were held in Nissen huts at the Long

Kesh airfield site. These special-category prisoners were effectively treated as prisoners of war and photographs of 'the Kesh' do indeed resemble images from Second World War PoW camps. Each of the paramilitary organizations was allowed to retain its own command structures, men wore their own clothes and they were not required to do duties or work expected of those convicted of criminal offences who were held in other prisons. In the mid-1970s the British government decided that paramilitary prisoners should be subject to the same rules and regulations as ordinary prisoners and a new prison complex was built on the site to house them. These became known as the H-Blocks from their design, which consisted of two long parallel wings connected in the middle by an administration block. The prisoners resisted the government's attempt to criminalize them, and requirements to wear prison-issue clothing and carry out work duties. Resistance began in 1976, when the first prisoner refused to accept a prison uniform, and escalated through various stages until it reached its climax in 1981 when republican prisoners went on hunger strike in demand for a restoration of their political status. The government eventually conceded the prisoners' demands but not before ten prisoners had died and the hunger strikes campaign had ended (O'Malley 1990). The Long Kesh H-Blocks achieved an international notoriety as a result of the hunger strikes and the IRA gained their most significant martyr in the figure of Bobby Sands who led the strikers, was elected Member of Parliament for Fermanagh and South Tyrone during his fast, and was the first of the ten to die.

The Belfast Agreement signed in April 1998 provided for an accelerated release of all prisoners associated with the paramilitary groups holding a legitimate ceasefire. This meant that all the prisoners held in the Maze would be released within two years and the complex would no longer be required as a prison. In fact the last prisoners were released in September 2000. Again there is no clear indication of what will happen to the prison buildings and site. Sinn Féin has argued that some of the complex should be preserved in some way and there have been suggestions that the site should be the location for a museum of the Troubles. However there has yet to be any serious consideration of the future of the Maze. If the views of Sir David Ramsbotham, Chief Inspector of Prisons, were adopted it would seem more likely that the site would be razed. In a newspaper report Sir David suggested that the structures should be demolished: 'If its days are numbered, I hope it will be razed to the ground as quickly as possible after it is finally emptied, and confined to history … so that no-one should be tempted to make expensive rehabilitation of its unsatisfactory structures.' (*Newsletter* 11 November 1998).

This gives some indication of the difficulties facing academics and historians when addressing the matter of structures related to the conflict. The Maze/Long Kesh is probably the most famous and infamous building of the Troubles. Everybody in Ireland knows of it, as do many people around the world, although few people have any direct experience, or knowledge, of the place. It is difficult to get any clear view of the site from outside, beyond the scale of the walls and the complex of lights and electronic security devices. It is a large site but there does not appear to be any pressing need or demand for the land as there might be for the Crumlin Road buildings. The recommendation to demolish the buildings would appear to be driven by a desire to erase the political memories of the place, to remove all physical traces of a locale where the government won the battle with the hunger strikers but lost the war with the prisoners who ended up exercising a significant and well-documented control over the legal authorities. The Maze may not have the architectural or historical significance of the Crumlin Road Prison, which more readily reflects the ideal of penal institutions and does have a certain bleak Victorian grandeur, but the H-Blocks have a more powerful symbolic status and they remain a unique experiment in penal control. The Inspector of Prisons' desire to see the site razed seems to balance the welcome that republicans give to the removal of British army bases in their desire for the removal of powerful symbols which will serve to stir unwelcome memories.

Prisons can be difficult buildings to deal with when society is moving from conflict to peace. They are the location for a complex array of memories and emotions depending on whether one was a prisoner or part of the prison service, a relative of a prisoner or a victim of the actions that led to incarceration. They are the places where the state has, and is able to exercise, fullest control over those who are trying to force the pace of change. A place where ideological enemies come face to face in a space marked out by total imbalance of power and authority, and where the state and its agents are able to exercise brutal discipline and revenge with a minimum of fear of reprisal (Foucault 1977; Millett 1995). But equally often they are key sites of resistance, emblems of spirit and determination, a place for the consolidation of alternative structures of authority, centres of thought and learning. Prisons symbolize both the physical power of the state and its weakness; they symbolize the vulnerability of individual prisoners but also their strength. Being able to deal with the memories of the prison is perhaps a key feature of dealing with the past, but there are no blueprints for confronting the issue. In South Africa, Robben Island Prison has become a part of the tourist itinerary only a few years after the release of Nelson Mandela and other political prisoners (Clark, this volume). In Dublin, Kilmainham Gaol, host to political prisoners from Henry Joy McCracken in 1798 through to the leaders of the Easter Rising in 1916, was closed following the release of future president Eamon de Valera at the end of the civil war in 1924. Thereafter it was allowed to decay. The government remained uncertain whether to demolish or restore the ruin and quietly ignored the structure until volunteers took on the job of restoring the site in the 1960s. It is now a major memorial site, museum and tourist attraction (Cooke 1995).

Because they contain such diverse and ambiguous memories it can seem simpler to make a knee-jerk reaction and physically remove prison structures, clear the ground and start again rather than allow the time and space for more considered reflection. This issue highlights some of the difficult questions raised by the process of moving out of conflict and dealing with the recent past while memories are still vivid, while personal experiences are still recent, while wounds are still raw, while combatants are still trying to adjust to new roles as statesmen, while peace is still fragile, while no one is sure who won and who lost, and while there is no common interpretation of what actually happened. In such a situation the maxim that history is written by the winners is of no help. The prison site may be the venue where all the dislocating uncertainties of the recent past are brought most clearly into view. The process of recording, documenting and preserving the most significant artefacts and structures is thus made more complex, and thereby opens the possibility that things will be destroyed in the haste to heal hurt and conceal unwelcome reminders of the past. Given the importance that prison issues and paramilitary prisoners have had within the Troubles, in many ways the Maze Prison would seem to be the ideal site to represent them in their historical context. But the example of Kilmainham illustrates the sensitivities that can surround such places and the time it can take for such attitudes to change. It took forty years of decay before Kilmainham was acknowledged as a significant historical site and it was converted into a museum and became an important tourist attraction. One wonders how long it might take before the Maze Prison could be viewed in such a way, and whether the time will be available to allow a dispassionate and reflective view of its significance to be formed.

MURALS AND MEMORIALS

The apparent lack of any significant public discourse on the merits of the preservation of the architecture of the Troubles does not mean that people are not commemorating the recent past. It rather implies that there is no common understanding of what and who should be remembered, and how the process of memorialization should take place (Bloomfield 1998). In fact there are a large number of memorials and informal installations that mark sites of physical violence and death and a wide range of more general, local memorials. These in turn are part of a large group of artefacts that have been created as part of, or in response to, the political situation and the recurrent violence. When one moves away from the more obvious and overt military and security structures, questions arise about what constitutes the material culture of conflict. In a situation such as Northern Ireland where the war is fought out over a long period of time, where daily life carries on amidst military and paramilitary campaigns, and where there are huge variations between the military capacities of the various sides, the nature of the material remains will be diverse. While the British army and the RUC can build substantial physical structures to define the areas they control and to protect their personnel, the paramilitary groups map out their zones of authority in a different way and by utilizing different media. One way in which the paramilitaries have defined their territory and refined their arguments has been through political murals on the walls of houses (Fig. 24.4).

Protestants have painted political murals in Belfast since before the First World War (Rolston 1991; Jarman 1997), but the practice was almost moribund by the 1960s. It was only given a new lease of life when republicans started painting murals as part of the campaign in support of the hunger strikers in 1981. In the 1980s there was a dramatic outpouring of new images with paramilitary emblems, hooded gunmen, historical icons and political statements replacing the earlier symbols of the Orange Order and expressions of loyalty to the British monarchy. Since that time there have been hundreds of murals painted across the city. The quality of the

Figure 24.4 Wreath-laying parade at a UVF commemorative mural on the Shankill Road

Source: Author

images has steadily improved; the subject matter has increased in range and the practice spread to other towns across the north. Murals have become the most distinctive material remains of the Troubles and are widely used in newspapers, television reports and films to illustrate the symbolic complexities of the conflict (Jarman 1996).

But despite their importance as a medium of propaganda, murals have an uncertain life span. Some last only a few weeks before they are damaged by graffiti, begin to decay because of the poor quality of paint, or are painted over with a new image. A number have become targets for more focused attack. A small number of republican paintings have been deliberately targeted by members of the British army and the RUC, who have defaced the images by throwing paint-bombs at the walls in a strange replication of republican petrol-bomb attacks on the security forces. Some paintings remain in place for years and a small number of these are painted or maintained as a memorial and regularly repainted to keep them fresh and bright. The gable wall in Derry's Bogside, which was used to announce 'You Are Now Entering Free Derry' when the barricades went up in 1969, has been maintained ever since even though the rest of the terrace has long been demolished. It remains as a key symbolic marker in the city and in recent years a number of adjacent walls have been adorned with images relating to the early years of the Troubles to create a kind of outdoor visual gallery commemorating a nationalist perspective of the conflict. Others have been painted as more personal memorials: paintings of Bobby Sands on the Falls Road and loyalist leader John McMichael on Roden Street in a loyalist area of south Belfast have both been carefully maintained since the early 1990s. The Sands mural was even repainted after the building it graced was demolished and rebuilt. In the years following the cease-fires, a number of other such memorial murals have appeared across the city as the paramilitary groups have sought to mark the formal end to the campaign by honouring their dead. The content of the murals has shifted from strident expressions of a defiant resolve to carry on the war regardless of the cost, to more sorrowful expressions of the very human price that has been paid. They thus stand at one relatively fragile extreme of a range of memorials and markers that impose themselves on the landscape and jolt the memories of those who come into contact with them. Mural paintings may not seem an obvious category of artefact to include within the matériel of conflict, but their relative transience and their status as targets of violence makes them such a part of this larger category.

CONCLUSION

All the features that have been discussed in the preceding sections are linked by their impermanent status. Even those murals that are currently maintained and preserved are subject to the ravages of time, the foresight of the developer and the loss of interest of the faithful. All structures of war are seen as temporary and expendable, as liable to attack, damage or destruction and as targets for removal once the situation returns to normal. They are abnormal constructions constructed in response to an abnormal social situation. Security structures are not obviously seen as examples of modern architecture nor murals as works of modern art although both can be seen within such categories. The way that they are viewed: as partisan constructions, as politicized impositions on a landscape, as bearers of painful or ugly memories, furthers the perspective that welcomes their removal and destruction in the search for the normal.

To date there is no informed or considered debate about what should happen to the remnants of the conflict; no public discussion about what should be preserved or how structures should be preserved. The populist view of most remains of the conflict would be to say 'get rid of all traces of the Troubles and get on with our lives'. Nationalists favour the rapid removal of all military structures, but favour preservation of some buildings such as The Maze or Crumlin Road Prison. Unionists have been mute on the matter. Responses to the need to preserve the built environment are thus varied; there is no common voice. Many thousands of buildings have already been destroyed by the violence of the Troubles; others are at risk because of rapid redevelopment of Belfast and other towns. Government policy is to dispose of surplus buildings as long as those which are listed have that status respected. But many of the important structures are not old or elaborate; it is only their mundaneness which makes them interesting. The British army has rapidly dismantled any unused or unwanted bases or other structures and many of the less formal features of security or defensive architecture will also disappear relatively quickly. Meanwhile the heritage department is attempting to record and document what they can of a range of physical constructions as diverse as police stations and mural paintings, while the army has suggested that architectural plans and documents will eventually find their way into the public domain.

Amidst the slow and sometimes faltering moves towards peace in Northern Ireland it is perhaps too difficult, and too soon, to take time to reflect upon what should be remembered in years to come, how it should be remembered and where it should be remembered. The bus companies and tour operators have already expanded their operations to include the murals, the peace-lines and the security architecture on their itinerary and the thriving 'terror tourism' industry continues to grow. But the question of how such popular and opportunistic approaches should be balanced by the state has yet to be debated. Unlike the documentary archives, which are carefully preserved for a generation and more before they are subjected to public scrutiny, it seems as if much of the matériel of war will be removed as rapidly as possible until few of such troubling remnants remain.

REFERENCES

Bloomfield, K. (1998) *We Will Remember Them: Report of the Northern Ireland Victims Commissioner*, Belfast: The Stationery Office.

Cooke, P. (1995) *A History of Kilmainham Gaol, 1796–1924*, Dublin: The Stationery Office.

Foucault, M. (1977) *Discipline and Punish: The Birth of the Prison*, Harmondsworth: Allen Lane.

Heatley, F. (1983) 'Community relations and the religious geography, 1800–86', in Beckett, J.C. *et al.* (eds) *Belfast: The Making of the City*, Belfast: Appletree Press, pp.129–42.

Jarman, N. (1993) 'Intersecting Belfast', in Bender, B. (ed.) *Landscape: Politics and Perspectives*, Oxford: Berg, pp.107–38.

Jarman, N. (1996) Violent men, violent land: dramatizing the troubles and the landscape of Ulster, *Journal of Material Culture* 1(1): 39–62.

Jarman, N. (1997) *Material Conflicts: Parades and Visual Displays in Northern Ireland*, Oxford: Berg.

Jarman, N. and Bryan, D. (1996) *Parade and Protest: A Discussion of Parading Disputes in Northern Ireland*, Coleraine: University of Ulster.

Jarman, N. and O'Halloran, C. (2001) Recreational rioting: young people, interface areas and violence, *Child Care in Practice* 7(1): 2–16.

Millett, K. (1995) *The Politics of Cruelty: An Essay on the Literature of Political Imprisonment*, Harmondsworth: Penguin.

O'Malley, P. (1990) *Biting at the Grave: the Irish Hunger Strikes and the Politics of Despair*, Belfast: Blackstaff Press.

Rolston, B. (1991) *Politics and Painting: Murals and Conflict in Northern Ireland*, Cranbury NJ: Associated University Press.

25 Displaying history's violent heritage: how does the archivist approach exhibiting documents which relate to violent events?

ANNE GEORGE

In his first presidential address to the Society of Archivists in 1955, Sir Hilary Jenkinson stated that the essential and primary responsibilities of the archivist are 'the duties of conserving the evidence and of communicating it to the student public' (Jenkinson 1956). This was true then and is even more so now, nearly fifty years later, when improved awareness of and accessibility to archival collections, outreach and the exploitation of resources are increasing concerns. Archivists are the preservers of the recorded past: they seek out, classify and catalogue the documentary heritage in whatever format it comes, whether in medieval manuscript or modern electronic text, in image, or in sound files; they make it available for research and safeguard it for the future. Archival institutions exist to house collections of records to nationally adopted standards and to keep them safe against the time when they may be called up to further some kind of research or answer an enquiry. They are kept equally, even if no one uses the material for years: historical evidence should surely be conserved simply because history exists.

The process of 'making available' includes a range of different practices and some of these require special considerations due to the very nature of the archives involved. The survival of the record in the first place, its acceptance or selection for permanent preservation, the constraints imposed upon it by the owner or its creating body all affect how it is treated once it has reached the stage of being an 'archive', rather than a piece of information still required for current reference. Some archives pose no particular difficulties, but there are many classes of document which must be treated with especial care, due to the nature of information they contain and the conclusions which may be drawn from them. The information may be controversial or sensitive. It may describe, in words or in images, events of great violence, horror or the suffering of individuals or whole peoples. It is these sorts of records that the archivist should consider carefully before putting them in front of the public. Having them accessible for an individual's private research is one matter. It is something very different to use them in exhibitions which may well be seen by a wide range of people, of all ages and backgrounds. As with other heritage officers, museum curators and custodians of particular sites and buildings, distress and controversy can be inherent in much of what archivists deal with on a day-to-day basis.

Any County Record Office in England will house classes of archives such as those of the Boards of Guardians – administrators of the poor law until well into the twentieth century – whose records can cruelly illustrate the sufferings, both physical and mental, of our ancestors. To use as display objects records such as their registers of restraint may be quite unacceptable in many contexts. More notably, there are a number of national institutions and specialist repositories in Great Britain whose collecting policies focus on particular individuals or events which relate to the unpalatable or even unacceptable faces of the past. It is as essential that these archives are preserved as properly as those more prosaic and less controversial collections. Indeed, it can be politically easier, let alone far more interesting, to have the high profile of housing thought-provoking, sensitive or challenging collections than rather more 'routine' ones.

Repositories such as the Public Record Office and the Imperial War Museum are widely known to house collections which record the horrors of conflict, war and its aftermath, but there are equally a host of smaller institutions which house similar kinds of archives. An example of one such repository is the University of Southampton Library's Special Collections Division. For almost twenty years it has been receiving for safekeeping collections of national and international importance, focusing principally on nineteenth- and twentieth-century political and military themes, and on Anglo-Jewry. Briefly, these comprise the archives of the Duke of Wellington, including extensive papers from the Peninsular War period; and the Broadlands Archives, records deriving from the Hampshire home first of Lord Palmerston, Prime Minister and Foreign Secretary, and later of Earl Mountbatten of Burma. Mountbatten's papers cover his early family life and extend throughout the Second World War and beyond to his career as the last Viceroy and first post-independence Governor General of India. The third significant strand of the Division's collections relates to Anglo-Jewry and the relations between Jews and other peoples, having as its nucleus the working library of the Reverend James Parkes, a founder member of the Council of Christians and Jews. This has attracted the acquisition of over 500 collections of nineteenth- and twentieth-century manuscripts relating to Jewish communities, individuals and organizations.

The dissemination of information about the archives available in any given repository for study is of paramount importance to the professional. The publication of guides and the transferring of catalogues of archival collections onto the Internet are well-established methods used to this end, as is the mounting of exhibitions. The main aim of staging an exhibition may be to encourage use of the whole spectrum of material available for academic or other research, by displaying examples. These can provide a taster of the wide range of documents to be drawn upon to describe any given theme or event. Exhibitions are formed by a process of selection from the material available. This naturally leads to the foremost consideration, that of the general nature of the archive, its creating body or individual, and the purpose for which the records were made in the first place. The records at the professional's disposal for use in displays have also been deliberately shaped by the institution's agreed collecting policy. Short of borrowing items from another source, any choice could be perpetuating a partial truth in showing only one side of a many-faceted event. For example, the information gathered to back up a particular theme, such as war crimes papers, may reveal only one point of view and one that could be open to the conflict of controversy. If there is controversy or suffering to be wrought from any exhibition, it must be left to the viewer to interpret any given item as controversial or painful, and to develop that interpretation. An archivist is not an historian and must be cautious not to run the risk of imposing a particular theory of history or misrepresenting fact by not displaying the whole picture. The professional must seek to present an informative picture in a dispassionate way, in order to allow the widest interpretation of the documents by people of widely differing views. The selection of what documents to exhibit is a heavy responsibility. It must present an objective and acceptable corpus of material, which should be displayed in an appropriate way. The object is to inform, but not in a dictatorial or polemic way; to present items appropriate to the aims of the exhibition, but not to shock unnecessarily.

With the collections of Jewish-related archives at Southampton University, it would be easy to pander to the invited or pre-arranged audience and to tailor what is displayed to take into account the personal sensitivities of at least an older generation. One could be guilty of censoring at the outset what is chosen, because of the sensitivities of the viewers to the most emotive themes. It is wrong to use shocking images or indeed shocking written reports just for effect: they must be used to support a valid historical point – but one which should also relate in some part to audience expectations. Documents and images which inform and illustrate should be selected, but ones which do not cause unacceptable distress to those to whom the issues are too close, personal and harrowing. This must be the professional's attitude, but the line may be thin between genuine care and thoughtfulness and the suppression of the evidence. The degree of objectivity or evasion to be employed can be hard to equate. What should be done, for example, about exhibiting items from the graphic reports, with photographic evidences, relating to war criminals, found amongst Jewish archives? Can there be an acceptable way that these can be included without running the risk of the smack of sensationalism, of provoking great anxiety and rousing all sorts of other personal issues? Or what about the so-called Exodus papers which relate to the incident when German Jews, concentration camp survivors, arrived in Palestine in 1947 to start life anew, only to be turned back from Haifa at the insistence of the British government? These Jews were shipped back to Germany and were forcibly disembarked at Hamburg. Their pathetic appeal to British soldiers not to carry out their orders, and the notice of their hunger strike, are incredibly emotive documents.

The physical arrangements of the exhibition space, its layout and general style are all tools which can be used to create a particular atmosphere. Background music and lighting can create an aesthetically pleasing environment or one which can increase the discomfort of the visual display. Wallboards with enlarged images or words have immediate impact, but the images chosen for display in such a way must not be chosen solely for their effect. They must be used to support or further the other historical information being shown within the context of the theme of the exhibition. Images of emaciated holocaust corpses at the time of the liberation of the concentration camps are the strongest visual evidence for what happened, but they should be used appropriately.

An exhibition held at Southampton University Library to mark the fiftieth

Figure 25.1 Mountbatten with his wife and party inspecting riot devastation, 1947

Source: Broadlands Archives (MB3/N14/15)

anniversary of independence for India and Pakistan caused much consideration of the resources available and their context. It would, it was hoped, attract a diverse audience. Southampton is very much a multi-ethnic city and the event was publicized to the local community as well as through university circles. On display in the library foyer were copies of documents, photographs and coloured maps, largely drawn from the Broadlands Archives. The screens illustrated the chronology of the process undertaken which led to the transfer of power to the two new nations, created by the partition of the sub-continent in August 1947, and its aftermath. These were events which affected 450 million people, one fifth of the world's population at that time. Mountbatten arrived as the new Viceroy in March 1947 and preparations for independence, already in hand, were intense during the 71 days between the announcement of the partition plan and the date set for the transfer of power. Included were copies of meeting minutes and reports narrating the approval for the plans and announcing them to the Indian leaders, papers of the Commissioners who delineated the borders between the two new dominions, and of the Partition Council, whose remit was to divide between them all India's assets, from the armed forces and the railways down to the individual books in branch libraries and paper clips in the lowest clerk's office. Some books were simply torn into two. The artificial boundaries proposed to cut up the Punjab and Bengal and their 100 million inhabitants and divide them between India and Pakistan provoked bitter criticism and violence on a massive scale. Photographs were shown of the scenes of shocking devastation in Amritsar, the Sikhs' holy city, ruined buildings, piles of rubble with the Viceroy and his wife and staff inspecting the damage (Fig. 25.1). There were extracts from celebratory speeches given on independence day and photographs of

Figure 25.2   Refugee convoy, August 1947

Source: Broadlands Archives (MB3/24/2)

the ceremonies; equally there were items reflecting the horrific suffering of the estimated 14 million people caught up in the ensuing mass relocation (Fig. 25.2), in the communal violence between Hindu, Muslim and Sikh, in the disease and starvation of the refugee camps. There were graphic images and reports of attacks on refugee trains (Fig. 25.3), official records of the extent of the atrocities and letters of protest from Gandhi. But there were no specific images of any dead, neither Muslim, Hindu nor Sikh.

With an exhibition of this nature, careful consideration was given to how to proceed. An attempt was made to do it in an entirely neutral and open way, with short, to-the-point explanatory texts and captions. A point was made of trying to represent different viewpoints equally, and simply, for instance by including images of Gandhi and Jinnah in equal number. The photographs and reports spoke for themselves to a great extent, but items had to be placed in their context. However, the expectations of the audience to see things which truly reflected the violence of this occasion, had to be met. It was quite unavoidable not to impose choice and a sort of censorship: although written reports referred to numbers of dead, there was no pictorial representation of the bloodshed. Black and white typescript papers, even when interspersed with manuscripts, can look very dull, so attention-attracting posters and photographs were selected. Can this be construed as seeking to sensationalize the devastating effects of the inter-communal riots? Visual evidence has, after all, a much more overwhelming impact that the written word.

Images may, nevertheless, have to be used with caution. The manipulation of the subject is a common artifice and one which has been used for years to show a partial

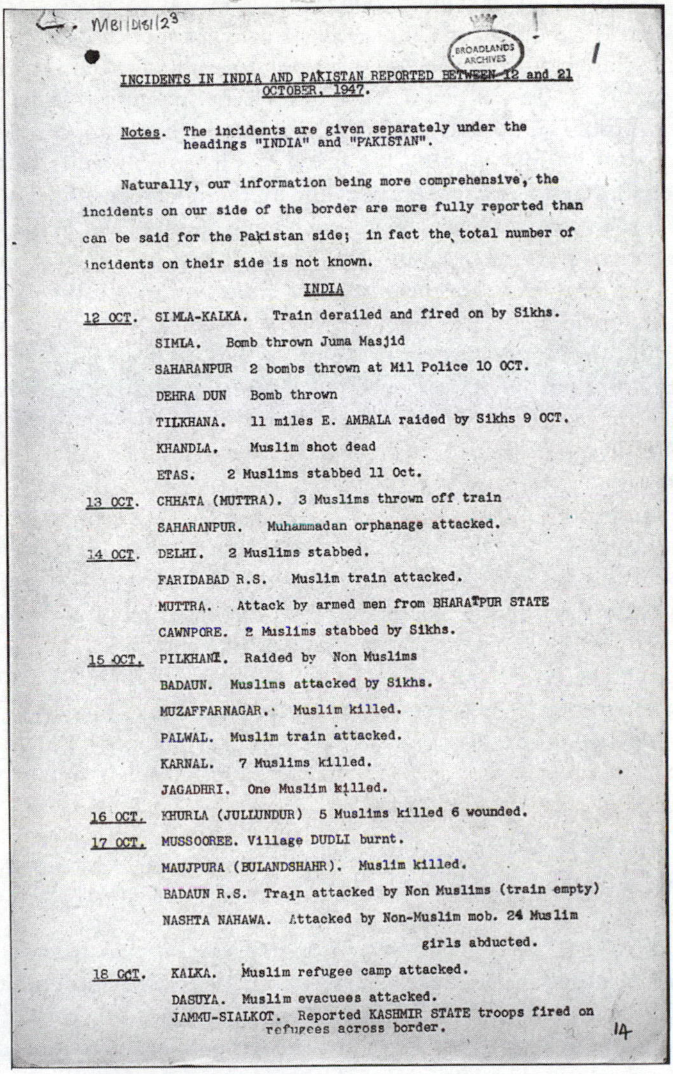

MB1/D181/2³

BROADLANDS ARCHIVES

INCIDENTS IN INDIA AND PAKISTAN REPORTED BETWEEN 12 and 21
OCTOBER, 1947.

Notes. The incidents are given separately under the
headings "INDIA" and "PAKISTAN".

Naturally, our information being more comprehensive, the
incidents on our side of the border are more fully reported than
can be said for the Pakistan side; in fact the total number of
incidents on their side is not known.

INDIA

12 OCT. SIMLA-KALKA.   Train derailed and fired on by Sikhs.

SIMLA. Bomb thrown Juma Masjid

SAHARANPUR 2 bombs thrown at Mil Police 10 OCT.

DEHRA DUN   Bomb thrown

TILKHANA.   11 miles E. AMBALA raided by Sikhs 9 OCT.

KHANDLA.   Muslim shot dead

ETAS.   2 Muslims stabbed 11 Oct.

13 OCT. CHHATA (MUTTRA). 3 Muslims thrown off train

SAHARANPUR. Muhammadan orphanage attacked.

14 OCT. DELHI.   2 Muslims stabbed.

FARIDABAD R.S.   Muslim train attacked.

MUTTRA.   Attack by armed men from BHARATPUR STATE

CAWNPORE. 2 Muslims stabbed by Sikhs.

15 OCT. PILKHANI. Raided by Non Muslims

BADAUN. Muslims attacked by Sikhs.

MUZAFFARNAGAR. Muslim killed.

PALWAL. Muslim train attacked.

KARNAL.   7 Muslims killed.

JAGADHRI. One Muslim killed.

16 OCT. KHURLA (JULLUNDUR) 5 Muslims killed 6 wounded.

17 OCT. MUSSOOREE. Village DUDLI burnt.

MAUJPURA (BULANDSHAHR). Muslim killed.

BADAUN R.S. Train attacked by Non Muslims (train empty)

NASHTA NAHAWA. Attacked by Non-Muslim mob. 24 Muslim
                                    girls abducted.

18 OCT. KALKA. Muslim refugee camp attacked.

DASUYA. Muslim evacuees attacked.
JAMMU-SIALKOT. Reported KASHMIR STATE troops fired on
               refugees across border.

14

Figure 25.3 Incident report, October 1947

Source: Broadlands Archives (MB1/D181/2)

view or stress a particular aspect of an event. Were the photographs taken to show the extent of some kind of violence, or simply to depict the concerned and caring face of authority? Some views, for example, of the Viceroy's tour of the devastation in India may well have been mere posed publicity shots. This concept holds true of some Jewish photographs: some of the images of concentration camps, though truly appalling, could be construed as stage-managed propaganda. There is often a difficult ambiguity in representation.

Inviting comment on an exhibition is the obvious way to gauge reaction to any themed event. Reactions to the India/Pakistan independence exhibition made it emphatically clear how alive the issues of the process and the aftermath of independence still are. There was heartfelt and bitter criticism of the role the British had played in the process. One respondent took the view that it is impossible to display a history or even attempt to disclose a history which is still being written in the blood of countless innocent people struggling for their independence. In the case of this exhibition, constraints had been imposed by the limit of the archive collection itself. The records were, after all, those of Mountbatten the Viceroy, an official of the British government. So there was nothing to reflect the opinion that Mountbatten forced events through too quickly, which led to the appalling massacres. Many of the photographs were taken by approved photographers: they may present a sanitized version of the scenes. No comment was made in the explanatory texts to the issue of the number of casualties in the Punjab – which ranged from under 200 000 in some official British reports to over one and a half million in some Indian opinion.

Archive institutions must preserve a neutral stance and present an unbiased and open view of the past from their collections. It is sometimes important to be somewhat low-key and less emotive than could be the case, given the materials which have been preserved and are available. This outlook matches the professional's stance as custodian, encouraging the use of material by historians of radically different outlooks. At the same time, it is the archivist's responsibility to present and promote the scholarly debate. Unnecessary provocation and the riding roughshod over deep and long-lasting sensitivities is not appropriate. The professional brief is to have an understanding of the past and of its present implications and to present the collections to the public in this context.

ACKNOWLEDGEMENTS

This chapter is based on a paper given at the third annual Cambridge Heritage Seminar on 'Heritage that Hurts' held in March 1998, at which time the author was an archivist at the University of Southampton Library. The author is grateful to the trustees of the Broadlands Archives for their permission to reproduce items from their collection in the University of Southampton Library. Thanks for helpful discussions are also given to Dr Christopher Woolgar, Karen Robson, Rosie Hayden and Allen Packwood.

REFERENCE

Jenkinson, Sir H. (1956) The future of archives in England, presidential address delivered at the society's AGM on 15 December 1955, *Journal of the Society of Archivists* 1(3): 57–61.

26 The hammering of society: non-correspondence and modernity

ROLAND FLETCHER

Column by column in a cloud of dust
They marched away enduring a belief
Whose logic brought them, somewhere else, to grief.
(W.H. Auden, The Shield of Achilles)

COLLIDING WITH MATERIALITY: THE EXPERIENCE OF TWO CENTURIES

In the nineteenth century the Western world began to experience the onslaught of materiality as industrialization smashed into the conservative social world of European daily life. That shock wave was exported to the rest of the world and now tears at the social fabric of every society. During the Industrial Revolution and the associated immense urban transformation, severe non-correspondence began between the material component of social life and the sociality of verbal meaning and human action. An appalling dissonance developed between materiality and sociality, most brutally expressed in the consequences of mechanized warfare and industrialized killing.

Humanity has been taught the sharp lesson that the material is not merely our servant, that it is not merely an epiphenomenon consequent on human intent and action that serves human progress, but also is a factor in its own right whose inertia and energy threatens our daily life. In nineteenth-century Europe the rapidly growing cities created appalling, unhealthy environments for millions of people, a process that now impacts to varying degrees on every urban society. In the twentieth century the West decisively learned that technological innovation was not progressive. Industrial expertise and technology were applied to killing human beings. The debris of Auschwitz, Sobibor and Treblinka was left behind, trapping our rational minds in grief, denial and an agony of unease. The development of nuclear weapons ended the assurance that innovation would serve humanity. Instead, we created a tool that threatens our biological existence. The ambivalence and contradictions of the first primitive nuclear weapons in 1945 are well expressed in the conflicts over the Enola Gay exhibition at the Smithsonian National Air and Space Museum in 1993 (Nobile 1995). A monument to progressionism, it sought to present the problem through a careful display of the development and consequences of nuclear weaponry, only to discover that the by-then retired, sensible people who had served in the US armed forces in the Second World War could not countenance the awful implications. In some ways even more troubling for our sense of self-assurance, because it is so pedestrian a matter, is the realization that we are even threatened by our garbage (Rathje and Murphy 1993), let alone that the material products of industry have started to warm the atmosphere of our planet (Nordhaus and Boyer 2000).

However, along with this rising awareness of the threat of materiality we are also aware that sociality, at least in the already industrialized world, is slowly gaining some ascendancy over the material. Labour union power, pragmatic morality, democracy and humanism have played key roles. Many of the disgraceful consequences of uncontrolled capitalism, factory labour and urban housing have been mitigated. In 1852, 52 per cent of the working-class families of Preston in the UK lived below the poverty line (Hobsbawm 1975: 260). For all the exigencies of incessant, contemporary economic change that situation would now lead to outrage in the West. There is even some hope that sociality might yet gain control over nuclear weaponry. In *Humanity*, Glover (2001: 222–3) argues that the moral of the 1962 missile crisis, when the USA and the USSR confronted each other over Soviet nuclear armed missiles in Cuba, is that we survived because Kennedy and Khrushchev did not make heroic decisions, offered ways out and did not engage in tribalism. The sociality of their decision-making was consistent with the material circumstances. Khrushchev remarked, 'Don't ask who lost or who won. Mankind won. Human reason won' (quoted by Glover 2001: 200). By contrast, in the First World War, the nations of Europe trooped into a collision with industrialized warfare using the social postures and tribal morality of the preceding two centuries of European sociality. In August 1914 the rectors of the Bavarian universities issued an appeal to arms. 'And so the *furor teutonicus* bursts into flames once again. The enthusiasm of the wars of liberation flares, and the holy war begins' (Keegan 1993: 358; quote sourced to Eksteins 1989: 93). Auden, in three terse lines of the 'Shield of Achilles' (1966), provides a brutal summary of what followed.

What I wish to follow up are the implications of the elementary point that materiality and sociality do not inevitably correspond with each other. They can do, leading to adequate functioning, but are just as likely not to – leading to dissonance and to potentially devastating outcomes (Fletcher in press). What is interesting and complex is that either end of the spectrum is possible. Neither materiality nor sociality determines the other, despite the short-term perspective that sees verbal meaning and human action creating the material. What the short-term view neglects is the mundane reality that actions have unanticipated consequences, action becomes depended on the material and the material possesses inertia, allowing it to continue its impact long after the actions have passed into memory or been forgotten. The material component of human behaviour acts as an independent variable in the trajectories of social life (Fletcher 1992, 1995, 1996).

To pursue this proposition requires first an outline of the relationship between materiality and the combination of verbal meaning and social action. The issue of the gradual recovery of social ascendancy over materiality will be discussed using the example of twentieth-century warfare. The analysis has implications for archaeology, for the way we view post-modern theory and, more specifically, the role of historical archaeology.

MATERIALITY AND REPLICATION

The essential point in the relationship between materiality and sociality is that this is not a dichotomized relationship. Instead it is a plural relationship spread across verbal meaning and social action and also across many scales of size and rate of replication. The material component of human behaviour contains massive constructions which are rarely replicated and can endure for centuries, numerous middle-sized objects such as tables and chairs – more frequently replicated but still capable of lasting for decades, and a myriad small items such as knives, pots and bracelets, incessantly reproduced and trashed. Some may last but most are disposed of within a few years or even less. The larger the material items the slower their aggregate replication rate and the greater their inertia. Because the material is differentially replicated and enduring an actual assemblage cannot have a simple relationship to human action and verbal meaning which are themselves replicated at different rates (Fletcher 1992, 1996). Because the latter is comparatively fast and can change most readily it is always liable to diverge from and be laid over the material actuality of daily life. There is non-correspondence. Only the very small and readily replicated material items will provide the rates of replication capable of tracking the changes in verbal meaning and action that make up sociality. We might therefore expect some correspondence between small-scale materiality and the usual pace of sociality but cannot suppose that coherent correlation exists throughout the aggregate of a community's material, active and verbal behaviour (Fletcher 1996).

What is complex and problematic is that materiality and sociality both correlate and do not correlate concurrently and to varying degrees even within one society. The implications for archaeological practice and historical interpretation are serious. The former must abandon seeking to reconstruct the 'social' in terms of purported correlations with the 'material' and replace that practice by studying the relationship between the degree to which correspondence occurs between those phenomena and the outcome of the engagement (Fletcher in press). Why this is of consequence for historical interpretation is then easy to perceive.

Historians have long recognized that the Industrial Revolution in nineteenth-century Europe was at odds with and overwhelmed the existing social order of daily life (Hobsbawm 1994: 15–16). It is, after all, a fundamental tenet of Marx. But what the material rates of change viewpoint serves to emphasize is that over the past two centuries a very unusual circumstance arose in which even the production and replication of the massive material component of social life came to outpace the rates of change in aggregates of social action and verbal meaning. That remarkable time was one in which changes in coherent sociality struggled not just with the inertia of the material but also with a massive material world that was being generated at immense speed. London grew by an average of 50 sq km per annum in the second half of the nineteenth century, from less than 100 sq km to over 2500 sq km. Though the 'social' could start to find identity in the myriad small items pouring from industrial production it could not find its expression in human action by engagement with the new massive framework. That was so vast that it had damaging ecological effects of its own, well represented by the appalling housing conditions of nineteenth-century European industrial cities and their consequences for human health (Gauldie 1974). The same massive productive capacity also led to an ecology of warfare that, in turn, tore apart the sociality of the old Europe in the early twentieth century.

WARFARE AND SOCIALITY IN THE TWENTIETH CENTURY: REGAINING SOCIAL ASCENDANCY

The point of my commentary in this chapter is that the history of the nineteenth and the twentieth centuries has been the story of the collision between materiality and the social world of daily life. That story continues into the twenty-first century. After a series of technological changes and a new combination of material features in the late eighteenth and early nineteenth century that assisted a massive urban transition (Fletcher 1995: 127–9), the scale and the productive rate of the material accelerated enormously in Western Europe. The sociality of daily life in that time and place was not adequate to deal with the consequences. The people of Europe and then the USA and Russia had to learn how to cope with and exploit mass production (see Miller's key work 1987). They also had to learn how to control the military consequences of industrialization.

Civil society today tends to look with horror on the continual improvement of weapons to increase their efficiency as killing and maiming devices. But we might instead consider that what has gone on over the past hundred years is a process of gradually increasing control by the societies of the weapon makers and users over the impact and the unanticipated effects of warfare. I do not dispute that cheap automatic weapons and anti-personnel mines have served up catastrophe to millions of people, especially in the under-industrialized world. However, the major warmaking nations have sought to create weapon environments that minimize their own casualties and have even begun to develop weapons to do precisely what is required rather than create extensive 'collateral damage' around legitimate targets.

The First World War was a generally unanticipated, titanic disaster. The decision to go to war in 1914 was, in the main, greeted with popular enthusiasm (Taylor 1987: 21) though some politicians seem to have been graced with premonitions of tragedy (Glover 2000: 184–5). Men volunteered in huge numbers. They set out with varied national conceits of superiority and delusion: the war would be over by Christmas – war was seen as sport or an adventure, or as a task for the Christian knight. Obedience and respect for authority locked them in. What these men collided with was the reality of mechanized warfare – industrial production of barbed wire, the machine gun, factories making thousands of artillery shells. The effects are well known, memorialized by the great war poets such as Siegfried Sassoon. A classic example is the first day of the Battle of the Somme on 1 July 1916 when the British Army suffered 60 000 casualties in a morning and won no significant ground because it marched thousands of men at a walking pace towards the entrenched and undestroyed machine guns of the German Army. Of about 8.9 million men mobilized by the UK in the First World War, about 900 000 died and 35 per cent became casualties (Spartacus online). Attack could not prevail because the means to effect and direct an assault were not available. As Keegan writes so grievously well, the soldiers reverted to the communications of the Napoleonic wars when they stepped into 'no-mans' land' (1976: 247, 260–1). Runners and flags were among the only means of signalling that they had reached the German trenches. The massed lines of men were necessary because the deafening chaos of the battlefield prevented precise and flexible control. Only when field radios could be used effectively in the last year of the war did control improve. Then the 'stupid' generals, like Haig, who had slaughtered their own troops in 1916 and 1917, proved to be skilful commanders of the highly mobile battles that held off and then wrecked the German army (Terraine 1978). What had changed was the means to control soldiers and new weapons systems, like tanks, that could break the ascendancy of the defence on the First World War battlefields.

By the time the Second World War started, the new senior commanders like Montgomery and Guderian, who had been junior officers on the battlefields over twenty years earlier, had already planned to prevent the shocking casualties of the earlier war. 'Matériel' and blitzkrieg were the desired solutions. Either employ vast quantities of machinery to spare soldiers' lives or operate at such speed that armies would collapse and attrition warfare would cease. Though conditions on the Soviet–German Eastern Front led to horrendous casualties, the Western democracies kept their battle casualties remarkably low – about 245 000 for the UK and about 290 000 for the USA worldwide (Groslier online). The Allied forces applied information technology to cracking enemy codes, building action on detailed knowledge of their opponents' intent and capacity. Radar provided forewarning for defence and locational details for attack. By 1945 proximity fuses increasingly ensured hits on target. Note that, by contrast, in the First World War, millions of artillery shells were fired and many never exploded. Their lethal contents are still dug from the earth every year in France (Webster 1997). By the Gulf War of 1992, 107 Hellfire missiles fired from Apache helicopters in less than one hour could destroy 102 vehicles (Scales 1997: 314).

In the Second World War proportionately high casualties among both the attackers and the defenders did occur in the European air-war where the Western democracies had yet to learn a new mode of warfare. What was meant to be precision bombing proved ineffectual because the aircrews could not navigate accurately enough nor did they have bomb-aiming capacities good enough to hit anything smaller than a city. In 1941, two thirds of aircrews missed their targets by 5 miles or more. (Glover 2001: 70). As a result, the aircrews had to operate in huge slow bomber streams, the British and American together suffering about 160 000 deaths in Europe (USSBS 1945: 1). The choice of cities as targets slaughtered 40 000 civilians in a night in Hamburg in July 1943 and over 100 000 in Tokyo in 1945. The latter figure, caused by the conventional use of incendiary weapons, produced casualties exceeding those of each atomic weapon attack in August 1945. In Europe the bombing campaign was not a success. Though industrial production was adversely affected the war on the cities was not decisive; most obviously, the morale of the civilian population did not collapse. The transformation of air warfare since 1945 neatly illustrates the rising power of sociality over materiality. Between the 1940s and the 1990s we have moved from city-smashing bomber streams of over a thousand aircraft to the development of 'smart' bombs and cruise missiles, which can hit single buildings and avoid the massive civilian casualties of the Second World War.

The Western military and the politicians have increasingly gained more precise control over the means and the ends of warfare. In the Gulf War in 1992, out of a field army of over half a million, the US-led coalition suffered only 140 dead (Scales 1997: 383). Instead of seeing the great world wars and their casualties as the enduring norm of the industrializing world, we can usefully see them as a brief phase in the development of mechanized warfare. With the application of electronic data management and acquisition both to intelligence collection and to the control of personnel and weapons the blanket onslaughts of the first half of the twentieth century are now at an end in the Western world. Politicians increasingly possess graduated, precise and selective tools for military action. They can direct the military to choose very specific targets and be far more careful about limiting civilian casualties. Regrettably that art has not extended to embargoes and blockades. But the shift to a viable sociality of mechanized war has begun, moving away from the pact of blood and honour that bound warriors together on the pre-industrial battlefields of Europe, to the quintessentially American approach in which 'war is work' (Keegan 1997). As Scales notes, ' The Army has a moral obligation to the American people to lessen the cost of the battle in American blood. To honor such an obligation, there is no such thing as a fair fight. An eye-to-eye battle is not a boxing match or a football game. An even match in either quality or quantity only serves to prolong the horror with needless casualties on both sides' (1997: 367). It's just a job.

IMPLICATIONS FOR ARCHAEOLOGICAL THEORY AND THE ROLE OF HISTORICAL ARCHAEOLOGY

Because a correspondence between materiality and sociality can develop after the material is established, the specific sociality that eventually works well with a particular material system cannot be a sufficient explanation either of why the material developed or what social institutions may co-exist, for a while, with the material. Historical archaeology, in particular, confronts archaeology with the central point that the material and sociality cannot be sufficient explanations of the other. Unavoidably, the literature and the documentary records of the recent historic past in the European world demonstrate that the relationship was as much a collision of difference as it was a concurrent development of the sociality that would work in the new industrialized milieu.

The irony of much post-modern literature is that though this disjunction is recognized, discourse is still dominated by verbality and verbal meaning. Indeed, on being borrowed and inserted into archaeology, post-modern propositions are declared to be about the verbal as the defining condition of enquiry, as is advocated by scholars such as Tilley (1999). Given that non-correspondence of sociality and the material is apparently usual, any efforts to continually merge the two and to collapse the critical component of time are likely to generate the complex writing styles and expressions of the post-modernists. While this is probably unavoidable, and perhaps even necessary for describing and interpreting the contemporaneous moments of recent and present society, it may be neither necessary nor sufficient for dealing with long time spans. The relationship of materiality and sociality may also be less complex to describe over the longer term since the differing rates of operation can be teased out and the relationship can be analysed in terms of 'outcomes' (Fletcher in press). Archaeology may be able to develop a simpler and more comprehensive way of describing this relationship than has been provided by the 'post-modern' philosophers of social science.

The era of industrialization is critical to our understanding of sociality because it is one of those rare periods when the operational consistency of fast sociality and slow large-scale materiality was disrupted. The formation of early urban agrarian growth and the formation of sedentary communities were probably the two other great equivalent transitions (Fletcher 1995: 69–98). During these transitions material change was phenomenally accelerated. The industrial revolution, and particularly the military transformation which it made possible, suggest that sociality takes time to accelerate to the same degree and thereby regain control of the material. The effects are of great interest. When material replication is accelerating in this way it is so powerful that it operates as a profound directive agency creating a trajectory into the future. This is, in essence, in the nature of material and should be a feature of the few, rare occasions when such great transitions occur. On this reading, 'modernity' is what happens in such a situation because of the power of the material. 'Post-modernity' then develops when the social has regained some ascendancy but can never actually regain complete control, enabling a myriad, varied associations to develop. On this view, the post-modern is the normal, piecemeal nature of human existence and has generally been the condition of human life. The 'modern' as a condition, rather than as a period from the eighteenth to the mid-twentieth century, is then rare and highly structured.

What is therefore crucial about historical archaeology is that its eighteenth- to twenty-first-century field of enquiry concerns one of those rare transition periods in which material production rates enabled the massive material framework and the high energy material systems to replicate faster and on a far greater scale than the then-habitual rates of change in social action. The strong implication is that this is the real topic of historical archaeology and its real power as a field of enquiry. We can study the impact of that collision on sociality and see how human intent, action and verbal meanings engaged with or failed to cope with the material changes.

Because the presence of documentary and oral records allows us little latitude to invent social systems and suites of meaning, we cannot readily indulge in invented 'social' pasts for this period. Simultaneously, the substantial material record gives us a picture independent of the selective nature of 'verbal' sources. We can use the archaeology of industrial expansion to rigorously study the complex of relationships without possessing the latitude to invent a social past that would merely suit our assumptions. It is not, therefore, some 'social' or historical label such as 'Capitalism' that is the proper theme of historical archaeology: that approach is liable to trap us within an agenda set by some other discipline. Instead we can study the vast story of the relationship between the social patterns of daily life and the transforming material giant within which they sought to function. In the late nineteenth and early twentieth centuries we can recognize the appalling plight of families jammed into the dank, small rooms of multi-storey housing blocks in the huge European cities and the tragedy of soldiers bound by obsolete loyalties, dying for them in the rending lash of machine-gun fire or smashed into the filth of mud, dead horses, wire and vomit. How sociality lost and is beginning to regain ascendancy is the real agenda of historical archaeology. The lesson it delivers to the rest of archaeology is that we must learn how to understand the fickle and unstable relationship between sociality and materiality over the entire span of human existence. We must avoid reconstructing assumed social correlates of the material when the problematic nature of those associations should be precisely the purpose of our enquiry.

ACKNOWLEDGEMENTS

As a participant in the 1999 World Archaeological Congress in Cape Town I sat in on the session that was the ancestor to this book. While I have long been interested in the history of modern warfare I had only just begun to combine that interest with my concerns about archaeological theory. In another session I had presented a paper on the ghastly impact of materiality on the industrializing societies of Europe. My thanks to Neil Silberman for his generous compliment on my paper and a great thanks to John Schofield and his colleagues for inviting a stranger in their session to participate in this book.

REFERENCES

Auden, W.H. (1966) 'The Shield of Achilles', in *Collected Shorter Poems 1927–57*, London: *Faber and Faber*, pp. 294–5.
Eksteins, M. (1989) *Rites of Spring: The Great War and the Birth of the Modern Age*, New York: Houghton Mifflin.
Fletcher, R.J. (1992) 'Time perspectivism, *Annales*, and the potential of archaeology', in Knapp, A.B. (ed.) *Archaeology, Annales and Ethnohistory*, Cambridge: Cambridge University Press, pp. 35–49.
Fletcher R.J. (1995) *The Limits of Settlement Growth: A Theoretical Outline*, Cambridge: Cambridge University Press.

Fletcher, R.J. (1996) 'Organised dissonance in cultural message systems', in Maschner, H.D.G. (ed.) *Darwinian Archaeologies*, New York: Plenum Press, pp. 61–86.

Fletcher, R.J. (in press) 'Materiality, space, time and outcome', in Bintliff, J.R. (ed.) *The Blackwell Companion to Archaeology*, Oxford: Blackwell.

Gauldie, E. (1974) *Cruel Habitations: A History of Working-Class Housing 1780–1918*, London: Allen and Unwin.

Glover, J. (2001) *Humanity. A Moral History of the Twentieth Century*, London: Pimlico.

Groslier online (2001) gi.groslier.com

Hobsbawm, E. (1975) (1997 edn) *The Age of Capital*, London: Abacus.

Hobsbawm, E. (1994) *Age of Extremes: The Short Twentieth Century 1914–1991*, London: Michael Joseph.

Keegan, J. (1976) *The Face of Battle*, London: Jonathan Cape.

Keegan, J. (1993) *The History of Warfare*, London: Random House.

Keegan, J. (1997) *Warpaths. Fields of Battle: The Wars for North America*, New York: Vintage.

Miller, D. (1987) *Material Culture and Mass Consumption*, Oxford and New York: Basil Blackwell.

Nobile, P. (ed.) (1995) *Judgment at the Smithsonian*, Smithsonian script by the curators at the National Air and Space Museum; afterword by Barton J. Bernstein, New York: Marlowe.

Nordhaus, W.D. and Boyer, J. (2000) *Warming the World: Economic Models of Global Warming*, Cambridge MA: MIT Press.

Rathje, W. and Murphy, C. (1993) *Rubbish!: The Archaeology of Garbage*, New York: Harper Perennial.

Scales, R.H. (1997) *Certain Victory: The US Army in the Gulf War*, Washington: Brassey.

Spartacus online. www.spartacus.schoolnet.co.uk

Taylor, A.J.P. (1987) *The First World War*, Harmondsworth: Penguin.

Terraine, J. (1978) *1918, The Year of Victory*, London: Sidgwick and Jackson.

Tilley, C. (1999) *Metaphor and Material Culture*, Oxford: Basil Blackwell.

USSBS (1945) *United States Strategic Bombing Survey. Summary Report. Presumed*, United States Government: Washington DC.

Webster, D. (1997) *Aftermath: The Remnants of War*, London: Constable.

Index